CHARLES L. LUMPKINS

American Pogrom

THE EAST ST. LOUIS RACE RIOT AND BLACK POLITICS

Ohio University Press   Athens

Ohio University Press, Athens, Ohio 45701
www.ohioswallow.com
© 2008 by Ohio University Press
All rights reserved

To obtain permission to quote, reprint, or otherwise reproduce or distribute material
from Ohio University Press publications, please contact our rights and permissions
department at (740) 593-1154 or (740) 593-4536 (fax).

15 14 13 12 11 10 09 08   5 4 3 2 1

Library of Congress Cataloging-in-Publication Data

Lumpkins, Charles L.
    American pogrom : the East St. Louis Race Riot and Black politics / Charles L. Lumpkins.
        p. cm. — (Ohio University Press series on law, society, and politics in the Midwest)
    Based on the author's thesis (doctoral)—Pennsylvania State University, 2006.
    Includes bibliographical references and index.
    ISBN-13: 978-0-8214-1802-4 (alk. paper)
    ISBN-10: 0-8214-1802-5 (alk. paper)
    ISBN-13: 978-0-8214-1803-1 (pbk. : alk. paper)
    ISBN-10: 0-8214-1803-3 (pbk. : alk. paper)
    1. East Saint Louis Race Riot, East Saint Louis, Ill., 1917. 2. Race riots—Illinois—East
Saint Louis—History—20th century. 3. East Saint Louis (Ill.)—Race relations—History.
4. East Saint Louis (Ill.)—Social conditions. 5. African Americans—Crimes against—
Illinois—East Saint Louis—History—20th century. 6. African Americans—Illinois—
East Saint Louis—History. 7. African Americans—Illinois—East Saint Louis—Social
conditions. I. Title.

F549.E2L86 2008
977.3'89—dc22
                                            2008012838

CONTENTS

ILLUSTRATIONS

TABLES

PREFACE

When I began researching African American life in the formerly industrial city of East St. Louis, Illinois, I wondered about the extent of black residents' community building and political involvement before and after the infamous race riot of July 1917. I found fragmented accounts of the influence and actions of black East St. Louisans in a few pre-1945 sources, primarily state and federal government documents and white-owned publications. My research revealed that before the race riot, African American political activity, as seen by some city leaders, so threatened white entitlement to resources and power that white townspeople organized for mass antiblack violence. For a few decades after the riot, black residents continued their activism but avoided the appearance of challenging the racial hierarchy.

I revisited the argument, advanced by sociologist Elliott Rudwick and others, that social strain brought about race riots in East St. Louis and elsewhere in the nation, especially those that occurred in 1919 and in the early 1920s. These scholars saw the riots emerging principally from white workers' fear of black competition for industrial employment during the Great Migration of black southerners to northern cities during World War I. But through my research, I found more explanatory power in the arguments of Roberta Senechal and other historians who situated nineteenth- and early twentieth-century American race riots within the historical continuum of antiblack violence by white groups seeking to end black people's quest for equality.[1]

I came to view the events in East St. Louis in July 1917 as something other than race riots. I found myself in agreement with, for example, Jewish American sources that referred to the East St. Louis turmoil as a pogrom: an assault, condoned by officials, to destroy a community defined by ethnicity, race, or some other social identity. I came to see the East St. Louis episode as another example of the ethnic cleansing campaigns described by James Loewen in *Sundown Towns: A Hidden Dimension of American Racism* and by Elliot Jaspin in *Buried in the Bitter Waters: The Hidden*

History of Racial Cleansing in America. I also drew parallels between anti-black violence in the United States and ethnic violence during the same time in regions that underwent nationalist ferment and social turmoil related to industrialization, for example, against Jews in czarist Russia and against Armenians in Ottoman Turkey. By centering African Americans in the race riot narrative, I saw more clearly that mass antiblack violence in East St. Louis had deep political significance that the term pogrom accurately conveys.[2]

The further I delved into my research, the more I understood the relationship of black East St. Louisans to the real estate men who controlled city politics and directed economic development. I saw black-white contestations around urban landownership and land use extending beyond residential segregation and landlord-tenant relations to include access to political power. I realized that black townspeople's efforts to gain independence from white control lay at the core of attempts by white city leaders first to channel and then, in 1917, to suppress African American politics. And I found that though the legacy of the pogroms weighed heavily on the collective memory of African Americans, black townspeople who remained in the city, augmented by new arrivals of black southern migrants, returned to the political arena but conducted their activities in ways that the local elite considered nonthreatening.

Black people persevered in their political struggles, gaining for East St. Louis iconic status in African American history. They knew that this status included building community institutions and overcoming hardships. But black townspeople could not achieve political equality as long as local white politicians and businessmen regarded black aspirations as problematic. By 1945, black East St. Louisans were readying themselves to embark on civil rights campaigns; but they did not know, as a few city leaders did, that decades of urban mismanagement had made East St. Louis vulnerable to economic dislocations and incapable of fulfilling black people's hopes for substantive social advancement. As *American Pogrom* makes clear, black East St. Louisans' history represents the African American quest not only for freedom, citizenship, and equality but also for political empowerment.

ACKNOWLEDGMENTS

I truly appreciate the assistance I received while writing the doctoral dissertation and, after earning the doctorate in 2006 at the Pennsylvania State University, as this book emerged from that dissertation. I am grateful for the Ford Foundation Minority Dissertation Fellowship, the Huggins-Quarles Dissertation Award of the Organization of American Historians, the King V. Hostick Award of the Illinois Historical Society, and other funding sources that enabled me to accomplish the gargantuan task of digging through archival collections for sources relating to African American politics in East St. Louis, Illinois. Special thanks go to Gillian Berchowitz, senior editor at Ohio University Press, who observed my presentation on African Americans in East St. Louis at the Barnes Conference in 2005 at Temple University and who, with boundless confidence, along with her colleagues at the press and anonymous readers, guided me through the publication process.

I consider myself fortunate to be part of a small, but expanding, coterie of scholars interested in connecting East St. Louis to national and international historical and political currents. In particular, I thank Dr. Andrew J. Theising, professor of political science at Southern Illinois University at Edwardsville, and Dr. Malcolm McLaughlin, professor of American studies at the University of East Anglia in Great Britain. Andrew was most gracious with his support, sharing his collections of documents, photographs, memorabilia, and other materials; his knowledge of the history, politics, and current affairs of East St. Louis; and his hospitality and guided tours of East St. Louis and environs. Andrew also put me in touch with Dr. Malcolm McLaughlin, who, though deep into completing his own dissertation, was generous with his time.

I thank Mrs. Lee Annie Bonner, Mrs. Jeanne A. Faulkner, Mrs. Mattie Malone, Dr. Lillian Parks, Mrs. Frances Nash Terrell, Mrs. Claudia Nash Thomas, Dr. Lena Weathers, Dr. Katie Wright, attorney Richard Younge, attorney Wyvetter Hoover Younge, and other East St. Louisans who found time in their busy schedules for me to interview them, giving me a glimpse of what life was like for black residents in twentieth-century East St. Louis.

I thank for their valuable assistance the archivists, librarians, and staff at the Belleville (Illinois) Public Library, the Chicago Public Library, the Illinois State Archives, Cheryl Schnirring at the Illinois State Historical Library (now the new Abraham Lincoln Presidential Library), the Illinois State Library, the Manuscript Division at the Library of Congress, Walter Hill at the National Archives at College Park, Maryland, Michael Tuohy at National Archives–Great Lakes Region in Chicago, the National Archives in Washington, D.C., the Pennsylvania State University, Steve Kerber at Southern Illinois University at Edwardsville, University of Missouri at St. Louis, Washington University in St. Louis, and other facilities.

I profited from Barbara Gannon and other scholars who asked probing questions and friends who encouraged me to stay the course. And I owe a special thanks to Rita, my better half, and to my son, Charles E., who gave me the support and love that only a family could provide to one deeply engaged in researching and writing from the dissertation through the manuscript to the monograph.

Introduction

ON JULY 2 and 3, 1917, rampaging white men and women looted and torched black homes and businesses and assaulted African Americans in the small industrial city of East St. Louis, Illinois. The mob, which included police officers and National Guardsmen, wounded or killed many black residents and terrorized others into fleeing the city. The rampagers acted upon a virulent form of racism that made "black skin . . . a death warrant," in the words of white newspaper reporter Jack Lait of the *St. Louis Republic*. According to one African American eyewitness, "When there was a big fire, the rioters . . . stop[ped] to amuse themselves, and [threw black] children . . . into the fire." The riots disrupted interstate commerce and industrial production, prompting Illinois authorities to mobilize additional National Guard units to suppress the mass violence. When the terror ended, white attackers had destroyed property worth three million dollars, razed several neighborhoods, injured hundreds, and forced at least seven thousand black townspeople to seek refuge across the Mississippi River in St. Louis, Missouri. By the official account, nine white men and thirty-nine black men, women, and children lost their lives. Some thought that more white than black people had been killed. And others said that more than nine white people and many more—perhaps up to five hundred—black citizens had perished.[1]

Scholars generally think of East St. Louis, Illinois, as the site of the first of the major World War I–era urban race riots. They attribute the clashes mainly to interracial competition for jobs and housing in the city, then a railroad freight center second in size only to Chicago and the industrial hub of meatpacking plants, iron, glass, and aluminum processing factories, and other manufacturers for the St. Louis, Missouri, metropolitan region. The publications of pre-1945 residents no longer exist, but the voluminous transcripts of a congressional investigation of the July violence are readily accessible, leading scholars to assign the causes of the racial tumult to white reactions to job-seeking black southern laborers rather than to the increasingly assertive black drive for independence from white political machines. In one of the two scholarly monographs that examine pre-1945 East St. Louis, sociologist Elliott Rudwick uses social strain theory to argue that the Great Migration of black southerners moving north to fill labor shortages during World War I exacerbated racial animosity and existing tensions between black and white working people over employment, housing, politics, and other issues. Rudwick finds white industrial workers chiefly responsible for the horrific massacre. Similarly, American studies scholar Malcolm McLaughlin explores "why the local white community broke out in such savagery on 2 July." He discusses, more so than Rudwick, the city's saloon culture, connections between organized criminals and local politicians and businessmen, the presence of white women rioters, and black residents' armed self-defense during the riot. Still, McLaughlin accepts Rudwick's argument that white workers bore major responsibility for the antiblack atrocities.[2]

American Pogrom centers African Americans in East St. Louis, from the colonial era to 1945, in the context of the black quest to achieve freedom, a multiracial democracy, and human rights.[3] It concurs with the findings of Rudwick and McLaughlin on many of the particulars, but places the violence within context of African American politics and grassroots efforts to attain equality and power. Politics, in this sense, encompasses not only political parties and government but also a wide array of groups, including community institutions and voluntary and advocacy organizations, interested in influencing events, shaping policy, and wielding power. *American*

Pogrom follows a community-centered approach similar to that used by historian Richard W. Thomas in his treatment of African Americans in Detroit, Michigan. Thomas sees "the community building process as the sum total of the historical efforts of black individuals, institutions, and organizations to survive and progress . . . and to create and sustain a genuine and creative communal presence" in the context of the black "struggle for freedom and equality." But in adopting this approach, this work neither negates nor minimizes African American struggles that occurred, for example, at the workplace. African Americans often tied noncommunity issues to concerns of their community and used their culture and institutions to shape and sustain their workplace and other noncommunity experiences. *American Pogrom* regards the May and July 1917 violence as a political watershed, when white city leaders derailed the black quest for power by institutionalizing limits on black residents' ability to advance black community interests. Black East St. Louisans continued to participate in the political arena, and their participation was tolerated, if not welcomed, as long as they neither challenged white residents' entitlement to resources and control of city government nor asserted independence from white political leaders.[4]

This work sees the origins of mass racial violence, in the words of historian William Tuttle Jr., "embedded deep in the social, economic, and political structure[s]" of cities. It concurs with sociologist Allen D. Grimshaw that no direct relationship exists "between the level of social tension and the eruption of social violence" and agrees with historian Roberta Senechal that social strain theory lacks the precision to explain adequately why race riots occur. Senechal observes that since the 1830s, social instability and racial tension had been persistent features in northern cities but notes that only some of these cities experienced race riots. Placing the East St. Louis race riots within a long-term historical framework demonstrates that social strain and racial animosities had existed for decades before and after the 1917 race riots. The race riots, therefore, had much to do with white reaction to perceived threats to white racial entitlements by black community building and politics in context of the historic African American quest for freedom and equality.[5]

American Pogrom reconstructs black residents' community building and political actions, including their pursuit of patronage—a form of resource distribution—and political power. African American voters in East St.

Louis had recognized before the end of the nineteenth century that patronage provided a modicum of representation and a sense of empowerment (an understanding shared by other communities, as noted in William Grimshaw's scholarship on black Chicago). Black East St. Louisans interacted significantly, and at times dramatically, with white working-class residents and employers. But their relations with land-interest politicians and businessmen were pivotal, largely because these men controlled patronage, directed the local economy, and wielded much political power. Most politicians in East St. Louis, including the political bosses, were businessmen involved in real estate activities, from rental and sale of commercial and residential properties to land speculation and development. African Americans engaged influential local real estate factions not only over issues of housing, residential segregation, and landlord-tenant relations but also concerning matters of urban land development, landownership, homeownership, and private property rights. From the 1890s into the 1940s, black townspeople confronted this coterie of real estate politician-businessmen and their allies who sought to control, channel, or otherwise restrict black people's community institutions and political actions. In 1917, some of these land-interest men, with the assistance of the police, used mass physical violence against the black populace and nearly succeeded in turning East St. Louis into an all-white, or sundown, town. For several years after 1917, black residents struggled to overcome that violent political derailment that brought in its wake ghettoization, intensified de facto housing segregation, and widespread discrimination. By the mid-1920s, they had rebuilt their political infrastructure and continued their historic quest against those who sought to deny them political equality and participation in municipal government.[6]

In the late nineteenth century, African Americans in East St. Louis were busily building institutions and expanding their political influence. African Americans established a vibrant community in a border region where northern industrial and southern folk cultures overlapped. Like African Americans in Ohio River border cities such as Pittsburgh and Cincinnati, black East St. Louisans confronted varying patterns of racism, cleaved into social classes, and engaged in many forms of political action. African Americans in East St. Louis, like those in Chicago, Cleveland, Detroit, and other industrializing midwestern cities, lived and worked among white people yet apart from them. After 1870, black East St. Louisan men voted and exercised other rights of citizenship; all black residents availed themselves of integrated public transportation and, earlier than black Americans in other cities, entered industrial employment in appreciable numbers. But like African Americans in much of the United States, black East St. Louisans endured segregation and discrimination in employment and public education. The vast majority of the men, barred by employers and trade unions from higher-paying, skilled positions, found themselves in manufacturing occupations in meatpacking, iron founding, glassmaking, railroad yards, and freight houses. Most women who entered the workforce toiled as domestics and laundresses. Black children attended segregated schools, even though black families resided within majority white neighborhoods across the city despite state legislation banning school segregation. Black residents, however, pursued their interests by using their community institutions and politics to extract patronage and other concessions from city leaders.[7]

Leading white politician-businessmen who shaped industrial East St. Louis held the key to black townspeople's social, political, and economic advancement. These men, including mayors John Bowman, Melbern M. Stephens, and John Chamberlain as well as machine boss politicians like Thomas Canavan and George Locke Tarlton (generally known as Locke Tarlton), positioned themselves at the center of the city's economic and political development, combining real estate ventures with politics. Just as scholar Edward Greer describes local businessmen as decisive political actors in Gary, Indiana, an industrial satellite of Chicago, so, too, were the politician-businessmen of East St. Louis. Similarly, in industrializing nineteenth-century American cities like Paterson, New Jersey, as historian Herbert Gutman illustrates, it was nonindustrial property owners, not industrialists, who commanded local politics and economic growth. Politician-businessmen in East St. Louis, no different from their counterparts in Gary or Paterson, maintained their rule over challengers, including industrialists and black and white working-class and middle-class residents.[8]

Black East St. Louisan voters, politicians, and activists devised various tactics and strategies in their increasingly difficult encounters with the politician-businessmen, who commanded politics, directed economic growth, and tolerated, if they did not actually encourage, a saloon culture of gambling, prostitution, and organized crime. African American residents held their own in the political arena, swinging closely contested elections, demanding and receiving patronage, and running for—and sometimes winning—political office. They achieved such gains while the city's black population was on the increase, swelled by the continuous arrival of black southerners who joined with long-term black residents in using the ballot to exert political influence. But while black townspeople positioned themselves to obtain their share of resources and power, white politician-businessmen began to view them as a threat to their political interests.[9]

The period from 1900 to 1915 witnessed a black East St. Louisan community full of political vitality and social ferment, one ready to protest to improve conditions and to maintain rights of citizenship—not a nadir of deteriorating race relations. Like African Americans in other locales, those in East St. Louis often faced a seemingly "tragic sameness" of "caste-like discrimination and prejudice," as described by David Katzman and other historians. But in East St. Louis, black people did more than just react to white hostility; they organized their community to advance their interests. They built institutions and a rich urban culture, and, as historian Joe William Trotter Jr. observes regarding African Americans in the border region of the Ohio River valley, they developed complex patterns of "occupational status and class structure." In addition, black activists in East St. Louis formed numerous political and social clubs to achieve specific objectives as they confronted a multifaceted racism. Black East St. Louisans did not face unrelenting racial hostility: their leaders did succeed in winning a certain level of patronage as well as appointive and elective offices. But this success in the political arena concerned white political bosses. Black community leaders remained influential in city government, for instance, gaining political positions while African Americans in Detroit, Cleveland, and other cities saw their opportunity to seek office drastically diminished when white officials rendered the black vote ineffective through the institution of citywide direct primary elections. Black East St. Louisans' achievements in the political arena also worried progressive reformers who saw African American influence in city government as a black cog in the white political machine they sought to dismantle. These reformers considered black people's support of white bosses to be evidence of an African American proclivity, dating back to Reconstruction, toward inefficient and corrupt government. By 1915, African Americans found themselves at the center of a heated power struggle between white machine politician-businessmen and progressive reformers as these groups vied for control of city hall and the future of East St. Louis.[10]

Unsure of the outcome of this struggle, certain politician-businessmen decided to employ mass racial violence to eliminate the threats that they perceived from rapid shifts in East St. Louis's political culture between 1915 and mid-1917. The mass antiblack violence of May 1917, relatively benign when compared to the July massacre, revolved not around social strain between black and white workers but around politicized interactions between black residents and various white groups. Black and white factions pursued their interests during the booming wartime economy, and the sharp upsurge in the number of black southerners arriving in East St. Louis as part of the Great Migration altered the existing political balance. Black politicians, noting that migrants boosted the African American vote, demanded more patronage. Several black politicos, thinking they had the numbers and votes to compete effectively with political machines, began renegotiating their relationship to white boss politicians. They maneuvered to end their status as a political "submachine" by forging an independent black political apparatus. Their actions worried not only machine boss politicians and progressive reformers but also Central Trades and Labor Union (CTLU) officials. Union leaders, viewing industrial labor shortages and workers' willingness to strike as opportunities for mass union organizing, prompted white laborers to unionize by raising fears of black migrants. The labor organization ignored the fact that black workers often cooperated in work actions and strikes with white workers, occasionally acted as strike leaders, and usually refused to break strikes and that pro–labor union black politicians and workers had sought the CTLU's assistance in organizing African American laborers. At the same time, white political bosses—chiefly those associated with the real estate industry—orchestrated a terrorist assault in May in an effort to destroy a nascent black political machine capable of altering the balance of power. When these white leaders and their allies failed to achieve their desired results, they plotted another round of mass antiblack violence.[11]

The East St. Louis massacre of July 1917 and its immediate aftermath represent one violent episode in the ongoing American story of mobilizing people by race to achieve certain objectives. White machine politicians, through their proxies, unleashed murderous antiblack violence to terrorize African Americans into leaving the city en masse. The July event was an American pogrom, or ethnic cleansing, in which officials directed the organized, physical destruction of a racially defined community. The July rampage followed nearly three decades of an unbroken series of mass antiblack attacks, a number of which also deserve the label "pogrom." The most dramatic and best-known of these episodes occurred in 1898 in Wilmington, North Carolina; in 1900 in New Orleans and New York City; in 1906 in Atlanta; and in 1908 in Springfield, Illinois. In each case, local white business and political leaders, policemen, and others instigated, encouraged, or participated in assaults to destroy African American businesses, institutions, communities, and lives. The July havoc served as a model for later mass antiblack violence, for instance, in August 1917 in Houston, Texas; in 1918 in Philadelphia; in 1919 in many urban and rural locales, including Chicago, Washington, D.C., and Elaine, Arkansas; and in 1921 in Tulsa, Oklahoma. The East St. Louis pogroms were but one episode in a violent and protracted struggle by various white factions to maintain legalized racism in the South and to reconfigure white supremacy into a form appropriate for the urban industrial North. The violence dramatized the limitations imposed upon any attempt by black Americans to build a political structure that advocated African American interests in a manner equal to and independent of white-dominated political institutions. Local authorities, progressive reformers, and real estate men used the pogrom to oust black politicians from office; to neutralize, if not eliminate, African American influence in electoral politics; to reconstruct city government; and to institute a rigorous de facto residential segregation.[12]

Between 1917 and 1929, black East St. Louisans engaged in a wide range of political activities as they recovered from the violence of July 1917. They articulated through various New Negro movements such ideals as militant defense against mass racial violence, economic self-help, building a black city within a white city, and racial solidarity. These New Negro actions spanned the ideological spectrum from working outside the white-dominated political system to asserting African American interests within mainstream politics. At the same time, African American men and women, many arriving from the South, obtained industrial employment, expanded black community institutions and culture, and, together with established townspeople, rebuilt black political influence. Black residents used ghettoization, a process by which white authorities created all-black residential districts, to mobilize for various causes, from improving neighborhoods to regaining political power. By the mid-1920s, black East St. Louisans concentrated their efforts on political actions to improve their conditions and gain patronage. They overcame their fear of another outbreak of mass racial violence and again challenged white politician-businessmen and others for a share of resources and power, but this time within the framework of established political parties. Black politicians and activists, both men and women, rebuilt their presence in the city's political arena through the precinct committee system, the very structure that progressive reformers had instituted after July 1917 to replace ward-based elections in an attempt to weaken black political strength.[13]

African Americans, working against the legacy of the pogroms, built interracial coalitions to overcome economic privations of the Great Depression and to end segregation and discrimination at the workplace during World War II. They made social and economic advances and formed alliances with all-white or white-dominated organizations and institutions as diverse as labor unions, the Communist Party of the United States of America, and the Democratic and Republican parties. Black Americans saw their need for economic relief addressed by several New Deal agencies whose high-level administrators included them in job programs. Black workers became deeply involved in the labor movement, especially in organizing unions through the Congress of Industrial Organizations, which welcomed black working people into its ranks. Their campaign for equal access to industrial employment received a boost when President Franklin Delano Roosevelt agreed to demands advanced by the leaders of the March on Washington Movement to end discrimination in war production industries. They also utilized government agencies—the Fair Employment Practice Committee, for example—to obtain war production jobs that had been denied them. Still, African Americans, depending in part upon their social class and gender, encountered varying levels of segregation or discrimination in employment, housing, public facilities, and other arenas of public life. Black East St. Louisans, even working through interracial coalitions, failed to break the power of the real estate politician-businessmen or to dismantle segregation, eliminate discrimination, and secure civil rights. But black and white civic, labor, political, and business leaders, remembering the July pogrom, congratulated themselves that East St. Louis did not erupt into mass racial violence, as Harlem and Detroit did during World War II.[14]

This study of African American political actions in East St. Louis ends in 1945, on the eve of the post–World War II civil rights movement that came to galvanize the nation in the 1950s and 1960s. The movement in East St. Louis began in earnest in the late 1940s, when black men, women, and youth at the grassroots level, through the local chapter of the National Association for the Advancement of Colored People, embarked on a program of militant but nonviolent action to desegregate the school system. Their actions proceeded without mass racial violence largely because black and white leaders had reached an accord. City officials included black residents in postwar planning and political life, hoping to avoid racial strife in order to attract industry for economic growth. White politicians acknowledged that East St. Louis had failed to expand its industrial base during the 1920s and the booming economy of the World War II years, as major postwar manufacturers chose to locate new plants elsewhere, and existing industry continued to vacate. Political and business leaders remained wedded, however, to a pre–World War I industrial economic policy, financial indebtedness, and machine politic—and their legacy was a deindustrialized, mainly impoverished, majority African American, and politically black-dominated East St. Louis.[15]

ONE

Historical Roots of an African American Community, 1800–1898

BLACK PEOPLE in nineteenth-century East St. Louis built a community that met their social and cultural needs and served as a platform to sustain a political tradition forged from their struggles to end slavery and attain citizenship. After the final destruction of chattel slavery in 1865, postbellum African Americans found the freedom to build and expand their churches, mutual aid organizations, secret societies, social clubs, and political institutions. They used their organizations in conjunction with family and neighborhood networks to nurture a vibrant urban culture and to obtain city resources, influence the labor movement, oppose those seeking to prevent their advancement, and claim a share of political power. Black East St. Louisans shaped their community in response to white hostility and agitated around issues that addressed their political interests. Through their institutions, they exerted the influence necessary to shape and reshape the city's political culture in ways that favored their interests. African American men and women connected local concerns to national ones, making nineteenth-century East St. Louis a historical microcosm of urban African America and a harbinger of twentieth-century urban black politics.[1]

Prominent narratives of the mass racial violence that occurred in 1917 in East St. Louis have been framed outside the context of black residents' resolve to maintain their community as a space for their own cultural activities and as a vehicle for attaining equality and political power. These narratives see the violence as resulting from a confluence of events set in motion by World War I and the Great Migration of black southerners to northern cities. They highlight the idea that the war and migration brought "to a climax racial tensions and animosities in labor, housing, and politics that had threatened to erupt for years." But these accounts of the riots do not stress that episodes of mass racial violence formed only part of a larger national story of how the black community made possible the African American quest for equality and human dignity.[2]

As late nineteenth-century East St. Louis industrialized and the African American community expanded, black men and women entered industrial employment in greater numbers and earlier than did African Americans in other locales. As black workers increased their presence in factories and foundries, they came in contact with the white-dominated trade and labor unions that tolerated, if not embraced, their presence in the labor movement. Black wage earners in East St. Louis certainly encountered workplace discrimination, occupational segregation, and skill and wage disparities that white industrialists and white workers perpetuated. But they also joined or established union locals and secured unskilled and sometimes even skilled industrial jobs. Most importantly, black townspeople used labor's prominent voice in East St. Louis politics as one way to assert political influence.

Black East St. Louisans achieved a level of political clout beyond that of many African Americans elsewhere in the 1890s, in part because of the history of African Americans in Illinois and in part because of their increasing proportion of the city's population. They had experienced the sharp issues and conflicts relating to slavery and freedom in a border region divided during the antebellum era between Illinois, a former slave labor state turned free labor state, and Missouri, a slave labor state. They also had found themselves immersed in the tumultuous politics of Reconstruction. Black residents drew on their history to build a collective behavior of political action whose roots were forged under slavery and Reconstruction. But black East St. Louisans began to make effective use of their collective politics only when the proportion of black residents in the total (mainly white) population reached a level at which white politicians needed their votes: black voters then found themselves courted by whites who offered them patronage in exchange. Black East St. Louisans, their political strength continually augmented by black migrants, capitalized on a higher black-white ratio than existed, for example, in Chicago or Cleveland (see table 1.1). Additionally, African Americans in East St. Louis benefited from an established political tradition in Illinois, a free state longer than Missouri and one with a less repressive climate. This was one reason they attained more political effectiveness than black inhabitants of St. Louis, Missouri, which had a slightly higher black-white ratio. And though black East St. Louisans did not experience the degree of racial egalitarianism that African Americans were said to have enjoyed briefly in Cleveland, neither did they face systematic legal repression of their rights or widespread violent racist terrorism as did African Americans across the South and in other locations.[3]

In East St. Louis, African Americans struggled to win a share of political power in the face of a key group of white residents, politician-businessmen who derived their wealth and income from the sale or rental of commercial

Table 1.1. Black Population: Chicago, Cleveland, East St. Louis, and St. Louis, 1870–1900

	Chicago				*Cleveland*		
Year	Total	Black	% Black		Total	Black	% Black
1870	298,977	3,691	1.2		92,829	1,293	1.4
1880	503,185	6,480	1.1		160,416	2,062	1.3
1890	1,099,850	14,271	1.3		261,353	3,035	1.2
1900	1,698,575	30,150	1.9		381,768	5,988	1.6
	East St. Louis				*St. Louis*		
Year	Total	Black	% Black		Total	Black	% Black
1870	5,644	100	1.7		310,864	26,387	8.4
1880	9,185	513	5.6		350,518	22,256	6.3
1890	15,169	772	5.1		451,770	26,865	5.9
1900	29,655	1,799	6.1		575,238	35,516	6.1

Sources: Data for Chicago from Allan H. Spear, *Black Chicago: The Making of a Negro Ghetto, 1890–1920* (Chicago: University of Chicago Press, 1967), 12. Data for Cleveland from Kenneth Kusmer, *A Ghetto Takes Shape: Black Cleveland, 1870–1930* (Urbana: University of Illinois Press, 1976), 10. Data for East St. Louis and St. Louis from U.S. Bureau of the Census, *Thirteenth Census of the United States, 1910.*

Note: Figures for the black population refer to African Americans and do not include other nonwhite people. East St. Louis became its own census area after its incorporation in 1862.

and residential property and the development of urban infrastructure. Black residents had only their community and the votes that they used to confront real estate entrepreneurs who, like their counterparts across the United States, made land a commodity and personally gained from urban growth. Black East St. Louisans interacted with real estate men in matters of landlord-tenant relations and residential segregation as well as in questions of patronage, a form of access to resources and formal political power. Black townspeople mobilized through their institutions and organizations to secure patronage that white land-interest political bosses controlled. They made progress toward improving their conditions by negotiating with politically powerful real estate men such as Mayor John Bowman in the 1870s and 1880s, Mayor Melbern M. Stephens in the 1880s and 1890s, and political bosses Locke Tarlton and Thomas Canavan at the turn of the twentieth century. These men wielded considerable power at the local level, had material investment in maintaining power, and managed the city at the expense of residents. As black East St. Louisans exerted their influence, their institutions became vulnerable to politician-businessmen whose control of land maximized their power and who often used that power to the detriment of the black community.[4]

Toward the end of the nineteenth century, black East St. Louisans retained their political influence even as racism intensified against African Americans throughout much of the United States. They forged their political actions in the context of the city's black-white ratio, border location, and industrial labor connections. Black residents experienced an adversarial interaction with white townspeople, but they never lost their political rights to the same extent as did African Americans in the South, nonwhite Americans in the trans-Mississippi West, or nonwhite people in Hawaii and the Philippines after those territories fell under American rule. As the 1890s drew to a close, black East St. Louisans found themselves in a stronger political position than at any time in the past, including Reconstruction, largely because the community they built supported a political trajectory that exploited fissures in city politics.[5]

Origin and Expansion of Black East St. Louis

People of African descent had been living as early as the eighteenth century on the site of the future East St. Louis. The settlement was located in an area of St. Clair County known as the American Bottom, a fertile flood-plain stretching for miles along the eastern bank of the Mississippi River in southern Illinois. Enslaved Africans and African Americans in French colonial Illinois, a frontier society, did not produce commodities for the world economic market as did slaves in the plantation regions of the Caribbean and Latin America and in the southern colonies of British North America. Instead, they engaged in a variety of tasks, from clearing land to laboring on farms and in workshops. Their enslavement remained the same after 1763, when France ceded Illinois to Great Britain upon the cessation of the French and Indian War (the American theater of the Seven Years' War in Europe), and after 1783, when Great Britain handed the territory over to the United States after the American Revolutionary War. Slavery continued under the Northwest Ordinance of 1787, which banned the importation of new slaves into the region but allowed resident slavehold-ers to retain the slaves they already held. This institution of enslaved labor remained in force when Illinois achieved statehood in 1818, coming under tighter control in 1819 with the enactment of the Black Laws, modeled after the Ohio Black Laws. But by then, slavery had already come under attack from antislavery white Illinoisans who sought to end that labor system for fear that they would lose out to wealthy slaveholders in the competition to purchase the best farmland.[6]

Illinois abolished slavery in 1823, but black people in the state experi-enced a precarious freedom. First, abolition brought not an abrupt end to slavery but a gradual emancipation for adult slaves and freedom for chil-dren born to enslaved parents after emancipation. Free black people and manumitted or fugitive slaves disapproved of legislative enactments ban-ning black people from migrating to Illinois. They also knew that freedom was not guaranteed as long as the United States protected slavery, denied citizenship to free African Americans, and required white citizens to return fugitives to their masters. Black people, however, ignored such laws, knowing that they had more opportunity to build stable families and communities in free labor Illinois than they had in slave states. Some black individuals in 1828 and 1829 took advantage of policies that led to the federal Pre-emption Act of 1830 that allowed people who squatted on and farmed land to purchase the improved acreage. Even white Illinoisans ignored anti-black residency laws at certain times, for example, when they needed temporary labor.[7]

Black people settled on the American Bottom in close proximity to slave-holding Missouri across the Mississippi River. In 1850, nearly half the black population in the district was Missourian by birth. These people, either manumitted or fugitive slaves, may have chosen to remain in the area because they had enslaved friends and relatives in St. Louis and other nearby Missourian towns. Black residents of the American Bottom had to remain vigilant; slave catchers not only captured and returned fugitives to their masters but also kidnapped free black people and sold them down river.[8]

Many African Americans in the American Bottom district during the antebellum years lived in what became known as Brooklyn, a village a few miles northwest of the future East St. Louis. Free people of color and fugitive slaves established Brooklyn in the 1820s, making that settlement, according to historian Sundiata Keita Cha-Jua, the first continuously all-black town in the United States. The town was first incorporated as Lovejoy, named in honor of the white abolitionist and newspaper editor Elijah Lovejoy, who was assassinated by a proslavery mob in 1837 in nearby Alton, Illinois. Black Brooklynites vigilantly protected their politics and government from encroachment by the white resident minority and the government of St. Clair County. But Brooklyn, the center of African American life and culture on the American Bottom for much of the nineteenth century, lost its leading position in the decades after the Civil War, when manufacturers sited more of their facilities in East St. Louis. As a consequence, many black people settled there in order to live closer to industrial jobs.[9]

African American migration had a long association with East St. Louis and southern Illinois, a border region similar to the Ohio River valley where broad patterns of northern industrial and southern folk cultures overlapped. African Americans began to migrate in earnest after 1870 from former slave states, principally Mississippi, Missouri, and Tennessee, to East St. Louis. Some left the South during the last few years of Reconstruction when "redeemers," white supremacists who abhorred the political rule of the Republicans, regained control of local and state governments through terrorism and other means, ending any possibility of interracial democracy. Migrants also sought to escape a depressed southern economy and an increasingly regressive sharecropping system that severely limited opportunity for economic advancement. One wave of migratory enthusiasm, which had an early impact on East St. Louis, culminated in the Exodus of 1879 when black southerners, known as Exodusters, headed to

Kansas to find farmland. An unknown number, for a variety of reasons, never reached their destinations and settled in towns and cities en route to Kansas. For example, in 1876 a migrant agent left fifty black people stranded in East St. Louis, presumably either because the agent was unscrupulous or because the migrants ran out of money to pay him to continue their journey. Black southerners continued to migrate after the 1870s, especially during the 1890s when various groups of white southerners, with support from white northern factions, legalized and systematized white supremacy. Migrants sought freedom from the intensification of racial subordination, lynching and other forms of terrorism, disfranchisement, and segregation.[10]

The African American population in East St. Louis increased in the last quarter of the nineteenth century. Black people, more than before, resided in enclaves scattered across the city; the ghettoes of other northern and border locales had yet to appear in East St. Louis. Many resided in the city's oldest districts bordering or near the Mississippi River, notably on "Bloody Island" and in "the Valley," both west of what is now Tenth Street—the street that, before the 1890s, formed the city's eastern boundary (map 1.1). Most low-income African Americans inhabited substandard housing nestled around railroad yards, factories, and open fields in the western half of the city. During the 1890s, greater numbers of black townspeople often found

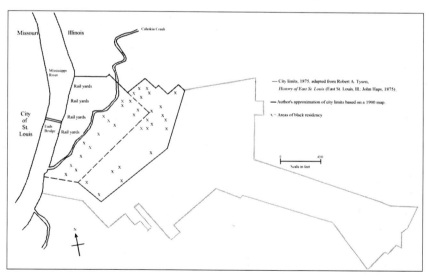

Map.1.1. African American residency, 1900 (selected places from 1900 census manuscript). *Map by author*

themselves living in the south end neighborhoods of Denverside and Rush City and in the north end section known as Goose Hill. Still, by the end of the nineteenth century, black residents lived in every city ward.[11]

An expanding black East St. Louis brought a proliferation of African American institutions. Black townspeople established churches, the traditional and most important centers of black communities, as well as civic and fraternal clubs, lodges, and other organizations where they affirmed their dignity as a people and gained skills required for political leadership and agitation. Between 1865 and 1870, they erected their first institution, a Baptist church, on Brady Avenue. Other churches followed—for example, St. Luke's African Methodist Episcopal Church in the late 1880s and an African Methodist Episcopal Zion church in 1887. In 1895, Mississippi-born laborer Timothy Peacock and his Missouri-born wife Charity, John and Minerva Williams, Missouri-born Mary Chism, and Arkansas-born Zelphia Williams organized St. Paul's Baptist Church, holding services in private homes before building a house of worship on Seventh Street in 1897. Jennie Thomas and others organized the Mount Zion Missionary Baptist Church in 1901, conducting worship in her home until the congregation raised enough funds to construct a church. Mississippi-born reverend James Lampley and his followers in 1910 formed the Truelight Baptist Church. Black Roman Catholics, like their Protestant brothers and sisters who had withdrawn from white churches in the few decades after the Civil War, became independent of white Catholics and in 1921 built their own house of worship.[12]

Men and women also founded lodges, societies, and other secular institutions, though specifics regarding the activities of these organizations remain to be ferreted out in future research. They pursued objectives similar to those of fraternal organizations in other cities, such as the provision of beneficiary or mutual aid to their members. Civil War veterans founded Pennock Post No. 749 of the Grand Army of the Republic and the St. George Lodge No. 1524 of the Grand United Order of Odd Fellows in the decade after the war. Fifty Odd Fellows conducted their first meetings in East St. Louis in 1876, presumably offering sickness and death benefits as Odd Fellows chapters did in Detroit and elsewhere. Another society, St. Paul Lodge No. 42, said to be the city's oldest black Masonic lodge, was founded in the 1870s by laborers Henry L. Jones and John Woods. Some women chartered a branch of the International Order of Twelve of the

Knights and Daughters of Tabor, a militant black abolitionist organization founded in the 1840s in St. Louis. Women also established clubs such as the Sunrise Council of the Daughters of Africa, the Mysterious Ten of the Court of Calanthians, the Daughters of the Tabernacle, and the Sisters of the Golden Gate.[13]

A primary reason that black men and women could build their community so rapidly was that they easily obtained jobs, albeit often the least remunerative jobs, in an industrializing East St. Louis. Over the last four decades of the nineteenth century, many men shifted from agricultural and other nonindustrial work to employment in such areas as railroading, meatpacking, and manufacturing. A few secured skilled positions such as butchers in meatpacking plants, while others worked in nonfactory jobs as brick masons, carpenters, coopers, foundry men, hod carriers, janitors, porters, and teamsters.[14]

African American women must have been wage earners in appreciable numbers, even though census manuscripts and city directories for East St. Louis have little to say about female employment. Perhaps in the mid-nineteenth century, some earned income selling garden produce, attending births as midwives, or lodging travelers. In the 1890s, black women increased their presence in paid employment by working as cooks, glass factory workers, janitors, laundry workers, sack makers, seamstresses, and laborers; the records also show one as a railroad laborer and one as a stockyard worker. Some labored in meatpacking and in odd factory jobs. But if histories of Atlanta and other cities provide any guidance, then probably most black women in East St. Louis toiled as domestics and laundresses. More likely than not, domestics commuted to work rather than lived in their employers' homes, and laundresses washed clients' clothes in their own homes rather than at clients' residences. These working women preferred to minimize contact with white employers in many instances in order to lessen their chances of being sexually harassed or raped.[15]

Black people arrived in East St. Louis in significant numbers in the 1890s when the city was already heavily industrialized. Clearly, by 1900, black men and women had obtained employment in nonindustrial positions. They also entered the manufacturing sector in numbers proportionately larger than did African Americans in northern cities like Chicago (table 1.2). African Americans may have fared relatively well in securing unskilled factory jobs in East St. Louis because eastern and southern European immigrant

Table 1.2. African Americans in Manufacturing, Chicago and East St. Louis, 1900

City	Total Employed (all races)	Total in Manufacturing (all races)	Total Black Employed	Total Black in Manu-facturing	% Black in Manu-facturing
Chicago	704,382	251,586	17,986	1,664	0.6
East St. Louis	23,677	4,308	938	225	5.2

Sources: Data for Chicago from Allan H. Spear, *Black Chicago: The Making of a Negro Ghetto, 1890–1920* (Chicago: University of Chicago Press, 1967), 30–31. Data for East St. Louis from U.S. Bureau of the Census, Special Reports: Occupations at the Twelfth Census, (1904), 440, 442. The Twelfth Census did not break down figures by race for cities of less than 50,000 inhabitants. Data for total black employed and for black employed in manufacturing derived from census manuscript for 1900. All tabulations from the census data are by the author.

laborers did not dominate the unskilled workforce as they did in many other industrial cities. Or perhaps African Americans had established enough of a presence in East St. Louis, moving into low-wage industrial jobs in the city, before large numbers of eastern and southern Europeans arrived in the United States. Yet another possible reason African Americans held their ground is that southern Illinois, with its strong orientation to southern folkways, was an area where they had long been regarded as the working-class population best fit for doing the least desirable jobs. But consistent with a national pattern, black workers lost to immigrants in the competition for industrial employment in factories several miles north of East St. Louis in the newly established towns of Granite City, Venice, and Madison. In addition, African Americans had been banned from residing in many, if not all, sections of that tri-city area. But in East St. Louis, black people maintained a presence largely because their role as swing voters proved useful to machine politicians who directed economic and urban growth.

Land Interests Shape the City

Various entrepreneurs and economic speculators developed East St. Louis with one overarching objective: to obtain personal wealth from activities connected to the economy of St. Louis, Missouri. As political scientist Andrew Theising notes, these men founded, governed, and planned East St. Louis and its economy, making their business interests, not the general welfare of residents, their foremost, if not their single concern. These men implemented policies that magnified their power to the detriment of the city's treasury and the residents of East St. Louis. The pro–economic growth businessmen of East St. Louis, like their counterparts in St. Louis, Pittsburgh, Cincinnati, and other towns and cities, were centrally involved in landownership and land transactions and sought to industrialize their town.[16]

The early generations of economic speculators began with pioneer settler and American Revolutionary War veteran Captain James Piggott. In the 1790s, he founded the village of Washington, which became part of the future East St. Louis. Piggott, who established a passenger and cargo ferry service, worked with others to build an economy that provided agricultural surpluses to St. Louis, a rapidly expanding city that had evolved from a French colonial trading post on the west bank of the Mississippi River. By the 1830s, city boosters in East St. Louis, like those in other municipalities, encouraged the development of railroads to bolster economic growth. Louis Boismenue and other local businessmen joined former Illinois governor John Reynolds in 1837 to finance and direct the construction of a six-mile horse-drawn railroad to carry coal from mines on the nearby bluffs overlooking the American Bottom to the village of Washington, by then renamed Illinoistown, for shipment to St. Louis.[17]

Like many urban boosters in antebellum America, East St. Louisan businessmen and politicians recognized the railroad as an important factor in developing the local economy, and they encouraged railroaders to locate their operations in the area. East St. Louis was the closest point on the east bank of the Mississippi River to St. Louis and thus a logical location for railroad terminals. In 1852, city leaders welcomed the first steam railroad, the Ohio & Mississippi, to their town. Within a few decades, railroads laid tracks running straight as arrows through miles of open country. East St. Louis joined cities like Chicago and Atlanta in becoming railroad centers for passenger and freight service, expanding in population, territory, and infrastructure. The city grew around the rail lines, train yards, and freight houses that dominated the riverfront and emerged before the end of the nineteenth century as a railroad hub second in volume of freight traffic only to the nation's largest, Chicago.[18]

A new generation of economic promoters appeared during the middle third of the nineteenth century, possessed by the single-minded purpose of making East St. Louis the dominant economic force in the Midwest. Some of these boosters combined their real estate businesses, which included land speculation and the renting and selling of property, with their activities as local and county politicians. They sought control of city hall to facilitate the conversion of land into profit and to transform the city into an economic growth machine. Among these real estate politician-businessmen was John Bowman, who became an aggressive economic growth advocate and a leading spokesman for these land-interest men.[19]

Bowman, a fitting representative of the real estate faction in local politics, used city hall to turn East St. Louis into an economically vibrant town and also to boost his personal income and wealth from land transactions. Born John Bauman near Mannheim in Baden, Germany, he fled his native country after the defeat of the liberal revolution of 1848. Bauman arrived in the United States in 1855 and secured employment as postmaster in Missouri in 1856. He adopted the name Bowman, a misspelling of his name that appeared on his post office commission paper. In 1858, Bowman moved to East St. Louis, and the following year he won election as justice of the peace, opened a real estate and insurance office, began practicing real estate law, and became an agent for the Connecticut Land Company. While serving as mayor, Bowman directed city government to industrialize East St. Louis. He also set a pattern of using political office for personal gain. Bowman exploited his position and influence in city government by selling land that he or his associates owned to industrialists who had decided to site their facilities in the district. For example, in 1873, after recruiting the St. Louis National Stockyards Company, a corporation consisting of John B. Dutcher of the New York Central Lines Railroad, meatpacker and financier Samuel Allerton of New York, and other railroad men, livestock operators, meatpackers, and financiers, Bowman and a business partner sold 400 acres of their land to the company.[20]

East St. Louisan businessmen thought their city had the opportunity to surpass St. Louis economically, especially after East St. Louis became the terminus of rail traffic for St. Louis. No bridge spanned the Mississippi River at St. Louis until 1874, when the Eads Bridge was constructed. City boosters took advantage of the St. Louis-Chicago rivalry in hopes of propelling East St. Louis into industrially outdistancing St. Louis. They had to be aware that during the 1850s and 1860s, economic leadership of midwestern cities had shifted from St. Louis to Chicago, for several reasons. First, an influential group of St. Louisans had emphasized river over railroad commerce, giving little thought to Chicago's economic growth based on rail connections to populous, industrializing cities in the Northeast. Second, some eastern financiers, worrying that national politics over slavery made the business climate in the 1850s in St. Louis uncertain, moved their investments from St. Louis to Chicago. Finally, by 1861, St. Louis's leaders, favoring river over rail transport, saw plans to build their city's economy collapse when the southern states seceded, severing shipping lines on the Mississippi River. In addition, Chicago's aggressive railroad expansion had taken productive hinterland of the upper Midwest away from St. Louis. The Missouri metropolis continued, however, to attract eastern financiers, capitalists, and railroaders like J. L. Pennifill of the Springfield, Jerseyville & St. Louis Railway, seeking to tap that city's still-lucrative commercial markets.[21]

East St. Louis politicians and businessmen eagerly began promoting their city to industrialists. They enticed manufacturers by publicizing the town's dense rail network and its geographic advantages, including inexpensive flatlands for factories, close proximity to St. Louis, and access to cheap coal from southern Illinois. They also stressed the advantages for corporations in dealing with one rather than several municipalities. In 1861, led by John Bowman, a majority of voters in Illinoistown and neighboring settlements agreed to unite into one jurisdiction so that corporations would only need to interact with one local government. Townspeople approved of incorporating the town under the name of East St. Louis, hoping to profit by association with St. Louis's favorable image as a cultural center. Bowman and attorneys William G. Kase and Mortimer Millard obtained in 1865 a charter from the state legislature authorizing a change in municipal organization from that of town to city. Prominent landowning families such as Abt, Kurrus, Lovingston, Sexton, Weiss, and Winstanley expanded East St. Louis by annexing Illinois City, St. Clair, New Brighton, and other villages.[22]

City businessmen, however, disagreed over the issue of flood control. They knew of manufacturers' reluctance to locate on a floodplain unless city and county governments offered protection from floodwaters. John Bowman led a faction calling for a strong, proindustry city hall that would show a willingness to finance expensive flood control projects, including the creation of a system of levees and drainage canals. They above all insisted upon undertaking a bitterly controversial project, the high-grading, or elevation, of principal streets and public buildings above the highest known flood level. In 1866, Bowman, as city mayor, and lumber dealer John B. Lovingston, a board member of Workingmen's Bank and a city councilman, signaled to railroaders and manufacturers that high-graders were ready to commit the city to flood control projects and welcomed on the city council corporate representatives such as Patrick Vaughan of the Indianapolis & St. Louis Railroad and John Doyle of the St. Louis Transfer Railway Company. High-graders argued for approval of bonds and loans for flood control and related infrastructure work, including the paving of streets and the installation of sewers, water lines, and sidewalks.[23]

Opponents of high-grading charged that the project had the potential to plunge the city into massive debt. Some feared that the high-grader-dominated city hall planned to confiscate property that fronted streets to be elevated. In 1877, the opposition, angered by several years of political maneuvering by the Bowman faction and its industrialist allies on the city council, rose to action, instituting their own city government and police force. Grocer Maurice Joyce presided as mayor of the anti-Bowman government, while Thomas Winstanley, a board member of East St. Louis Bank and a Bowman protégé, headed the high-graders' council and police department. In 1878, members of the two factions engaged in occasional street fighting, and the two police departments became involved in gun battles that sometimes resulted in fatalities. Bowman had left political office by the time the dispute ended in 1880 and the Illinois Supreme Court ruled in favor of the anti-Bowman government. But his political enemies did not forget him. In 1885, one or more persons assassinated Bowman, leading to a public outcry that spelled the downfall of the Bowman opposition and returned high-graders to power. The latter rallied around Bowman protégé Melbern M. Stephens, a former engineer for the Ohio & Mississippi Railroad and later real estate man, and elected him mayor in 1887, knowing that he would continue high-grading and its accompanying public works projects as the keystone of city development. Opponents' fears of a city deeply in debt did materialize, but not until the first decade of the twentieth century. Meanwhile, local businessmen oversaw the rapid industrialization of East St. Louis in the 1890s.[24]

Rather than dominating St. Louis economically, East St. Louis under city leaders' economic planning became an industrial satellite of St. Louis and acquired a host of problems that other industrial suburbs of large cities also experienced. East St. Louis, like other suburbs separated from a metropolis by a state boundary, suffered from differences in state laws and municipal ordinances regulating industrial production. Often industrial suburbs attracted corporations that metropolises with rigorous health or environmental laws did not want within their jurisdictions. Like Camden, New Jersey (a neighbor of Philadelphia, Pennsylvania), and Gary and East Chicago, Indiana (adjacent to Chicago, Illinois), East St. Louis attracted industry known for generating noxious air, water, noise, and olfactory pollution that damaged employees' and residents' health and homes.[25]

While some industrial suburbs had basically a one-industry economy (for example, Gary, Indiana, relied on U.S. Steel Corporation), East St. Louis gained a diverse array of manufacturers, none of which governed the local economy. By 1900, East St. Louis and its environs hosted a major stockyard, several meatpacking plants, glass works, food processing plants, a lead smelter, iron foundries, steel mills, breweries, lumberyards, roofing and other building material companies, cement-making firms, and paint factories, among numerous others. There were acres of railroad yards dotted with freight houses and train repair facilities.[26]

Many of the companies recruited to the East St. Louis district, according to Theising, were "intermediaries." Such firms processed raw materials into components that other companies then converted into products. These manufacturers occupied "a position between some market-driven commodity and the capacity of some client firm to create or retail the consumable good." Intermediaries lacked control over the prices of either the raw materials or the finished products and operated on narrow profit margins. For example, in 1889, the meatpacker Armour and Company earned a net profit of fifty-nine cents per sale of 710 pounds of dressed beef at five and three-eighths cents per pound in the New York City market. Intermediaries had direct control of only "overhead, wages, and facility/transportation costs." The livestock and meatpacking, railroading, iron and steel, and other labor-intensive intermediaries that composed East St. Louis's diverse economic base maintained low overhead, high volume of production, and high transportation costs. They demanded low corporate tax rates and relied heavily on unskilled, low-wage labor to perform grueling, often dangerous tasks.[27]

Livestock and meatpacking corporations numbered among East St. Louis's chief industrial intermediaries. In 1873, the St. Louis National Stockyards Company sited its facility on the other side of the city's northern boundary. The company that held, transferred, and sold livestock became one of the world's largest horse and mule markets. Meatpackers drew upon the National Stockyards for cattle, hogs, and sheep to process into meats and other products, including fertilizer. The first meatpacker in the area, Kent, Hutchinson and Company, began its operations in 1873 on National Stockyards property. Meatpacker Nelson Morris and Company arrived in 1889, employing around 1,200 men. Two giants in the meatpacking industry followed, Swift and Company in 1893 with 1,650 workers and Armour and Company in 1902 with 3,000 workers.[28]

Steel and iron firms were another important industry that employed significant numbers of workers making products for the national market. By 1902, the oldest iron works in the city, the Republic Iron and Steel Works, formerly the Tudor Iron Works, provided jobs for 1,200 men who primarily manufactured railroad rails, spikes, and bolts. The Elliott Frog and Switch Company produced railroad frog switches, special sections of rail that allow a train to "leap across" intersecting rails. It opened its East St. Louis facility in 1874 with 350 laborers and by 1915 employed between 700 and 800. Missouri Malleable Iron Company initially maintained a workforce of 800 men, producing railroad specialties and wagon skeins (metal thimbles that protect the spindles of wooden axles); it eventually carried on its payroll between 1,000 and 1,500 workers. One cast steel plant, Leighton and Howard Steel Company, employed 1,400 workers. Another, established by American Steel Foundries Company, had in its employ 2,000 men, who daily produced 150 tons of finished castings.[29]

Other intermediaries, including cotton compresses, food processors, foundries, lumberyards, bakeries, and manufacturers of office fixtures, agricultural implements, and roofing materials, further diversified the city's economy and solidified its reputation as a national industrial center. The W. H. Hill Lime and Cement Company, founded by W. H. Hill Sr. in 1872, employed from 30 to 35 men in the production of lime and cement products. In 1892, the Obear-Nestor Glass Company sited a facility in East St. Louis that provided jobs for 600 workers producing mainly flint and green bottles for breweries, canneries, and other corporate consumers. Southern Illinois Construction Company, founded by contractors C. L. Gray and William J. Edinger in 1898, planed lumber and cut stone. Established in 1902 by businessmen from Iowa, Indiana, and East St. Louis, the East St. Louis Walnut Lumber Company received walnut logs primarily from Tennessee, Missouri, and Kentucky and prepared the wood for the European market. The Pittsburgh Reduction Company, an aluminum processor, opened an East St. Louis facility, the Aluminum Ore Company, in 1903. Pittsburgh was later renamed the Aluminum Company of America and went on to gain international importance as the corporate giant Alcoa. The Aluminum Ore Company was the sole firm in North America to turn bauxite ore into alumina that other Alcoa plants fabricated into aluminum wares.[30]

Businessmen welcomed the population surge brought about by the arrival of intermediary firms that employed from several dozen to a few thousand mainly unskilled workers. Their dream of making East St. Louis at least a twin city of St. Louis, if not the dominant of the two municipalities, depended upon encouraging rapid industrialization and urbanization. City boosters advertised that industry offered numerous opportunities for employment. Real estate men, who had much to gain from an expanding population, figured prominently among the boosters. Those who did not earn their wealth through land transactions with capital investors sold or rented residential property to working men and women and their families searching for housing close to their places of employment.

The white population expanded dramatically from 5,544 in 1870 to 52,646 in 1910 as native-born migrants and European immigrants settled in rapidly industrializing East St. Louis. In 1900, the foreign-born made up at least 14 percent of the city's white population, and in 1910 their percentage increased slightly (table 1.3). Unlike in Chicago and other northern cities, in East St. Louis native-born and "old immigrants," primarily of English, Scottish, Welsh, Irish, French, German, and other western and northern European heritage, constituted a numerical majority among white people. The majority of old immigrants were mainly of nonpeasant background, possessed industrial skills, and practiced some form of Protestantism. The Catholic Irish were the exception: they came from peasant backgrounds and formed a significant percentage of unskilled industrial and service laborers (see table 1.4 for the largest white ethnic groups). In this sense the Irish resembled the "new immigrants" who began entering the United States in large numbers in the 1880s, coming from the Russian and Austro-Hungarian empires, Greece, Italy, and other areas of eastern and southern Europe. These new immigrants were overwhelmingly of peasant stock, possessed few if any industrial skills, practiced either non-Protestant

Table 1.3. Nativity of White Inhabitants, Chicago and East St. Louis, 1900 and 1910

Chicago

Year	Total White Population	Native White with Native Parents	Native White with Foreign/Mixed Parents	Foreign-Born White
1900	1,667,140	354,379	727,341	585,420
% of Total White Population:		21.2	43.6	35.1
1910	2,139,057	445,139	912,701	781,217
% of Total White Population:		20.8	42.7	36.5

East St. Louis

Year	Total White Population	Native White with Native Parents	Native White with Foreign/Mixed Parents	Foreign-Born White
1900	27,842	14,455	9,484	3,903
% of Total White Population:		51.9	34.1	14.0
1910	52,646	30,447	12,799	9,400
% of Total White Population:		57.8	24.3	17.8

Source: Data from U.S. Bureau of the Census, *Thirteenth Census of the United States, 1910: Bulletin, Population: Illinois* (1913), 30.

Christianity or Judaism, and expressed cultural perspectives that native-born white Americans considered alien.[31]

White newcomers, both native-born Americans and immigrants, came to East St. Louis to obtain industrial employment. Though profiles of these new white arrivals need to be built from further research, they displayed employment patterns similar to those of white migrants elsewhere. Many entered a split labor market created by employers eager to divide the labor force by ethnicity and skill level. Native-born and old-immigrant workers dominated higher occupational levels in terms of wages and skills and generally shunned the less remunerative, unskilled and semiskilled positions, leaving such jobs for new immigrants. In the packinghouses, for instance, unskilled Irish American and English American workers moved into skilled jobs as new immigrants entered the ranks of common laborers.[32]

New immigrants supplied the muscle for unskilled industrial production. They arrived at a time of rapid expansion of postbellum industrialization,

Table 1.4. Five Largest White Nativity Groups in East St. Louis Compared to Same Nativity Groups in Chicago, 1910

East St. Louis

Country of Nativity	Foreign-Born White		Native-Born White with Both Parents Born in Country of Nativity	
	Number	%	Number	%
Austria	1,672	3.2	505	1.0
Germany	1,427	2.7	3,048	5.8
Hungary	1,807	3.4	260	0.5
Ireland	998	1.9	2,155	4.1
Russia	1,690	3.2	513	1.0

Chicago

Country of Nativity	Foreign-Born White		Native-Born White with Both Parents Born in Country of Nativity	
	Number	%	Number	%
Austria	132,059	6.2	85,208	4.0
Germany	182,281	8.5	244,185	11.4
Hungary	28,938	1.4	8,286	0.4
Ireland	65,963	3.1	99,346	4.6
Russia	121,786	5.7	58,417	2.7

Sources: Data from U.S. Bureau of the Census, *Thirteenth Census of the United States, 1910: Bulletin, Population: Illinois* (1913), 30.

Note: The total number of white inhabitants in East St. Louis in 1910 was 52,646. The total number of white inhabitants in Chicago in 1910 was 2,139,057. A breakdown by nativity for census years before 1910 is not available for East St. Louis, indicating a need for future research in the census manuscripts. Hungarian-born residents did not rank among the five largest white nativity groups in Chicago.

when native-born and old-immigrant workers had already established their presence in the upper echelons of the industrial workforce. By 1910, new immigrants made up a significant percentage of the unskilled industrial workforce. They were relegated to lower job categories largely because they were considered racially different from native-born white Americans, who generally regarded the newcomers as "not white" or at least as not acculturated to being white in the United States. Employers thought them "racially" fit for undesirable working conditions. For example, managers regarded Ukrainians and other Slavic-speaking people as docile and capable of working most efficiently under strict supervision in dusty and smoky environments and Turks and Armenians fit solely for unskilled positions. At various moments native-born and old-immigrant white workers prevented new-immigrant laborers from obtaining even unskilled positions in factories that white workers considered desirable places of employment. For example, in April 1908, native-born white workers, joined in this instance by black laborers, fought and routed eastern and southern Europeans waiting to be hired at an Aluminum Ore Company factory gate. But within a few years new immigrants did find jobs at Aluminum Ore.[33]

In East St. Louis, new-immigrant workers provided much of the unskilled labor power at industrial intermediaries, but enough openings existed to allow the hiring of significant numbers of African Americans. For reasons still needing further research, new immigrants did not populate East St. Louis in as great numbers as they did Chicago and other large northern industrial cities. Though black East St. Louisans faced strong competition from white workers, they found a niche in the urban industrial economy much earlier than did black people in other northern industrial cities. But both white and black workers came to realize that though industry brought much employment to East St. Louis, they neither enjoyed job security nor earned decent wages. Thus, workers began to build a labor movement to improve their situation.[34]

The Labor Movement in Local Politics

As cities industrialized in postbellum America, industry first eroded, then later destroyed the artisan-based work system that had provided the livelihood of countless white Americans and European immigrants. African Americans were overwhelmed by white working people streaming into cities like Chicago, Buffalo, Cleveland, Atlanta, Detroit, and East St. Louis in search of industrial jobs. In the competition for employment, especially for semiskilled and skilled jobs, African Americans frequently lost out to white workers who claimed an entitlement to factory jobs and who, along with employers, shut black workers out of many occupations. Nevertheless, many black men and some black women did obtain unskilled industrial employment. Once employed, at least in East St. Louis, African

Americans sought to improve their chances for economic advancement by joining the white-dominated labor movement.[35]

White workers across the nation sought to reform the industrial order by building a movement to institute collective bargaining. They opposed industrialists' efforts to manage work processes and transform workers, especially those with specialized skills, into tightly controlled unskilled or deskilled laborers and factory operatives. In East St. Louis, workers began demanding the right to collective bargaining and an eight-hour workday in 1866. Railroad employees, a powerful bloc of industrial workers in the city, formed the core of the local labor movement. In 1873, railroad worker Thomas Calhoun led brakemen in forming the area's first major labor union. Two years later, railroad engineer Melbern M. Stephens, who later became a real estate man and the mayor of East St. Louis, founded a Brotherhood of Locomotive Firemen local. Other railroad workers established a local of the Brotherhood of Locomotive Engineers.[36]

Railroad workers in East St. Louis laid the foundation for a labor movement that became a significant political force in city affairs during the nationwide Great Railroad Strike of 1877. They first pressed for a resolution of their grievances during an economic depression that stretched from 1873 to 1877, a period when corporations eliminated jobs, slashed wages, and crushed union organizing drives. The Great Railroad Strike, initiated by Baltimore & Ohio Railroad employees in Maryland and West Virginia on July 19, 1877, quickly swept westward to Chicago, St. Louis, and Kansas City, Missouri. On July 22, 1877, strikers and sympathetic nonrailroad workers in St. Louis and East St. Louis established committees to coordinate a general strike in which workers in both cities took command of their respective municipal governments. In East St. Louis, strikers led by brakemen Alex Kissinger of the Wabash Railroad, Jack McCarthy of the Vandalia Railroad, and Harry Eastman of the Narrow Gauge Railroad halted rail traffic except for passenger and mail trains and took control of the Eads Bridge and telegraph lines. Strike leaders found a useful ally in East St. Louis mayor and real estate man John Bowman, accepting him as their arbitrator and even consulting him on matters of municipal governance. Unlike in Pittsburgh and other locales where strikers or their supporters destroyed railroad property, strikers in East St. Louis, through a special police force appointed by Bowman, maintained law and order. Their peaceable intentions won praise from the business community and laid the foundation for labor's future participation in government in East St. Louis.[37]

The strike in East St. Louis differed from the one in St. Louis with respect to the use by antistrike forces of racism and patriotic appeals to break the strike. In St. Louis, businessmen and others blatantly employed racist language to divide black and white workers. Perhaps in East St. Louis black workers numbered too few for antistrike elements to bother trying to foment a racist backlash. Strike leaders in St. Louis, as opposed to those on the east side of the river, held socialist views. Members of the socialist Workingmen's Party roused the anger of industrialists who feared an American version of the working people's government that briefly appeared as the Commune in 1871 in Paris, France. The nonsocialist strike committee in East St. Louis directed by Eastman and other leaders shunned the politics of their radical St. Louis colleagues so as not to alienate Bowman's business constituents. Strikers in both cities ended their rule on July 28, when federal and state troops arrived and returned the reins of government to elected officials.[38]

After the Great Railroad Strike of 1877, union organizers and their supporters sought to unionize black and white workers, reform city government, and improve working and living conditions. White labor leaders Harry Eastman, Alex Kissinger, and others recruited black and white workers to organize unions and campaign for labor candidates for city offices. Their message of equality between black and white workers resonated with black East St. Louisans. In the municipal election of 1878, for example, black voters supported white politician Mr. Wider (first name not given), who promised them city jobs and "equal privileges with the white laborers." Labor activists used for their vehicle the Knights of Labor, a national industrial union that aimed to abolish the wage labor system and unite white and black workers. Some unionists, seeking to install a prolabor government in city hall, railed against the corruption and violence that marked the municipal election of 1885 when their opponents, local Democratic Party operatives, won the election allegedly by stuffing ballot boxes. Approximately 3,500 votes were cast in a city of 1,500 registered voters. In addition, unionists mourned the death of their friend John Bowman that year when gunmen, presumably his political enemies, assassinated him outside his home. In 1886, the Knights disbanded when local and national authorities crushed a national railroad strike. The demise of the Knights of Labor left the labor movement primarily in the hands of labor organizers who concentrated on organizing skilled workers into craft or trade unions.[39]

Some local labor organizers persevered in calling for social betterment for working people in their agitation against corrupt city officials. These organizers and their allies, including the district's U.S. congressman, Jehu Baker, saw the need for a new local political party to oppose political machine bosses in the election of 1887. In that year, unions and anticorruption factions established the Citizens' Party of East St. Louis to conduct nonpartisan local elections, bring "sound business management and honest and efficient officers" to city government, and promote racial and class cooperation.[40]

Throughout the 1890s, the Citizens' Party promoted class harmony, industrial development, and a stable political culture, attracting white and black residents of all social classes. Its ranks included Republicans, Democrats, Populists, socialists, trade unionists, and others favoring progressive reform of urban life and politics. Citizens' Party politicians, gaining control of city hall, sponsored public works projects such as the installation of paved streets, sidewalks, streetlights, and water supply lines, and the improvement of schools. The party modernized the police and fire departments, expanded municipal services, and improved the city's infrastructure by, for example, constructing bridges and viaducts. It attracted working people who supported corruption-free city government, economic growth, more jobs, higher wages, and an eight-hour workday.[41]

Some unionists and their supporters placed neither interracial working-class solidarity nor organizing black workers on the agenda when they formed the Central Trades and Labor Union of East St. Louis (CTLU) in 1892. These organizers sought to build mainly trade unions, each having jurisdiction over a specific craft or trade and composed of skilled workers, nearly all of whom were white men. They structured the new organization to coordinate the activities of union locals and strikes and to advance labor's cause in city government. The CTLU affiliated itself with the American Federation of Labor (AFL), an association founded in 1886. It followed the AFL's program of business unionism, which involved winning union recognition, higher wages, a shorter workday and work week, and better working conditions, ideally through arbitration rather than through strikes. The CTLU organized barrel makers, carpenters, bricklayers, barbers, bartenders, and other skilled workers who retained a certain degree of control over their work processes. In emphasizing business unionism and organizing craft workers, CTLU leaders, like their counterparts in the AFL, showed little interest in unionizing unskilled workers, whether black or white, male or female. Some trade unions explicitly barred even skilled black workers from becoming members. The CTLU, with few exceptions, largely pushed black working people to the margins of the labor movement, thus forcing them to look for allies elsewhere. Black working people united with other black townspeople to forge a multifaceted African American politics that gained influence in city affairs and that at times competed with the CTLU for patronage and a share of political power.[42]

African American Politics

Black people in East St. Louis fashioned their politics in relation to white factions like the Central Trades and Labor Union, but also, more importantly, as a microcosm of the larger national quest by African Americans to attain freedom and the power to control their lives. Like African Americans elsewhere, black East St. Louisans relied upon their churches, secret societies, political and social clubs, and other institutions to gain access to local government resources and services and a voice in city hall. They constructed a tradition of community activism to advance their interests as a people and overcome various injustices rooted in class and racial inequality. Black workers had moments of interracial solidarity with the white-dominated labor movement and found a niche in the industrial economy. In addition, black townspeople won patronage and some services from white politicians. But they did not win the necessary level of support from city leaders to improve their conditions and status. To make substantial gains, black East St. Louisans, like their kin and kith in other regions, had to rely upon their own institutions and build a political tradition drawn from the experiences that they had gained during the Civil War and Reconstruction.

African Americans in Illinois and across the nation took a dramatic leap toward freedom as a result of the Civil War. Free and enslaved black people, whenever and wherever possible, seized the opportunity to strike a blow against slavery, working to transform the national conflict into a war for abolition. African Americans, especially the slaves who made their way to federal troop lines and encampments, influenced the administration of

President Abraham Lincoln in 1862 to make emancipation one of its major war objectives. Men and women contributed mightily to Union victory as soldiers, sailors, laborers, nurses, spies, guides, teamsters, laundresses, and cooks, among other roles. To cite just one example, Henry Mitchell, from a seemingly comfortable black middle-class family in Centreville, located just south of East St. Louis, enlisted in 1864 in the federal cavalry. Following northern victory and abolition in 1865, Mitchell moved to East St. Louis, where he became active in community building and a statewide movement to secure citizenship rights for black people.[43]

Beginning in 1865, African Americans explored the freedoms they had won through warfare. Black men and women seized the opportunity to build their family lives and community institutions without the disruptions they had endured from proslavery forces. But they knew their situation would remain precarious until they achieved full rights of citizenship and some degree of economic stability. African Americans entered into a series of protracted struggles from Reconstruction into the 1890s for landownership, labor rights, and political power. Their confrontations with implacable foes in the North, though less frequent than those in the South, became just as bitter, sharp, and bloody.[44]

Black Illinoisans agitated for landownership and civil rights after the repeal of the state's Black Laws and the ratification of the Thirteenth Amendment in 1865. Fifty-six African Americans convened the Illinois State Convention of Colored Men in Galesburg in 1866, evoking the memory of black loyalty to Illinois and the federal government during the Civil War as the basis for a claim to citizenship. Conventioneers passed resolutions, including those for equal education, voting rights, and acquisition of farmland for economic security. Though land reform was not as central an issue in Illinois as it was in the South, where ex-slaves demanded land, the convention goers' call for farms signaled that black Illinoisans agreed with their southern counterparts that political liberty rested upon an economic foundation.[45]

After the ratification of the Fourteenth Amendment in 1868 and the Fifteenth Amendment in 1870, black Illinoisans began exercising their rights of citizenship in social arenas such as schools and public accommodations that lay outside the protection of the federal government. Though the Fifteenth Amendment extended voting rights only to men, African American women remained influential in informal politics, participating in civic clubs, rallies, and other activities. African Americans in East St. Louis voted, ran candidates for office, and generally participated in electoral politics in an effort to maintain what hold they did have on formal political power. In 1873, political activists in the East St. Louis chapter of the Union League, a pro–Republican Party club, called upon black people to support the candidacies of equal rights politicians. Like its sister chapters elsewhere, the one in East St. Louis demanded full protection of citizenship rights, including the rights to sit on juries and to send their children to public schools. Led by African American state assemblyman John W. E. Thomas of Chicago, black East St. Louisans along with other black Illinoisans successfully pressured the General Assembly in 1874 to ban segregation in public schools and in 1885 to prohibit racial discrimination in public accommodations.[46]

African Americans in many northern and southern locales experienced a nadir in race relations after the war, facing terrorism, legalized segregation, and disfranchisement. It was a period of political and intellectual ferment as they debated how to oppose an intensified racism. Black people in the border regions of southern Illinois and the Ohio River valley engaged in similar struggles to arrest the deepening of racial subordination. Their battle over public schooling was one of many sharp contests for equality. In East St. Louis, black townspeople made access to public education a major concern by confronting exclusionism that denied African Americans access to public schools. In 1867, upon gaining citizenship, black residents brought about an end to exclusionism by forcing the school board to provide a school for their children. Parents accepted the board's offer of a segregated facility after white people threatened violence. They witnessed in 1875 an attempt by some white Illinoisans to establish de jure segregation. In that year, for example, a Mr. Plater (no first name given) of the Illinois General Assembly filed a bill to allow voters of a school district to authorize segregated schools. Though the bill died in committee, black residents knew that segregation could exist without being embodied in law.[47]

African American parents demanded that the East St. Louis school board either allow black children to attend white schools or improve black schools. In August 1875, black residents decided against sending their children to classes in a building in need of repair. At least eighteen black men and women met at the black-owned Brady Avenue Baptist Church to discuss public education. They formed an ad hoc group with the Reverend

B. Saunders as president, laborer and minister the Reverend Park Hutchinson as vice president, and William Eagleson as secretary, and together they petitioned the school board to provide equal education to black children in safe facilities. Led by ex-slave and Civil War veteran Captain John Robinson, formerly of Virginia, 200 black people demanded a new school for their children. On September 9, 1875, parents sent their children to the all-white Douglas and Franklin schools. Black residents ceased protesting after white teachers convinced them that the school board would find a solution for the children who resided near the Franklin school and would provide a separate classroom and an African American teacher for the children who lived in close proximity to the Douglas school. Parents renewed their protest upon hearing that M. M. Hayes, the black schoolteacher, decided not to proceed with class when he found the door to the black schoolroom tightly barred. Five days later at one of these schools, twelve children and their mothers confronted white students and adults who barred them from entering and threatened physical violence. The next day, Robinson led the twelve children, and presumably their mothers, into the white school, guarded them, and informed white parents that all children had a right to an education in decent schools.[48]

Black East St. Louisans knew before the end of the 1870s that school integration had ceased to be a possibility, and they worked to weave their segregated schools into the fabric of their community. They used their educational facilities as centers to offer black people, divided by church membership and other social affiliations, a chance to share recreational, cultural, and social interests. Black children attended segregated schools that spared them the daily racist insults that African American pupils had endured in integrated schools. In addition, black schools provided employment through the political patronage system for African American teachers and nonteaching personnel. Black East Louisans understood that their teachers enjoyed more freedom in what they taught than did their teachers' southern counterparts. But black townspeople also knew that ultimate control of their schools remained with the white school board and the politicians who controlled patronage and access to other resources. They realized that they had to enter city politics if they wanted access to resources and political power.[49]

Beginning in the 1880s, African Americans in East St. Louis vigorously engaged in electoral politics as a means to extract patronage from city government. Patronage supplied jobs that offered black people a steady income, increased their social status, and afforded them greater access to city hall. But most importantly, black East St. Louisans saw patronage as signaling white politicians' willingness to share a measure of power. Black residents saw one of their own run as a candidate (his name is not mentioned in the source) in the 1886 election when the Knights of Labor included an African American worker among their seventeen nominees for various positions in city government. White voters swept fifteen of the seventeen into government but rejected the sole black office seeker. Still, African American residents continued their involvement in formal politics, supporting whichever party promised the most patronage. For example, though black voters often voted Republican, especially in national elections, they occasionally cast their ballots for the local Democratic Party when it promised generous patronage, even though the national Democratic Party boldly proclaimed itself the party of white supremacy. In one such instance in the 1893 municipal election, black East St. Louisans voted for the People's Party, another name for the local Democratic Party, which guaranteed black citizens janitorial jobs in all public buildings if the party won.[50]

The People's Party and other organizations frequently reneged on promises of patronage after winning control of city hall or other political offices on the strength of the black vote. As a result, most African American residents during the 1890s allied with the Citizens' Party of East St. Louis. Black support for the Citizens' Party began in earnest in 1894 when Andrew J. Morgan and B. F. Goff organized and led citywide political education meetings for black voters. Morgan and Goff set about welding a black voting bloc for the 1894 presidential and the 1895 municipal elections with the objective of winning patronage from city hall. In petitioning for patronage, club members found Citizens' Party leader Mayor Melbern M. Stephens agreeable to black representation in the police, fire, and street departments. In August 1894, Captain John Robinson and Daniel Jenkins, the president and secretary of the pro–Citizens' Party club, now the Murphy Republican League Club No. 1, continued to mobilize the black vote. During the election of 1895, they marshaled black voters for the Citizens' Party, which promised more patronage than the People's Party. During a mass meeting in 1896 that signaled a loss of confidence in the People's Party, Captain Robinson and another

Citizens' Party advocate, Morton Hawkins, led the audience in denouncing a call made by a Mr. King (first name not given) for a black People's Party club.[51]

An increasing number of African American residents, through their clubs and ward committees, lent their support to the Citizens' Party because it met their expectations with respect to disbursing resources, awarding positions in city and county governments, and funding improvements, such as the extension of streetcar lines into and paving of streets in black neighborhoods. In 1897, most black voters supported Citizens' Party candidates Melbern M. Stephens for mayor and James Reese, a black resident, for county assistant supervisor. Though Reese lost his election, black voters remained loyal to the Citizens' Party, which in turn was grateful to have regained city hall with the black vote.[52]

African American townspeople also supported the Citizens' Party because of the efforts of the Afro-American Protective League of Illinois through its East St. Louis chapter. The league formed in 1895 when black Illinoisans became concerned about the erosion of their citizenship rights, and it quickly gained much influence in local black politics. The Illinois league affiliated with the National Afro-American League, founded in 1890 by black activist and newspaper editor Timothy Thomas Fortune. Combining notions of self-help, self-defense, political agitation, and accommodation, the Illinois league had as its goal the elimination of racial inequality. The organization opposed rising antiblack prejudice, segregation, and racial discrimination that, according to Illinois league president John Chavis, impeded "the rapid progress of the Negro."[53]

The National Afro-American League and the Afro-American Protective League of Illinois formed at a time when black people, especially those in the South, opposed a virulent, multifaceted assault upon their rights and persons. These organizations publicized black southerners' confrontations with white attempts to control African American labor and social and economic advancement through legal and extralegal coercion, disfranchisement, and segregation. By the 1890s, African Americans and a dwindling circle of white allies had failed to reverse the rise of antiblack hostility that led to violations of the Fourteenth and Fifteenth amendments. Their loss of political ground became evident in 1896 when the U.S. Supreme Court legitimized white hostility in *Plessy v. Ferguson,* which declared segregation constitutional under the doctrine of "separate but equal."[54]

Facing an uncompromising and murderous brand of white supremacist aggression, African Americans debated strategies and tactics to reverse
the erosion of their civil and political rights. Two major schools of thought
emerged on how best to advance black interests. One coalesced around
educator Booker T. Washington, founder and head of the Tuskegee Institute in Alabama, and the other around Washington's various opponents.
Washington, a spokesperson for a broad cross section of black America,
advocated accommodation as a principled strategy. He argued against black
political involvement and agitation for fear of sparking a massive, violent
white retaliation. Nicknamed the Wizard of Tuskegee, he promoted self-help
based upon land acquisition and the development of occupational skills and
businesses to sustain black social advancement. Not realizing that Washington also secretly maneuvered to oppose laws that disfranchised, segregated, or discriminated against African Americans, his detractors launched
a barrage of criticism against him, attacking his policy that in their view
called for making peace with white supremacists. One adversary, journalist and militant activist Ida B. Wells-Barnett, taking issue with Washington's pacifism, proposed that black people mount an armed self-defense
against white mobs. African Methodist Episcopal bishop Henry McNeal,
arguing that white southerners would never befriend black southerners,
urged black emigration to Africa. And W. E. B. Du Bois, a chief critic of
Washington, joined radicals like William Monroe Trotter in advocating
that African Americans engage in political agitation in order to restore
their citizenship rights.[55]

In 1897, however, members of the East St. Louis chapter of the Afro-
American Protective League of Illinois did not see Washington's strategies
of accommodation and his radical opponents' advocacy of political agitation as mutually exclusive. Perhaps some thought the Tuskegeean had served
up a policy of accommodation only to placate white southerners, as Washington's black northern supporters presumed. Chapter leaders continued
to seek patronage and political office as they accommodated to the harden-
ing of segregation. For instance, East St. Louisan realtor Pearl Abernathy
was a Protective Leaguer and a member of Washington's National Negro
Business League, which advanced self-help through black-owned businesses. He openly participated in local politics to gain patronage and political office. Abernathy knew that segregation helped his business among
black homebuyers, whom white realtors ignored. Unlike Washington,

East St. Louis leaguers openly condemned violence against black people: they denounced lynching as a barbaric "enemy of civilization" and called upon the federal government to enforce equal protection laws. Even though, as they knew, Washington possessed the power to derail individuals and groups involved in political actions, Washington and his allies made no attempt to disrupt the Illinois league. Perhaps Abernathy and fellow Afro-American Protective Leaguers had been shielded from attacks by Washington's followers because of Timothy Thomas Fortune's friendship with Washington.[56]

The East St. Louis chapter of the Afro-American Protective League and other black political clubs allied with the Citizens' Party to obtain political and economic benefits. The league endorsed the party in 1898, noting that within ten months of the party's retaking of city hall in 1897, black residents employed by the city were collectively drawing over $5,000 annually in salaries. It stressed that Citizens' was "the only party in East St. Louis that [had] ever put a colored man on the ticket and then stood by him and [saw] that he got his office when the Democrats [i.e., the People's Party] had counted him out." The league calculated that African American participation in the Spanish-American War, including that of nearly 300 East St. Louis–area men recruited into the army by Captain John Robinson, had convinced white Illinoisans of the need for racial equality. The organization sought to increase black political strength and gain patronage and representation in local and state governments. In April 1898, it worked to swing the African American vote behind black candidates running for the Illinois General Assembly. In September, the league campaigned around the issues of fair treatment for black Spanish-American War veterans, patronage for black people proportionate to their numbers in Illinois, union protection for black laborers, and open access to all public schools. Though black candidates failed to win seats in the state legislature, the league welcomed the growing influence of the black vote in local politics. In 1899, the league urged black East St. Louisans to reelect Mayor Melbern M. Stephens of the Citizens' Party, who had "done much along the line of giving all nationalities representation in accordance with their numerical strength."[57]

Black townspeople enjoyed the patronage the Citizens' Party bestowed. Captain John Robinson won appointment as superintendent of janitors in the Illinois Statehouse in 1897 and as Senate cloakroom superintendent in

1905. Self-employed teamster Morton Hawkins became a City Hall janitor in 1898, James Reese was appointed street commissioner in 1900, and Robinson and William Jackson served as Citizens' Party precinct representatives in 1903. Daniel Adams and others in the Negro Council Club who had worked to solidify ties between black voters and the Citizens' Party were rewarded with ward representative appointments in 1900. Adams was also nominated for the position of assistant supervisor of St. Clair County. Black voters expected Adams, one of the party's two candidates opposing Democrats for assistant supervisor, to win his election because white residents held the Citizens' Party in high regard. But in the April election, Adams was the only Citizens' Party candidate to be defeated, losing by just 52 votes. Black activists concluded that even though Adams had the backing of the immensely popular Citizens' Party, the majority of white East St. Louisan voters, following white supremacist sensibilities, had cast their ballots for his white opponent.[58]

From the Civil War into the 1890s, African Americans in East St. Louis constructed their community in the context of several factors, including the rise of the labor movement, industrialization, and urbanization. Black East St. Louisans began building their institutions in earnest after the Civil War ended the chattel slavery that had been a constant threat to the development of black communities. During the last quarter of the nineteenth century, their community experienced accelerated growth as more African Americans settled in East St. Louis, mainly black southerners who left behind a South of grinding poverty and deepening racial oppression to seek industrial employment outside the region. Black native-born residents and newcomers alike seized the opportunity to improve their lives in a rapidly industrializing East St. Louis. They established churches, fraternal societies, political and social clubs, and other organizations and entered the industrial working class, mainly as unskilled laborers in railroading, meatpacking, and iron, steel, and glass manufacturing.

African Americans in East St. Louis possessed a well-developed tradition of political action that had its roots in the antebellum and Reconstruction eras. They fashioned an activism that depended on having a community anchored to institutions that black people clearly called their own. Black East St. Louisans thought their most viable path to further economic and social advance was to use their community as a platform to allocate resources and attain political power. Black townspeople therefore made their community institutions key in their drive to take control of their destiny. As they worked toward their objectives, they mobilized their community, tailoring their actions to a region that presented African Americans with both opportunities and limitations.

But black people in East St. Louis shaped their community and political actions under the thumb of land-interest politicians and businessmen who wielded an inordinate degree of control over city and county government. Black—and white—residents encountered the spectacle of city leaders and economic boosters turning the municipality into an economic growth machine that brought excessive debt and myriad social problems that in turn had a negative impact upon their living conditions. But when an intensification of racism in late nineteenth-century America closed avenues to economic and social advancement for African Americans elsewhere, black East St. Louisans continued to participate in electoral politics in order to improve their living conditions and status. Their tradition of political involvement, combined with their increasing population, offered a degree of protection from the racial oppression that characterized African American life across much of the nation. Thus, African Americans in East St. Louis positioned themselves to challenge white city leaders for an even greater share of political power.[59]

The African American Political Experience, 1898–1915

AFRICAN AMERICANS in East St. Louis from the late 1890s to the mid-1910s fashioned a political trajectory that ran counter to that of African Americans across the nation. They asserted their influence with greater vigor upon witnessing racism in the military during the Spanish-American War of 1898, the American suppression of Filipino sovereignty after that war, the legalization of white supremacy in the South, and the recognition of de facto white supremacy in the North. Black East St. Louisans increased their political influence at a time when black people in many areas, especially in the South, experienced a loss of their political rights. Though their pre-1915 political involvement has not entirely escaped the attention of historians, their actions in the political arena have not been viewed by scholars as significant to the national historical narrative. African Americans in the small industrial Illinoisan city carved a path that held the promise of a share of political power while their counterparts elsewhere saw a reversal of their rights. African Americans in Wilmington, North Carolina, for example, lost commanding positions in local government to armed white insurrectionists in 1898. In New Orleans in 1900, Evansville, Indiana, in

1903, Atlanta in 1906, Springfield, Illinois, in 1908, and in other locales, African Americans experienced indifference or even violent treatment from police and municipal officials and little if any protection from murderous mass assaults. But black East St. Louisans continued to project their influence in city politics even in the face of increasing segregation, discrimination, and antiblack assaults. They accomplished what numerous African Americans elsewhere were prevented from achieving during the nadir of race relations from the 1890s into the 1910s: they amassed political power and built a black political infrastructure independent of white political bosses.[1]

But as black East St. Louisans began entering the urban industrial workforce, joining labor unions, electing black politicians, winning patronage and access to resources, and generally asserting their interests, they encountered white factions that took more frequent and more vigorous action to impede if not reverse their political, social, and economic gains. Black laborers competed with white native-born and immigrant workers for jobs in an urban industrial economy fraught with uncertainty brought about by frequent cycles of economic depression and unemployment. They faced the racism of employers and white working people that limited their occupational opportunities. Black townspeople witnessed white urban machine politicians who refused their demands for greater, more desirable, patronage. They confronted real estate men, particularly those involved in politics, who viewed the expansion of the African American community as a threat to their economic and political power. Black residents also contended with white progressive reformers who in the first two decades of the twentieth century gained enough influence to challenge the rule of machine politicians and curtail black aspirations. They found themselves at the center of reformers' explanations of what had gone wrong in the city when white politicians enacted policies that mismanaged urban growth and municipal government. But black voters, in spite of these obstacles, continued to employ tactics such as swing voting to divide white political factions in hopes of advancing African American interests.

Real Estate Politician-Businessmen and Progressive Reformers

During the last half of the nineteenth century and the first two decades of the twentieth, East St. Louis shared with numerous cities a host of problems created by rapid industrialization and urbanization, including rampant political corruption and graft, social and criminal violence, and over-crowded, unsanitary housing conditions. To a greater extent than other in-dustrializing cities, however, East St. Louis possessed an organized group of politicians among real estate men and other businessmen who occupied positions of authority and wielded extraordinary control of government and economic growth. This faction transformed East St. Louis into an economic growth machine and maintained the municipality as an attrac-tive place for industrial investments. City leaders maximized their economic and political strength and minimized their concern that East St. Louis had earned an international reputation as a wide-open town of unabashed corruption, debt, violence, industrial pollution, crime, and prostitution.

In the latter decades of the nineteenth century, politician-businessmen involved in real estate occupied the upper echelons of the city's leadership. In 1889, landowning real estate boosters J. T. McCasland, Henry D. Sex-ton, and John W. Renshaw founded a real estate association to coordinate the actions and collective interests of real estate men and their allies, in-cluding bankers and building contractors. In 1902, Thomas L. Fekete Sr. led the association, renamed the East St. Louis Real Estate Exchange, to command local planning. Exchange members wanted to attract manufac-turers in order to increase their opportunity to obtain personal wealth through real estate transactions with these industrialists. These men con-tinued the city's program of reshaping the topography and speculating in land in order to attract the industry that would bring people to whom they could sell and rent residential property.[2]

The real estate faction consolidated its power in the city and in neigh-boring towns on the American Bottom after a devastating flood in June 1903 covered sections of the city with thirty-nine feet of water. Real Estate Exchange member Sexton took the initiative in lobbying for a flood con-trol agency to build and manage a system of levees, dikes, and drainage canals in the American Bottom area of St. Clair and Madison counties. In 1908, Sexton, real estate man Locke Tarlton, and other land speculators organized a levee board to oversee flood control projects. Tarlton, a native son, used his real estate firm and the levee board to build his wealth and power and to underpin his role as a machine boss politician who bought and sold votes and disbursed patronage to loyal followers in the period from 1905 to 1917. In 1913, levee board members incorporated their organi-zation as a municipality, the East Side Levee and Sanitary District. Although they were elected by citizens of bottom district towns, board members operated independently of oversight from municipal governments. These officials used district money to influence city and county elections and to drain swampland they owned so they could sell it as improved acreage to developers.[3]

Politicians involved in real estate, banking, law, contracting, and allied pursuits enacted laws and extended tax breaks favorable to industry. They, like many city boosters, machine politicians, and urban growth advocates in other locales, ran a city government that favored the interests of corporations over those of residents. Over time, city hall shifted the tax burden from manufacturers to residents and consumers. For example, in 1911 Mayor Charles Lambert offered bonuses and other benefits, including a five-year tax exemption, to firms newly recruited to the city. These policies encouraged corporations to place their own concerns before those of townspeople.[4]

Railroad executives and others with interests in railroading led industrialists in responsibility for the imposition of financial burdens on East St. Louis. These corporate officials were often national figures making decisions in New York City and Chicago. For instance, New York–based banker J. P. Morgan owned the Eads Bridge, a railroad bridge spanning the Mississippi River between East St. Louis and St. Louis, and another New York–based financier, Jay Gould, owned the Missouri Pacific and Wabash railroads in the St. Louis–East St. Louis rail network. These and other railroad executives regarded East St. Louis merely as a site for economic exploitation and as a terminus for St. Louis's commercial markets. Their operations covered extensive acreage with rail yards, repair shops, and freight houses, limiting available building sites for other construction, such as residential housing. Chicago-based railroad managers levied discriminatory freight fees that slowed the economic growth of the St. Louis–East St. Louis region. Much to the ire of local businessmen like National and Union Live Stockyards chairman W. L. Tamblyn, railroads refused to equalize fees between eastbound and westbound freight traffic crossing the Mississippi River.[5]

Terminal Railroad Association of St. Louis, formed in 1889 as one of Jay Gould's concerns to represent railroads in East St. Louis and St. Louis, was particularly fierce in pursuing its own interests to the detriment of East St. Louis. In 1891, the association derived more than $400,000 in revenues from its ownership of two miles of track where 90 percent of railroad tonnage in Illinois was switched from one track to another. Terminal had become by 1900 a major actor in the local economy, charging higher fees, or "arbitraries," for westbound than for eastbound commodities, making westbound coal more expensive. Its actions convinced investors to site heavy industry on the east side of the river, where coal was cheaper and where Terminal also profited from renting its Illinois properties to them. Antagonized by the arbitraries that burdened its economy, St. Louis in 1906 began constructing a new bridge, the Municipal Bridge, to compete against Terminal. The bridge opened to rail and vehicular traffic in June 1917. Since St. Louis did not charge tolls, area residents nicknamed the Municipal Bridge the Free Bridge. (In 1942, the Municipal Bridge was renamed MacArthur Bridge in honor of General Douglas MacArthur.) The association, however, still dominated interstate commerce across the Mississippi River, determining freight charges through the ownership of ferries and toll bridges and depriving East St. Louis and even St. Louis of needed revenues for decades.[6]

Manufacturers and local political leaders mutually benefited from low assessed commercial property values and tax rates that contributed to the corruption of city government and to the financial weakness of East St. Louis. The former group, offering industrial capital and jobs, insisted on receiving tax incentives and secured lower taxes by donating money to the election campaigns of real estate politician-businessmen. The latter regarded themselves not as pawns or servants of corporate owners but as men who had knowledge, ownership, or control of land that manufacturers needed for their facilities. Over several decades city politicians helped corporate managers annually save tens or hundreds of thousands of dollars in taxes. In 1915, both sides gained immeasurably when Edward Miller, other politician-businessmen, and their friends sat on the county board of assessors, which assessed the value of a property and determined the amount of taxes to be paid, and the St. Louis County Board of Review, which set the final assessment and tax payments. Companies that won sharp reductions in their assessments included, for example, the Aluminum Ore Company, which saw its assessment lowered from $799,999 to $200,010; American Steel Foundries Company, from $507,000 to $454,990; Elliot Frog and Switch Company, from $24,420 to $9,000; Missouri Malleable Iron Company, from $519,000 to $132,000; and St. Louis Bridge Company, from $3,150,000 to $2,500,000.

More firms fared well with respect to taxes in 1916, when the board of review lowered the figures issued by the St. Clair County Board of Assessors. For instance, Armour and Company initially was to pay $420,057 in taxes before the board of review lowered its payment to $55,100. The East St. Louis Cotton Seed Oil Company saw its tax bill drop from $19,474 to $1,492, Morris and Company from $402,927 to $53,600, and Swift and Company from $428,619 to $54,110. In return for the lowered tax assessments and payments, Miller and his cohorts received gifts and donations from grateful industrialists while East St. Louis continued to endure crushing deficits.[7]

City leaders compensated for lost revenues by annexing territory that included prime factory and residential sites. Their reasons for annexation—to secure more resources, principally land, and enlarge the population base for more taxes—were no different than those of city boosters in other municipalities, including Boston, St. Louis, New York City, and Atlanta. Real estate men led campaigns to annex neighboring villages whose inhabitants initially welcomed access to city water and sewer systems, police and fire protection, and other services. Mayor Stephens oversaw in 1902 East St. Louis's absorption of Winstanley Park, Alta Sita, Denverside, Rush City,

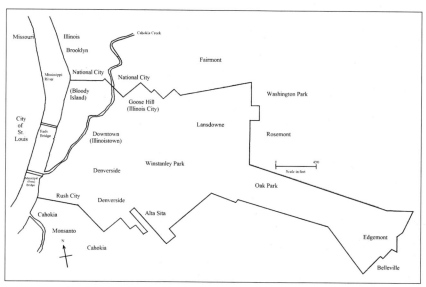

Map 2.1. Selected districts of East St. Louis, Illinois, 1910s (older names of districts in parentheses). *Map by author*

and other locales where the Obear-Nestor Glass Works (renamed Obear-Nestor Glass Company before 1910), the Shickle, Harrison and Howard Iron Works, and other manufacturers had established their facilities.[8]

By 1906, real estate men had begun to rethink their use of annexation as a tool for raising revenues. They faced increasing opposition from residents and industrialists in unincorporated territories they hoped to absorb. When, for example, city officials had secured enough votes for annexation mainly from white inhabitants of the villages of Klondyke and Tudorville, they encountered anti-annexation sentiment from many black villagers who hoped to incorporate into the village of Glendora, presumably to create a predominantly black town. (Sources do not indicate the locations of Klondyke and Tudorville, but presumably these settlements were situated along East St. Louis's present southern boundary.) Boosters also suffered a severe setback when St. Louis National Stockyards and the three meatpacking giants, Armour, Swift, and Morris, initiated an anti-annexation movement. These companies, eager to avoid paying taxes to any town, in 1907 invoked Illinois village incorporation laws to turn themselves into the municipality of National City. As a result of that incorporation, East St. Louisans were deprived of much-needed revenues even though they continued to provide services to National City and other corporate towns on the city's periphery. Annexationists saw their last acquisitions in 1908 with Lansdowne and in 1909 with the village of Edgemont.[9]

City politicians compensated for the loss of corporate taxes by relying upon licensing fees they collected from an ever-expanding number of saloons. Political leaders saw the possibility of covering revenue shortfalls fueled by their industrial growth policies as long as city expenditures remained within manageable limits and saloons proliferated.

By the early 1910s, the many saloons and their varied clientele made East St. Louis similar in at least one respect to other cities, large and small. Bars blanketed working-class districts, especially in the Valley, an industrial and racially mixed residential area centered along Third Street and adjacent alleys on the western edge of the downtown district, from Broadway on the south to St. Clair Avenue on the north. Many taverns were located across from factories and drew laborers who came to relax after work. Most notable of such locations was "Whiskey Chute," a string of bars along St. Clair Avenue across from the meatpacking plants and stockyards of National City. A few such drinking places attracted both black and white customers on a regular basis. Most integrated saloons, however, operated in nearby all-black Brooklyn; there the drinking houses resembled Chicago's "Black and Tan" saloons, which often doubled as dance halls. In general, saloons in East St. Louis remained segregated by custom. Some also served a mixed middle-class and working-class clientele, but most catered to mainly working-class male saloon-goers who enjoyed camaraderie and social drinking, turning such places into workingmen's clubs. These businesses, in addition to selling alcoholic beverages, functioned as headquarters for ward and machine boss politicians and their political operatives, employment offices for jobseekers, banks that cashed workers' checks, havens for trade unionists to organize workers, places to catch the latest news and gossip, restaurants for male and female customers, and meeting halls for neighborhood residents.[10]

East St. Louis reaped revenues and municipal government personnel and private citizens reaped an income from saloons, gambling houses, and places of prostitution. City hall collected from saloons an annual licensing fee that by 1915 amounted to $500 from each of the 376 legal taverns in town. Politicians considered saloons problematic only when saloon owners either failed to pay the fees or supported their political opponents. Some policemen supplemented their meager pay through dealings with saloon-keepers, gamblers, and prostitutes. By the early 1910s, several police officers, including assistant chief of detectives Frank Florence, owned brothels. Landlords collected monthly rents of $30 to $100 from prostitutes for housing that ordinarily rented for $15.[11]

Haphazard enforcement of antigambling and antiprostitution laws contributed to East St. Louis's reputation as a "wide-open town" that tolerated social and criminal violence. Authorities allowed the town to serve as "sin city" for St. Louisans seeking gambling and prostitution. City officials did little to interfere with such operations as these businesses brought money into the city treasury—and their own pockets.[12]

Politicians, police officers, businessmen, and others often ignored antiprostitution laws or violated these laws themselves. Like their counterparts in other cities, they tolerated prostitution as long as it occurred outside affluent neighborhoods. Authorities allowed prostitutes to ply their business within a block of city hall and in the Valley, and they seemed to look the other way when prostitutes, white and black, entertained both white and black men. Officials also often turned a blind eye when individuals forced women into prostitution. For example, they did not arrest dance hall owners John Peters and his wife, who pressed a fifteen-year-old white woman into the sex trade, or white saloonkeeper Steve Unk and his wife Lily, who coerced a white nineteen-year-old, Myrtle Gardner, to prostitute for eastern European immigrant workers. More often than not, policemen, bondsmen, and court personnel through bribes or other transactions offered legal protection to prostitutes and brothel owners as well as to dance hall owners and saloonkeepers who permitted prostitution on their premises. Police officers who ran prostitution businesses counted on their friends who were bailsmen, lawyers, judges, and fellow members of the police department to extricate them from difficult situations. Policeman Florence, for instance, on trial for the killing of police morality squad officer H. F. Trafton, who had conducted a raid on Florence's prostitution operation, had his friends arrange for his acquittal despite damaging eyewitness testimony.[13]

East St. Louisans who considered saloons, gambling, and prostitution unacceptable represented local variations of progressive reformers nationwide. Reformers vigorously accused city officials of perpetuating immorality and depressing the quality of life, and they challenged the rule of boss politicians, businessmen, and their allies. Like reformers in other cities, East St. Louis progressives positioned to enact political change came from the ranks of the white middle and upper classes. Including both men and women, they were clergy, newspaper publishers and other opinion makers, professionals such as social workers and lawyers, and corporate managers and business leaders active in clubs and civic associations. For example, a Baptist minister, the Reverend George Allison, emerged in the 1910s as the city's most influential progressive reformer, tirelessly attacking what he considered rampant immorality and city leaders who derived income from saloons and prostitution. Reformers also criticized machine politicians, especially those with real estate interests like Locke Tarlton and Thomas Canavan, for economic growth policies that fueled corruption, patronage, saloons, gambling, prostitution, and criminal violence. Reformers condemned politicians, police officers, and bondsmen who protected lawbreakers or recruited "thugs, pimps, loafers," saloon "bums," and gang members of clubs like the Cahokia Athletic Association to employ violence against political opponents.[14]

In East St. Louis, as across the country, progressive reformers pursued a wide array of issues, campaigning for government to impose a moral and efficient social order upon a nation undergoing seemingly chaotic social and economic transformations. They constituted an extremely heterogeneous, loose coalition of political movements concerned about the immigrant question, the labor question, and other social problems. Some progressives railed against managerial policies that provoked workers to strike. Many reformers, overwrought about the decline in public morality, prostitution, crime, and other perceived antisocial activities, sought to banish saloons and dance halls that native-born and immigrant working people patronized. Numerous progressives coalesced around campaigns to cleanse government of graft, corruption, nepotism, and inefficiency. Reformers in northern cities expressed concern that new immigrants lived in overcrowded and unsanitary tenements, participated in labor strikes, failed to Americanize themselves quickly, and voted for machine politicians.[15]

White progressives, especially those in the southern states and the border region, also discussed the "Negro problem," the proper social status of African Americans in a nation openly committed to white supremacy. Most progressives, like many white Americans influenced by scientific and cultural racism, thought black people contributed greatly to social disorder. They used racist imagery to build popular support for corruption-free government, the elimination of saloons and vice, and the segregation of African Americans. A few white reformers, including Chicago's famous settlement house activist Jane Addams, addressed the social problems that black people faced, but most sought to marginalize African Americans socially and politically. Some justified segregation, arguing that black people were socially maladjusted or inferior and that slavery had damaged the black family and psyche. Even the racial egalitarians among them, including Addams, generally regarded black people as predisposed to corruption, squalor, gambling, prostitution, vice, and criminal violence.[16]

Progressive reformers pushed to lessen, if not eliminate, black political influence, arguing that black people preferred patronage and government largesse to hard work and eschewed good citizenship. Reformers considered black people's dependency upon political machine patronage and agitation for equality to be disruptive, if not destructive, of ordered society. Social reformer Quincy Ewing, for one, wrote that white Americans generally thought that they must rid African Americans of the notion that black and "white [men] stand on common human ground." James Kirk, publisher of the *East St. Louis Daily Journal*, saw African Americans, like nonwhite people in the newly acquired American colonies of Puerto Rico and the Philippines, as unfit for democratic self-rule. While concerned progressives in the South denied black participation in electoral politics through disfranchisement, those in the North, by the 1910s, took a different tack. They found that the political influence of black voters, like that of white working-class voters, both native-born whites and naturalized immigrants, could be rendered "safe," perhaps even ineffective, by replacing ward-based with citywide elections and representation. Some progressives joined campaigns to segregate black people to a few residential districts when they realized that the black vote could be made superfluous by tying residential segregation to citywide elections, a practice common throughout the North.[17]

Class Development and Politics in Black East St. Louis

African Americans, and not just those in the South, underwent a reversal in the exercise of their political rights and witnessed an increase in legal or customary restrictions. In their daily lives, they experienced aggressive antiblack assaults from white people generally and indifference, if not hostility, from government at all levels. They faced a constant bombardment of indignities that reinforced their status as inferior citizens. For example, African Americans knew the symbolism of the protracted search for a white boxer to defeat heavyweight boxing champion Jack Johnson, an African American, whose intimate affairs with and marriages to white women infuriated numerous white—and black—Americans. As historian Kevin Mumford points out, the Jack Johnson story represented one facet of an expanding and determined northern commitment to white supremacy. Cultural works like the 1915 movie *The Birth of a Nation* served a similar social function in reinforcing a national commitment to white domination. In the rural South, black people under the oppressive rule of the plantation regime became further tied to sharecropping, debt peonage, and seasonal work in the context of a relatively dismal regional economy. Urban, primarily northern, African Americans found that white employers— often with the support of white workers—denied them factory employment. African Americans, regardless of social class, sought ways to end the segregation, disfranchisement, discrimination, and terrorism of rapes, lynching, and mass mob violence.[18]

Black men and women forged various strategies to reverse the descent into what became known as the nadir of race relations in the post-Reconstruction

United States. They counteracted racist assaults by founding social and political organizations to promote African American interests. African Americans across the nation formed political clubs that carried the message of national organizations like the Niagara Movement, established in 1905 to implement an aggressive program to achieve equality on all fronts for African Americans. Some looked to reshape national politics either by working closely with existing political parties or by establishing new ones. Some women, for example, hosted clubs that aimed to improve the lives, status, and image of black women. Others mobilized their energies to influence municipal government. Black people in East St. Louis, like African Americans in other border region cities, participated in formal politics at the local level. They made greater strides than their counterparts elsewhere toward gaining representation in local governance and building political organizations that could wrest some degree of independence from white politicians and attain a share of political power. Their expanding political strength in winning their share of patronage and influencing election results was due in part to the small but steady migration of black southerners to East St. Louis, where African Americans had gained a foothold in the urban industrial economy.

African Americans incorporated migration as a strategy to improve their situation, especially in terms of securing employment that offered the possibility of material advancement. Black southerners who had the means to leave the South, with its low wages and grinding poverty, saw border cities like East St. Louis as ever more attractive destinations for factory employment. They moved steadily north, but in small numbers since access to even unskilled industrial occupations remained limited by northern employers' preference for European immigrant laborers. Still, a significant percentage of black workers, men more than women, secured factory employment, albeit in mainly unskilled and menial positions. African Americans in East St. Louis entered the industrial workforce usually as common laborers in railroading, iron and steel founding, and meatpacking. Rural southern migrants, both men and women, who were familiar with butchering hogs either on farms or in abattoirs commonly obtained work in border region meatpacking firms. For example, 215 out of 1,762 employed black East St. Louisans in 1912 toiled in packinghouses, including 87 at Armour and Company and 99 at Swift and Company. A total of 253 black men worked for Mobile & Ohio, Southern, Louisville & Nashville, Illinois

Central, Terminal, and ten other railroad companies with facilities in the city. Black laborers composed by 1915 about 40 percent of Missouri Malleable Iron Company's unskilled workforce.[19]

Most African Americans obtained jobs as common laborers because they worked in a market where managers, structuring antiblack racism into the workplace, assigned the least skilled, most dangerous, or least remunerative positions to black men and women. Black workers at Illinois Central Railroad held positions as firemen, shop laborers, and brakemen because chief manager James Clarke, a former slaveholder, thought black people biologically unsuited for skilled tasks. Black men and women employed in packinghouses found themselves concentrated in hog-killing departments because managers like Frank A. Hunter of Swift and Company and Robert Conway of Armour and Company thought them more useful there than in the steadier work of cattle processing. Eighty percent of those assigned to hog killing at Armour and Company, for example, were black men. Women packinghouse workers toiled mainly as poorly paid pork trimmers while men performed the most odious jobs in meat-packing fertilizer departments. Some companies, including Aluminum Ore Company, rarely hired black workers. Gordon Crook and Elijah Smith, for example, were among only twelve black men, all in menial positions, who worked for Aluminum Ore between 1902, when the plant opened for production, and late 1916, when large numbers of black southerners began filling job vacancies.[20]

Black workers also endured problematic relationships with white working people and trade unionists. Some confronted white workers who restricted their access to various industrial occupations, denied them union membership, or physically attacked them. They knew that the Central Trades and Labor Union of East St. Louis, an affiliation of mainly craft unions within the American Federation of Labor, showed only sporadic interest in building interracial worker solidarity in the workplace. Poorly paid black workers lacked the funds to apply for union charters or sustain payment of union dues, giving white labor organizers a convenient excuse to rationalize their lackluster efforts in unionizing them. African Americans realized that the CTLU refused to address racism within the labor movement and that white working people generally asserted the notion of white entitlement to industrial employment, especially to skilled, higher-paying positions.

Black working people entered the urban industrial economy in noticeable numbers in East St. Louis as more employers embraced principles of scientific management that transformed work processes, forcing skilled white workers into protracted struggles to prevent the de-skilling of their tasks and furthering the difficulties of unionizing unskilled white laborers. Black men and women entering the industrial workforce only increased the concern of white men and women workers, who feared they would lose social status by laboring alongside black people. As more black East St. Louisans obtained manufacturing jobs, they faced greater efforts by white workers to bolster their racial identity in an unstable urban industrial economy by restricting black people's access to industrial jobs.[21]

African American workers sometimes formed alliances with white wage earners in certain locales, for example, in the coal mining region of Birmingham, Alabama, or in occupations like meatpacking where they constituted a significant percentage of the workforce. They engaged in momentary displays of interracial solidarity, winning concrete demands like higher wages, but failed to break down structures of racism in the workplace, such as seniority systems that favored white workers. Black laborers embraced unionization, through either integrated or segregated locals, in hopes of obtaining collective bargaining rights and higher wages and improving working conditions. In East St. Louis, black teamsters, coal miners, and molders joined integrated unions. Hod carriers and hotel and service porters, barred from existing union locals, formed their own all-black units. In August 1903, fifty-seven porters founded a union, electing Tennessee-born barbershop porter Edward Wilson as president and Tennessee-born bootblack Ambrose Jones as treasurer. Their union, an affiliate of the CTLU, quickly received an invitation to march in the CTLU's annual Labor Day parade. But over time, black East St. Louisan workers, though they did not reject unionism, realized that given white trade unionists' disinterest in ending racism within the house of labor, they had to look elsewhere to advance their political interests. One way was by forming alliances with middle-class black residents and white machine politicians.[22]

The emergence of a black middle class in predominantly working-class communities signaled the development of significant class divisions among African Americans. The black middle class did not mirror the white middle class in terms of economic power and structure, largely because in the latter third of the nineteenth century and the first two decades of the twentieth racism had intensified and hindered the black middle class from developing extensive economic networks and capital. The black middle class lacked highly placed professionals and corporate managers; it did not command any sector of the local, let alone national, economy. It included salaried and self-employed professionals and owners of small businesses, and its numbers and influence expanded in black communities as white professionals and businesses segregated or refused service to African Americans. Barbers, dentists, grocers, hostlers, ice and coal haulers, junk dealers, lawyers, ministers, morticians, newspaper editor-publishers, physicians, poolroom owners, realtors, restaurateurs, saloonkeepers, and schoolteachers formed the structural core of the African American middle class in East St. Louis. They relied heavily upon a black clientele for their livelihood, but a few individuals did provide services to both white and black people. For example, dentist Leroy Bundy, a native of Cleveland who also owned a small automobile sales and repair business, treated both African American and European immigrant patients. Missouri-born Pearl Abernathy, once a day laborer, became a realtor selling property to both black and white homebuyers. Born a slave in Georgia, Noah Parden, who became the first black attorney to argue a case before a justice of the U.S. Supreme Court, settled in East St. Louis in 1906 and opened a legal practice that attracted white as well as black clients. And ex-slave Captain John Robinson, a onetime laborer who became a community leader and saloonkeeper, held a series of patronage jobs at city hall and the statehouse where he formed friendships with white politicians. But out of 3,100 black adult residents in East St. Louis in 1912, only 120 people, or 4 percent, could be considered core members of the city's black middle class. Their number remained small mostly because black East St. Louisans found a wider range of needed services from black business owners and professionals across the river in St. Louis.[23]

African Americans of, or aspiring to, middle-class status gained a reputation among working-class black people as arrogant, self-appointed leaders of the race espousing the ideology of racial uplift. They included both those who held occupations commonly regarded as middle-class and those who merely expressed what they saw as middle-class respectability. Thus even black men and women who labored in what the white community commonly considered working-class occupations often sought entry into, or saw themselves as belonging to, the middle or "better classes." They advocated "middle-class ways—temperance, frugality, and hard work—as useful tools for living." Though the actual black middle class in East St. Louis was too small to exert much influence, the larger group of black working-class men and women who adopted a middle-class outlook took a prominent role in various racial uplift activities. In East St. Louis, as across the nation, such people engaged in an array of social movements aimed at demonstrating black people's capacity for good citizenship. They volubly criticized, for example, black patronage of saloons and dance halls, rollicking church services, and other activities they perceived as violations of refined sensibilities. They sought to assimilate African Americans into the mainstream of middle-class, white-dominated America and to transform less affluent African Americans into people capable of emulating their social "betters." Their efforts to uplift their race constructed an African American version of progressive reformism. Racial uplift advocates hoped that through social work and related activities among the black working class, they could persuade white Americans to relent in their racism and remove all impediments to African American economic, political, and social advancement.[24]

Black middle-class women and black women who aspired to the middle class stood in the forefront of racial uplift politics. They sought to instill morals and improve conditions among the less affluent, concentrating on the concerns of children and women. Toward this end, they established women's clubs such as the National Association of Colored Women, an affiliation of black women's clubs that formed in 1896 from the merger of the National Federation of Afro-American Women and the National League of Colored Women. These clubs worked to promote racial and gender equality and to meet social needs by establishing day nurseries, welfare and social work bureaus, and homes for the elderly, among other agencies. As they pushed forward these activities, clubwomen found themselves at the center of black progressive thought. Some also assailed what they considered the immoral or loose habits of working-class women, especially single mothers, whose presence, according to these black progressive reformers, fueled antiblack racism. In East St. Louis, under the slogan "Loyalty to Women and Justice to Children," Sarah B. Jones, who from 1910 to 1912 served as first vice president of the Illinois Federation of Colored Women's Clubs, led the federation chapter to instill middle-class values of frugality, sobriety, and industriousness among low-income black women and their families. Members advocated sexual self-control as one way to counteract racist imagery of black women as lewd and immoral. They also addressed working women's concerns such as employment, child care, and housing. In 1910, within the black progressive framework, Mary Martin and other black East St. Louisan women concerned about the welfare of orphans and the elderly formed an ad hoc committee with Mary Martin as president, Mary Parris as vice president, Alberta McKenzie as secretary, Mrs. Moore as treasurer, and Ruth Freeman, Annie McCraven, Mississippi-born Sarah Flood, and Alabama-born Rachel Ingram as club boosters. The women reorganized their committee in 1913 into the Colored Old Folks' Home and Orphans' Association, which quickly emerged as the city's preeminent black social work agency.[25]

A particular group of black men and women comprising entrepreneurs, workers, and others involved in the city's culture of saloons, gambling houses, and brothels occupied a niche within the black community, as well as between the black community and white East St. Louis. The number of individuals involved in such activities remains a matter of conjecture. According to the 1912 city directory, African American bartenders, saloonkeepers, and saloon employees totaled forty people. Black women in significant numbers counted among the hundreds of prostitutes plying their trade in the Valley and other sections of the city. Saloonkeepers, bartenders, saloon porters, professional gamblers, prostitutes, pimps, and others performed functions that some in the black community valued but others regarded as contributing to the city's social ills. African American saloonkeepers provided employment for black residents and operated as bondsmen for men and women who ran afoul of the law. Individuals in the saloon economy became targets of criticism from racial uplift advocates who desperately wanted African Americans to project an aura of respectability to white townspeople. Black saloonkeepers, prostitutes, and their ilk were regarded by white progressive reformers as exemplifying the extremes of African American racial proclivity to engage in immoral activities. Like their white counterparts, however, black saloonkeepers and prostitutes directly or indirectly provided revenues to city hall through licensing fees and bonds. In return, they often received a wink and a nod, if not protection, from municipal officials and police.[26]

African Americans, regardless of class or livelihood, faced white Americans' unrelenting resolve to relegate them to positions of social, political, and economic disadvantage. They often subsumed their own political or ideological differences within interclass alliances in order to oppose white impediments to black social advancement and antiblack violence. Black East St. Louisans encountered obstacles from politician-businessmen whose proindustry policies had fiscally weakened the city. Their attempts to acquire patronage and other resources began to be frequently restricted and rebuffed as city leaders found themselves squeezed by shifts in the national economy and the demands of their various constituencies.[27]

Black East St. Louisans knew that African Americans were not safe as long as most white Illinoisans held contempt for black people. For instance, in 1902, African Americans in Eldorado, a town about 130 miles southeast of East St. Louis, confronted an angry white citizenry who feared that a newly opened black industrial training school in their town would attract more black people to settle there. African American faculty, students, and residents confronted a mob eager to force them out of town. As events escalated into violence, an African Methodist Episcopal pastor, the Reverend Peter A. Green, used his gun to fend off a mob attacking his house. Black residents expressed relief when Governor Richard Yates Jr. sent in the militia to restore law and order. But black inhabitants, realizing they were not welcome, moved out en masse, turning Eldorado into a sundown town, a place empty of black residents. In the following year, African Americans in Belleville witnessed the spectacle of a white mob, estimated to number in the hundreds, storming the county jail and capturing a Mr. Wyatt (no first name given), a black schoolteacher accused of shooting a county school superintendent during a dispute over a job contract. The mob performed the lynching ritual, torturing and hanging Wyatt, riddling the corpse with bullets, burning the body, and afterward rushing to collect souvenirs of the victim's remains. Mass violence occurred in the state capital, Springfield, in 1908 when a mob, foiled in their attempt to seize a black man jailed on suspicion of raping a white woman, killed at least two other African American men, burned black homes and businesses, and drove hundreds of black people out of town before the state militia quelled the fighting. Black townspeople continued to maintain a presence in Springfield, knowing that they remained relatively safe in the state capital. In another episode of antiblack mass violence in Belleville in 1909, a lynch posse formed after police jailed a black man accused of murdering a popular white streetcar operator. In this case, white county sheriff Charles Cashel prevented a lynching by knocking one of the mob leaders to the ground and ordering his deputies to disperse the throng. Through lynching and mass racial violence, white Illinoisan terrorists, often with the support of the white community, sent the message to black people that they had little or no protection under the law.[28]

Black East St. Louisans responded to such antiblack terrorism through organizations determined to oppose the rising violence. Following the Wyatt lynching in 1903, they established the Imperial Social Club to pressure city authorities to enforce equal protection laws. They also organized local chapters of existing national associations. For instance, in 1915 a group of black East St. Louisans, including veterinarian Fred Halsey, physician William Baldwin, dentist H. T. Bolden, mortician Russell M. C. Green, and others, formed a local branch of the National Association for the Advancement of Colored People (NAACP). The NAACP, an interracial organization, had been founded in 1909 in response to the mass antiblack violence in 1908 in Springfield, to combat lynching and racial injustice and restore full citizenship rights for African Americans.[29]

Some African Americans linked antiblack violence and disfranchisement to American colonial suppression of the national sovereignty of people in the Caribbean and the Philippines. Anti-imperialists among them, especially veterans of the recent Spanish-American War who had seen the imposition of American-style racism on Filipinos and others, took the lead in weaving black concerns into local as well as national politics. East St. Louisans, including Spanish-American War veteran William T. Scott and several laborers from Missouri Malleable Iron Company, in 1901 formed the General Maceo Club, named after Antonio Maceo, an anticolonial freedom fighter of African-French-Venezuelan heritage and one of the chief leaders of Cuba's movement for independence from Spain. Scott took pride in the fact that Maceo and other Cubans of African descent had been formidable fighters in that country's anticolonial war. Maceo Club members participated with members of other local black political clubs in organizing voters for city elections and furthering African American concerns in electoral politics.[30]

Toward the end of the nineteenth century, while many African American voters remained wedded to the Republican Party, some black politicians in East St. Louis, including William T. Scott, maneuvered to make the Republican and Democratic parties compete for the black vote. Scott, for one, condemned the Republican Party for taking black support for granted. He and others attempted to break the Republican grip on African American voters by seeking an alliance with local Democratic politicians so as to swing the black vote to the Democratic Party. They must have been aware that black Chicagoans had been rewarded with patronage from Democratic mayors grateful for having been elected to office in 1885 and 1899 with the assistance of African American votes. In 1901, black Democrat Harvey T. Bowman formed the Third Ward Independent Club for the purpose of enlisting black political operatives to work closely with local Democrats.[31]

In the early years of the twentieth century, some African Americans began making tentative movements toward building an independent black political party. At a Negro National Democratic League meeting in 1900, Scott, as league vice president, condemned the Republican Party for conducting imperialist ventures overseas and condoning segregation. But he and other black Americans knew that the national Democratic Party remained steadfast as the party of white supremacy. A year or two later, Scott and other black political hopefuls dismissed both the Republican and Democratic parties and explored the possibility of establishing a national black political party committed to equality. In 1904 in St. Louis, he convened with AME Zion Church bishop Alexander Walters of New Jersey and other black leaders to form the National Negro Liberty Party. Scott promoted the African American cause and at the same time advanced his own political fortune when the party nominated him as its candidate for president of the United States. But the National Negro Liberty Party made little headway and failed to attract a nationwide following of African American voters, partly because most African Americans had been disfranchised and partly because most of those who still retained the vote refused to break from the major political parties. Perhaps of the several lessons learned, the most important was that African Americans needed to invest their energies in working with pressure groups for social change rather than become involved with all-black third parties that lacked leverage in national electoral politics.[32]

Black participation and increasing influence in formal politics made East St. Louis unusual at a time when African Americans in many locales had been forced out of the electoral arena. Black townspeople formed a voting bloc to mine opportunities as the local political culture fragmented from a combination of economic downturns and continuous mismanagement of the city. The economic depression that occurred from 1893 to 1897 had exacerbated the deleterious effects of the Citizens' Party's industrial growth policies. Townspeople's doubts about the party prompted newspaper owner and Citizens' Party insider James Kirk to remind voters that the party had worked for economic growth and prosperity for all East St. Louisans. By 1900, however, African Americans knew that the Citizens' Party had ceased to function as a unifying force in local politics. Black residents sought to protect their own interests as the Citizens' Party declined and competition for control of the city's political future intensified among influential, but dissatisfied, white Citizens' Party constituencies, principally railroad workers, businessmen, and progressive reformers.[33]

A substantial number of white railroad workers initiated a major realignment in city politics in 1900 when they broke from the Citizens' Party. Organized railroad employees, as members of craft unions, lacked interest in nonunionized, unskilled laborers whose ranks included black railroad laborers. In addition, dissident railroad workers claimed strong ties with the Democratic Party. They denounced both the Republican and Citizens' parties as servants of capitalists and praised the Democratic Party as the friend of the wage earner. Anti-Republican railroad workers formed the East St. Louis Bryan and Stevenson Railroad Men's Club to campaign for national Democratic Party candidates William Jennings Bryan for president and Adlai E. Stevenson for vice president. Their criticism of the Citizens' and Republican parties alienated most African Americans, who still supported both parties. Pro–Republican Party railroad employees were led by Illinois Central car repairer J. N. Luckett and yard master E. J. Payne and Mobile & Ohio yard master M. M. Walsh. They organized an East St. Louis McKinley and Roosevelt Railway Men's Club to prevent further worker defection from the Citizens' and Republican parties. Though Republicans won the district's congressional seat in 1900, many white workers in East St. Louis voted for Bryan and Stevenson. Their vote reflected a nationwide shift in white worker allegiance from the Republican to the Democratic Party.[34]

These white railroad workers, like white working people across the nation, emphasized antiblack racism as they built a labor–Democratic Party alliance locally and nationally. Railroad workers, especially skilled workers, in the brotherhoods systematically excluded black laborers from certain unions and from various railroad occupations altogether. As white working people strengthened their ties with the national Democratic

Party, they accepted the party's embrace of segregation and disfranchisement of African Americans in the southern states. White workers in East St. Louis through their unions became more interested in the local Democratic Party, and their leaders viewed the party as a platform for the advancement of labor concerns in city hall. The CTLU, to influence municipal affairs, sponsored large annual Labor Day parades, ran political education campaigns, and fielded labor candidates for city government offices. White railroad workers through the CTLU and other organizations began to lay the foundation for labor as an important, albeit junior, partner of the real estate–led faction in city government.[35]

Retail businessmen made up the core of the second major constituency to split from the Citizens' Party. They formed their own Republican Party club in 1901 to oppose the fiscal policies of the Citizens' Party. J. B. Sikking of the Retail Merchants Association of East St. Louis led these businessmen in forming a temporary coalition with the local Democratic Party to defeat the Citizens' Party. Sikking's faction anticipated further revenue shortfalls when city and county agencies lowered the assessment on industrial property from $5,359,000 to $4,500,000. They understood that any successor to the Citizens' Party had to rescue the city from the twin policies of unfettered economic growth through service to corporations and dependency upon saloons and an underworld economy to cover fiscal shortfalls. The business community, envisioning a city hall less generous with public works projects and patronage, placed itself on a collision course with the black community that relied upon municipal programs.[36]

A third major Citizens' Party's constituency, progressive reformers, slowly broke away from the party, and by 1910 they had organized the Progressive Citizens' Party to challenge political machine bosses. This new party included former members of the Citizens' Party. Some of the Progressive Citizens remained less than committed to the party's reform agenda. For example, real estate man Thomas Canavan, a boss politician and Locke Tarlton's business partner, continued his involvement in machine politics. The Progressive Citizens' Party, riding the tide of progressivism that swept across America, combined the politics of individual moral responsibility with the demand for honest government. The party allied in 1910 with former president Theodore Roosevelt's wing of the national Republican Party in opposition to party regulars who supported Howard Taft. The Progressive Citizens' Party accused the local Administration Party, successor to the Citizens' Party, of rampant corruption and campaigned for controlled economic growth, sound management of city government, good citizenship, and the restoration of law and order.[37]

Most black voters in East St. Louis continued to support the declining Citizens' Party at the start of an uncertain transitional period in the city's political culture, from 1900 to 1910, when factional battles between machine politicians and progressive reformers intensified. Black East St. Louisans favored the Citizens' Party because of its history of disbursing patronage and political resources to African Americans. In 1901, Georgia-born teamster J. H. Burkhalter and Arkansas-born delivery wagon driver Parnell Gibbs founded the Colored Men's Progressive Club to work for the Citizens' Party by backing Republican candidates for state and congressional seats. At a meeting of St. Clair County African American supporters of the Republican Party in 1902, the majority of those present denounced the Democratic Party, forcibly ejecting from the meeting hall Democratic supporter William T. Scott. Attendees appointed Daniel Adams of the Citizens' Party to head an ad hoc committee to issue resolutions to condemn the Democratic Party for its disregard of black people's rights and to reaffirm black support for the Republican Party.[38]

A few years into the new century, black East St. Louisan support for the Republican-oriented Citizens' Party began to falter. During the municipal election campaign of 1903, a number of black voters, approving of African American representation in the police and fire departments, aligned with white Democrats who had formed the local Independent Municipal Party, which outdid the Citizens' Party with promises of patronage. In the meantime, Republican stalwarts Captain John Robinson and Harvey T. Bowman of the Rush City and Tudorville Citizens' Club campaigned for the Citizens' Party ticket headed by Mayor Melbern M. Stephens. But a majority of black voters in the predominantly African American precincts in the second and third wards cast their ballots for Independent Municipal Party office seekers, including its candidate for mayor, Silas Cook. In May, black politicians, who had made the Independent Municipal Party victory possible, called upon party bosses to honor their promises of patronage, which the party later failed to disburse generously.[39]

Black Republicans stepped up their organizing drive in 1906 to counter local Democratic ascendancy among African Americans in East St. Louis. The newly formed Colored Lincoln-Roosevelt Republican League, with saloonkeeper Richard Freeman as president and Tennessee-born laborer Alex Lane as vice president, began rebuilding Republican ties with black voters. Leaguers extracted from the Republican Party promises of patronage, an aldermanic seat for the majority-black second ward, and judge and election clerk positions in an effort to prove to black East St. Louisans that the party valued their votes. But black residents received few rewards in 1908 after the Republican Party, on the strength of the black vote, won state and federal offices.[40]

As black political operatives became more adept at managing the black vote, they earned the ire of opposing party bosses whose sharp contests for control of the city left them with little patience for black political strategies. These operatives convinced black voters to cast their ballots for real estate men Locke Tarlton and Thomas Canavan, machine politicians whose allegiance fluctuated between the Democratic and Republican parties or their proxies. But black political workers often became targets of their bosses' enemies. For example, in 1907 black Citizens' Party worker James Turley received a severe beating from a police officer in the employ of one of Canavan's opponents. In 1908, Joseph Suttles and bartender William Mosely, campaign workers for the white state's attorney of St. Clair County, Mr. Tecklenburg (first name not given), a friend of Democrats Tarlton and Canavan, were arrested for selling liquor on the day of the Illinois primaries. The arrest was made by black deputy sheriff George Brockman, who acted on orders from his boss C. E. Chamberlin, a Republican trying to unseat Tecklenburg.[41]

Black East St. Louisan voters, whether skillful as a swing voting bloc or as ticket splitters, still failed to gain the level of patronage they sought, even when their candidates succeeded in winning political seats. During the municipal election of 1910, they received overtures from white politicians of the Administration Party (no connection to the Administration Party of 1902), the new name of the local Democratic Party, and the reformers' Progressive Citizens' Party as both organizations fought for control of the city. Attorney Noah Parden, for one, found the Progressive Citizens' Party attractive, connecting its platform for prosperity and sound municipal government with racial uplift, sobriety, and respectability. But other political operatives, viewing patronage as a stepping-stone to political power, backed the Administration Party. Black voters faced for the first time the prospect of splitting their vote between two well-known community leaders,

Progressive Citizens' Noah Parden and Administration's Leroy Bundy, who were both competing for a seat on the Board of Assistant Supervisors of St. Clair County. They saw either a Parden or a Bundy victory as opening the way for greater African American access to city hall. But when the Progressive Citizens, winning the election, credited their success to white voters' disgust with "vice, dishonesty, crime, and corruption," black residents expected little if any patronage, even though Parden won the assistant supervisor seat. In addition, the black vote for the Progressive Citizens' Party did not end reformers' use of racist imagery to blame black people for encouraging political corruption with demands for more patronage.[42]

From 1910 to 1912, black Republicans concluded that the Progressive Citizens' Party, like the local Democratic Party, had no interest in black residents. They made tentative moves to claim decision-making control of their wards so as to be independent of white political machines. Their effort to win political power received much impetus after the Progressive Citizens' Party boss, Republican congressman William A. Rodenberg, refused to award black people patronage other than janitorial positions. In 1912, saloonkeeper Addison King and hod carrier Anderson B. Woods formed the Colored Progressive Republican League of East St. Louis to oppose Rodenberg. They weakened the congressman in the eyes of black voters by criticizing his failure to assist a congressional committee investigating an altercation that had occurred in 1906 between 167 African American soldiers and white authorities in Brownsville, Texas, resulting in the jailing of the troops on false charges. Like many Americans, black and white, African Americans in East St. Louis expressed anger that then–Republican president Theodore Roosevelt dishonorably discharged the troops. Black residents were disturbed by Rodenberg's disinterest in the investigation of the Brownsville affair. So when the Colored Progressive Republican League started organizing anti-Rodenberg political clubs to mobilize black voters, it was able to exploit the rift within the local Republican organization between Republicans backing President Howard Taft, including Rodenberg, and Theodore Roosevelt progressives.[43]

The East St. Louis chapter of the Afro-American Protective League of Illinois emphasized to black townspeople that their vote illustrated the African American struggle for freedom and equality. The organization took a keen interest in wresting as much power as possible from white machine bosses. It used the annual commemoration of the day when the

Emancipation Proclamation was first announced to promote its program to support black political candidates for local and state government offices. For example, at a fiftieth anniversary celebration of the Emancipation Proclamation sponsored by the chapter in September 1912, speakers contrasted the document's promise of freedom with the expected curtailment of civil rights if Woodrow Wilson and his segregationist supporters won the White House in November. Leading black East St. Louisans also spoke about African American intentions to reshape the city's political culture, though details of their oration went unrecorded.[44]

Independent-minded African American politicians and operatives separated themselves from William A. Rodenberg, whose machine exerted much control over black Republicans. They did not have to wait long for Rodenberg to counterattack, which he did in 1912 by manipulating the voting process and intimidating his opponents. Anti-Rodenberg Republicans became targets when the machine assigned two black operatives, Terminal Railroad employee John Jefferson and driver John Green, to import African Americans from southern Illinois into East St. Louis for the purpose of padding voter registration rolls for the Republican Party. Additional harassment ensued when Rodenberg's black loyalists filed affidavits questioning the qualifications of dissident black Republican voters. Black politicians realized that Rodenberg used such tactics to discipline them into doing his bidding on election day. Lincoln High School principal Benjamin F. Bowles, an anti-Rodenberg Republican, became the first major casualty of the Rodenberg offensive in 1913 when the machine successfully pressured the school board not to rehire him. In 1914, Bowles accused Rodenberg of recklessly taking advantage of East St. Louis for his own profit and riding roughshod over black Republicans. The Bowles episode did not alter the balance of power, but it dramatized to those seeking a strong black political presence that machine politicians intended to squelch such a possibility.[45]

White machine politicians wanted to secure the black vote largely because their opponents who espoused some form of progressive reform of city government and politics had been gaining influence. From 1913 to 1915, political bosses and progressive reformers clashed for control of city hall in a dizzying dance of shifting alliances. Some politicians, including Canavan and Tarlton, played both sides, giving token support to reform in order to retain their grip in those areas of city affairs relating to economic development. In 1913, they backed progressive mayoral candidate John M. Chamberlin, who suppressed prostitution, gambling, and illegal saloons after he became mayor. His actions alienated Canavan, Tarlton, and others who benefited financially and in other ways from the operation of such enterprises. Republican political bosses Fred Gerold and Charles Lambert and their followers, who also opposed Chamberlin's moral cleansing program, decided to take their revenge against Chamberlin in the upcoming municipal election of 1915 by backing Canavan and Tarlton's Democratic candidate, Fred Mollman, for mayor.[46]

In election year 1915, Mayor Chamberlin's Administration Party, formerly the Progressive Citizens' Party (not to be confused with the Administration Party in 1910), saw its reform agenda compromised by the actions of some of its leading members who had profited from corruption and vice under his tenure. For example, Fred Gerold, city treasurer and tax collector, had stolen money from city hall by making duplicate payments of interest on several transactions and retaining a 2 percent commission on nearly $50,000. When Gerold later demanded payment for services rendered to the city, Mayor Chamberlin denied the request, thinking that by taking a stand against corruption he would ensure his own reelection. Instead, Chamberlin split his party into factions, sending members whom he had angered over to the Greater East St. Louis Party where they supported lawyer Fred Mollman as mayoral nominee.[47]

Progressives within the Administration Party who remained with Chamberlin saw an opportunity to implement their agenda and realign political power to favor reform. They regarded the April 1915 election for mayor and city council as key in the battle against political bosses. The Chamberlin faction claimed that Canavan, Tarlton, and their allies shamelessly exploited East St. Louis and that Mollman tolerated a "wide-open city" in which "everything goes." Reformers opposed Fred Gerold and Charles Lambert, advocates of unrestricted economic growth who had joined forces with machine boss politicians Canavan and William Rodenberg. They charged that these men had bankrupted the city and controlled mayoral candidate Fred Mollman. They also accused the Canavan-dominated levee board of extracting more revenue annually from townspeople than did city hall. According to Canavan's opponents, the levee board had channeled tax money to pay the interest, amounting to $370,000, on bonds issued for unnecessary construction work and had funneled the payments into an account at a local bank for the purpose of funding Mollman's campaign.[48]

As black East St. Louisan politicians and voters positioned themselves to swing the 1915 municipal election to their benefit, they witnessed a surge in the use of racist imagery and rhetoric by machine politicians and reformers. Black political operative "Kid" Amos became the focus of a racial fear campaign initiated by progressive reformers who denounced him for working with the Canavan-Tarlton faction. Amos symbolized the progressives' nightmare as reformers charged that African American politics led to black involvement in vice, corruption, and attempts to control the political life of East St. Louis. Amos, who had left East St. Louis during one of Chamberlin's moral cleansing campaigns, returned in 1915 to restart his brothel business in the Valley after Canavan and Tarlton promised him immunity from prosecution for running a brothel in exchange for his delivery of the black vote. The Kid Amos episode showed how East St. Louis followed a nationwide pattern of injecting racism into antiprostitution campaigns. African American residents found themselves in the middle as the machine signaled to white voters its ability to control black people and progressive reformers condemned black townspeople for causing corruption and demanding patronage and seats in local government.[49]

Black East St. Louisans had two reasons to anticipate additional patronage for their community after the election of 1915. First, they had been steadily gaining political influence as the number of black men of voting age increased from 649 out of a total of 9,841 voting-age men in 1900 to 2,286 of 21,005 in 1910, that is, from 6.5 percent in 1900 to 10.9 percent in 1910. In 1910, voting-age black men formed 70 percent of the total of 3,233 black males in a population of 5,882 black townspeople, or 55 percent of black East St. Louisans. Second, the black voting population further gained in numbers when African American women entered the formal political arena in 1913 after Illinoisan women won the right to vote in local elections. Though statistics by gender for the voting-age population are unavailable for the years between 1910 and 1920, the number of potential voters undoubtedly increased because local authorities noted an increase in the total number of residents from 58,547 in 1910 to an estimated 80,000 in 1915, the first year of the Great Migration. If ratio of black to white townspeople in 1910 remained about the same in 1915, then the city's black population in 1915 probably stood at about 8,000.[50]

Black women voters had to be a concern for white reformers who hoped to rally newly enfranchised women to the progressive cause. Though black clubwomen's message of racial uplift reinforced the reformers' moral appeals to eliminate prostitution and other perceived social ills, the clubwomen considered other issues as well, including elevating the political strength of their community. During the election of 1915, enough black women political operatives and voters, including Vella Bundy, wife of Leroy Bundy, opted for patronage, joining others in rejecting reformers' visions of honest government.[51]

Black voters in April 1915 saw the progressive reform candidates win a majority of aldermanic seats. Chamberlin lost the mayoral election even though a majority of women, presumably those of the white middle class, supported his ticket's moral, progressive message. He and his allies charged that the black vote had brought Mollman to victory. Chamberlin's Administration Party won five of eight aldermanic seats but lost the mayor's office to Mollman by just 27 votes. Progressives, thinking that their message for honest government had garnered wide appeal, began preparing for the next city election. All factions now expected Mollman to respond favorably to African American demands.[52]

Black Americans, especially those migrating from the poverty, disfranchisement, and racial violence of the South, found that the urban industrial economy held out the promise of a better way of life. Slowly but steadily, from 1900 into the 1910s, they gained a foothold in industrial occupations. Through this economy, African Americans hastened their transformation from a predominantly rural to an urban, mainly industrial, working-class people. Whether or not black men and women saw the promise of a better life fulfilled, they found social space in the urban industrial economy to build their communities and to shape relationships with organizations like trade and labor unions and political parties.[53]

African Americans in East St. Louis became skilled in mobilizing as a voting bloc, swinging elections, and winning patronage. They employed strategies and tactics as they related to machine boss politicians and progressive reformers. Like African Americans across the United States, black townspeople maintained an activist tradition through community institutions, labor unions, and political clubs that opposed segregation and antiblack violence and sought to attain political power. Black residents, including women who in 1913 won the right to vote in local elections, channeled their public actions into electoral politics to secure greater access to city government. By 1915 black residents had become, according to meat-packer manager Robert Conway, a source of fear for white inhabitants who thought that black voters held "the balance of political power." As an increasingly assertive black population reshaped the city's political culture, white political bosses and progressive reformers firmed their resolve to reverse the expansion of black political strength that they viewed as a threat to white entitlements. In 1917, agents of the state would opt for violence to solve the "Negro problem."[54]

THREE

The May Uprising

An End to Expanding Black Power

FROM 1915 to July 1917, black and white townspeople of East St. Louis, along with black and white migrants to that city, found themselves engulfed in a swirl of events that culminated in two outbreaks of mass racial violence: the first on May 28 and 29, 1917, and the second thirty-five days later, on July 2 and 3. The people involved, and later scholars as well, often cited the influx of black southerners as a key factor in fueling the antiblack violence. But the actions of black and white people made these years in East St. Louis more than just a history of black southern migrants seeking industrial employment, of managers recruiting migrants, and of white workers reacting to the migration. Though black—and white—migrants placed a strain on employment, housing, and resources, this tension had existed before the war years and did not cause the mass racial violence. The violence did not have to happen. Black and white East St. Louisans, by making certain political decisions and taking certain actions, created the possibility of violence. Black voters, one of several groups jockeying to increase their political strength, were on the verge of exerting much influence in city governance. This moved some white East St. Louisans to mete out antiblack violence in order to protect their entitlements to resources and power that they were accumulating before and during the war years.[1]

African Americans propelled major shifts in social relationships between black and white people during World War I. Black southerners in the hundreds of thousands shook the economy of the South by migrating to northern cities, where they entered the urban industrial economy that had been largely closed to them in the prewar years. Though many white southerners also migrated north, black working people had provided the crucial labor power for key sectors of the southern economy. Southern employers either had to make adjustments favorable to black people or find ways to thwart the northward migration. It also made relations between black and white people fluid, allowing African Americans the possibility of achieving equality, especially in the North. But white northerners, informed by national debates on the "Negro problem," chose to blame black newcomers and not white arrivals for heightening social problems in workplaces, public spaces, and neighborhoods. Black southerners encountered hostility from certain politicized, organized individuals among white people who wanted to return to rigid prewar race relations by imposing, at times through physical violence, limits on the extent of freedom that African Americans assumed was theirs to exercise.[2]

Black and white East St. Louisans gave African American migrants a mixed reception. Many African American residents welcomed the arrival of black southerners. Physician Lyman Bluitt, for instance, anticipated migrants' contributions to the growth of black community institutions, their patronization of black-owned businesses, and their support of black politicians. But some black East St. Louisans, at least according to real estate politician-businessman Thomas Canavan, expressed misgivings about the migrants, worrying that black southerners, lacking knowledge of northern folkways, would provoke white people's racism. Such opposition, however, remained muted, perhaps because the majority of established African American residents, or "old settlers," had southern origins or because migrants numerically overwhelmed the old settlers. White East St. Louisans overwhelmingly constituted the chief source of vehement antimigration sentiment. Many, like former mayor H. F. Bader and justice of the peace Russell Townsend, blamed migrants for crime, substandard housing, and other urban problems. Edward Mason, secretary of the Central Trades and Labor Union of East St. Louis, argued that black southern migrant laborers contributed to labor disputes as they displaced unskilled white factory workers. Other white people feared that the expanding number of voting-age migrants increased the possibility of black politicians winning seats on the city council or at least exerting greater influence in city governance. When the manager of Armour and Company meatpacking, Robert Conway, noted that the "negro [held] the balance of political power," he voiced a fear common among white residents who believed that black migrants had propelled the African American community into becoming a force in city affairs. White townspeople debated ways to maintain their position in the social hierarchy without legalizing segregation. White East St. Louisans with a racist political agenda were the first white northern urbanites during the war years to use mass violence to prevent black people from strengthening their political clout in order to gain greater access to city resources.[3]

By 1917, several groups stood at the center of the city's political culture and found themselves connected in one way or another with the Great Migration and the mass antiblack violence of May. Two groups in particular, black migrants and white workers, have received scrutiny from contemporaries and scholars. Black southern migrants came to East St. Louis to attain a better quality of life, but their numbers translated into African American political power at the ballot box. White workers, though often treated in the literature as a monolithic bloc, were a heterogeneous population. But the white workers at the center of the anti–black migration agitation or antiblack violence happened to be primarily nonindustrial workers, denizens of the saloon culture, and political operatives. The other participants at the center of East St. Louis's politics were black politicians and community activists and white corporate managers, local businessmen, city officials, city employees, and civic leaders. Some worked with or were themselves machine politicians or progressive reformers. Each group played a role in creating and shaping the events that made possible the mass racial violence that occurred on May 28, 1917.

The May race riot has been treated in the historiography as a backdrop or prelude to the larger conflagration that occurred on July 2, 1917. Overshadowed by the July event, the May riot became unmemorable simply because of the absence of widespread damage and riot-related deaths. But contrary to the impression given in the historiography, the May conflict was an important, indeed crucial, occurrence whose causes went beyond white workers' fears of competition from black southern migrants for jobs and housing or black swing voting in local elections. The May pogrom dramatized a violent reaction by northern white supremacists to sustained African American challenges to white entitlements, both resources and political power. The May event was instigated by the same people who later planned the July massacre. The disturbance, a bloodless version of the one that would occur in July, revealed on several levels the political dynamics of mass racial violence unfolding in East St. Louis, and by extension in other northern and southern locales. This violence represented the American equivalent of what has been referred to in the nineteenth and twentieth centuries in other nations as pogroms or during the 1990s as ethnic cleansing. White political leaders objected to black southern migrants' mere presence, not to mention their competition for jobs and housing, and with this as justification, the East St. Louis pogrom of May 1917 attempted to remove African Americans from the political arena and from the city itself. When the May event failed to achieve this result, antiblack elements found their opportunity to stage another clash in July.[4]

Black Southern Migrants

Black southerners cited numerous reasons for migrating north, including economic advancement, freedom from racial injustice, and opportunity for their children. They had struggled to control their own institutions and cooperative movements in the South, employing an array of strategies in the face of planters' efforts to decrease black landownership and coerce black churches, schools, and organizations into serving the interests of the plantation economy. African American southerners forged a political sensibility honed from fighting oppression that reinforced an imposed racial inferiority and class exploitation. Many black people left plantation districts, like the Mississippi Delta region, where they experienced grinding poverty and repressive planter rule. But as black working people fought to reverse their status as "displaced mill sills of southern industrial development," notes historian Carole Marks, they learned about opportunities to earn higher wages in the North. Once black southerners found out about favorable conditions in the North, many made the decision to migrate, bringing with them their political skills. They shaped the Great Migration into a self-directed, seemingly leaderless, grassroots social movement that brought about substantive changes in African American life.[5]

African Americans seized opportunities that emerged during World War I. They took advantage of manufacturers' need to expand industrial output so that the United States could supply Great Britain and France in the war against Germany. Black migrants filled job openings that were created as the war brought European immigration to a halt, as many European immigrant laborers returned to fight for their homelands, and as large numbers of native-born white and remaining immigrant workers moved into higher-paying war production jobs. Black migrants, observed dentist and entrepreneur Leroy Bundy, one of the leading black politicians in East St. Louis, saw the two-dollars-a-day wage in the North as superior to the one-dollar-a-day wage in the South.[6]

Migrants who came to East St. Louis learned about available jobs from a variety of sources. Some heard about openings from relatives and friends who resided in the city. Others read ads placed by managers of companies in the East St. Louis area, like Missouri Malleable Iron Company's superintendent John Pero, who placed ads in newspapers in southern locales such as Nashville, Tennessee, and Vicksburg, Mississippi. Black southerners also found out about employment from labor recruiters for companies like Obear-Nestor Glass. Others received assistance in finding work in East St. Louis from their churches and other community institutions. And after the initial wave of migrants established themselves in East St. Louis, they in turn became sources of information about employment opportunities for their friends and relatives.[7]

Black men and women migrants composed a diverse group in terms of work experience. Some had industrial or nonagricultural work experience prior to leaving the South. For example, Andrew Avery, a farmer in Kemper County, Mississippi, had worked in sawmills during the winter months. Alabama-born William Kings also had worked in a sawmill job for seven years in Laurel, Mississippi. Warren King, from Garretson, Alabama, had labored as a steel mill worker in nearby Birmingham. But many migrants, mainly sharecroppers and agriculturalists, had little or no urban industrial work experience. And many women who migrated north had been employed mainly as servants in white people's homes.[8]

By 1916, African American southerners controlled and sustained the networks that facilitated the migration. Kin, friends, and neighbors mobilized through personal contacts to move information as well as people who needed to know about jobs, housing, and city life. For example, George

Lewis and Sam Pettis, both from Oxford, Mississippi, and Alabaman William Kings received assistance from relatives and friends in obtaining jobs at the East St. Louis and Suburban Railroad Company. John Betts from Columbus, Mississippi, who had worked seasonally in sawmills, on farms, and for the Mobile & Ohio Railroad, got help from his wife's brother-in-law Henry Billips in securing a job at American Steel Foundries. Betts in turn sent money home to his wife, Daisy, who later followed him to East St. Louis where she obtained a job as a laborer at Obear-Nestor Glass Company, one of the few firms employing black women in significant numbers. Black southerners also relied upon community institutions, particularly their churches, for information about and leadership and organization of the migration. At times black ministers took a direct role in aiding migrants. The Reverend Thomas W. Wallace, pastor of St. John's AME Church in East St. Louis, for example, traveled to southern packinghouses, carrying an annual pass that he had received from meatpackers, to encourage black laborers to migrate north. Black southerners came to East St. Louis for employment and a better way of life for their families, but they also entered into the political calculus that turned them into a base of strength for those black politicians who hoped to create a black political machine.[9]

Building an Independent Black Political "Machine"

Black politicians and business owners in various northern cities generally welcomed black southern migrants, who expanded the size of the African American voting population and increased opportunities to attain patronage and access to political power. In East St. Louis, black politicians molded an expanding black population into a voting bloc to swing elections. Lyman Bluitt, for example, advised migrants when voting in local elections to vote not the party but the candidate, Republican or Democratic, who promised patronage. Bluitt and his colleagues hoped to maneuver both white Democratic and Republican office seekers into a dependency upon black voters.[10]

African Americans nationwide regarded the national election of 1916 as a critical test of their political strength to affect party alignments. They knew that the national Democratic Party aimed to weaken the African American vote in the North, where black people voted overwhelmingly

Republican. Many black voters faced the possibility of disfranchisement as local Democratic Party leaders accused Republicans of "colonizing" and illegally registering black migrants in northern cities. In East St. Louis, black— and white—residents dismissed the charge of colonization as groundless, agreeing that black southerners migrated on their own volition for jobs, not for the freedom to cast the ballot. But Democratic Party stalwarts, like CTLU labor organizer Earl Jimerson, accused Republicans of fraudulently registering at least 400 black migrant laborers and won a motion from the district court to examine the voter rolls. As a result of the examination, at least 200 black residents had their names expunged from registrant lists. Some black residents realized that the Democratic Party aimed to weaken the Republican Party's traditional base of support and at the same time prevent the formation of a black political machine.[11]

Black politicians and community organizers decided to take an independent course to oppose both Democratic leaders who disfranchised African American voters and Republican bosses who took their African American constituency for granted. In 1916, Bundy, Bluitt, attorney Noah Parden, and others took a step toward forging a strong black presence in the political arena by forming the Lowden Club to reelect Republican governor Frank O. Lowden. They planned to force local Republicans to reward loyal black voters with additional patronage. As Bundy stated, black people sought to be "independent of whites because . . . Negroes got no consideration [from Republicans] in the matter of division of office." Bundy had previously acted without consulting white bosses during the local election in April 1916, when he helped black laborer Sam Wheat defeat a political machine candidate for the position of alderman by 300 votes to his opponent's 94 in the predominantly black second ward. In October 1916, the Lowden Club, by this time renamed the St. Clair County (Colored) Republican League, moved against the Republican Party. The key figures were Bundy, Bluitt, and other leading league members including mortician R. M. C. Green, the Reverend Duncan (first name not given), realtor Pearl Abernathy, newspaper editor Thomas W. Wallace (who was also pastor of St. John's AME Church), carpenter Tom Huddleston, John Eubanks, Matt Hayes, and attorney William E. Lilly. They sent Republican bosses a list of demands that called for black control of the election campaign in African American districts and the awarding of the county offices of deputy coroner and assistant state's attorney to black politicians.[12]

Leaguers turned to the Democratic Party after Republicans rejected their demands. They decided to drive a wedge between white political factions as black southerners had done before the massive disenfranchisement of the 1890s. Leaguers endorsed national and state Republican tickets but supported a number of local Democrats: Charles Webb for state's attorney of St. Clair County, C. P. Renner for county coroner, and real estate politician-businessman Locke Tarlton and his associates for levee board.[13]

In mid-1916, African American Republican and Democratic Party operatives united in order to raise funds to finance the building of an independent black political machine. Members of the St. Clair County (Colored) Republican League, having been rebuffed by Republican Party bosses, decided to break from the party. In October, the Republican leaguers approached the officers of the Colored Democratic League—president John Clark, a laborer, along with first vice president James Dickson, second vice president Dallas Johnson, secretary Walter Demery, treasurer Joseph Wilson, and sergeant-at-arms Gus Johnson—and requested that the Democratic League mediate negotiations with Democratic Party boss Tarlton. Black Republicans received $300 from Tarlton to cover office expenses and campaign workers' salaries. They won additional support from the Republican-oriented Afro-American Protective League, which approved the St. Clair County (Colored) Republican League's endorsement of certain local white Democratic candidates. The Republican league positioned itself to be an influential organization in the upcoming November 1916 and April 1917 elections.[14]

Black Republican and Democratic operatives during the political campaign of November 1916 decided to form a pressure group in order to deliver the black vote to local Democratic candidates. They assigned highest priority to increasing the black community's share of patronage and forging an independent path for African Americans in local politics. But some African American politicians received directives from white city Democratic and county Republican machine bosses to deliver the vote without forming a black political machine. Noah Parden, who had continued to work with the Republican Party in expectation of an appointment as assistant state's attorney for St. Clair County after the election, found himself under intense pressure to remain loyal to the party. His boss, the state's attorney for St. Clair County and leader of the county Republicans, Hubert

Schaumleffel, had angered city Republicans by siding with the Democratic machine that had allied with the St. Clair County (Colored) Republican League. Parden knew that his bosses expected him to deliver the black vote. Black politician Leroy Bundy endured attacks from Democratic Party bosses who alleged that he had committed voter registration fraud and colonized black migrant voters in both East St. Louis and Chicago. Bundy, who had demonstrated a determination to build an independent black political machine around Sam Wheat's election, seemed too risky an ally for Democratic leaders. In addition, Bundy and black Baptist minister P. C. Parker became the center of progressive reformers' charges that African Americans sold votes and wallowed in corruption. Bundy topped the list of possible embarrassments for Democratic machine bosses, who knew that their progressive opponents had no qualms about connecting African Americans to a corrupt, debt-ridden city government.[15]

Black Republican and Democratic operatives calculated that the creation of a black political machine in East St. Louis was a real possibility if they skillfully exploited the fissures among white factions. They worked for the reelection of Mayor Fred Mollman, a Democrat and protégé of Tarlton and Canavan, during the municipal election campaign of April 1917 in which he was challenged by John Domhoff. A progressive reformer, Domhoff called for honesty in government and for the elimination of brothels, dance halls, gambling houses, and illegal saloons. In March 1917, under orders from Schaumleffel, Parden directed black Republican ward politicians and saloonkeepers, both men and women, to deliver the vote for Mollman. Parden also informed his operatives, especially those who owned or operated saloons or who acted as bondsmen, that Tarlton and Canavan had promised them continued opportunities to make money after a Mollman victory. These patronage seekers now knew that Mollman, Tarlton, Canavan, and their white allies had no intention of threatening their livelihood and source of power by removing saloons and other establishments that progressives deemed destructive to a moral social order. Parden and his campaign workers understood that a Domhoff win would mean not only a reform government run by progressives but also a certain end to patronage.[16]

Mollman's victory signaled that the St. Clair County (Colored) Republican, Colored Democratic, and Afro-American Protective leagues had succeeded in transforming the black community into a swing voting bloc. They expected political rewards after securing Mollman's reelection. Nearly 400 black politicians and political operatives, including Bundy, Bluitt, Parden, Russell M. C. Green, and P. C. Parker, celebrated Mollman's victory with a banquet attended by Mollman, ice and coal businessman John H. Drury, and other white politicians who had pledged to advance the interests of black residents. Some African American political operatives, however, fumed when they and other black voters received less money for selling their votes to Tarlton than black people had in 1914 for selling their votes to Edward Miller, a Republican Party boss, real estate and insurance agent, and former secretary to Congressman Rodenberg. Vella Bundy, wife of Leroy Bundy, and other black women activists bitterly criticized Tarlton for failing to pay them for their votes. But black politicians and residents never contemplated that Tarlton and other politician-businessmen planned to put an end to black political influence altogether. White leaders found the opportunity to do so by exploiting certain developments within organized labor.[17]

Organized Labor Builds an Anti–Black Migration Coalition

Central Trades and Labor Union leaders openly moved to the forefront among white East St. Louisans in expressing sentiment against black migration. They saw war-induced labor shortages as a golden opportunity to organize white workers. Labor officials hoped to unionize white workers by using the politics of racism, playing on fears that black southern workers would become strikebreakers and pawns of antiunion industrialists. The CTLU sought to bolster its case by building an anti–black migration coalition among white townspeople around issues that concerned the white community, such as housing and crime. The labor affiliation insisted that black southern migrants were the main ones responsible for devaluing residential property and increasing the crime rate. Some trade unionists hoped to use their positions within the city and county governments to have city hall and various political groups find ways to prevent black migrants from settling and working in the city. They included, for example, CTLU president Michael J. Whalen, who sat as city clerk in Mayor Mollman's administration, and Earl W. Jimerson, the financial secretary and business agent of the Amalgamated Meat Cutters and Butcher Workmen of North America union local, who sat on the St. Clair County Board of Supervisors.[18]

CTLU officials attributed labor problems to the upsurge in the number of black southern migrants entering the industrial workforce, even though far more white than black laborers had arrived in East St. Louis in search of jobs. Some, like the labor representative of Belleville, Alois Towers, had to work through inconsistencies in their views that black workers took jobs from white workers but at the same time took jobs that white workers shunned. Unionists worried that corporate managers, like the superintendent of the East St. Louis branch of the American Steel Foundries, Peter Ward, saw black migrants as an available pool of low-wage workers, even though they hired black workers to replace white workers in jobs that white men vacated. They shared with white trade unionists in other locales the opinion that low-wage black migrants disrupted efforts to unionize workers. CTLU leaders developed an anti–black migration strategy as a racist mobilization to unionize white workers rather than expend the association's resources to organize the entire workforce.[19]

White workers generally had misgivings about black migration, but those who expressed their antimigration and antiblack sentiments did not elevate their concerns to a position high on the agenda as CTLU officials did. If white working people feared black workers, especially those migrating from the South, as job competitors, strikebreakers, and union busters, then their fears were voiced not from their ranks but by CTLU and other union organizers, politicians, newspaper reporters, journalists, and years later, scholars. In 1916, white working people in East St. Louis, or at least those in the industrial workforce, gave little thought to the black migration. White workers proceeded to plunge area industries into a series of strikes, showing that fear of black workers taking their jobs or breaking strikes was not a concern in a border city that had already had a significant black presence in industry for at least two decades. White workers instead took advantage of labor shortages in an expanding wartime economy to strike for higher wages, reduced working hours, improved working conditions, and union recognition. Strikers at the East St. Louis and Suburban Railroad Company, the meatpacking firms, and Aluminum Ore Company became pivotal in the local labor movement because the number of employees in these companies together totaled several thousand. Workers' strikes caught the CTLU unprepared, because the affiliation had focused on using fear of the Great Migration as its chief organizing tool.[20]

In May 1916, employees at the East St. Louis and Suburban Railroad Company, a mass transit authority, sparked the area's first significant wartime strike, initially proceeding without the involvement of the CTLU. Strikers restricted commerce in East St. Louis and surrounding towns in St. Clair and Madison counties, affecting area residents who depended upon streetcars to commute to jobs, shop downtown, or cross the Mississippi River to St. Louis. Track workers demanded a pay increase from seventeen and a half cents to twenty cents an hour, a ten-hour workday, and collective bargaining rights. In response, the company fired strike organizers and told laborers to either return to work or lose their jobs. Strikers ignored managers' threats and continued the work stoppage, crippling public transportation and retail merchant operations in the region. They also affiliated their strike organization with the AFL and the CTLU. During the course of the labor dispute, strikers received support from CTLU leaders but also from East St. Louis–area merchants, real estate men, and politicians, who pressured the company to settle the dispute. In July, strikers won their demands for higher wages and collective bargaining rights. Not once did they raise the issue of black southern migrant laborers.[21]

In the eyes of CTLU officials and labor organizers, the East St. Louis and Suburban Railroad strike presented an opportunity to connect workers' strikes to the black migration. Union activists learned immediately after the transit strike that the company planned to destroy the new union by subletting work to contractors employing nonunion black and white laborers at $2.25 a day for work that newly unionized workers performed for $1.75 to $2.00 a day. They also discovered that managers, including company official Mr. Meyers, considered using black southern migrants as a club to destroy the new union, especially since, for some unknown reason, no black workers had become union members even though they had participated in the strike.[22]

In July, at least 1,800 black and white packinghouse workers, an influential segment of the area workforce, called for simultaneous strikes at Armour, Swift, Morris, and East Side Packing, demanding that managers reinstate employees who had been dismissed for union organizing. In response, meatpackers, according to a CTLU estimate that is most likely exaggerated, brought in 1,500 black and white strikebreakers from packinghouses outside East St. Louis. According to the CTLU, white strikers focused their fears upon black strikebreakers, even though African Americans composed a significant percentage of the packinghouse workforce, had gone on strike, and at a few worksites had acted as strike leaders. But strikers never publicly aired their concerns about black migrants in their demands.

Workers ended the strike on July 25 when managers, eager to resume production, agreed to rehire dismissed union organizers and allow union presence on the shop floor.[23]

Like CTLU officials, many northern labor leaders also expressed the opinion that black southern migrants spelled disaster for the labor movement. In October 1916, AFL president Samuel Gompers requested AFL district organizer Harry Kerr investigate and report on the black migration and its impact upon the labor movement in East St. Louis. Labor organizers assumed that employers were poised to crush unions by ensuring that the number of black migrant laborers rose above the number of available jobs. Earl Jimerson and other AFL and CTLU officials accused managers of flooding the labor market with migrants in order to drive down white workers' wages and living standards. Jimerson believed that companies hoped that white and black laborers would be at each other's throats, and he warned Mayor Mollman to expect white workers to kill black migrants if companies used them to break future strikes. Labor representative Alois Towers charged that unskilled black workers posed a direct threat to the job security of unskilled white workers.[24]

The next major labor confrontation, the Aluminum Ore Company strike of October 1916, became the tocsin for the CTLU. This event, unrelated to the Great Migration, set the stage for a second strike at Aluminum Ore in April 1917 that the CTLU immediately connected to the Great Migration. The October strike began when employees accused managers of instituting an unfair payroll schedule and walked off the job. Five days later, strikers won their demands for a wage increase and an eight-hour workday. The company quickly settled the dispute in order to avoid the possibility of workers coordinating their strike with one occurring at Aluminum Ore's bauxite supplier, the Arkansas Works in Bauxite, Arkansas. In November, 1,600 men at Aluminum Ore, nearly the entire workforce, decided to protect their gains by forming the Aluminum Ore Employees Protective Association (AOEPA), unaffiliated with either the CTLU or the AFL.[25]

Immediately after the strike, Aluminum Ore Company suddenly began hiring African Americans, specifically black southern migrants, to fill positions that either had been vacated by unskilled workers or had opened after the company fired those active in the October strike. Between 1902 and late 1916, Aluminum Ore had employed a total of twelve African

Americans. But after the October strike, the company carried on its payroll 280 black laborers in November, 410 in December, 470 in February, and 381 in April, depending on production needs. From the CTLU's perspective, Aluminum Ore clearly sought to discipline white workers by hiring low-wage, presumably antiunion, black laborers. But as long as Aluminum Ore managers maintained a segregated, racially hierarchical workforce in which all black employees occupied unskilled positions, the CTLU had to construct its argument carefully to show that black migrant laborers threatened white workers.[26]

On April 18, 1917, when Aluminum Ore managers refused to rehire former AOEPA members, employees downed their tools and demanded that the company rehire the nearly 600 October strikers, many with years of seniority, who had been fired between October and April. Before arriving at their decision to strike, employees had been counseled by the CTLU against doing so for two reasons. First, Aluminum Ore employees, according to the CTLU, received the highest pay among industrial workers in the East St. Louis district. And second, after the United States declared war on Germany on April 2, employees faced the possibility of impressment into military service if they disrupted the production of necessary war material at the sole aluminum ore processing plant in North America. But when 1,700 black and white workers struck to stop further layoffs and save the AOEPA from destruction, the CTLU had no choice but to support them. During this second, and very bitter, strike that ground toward the end of June, strikers never discussed—at least openly—the issues of black migration or black laborers being hired for positions that white workers once occupied. The AOEPA strike committee on April 17 did not mention anything relating to black migrants either in their typewritten demands to assistant superintendent R. F. Rucker or in their testimony in court proceedings in early May, when Aluminum Ore brought charges of malicious and disruptive behavior against several strikers.[27]

Aluminum Ore managers resolved to crush the strike. Like their counterparts at other industrial plants, company officials had hired black laborers to fill low-wage, unskilled positions both to cut labor costs and to send a signal to white employees not to unionize. General manager Charles B. Fox and Rucker understood that the key to breaking the strike involved bribery, coercion, hostile propaganda, and sheer resolve to outlast the strikers, not playing upon white workers' racial fears. Rucker offered strike leader

Philip Wolf a bribe in hopes of discrediting Wolf if he accepted it. When Fox purchased rifles and hired a private security force purportedly to protect strikebreakers and company property, his critics thought that he aimed to intimidate strikers. In early May, Fox secured a court injunction against strikers who he claimed had damaged company property and injured his chauffeur and several other people. Rucker and Fox, according to Wolf and prolabor critics, enlisted provocateurs to mingle among the strikers and create trouble so that the public would blame strikers for damaging property and injuring innocent people. In addition, Aluminum Ore attempted to smear strikers by labeling them unpatriotic, saying that they had been influenced by German spies seeking to sabotage American war production.[28]

CTLU leaders used the Aluminum Ore strike to ratchet up anti–black migration rhetoric. They, and not white Aluminum Ore strikers, formulated overt racist appeals. According to some observers, the CTLU created the impression that migrant competition for jobs underlay the strike at Aluminum Ore. Trade unionists, according to meatpacking manager Robert Conway, "manufactured a sentiment against negroes because they were negroes, and because they were taking the [jobs] of white men." The labor affiliation used racism to organize white workers to build unions, calculating that white working people harbored strong antiblack sentiments, often discriminated against black workers, hated black strikebreakers more than white ones, and embedded their racial identity in their construction of class consciousness. Alois Towers, like other labor organizers, thought antiblack racism a difficult barrier for any union to overcome, "even if all blacks were unionized." Organizers concentrated on unionizing white workers, knowing that white workers made up the majority of the local industrial workforce. CTLU officials, who often criticized employers' use of racism to divide employees, themselves inflamed white workers' racism and fear of black laborers in order to unionize them.[29]

CTLU leaders mobilized white workers around charges that black migrants engaged in strikebreaking and held antiunion views. They did so even though they knew that black laborers broke strikes primarily in those industries that discriminated against African Americans or where trade unions barred them from union membership. The CTLU also ignored the fact that all of the black workers hired at Aluminum Ore between October and April had been new hires, not strikebreakers. Furthermore, the association did not view white new hires as strikebreakers. Organizers conveniently ignored the issue of white strikebreaking, preferring to dramatize black migrants as strikebreakers. In addition, union activists rarely discussed the fact that black workers, including southern migrants, refused to break strikes. Black Mississippian Andrew Avery, for instance, quit after his first night on the job at American Steel Foundries upon learning that workers there were on strike. The CTLU also lacked interest when black and white workers united and went on strike in late April at American Steel. Neither did the organization support a predominantly black workforce at the East St. Louis Cotton Seed Oil Company that went on strike. In condemning the black migration, CTLU leaders made economic security for white workers, not the unionization of black workers, their central concern.[30]

The anti–black migration coalition that the CTLU sought to build outside the labor movement began to appeal to white people of all social classes, in particular real estate men and their business allies, landlords, and homeowners, when the organization stressed issues such as housing and crime. Some real estate men preferred to sell properties to highly paid skilled white workers or even low-wage unskilled white workers capable of moving up the economic ladder rather than to black working people who had few prospects for economic advancement. In addition, land-interest city boosters, like their counterparts elsewhere, operated in a volatile housing market characterized by high interest rates, large down payments, and short loan repayment periods. White homeowners sought protection from drops in home property value by maintaining the class and racial homogeneity of neighborhoods. They, like white residents generally, blamed black southern migrants for declining property values.[31]

Real estate men and white homeowners sought to impose rigorous residential segregation without resorting to segregation laws by relying on such devices as property rights laws, zoning, mortgage covenants, and threats of violence to prevent black people from moving into or continuing to reside in white districts. Though white East St. Louis homeowners did not resort to bombing black residences as some white Chicagoans did, they did terrorize African American homeowners and those seeking to buy or rent homes in white districts. In September 1916, for example, white members of Alta Sita Improvement and Protective Association warned three black families living in the Alta Sita district of East St. Louis to either move out or face violent consequences. Some white people telephoned death threats to white real estate man Nathaniel McLean, who had been selling and renting homes to African Americans in white neighborhoods.[32]

White East St. Louisans thought segregation a solution to racial conflict, a sentiment voiced by progressive social reformer the Reverend George Allison. White townspeople who favored integrated neighborhoods, according to Allison, played into the hands of unscrupulous real estate men who profited during periods of instability in the housing market by buying houses below market value from white homeowners and then selling these residences above market value to black homebuyers. Perhaps Allison had McLean in mind, but the minister did not name names. East St. Louisans watched as voters in St. Louis approved in a special 1916 election two segregation ordinances modeled after regulations enacted in Baltimore, Maryland, and other cities. A local court in St. Louis, however, invalidated the election results, ruling that such ordinances violated buyers' and sellers' constitutional rights. Interestingly, black East St. Louisan realtor Pearl Abernathy advertised to African Americans in St. Louis that East St. Louis welcomed them to live anywhere they chose in the Illinoisan city. The St. Louis court's ruling squelched any effort in East St. Louis to establish segregation through ordinances. White residents generally concluded that customary segregation held the promise of keeping black people and the perceived social problems they brought with them out of white neighborhoods.[33]

Black residents opposed both legal and customary forms of residential segregation and desperately sought to expand the geographic range of available housing. But African Americans found such segregation taking shape, placing East St. Louis in the same category as large northern cities with their expanding ghettoes. Though they still resided in many neighborhoods, black people found their housing options limited to the city's North End, in the Goose Hill neighborhood, and South End, in Rush City and sections of Denverside. These rapidly became predominantly black areas. The Reverend Edgar Pope, pastor of St. Mark's Baptist Church, though insisting that African Americans had the right to buy homes wherever they pleased, proposed in May 1917 to the Real Estate Exchange that new homes be constructed for southern migrants in black neighborhoods to defuse the mounting tension over housing. But Pope's suggestion did not elicit any response from the exchange.[34]

CTLU leaders found common ground with white townspeople who blamed black migrants for the housing shortage and who showed willingness to support the CTLU's anti–black migration campaign. They ignored the fact that housing problems, which had existed prior to the Great Migration, had become more acute as war production diverted construction materials to other projects. Neither did unionists talk about white migrants—mainly native-born white Americans, perhaps a significant percentage from the South, who were arriving in large numbers and moving into housing unfit for human habitation. Union officials blamed corporate managers for creating a housing shortage by recruiting black migrants without considering where to lodge them. Some unionists, like Harry Kerr, described black laborers' housing as a breeding ground for communicable diseases. Kerr expressed a concern common among white urbanites that African Americans, especially the poor among them, constituted a public health risk to white communities. Atlanta, Georgia, for example, was just one city where white homeowners and public health authorities alleged that black domestics, laundresses, and house servants carried communicable diseases into their white employers' homes and neighborhoods. In the meantime, the CTLU urged the Chamber of Commerce of East St. Louis, city hall, and corporate managers to resolve the housing problem.[35]

Corporate managers of the area's largest firms briefly explored ways to provide housing for black migrant laborers. Street Railway, Light and Power Company general manager D. E. Parsons, Missouri Malleable Iron Company president Frank E. Nulsen, and Aluminum Ore Company superintendent Charles Fox advocated improved living conditions for newly hired African American employees. They considered the substandard houses occupied by black migrants to be "menac[ing] the sanitary and moral conditions" of white citizens. Managers called upon the industrial secretary of the local Young Men's Christian Association (YMCA), Irwin Raut, to meet with them and discuss black workers' housing conditions. Raut, as an official in a national organization concerned about housing for young people, knew that housing problems in East St. Louis were similar to those in large northern industrial centers like Cincinnati and Toledo, Ohio, and Chicago. He considered hiring Mr. Hamlin (no first name given), an official at the headquarters of the African American YMCA in Washington, D.C. to devise plans to improve housing for black migrants. But for reasons never disclosed, managers tabled the discussion of housing for black southern migrant laborers and their families.[36]

CTLU officials also led white townspeople in blaming the Great Migration for what they alleged was a sharp increase in the crime rate. Labor and civic leaders cast part of the blame upon judges, policemen, bondsmen, saloonkeepers, and politicians whom they accused of leniency toward black southern migrants' involvement in crime and vice. Philip Wolf exclaimed that black men escalated lawlessness to such a level that white inhabitants held ill will "against the colored man." Alois Towers thought that the "low saloon element . . . control[led] all political issues" and made the crime wave possible. CTLU leaders and other social critics minimized the criminal activities of white migrants, transient workers, and habitués of the saloon culture. While some saw race as the significant factor in pushing black people to commit crime, progressive reformer the Reverend George Allison understood that poverty drove some black people to break the law. But as Elliott Rudwick, Malcolm McLaughlin, and other scholars note, American cities had long experienced rising crime rates in tandem with increased population growth, and East St. Louis was no exception.[37]

White residents framed discussion about black people committing crimes, frequenting saloons, and carrying guns in terms of race. St. Clair County coroner C. P. Renner, for example, claimed that the immoral proclivities of African Americans underlay the wave of burglaries and homicides that occurred from early 1916 to mid-1917. AFL organizer Kerr exaggeratedly claimed that black rapists created a "reign of terror" that made white women afraid even to visit their next-door neighbors at night. While white East St. Louisans, like their urban counterparts elsewhere, generally saw white saloons as social clubs, they viewed black people's saloons or "jook joints" as incubators of crime, immorality, and violence. White progressive reformer and publisher James Kirk devoted much space in his newspaper to fomenting racist sentiment and provided police with an excuse to disarm African Americans by printing articles about black men carrying guns. When authorities complained that many young black southern men had purchased firearms upon arriving in East St. Louis, they showed indifference to the possibility that some obtained weapons to protect their persons and families in a city with a long-standing reputation for criminal violence. As at least a few white city leaders must have known, some migrants realized that their new urban home presented a level of social violence that, coupled with local government indifference or hostility, forced black people to rely upon firearms for self-defense.[38]

Black townspeople criticized white labor, political, and business leaders for blaming the crime wave and other social ills upon migrants, arguing that the vast majority of the newcomers were hardworking and law-abiding. Black police detectives W. H. Mills and W. Green, who interviewed migrants in the course of their work, insisted that the new arrivals only wanted decent jobs and an opportunity to build a better way of life. Lyman Bluitt argued that the CTLU needed to "make an effort in good faith to unionize every laboring man" rather than expend energy on preventing migrants from obtaining jobs. In addition, black residents worried that lurid reports of African American criminals reinforced some white individuals' perceptions of African Americans as a dangerous people and prompted others to demand that the police disarm law-abiding as well as lawbreaking black people.[39]

Across the nation, black and white Americans contested employment, migration, housing, crime, and other such issues in the context of rapid changes in social relations that World War I set in motion. White industrial workers pressed forward, striking for higher wages and union recognition. White women, black men and women, and Mexican immigrants found employment in occupations that industrial managers and unionists previously had denied them. More importantly, black women and men challenged legal and customary practices of segregation and demanded, even expected, equality of citizenship. But most white people refused to extend equality—political, social, or otherwise—to African Americans.

In many urban locales outside the South, black and white Americans jostled with the notion of equality in one highly contested public space, the streetcar. Black commuters, especially newly arrived southern migrants used to segregated public transportation, enjoyed the freedom to sit wherever they wanted on trolleys. For some, undoubtedly, the simple act of sitting in a seat of their choice, especially next to a white passenger— forbidden in the Jim Crow South—reinforced their sensibilities of being free citizens in the North. Most white residents, however, viewed such an occurrence through a different lens. Aluminum Ore Company staff physician Albert B. McQuillan, for one, asserted with much exaggeration that black passengers sat "down on white women's laps," crowded white people out of streetcars, made "a great deal of noise," and rarely sat together in groups. Some white people with preconceived ideas of proper public behavior for women reacted disapprovingly to what they saw as "abusive and uncontrollable . . . language and actions" of black women. Thomas Canavan counted himself among those who despaired that black people, especially migrant southern laborers, had forgotten their place in the white-dominated racial hierarchy.[40]

While the CTLU built an anti–black migration coalition, corporate managers opposed the labor affiliation by preventing union drives or by hiring black migrants. Some employers prepared for another round of labor unrest. Those engaged in interstate commerce or production of materials for the war effort took advantage of offers of protection from the federal government. For example, East St. Louis and Suburban Railroad Company, anticipating another strike upon expiration of the labor contract signed in 1916, asked for and received assistance from a federalized unit of the state militia. One Suburban manager reportedly had stated that troops were necessary to intimidate workers from striking and to guard strike-breakers if work stoppages occurred. Knowing that various factions within the white community had been loudly protesting the migration, some industrialists and businessmen continued quietly to encourage black southerners to migrate north. Aluminum Ore manager Charles Fox, a member of the East St. Louis Chamber of Commerce, and E. M. Sorrell, the chamber's secretary, used chamber letterhead without permission to advertise available jobs in southern newspapers. Though Fox and Sorrell denied their role, some in the chamber sought to investigate whether the two men had encouraged migrants to come to the city. But according to Jimerson, Fox's and Sorrell's friends in the chamber prevented chamber member attorney Maurice V. Joyce from conducting an internal investigation.[41]

CTLU officials remained vociferous about preventing migrants from entering the city. They argued that migration had exacerbated the housing shortage, fueled a crime wave, increased job competition, and inflamed the Aluminum Ore strike. Labor leaders focused upon the strike because a worker victory there held the potential to energize the local labor movement. Unionists raised the issue of the large influx of black migrants into the city in order to emphasize the threat to white workers and townspeople. But as Rudwick points out, the labor affiliation never acquired evidence to support its allegations. The CTLU proposed that black migrants be given the same treatment that police gave to white vagabonds, who were escorted to the city line, beaten, and told not to return. Harry Kerr thought that Mayor Mollman and the aldermen on the city council had the responsibility to solve the vagrancy problem that Kerr said migrants had caused. The CTLU, hoping to force the mayor and aldermen into action, published an open letter in which the organization denounced the migration and blamed black southern migrants for intensifying labor disputes, crime, and white people's race prejudice.[42]

As much as CTLU leaders tried to influence city hall, Mayor Mollman and his political machine also had their own agenda, which ran counter to that of the labor affiliation. While McLaughlin makes a persuasive argument that white labor perceived, for a variety of reasons, that city hall ignored its interests, the Mollman faction did not in fact ignore labor. The mayor had to strive for balance, running the city as an economic growth machine, maintaining cordial relations with the CTLU and the business community, and responding to black voters' demands for an increased share of city resources. Most importantly, the Mollman administration, skilled in the art of extracting wealth from the city, had to continue implementing economic boosters' decades-long policy of industrial development. The mayor and his associates knew that the booming war economy created additional opportunities for personal gain through the recruitment of more corporations to the city, through the buying, selling, and renting of commercial and residential real estate, and through collection of licensing fees from an ever-increasing number of saloons. City hall had to placate industrialists who welcomed black southern laborers. Mollman had indirectly encouraged black migrants to come to the city when he boasted in April 1917 about plentiful jobs in East St. Louis during a business trip to New Orleans. Since the mayor depended on labor's vote, he signaled to the CTLU his interest in resolving the Aluminum Ore strike and the problems that the organization thought the migration had exacerbated.

Mollman realized that the black community had become an influential swing voting bloc in the April election. He found himself caught between strong challenges from progressive reformers and the crucial black vote. Mollman and his bosses worried about losing control of the black vote to African American politicians like Leroy Bundy, who sought to institutionalize an independent black political machine. Mollman also knew that to restrict the migration infringed upon black migrants' rights. He understood that he angered organized labor by refusing to stop the migration, but if he did stop it, he would face loss of support from assertive black politicians who depended on increasing numbers of African American migrants for votes. Mollman and his political bosses had to wait and see what the labor affiliation planned to do before they made their next moves to counter both assertive labor leaders and upstart black politicians.[43]

Organized Labor and the Mass Racial Violence of May 1917

CTLU officials arranged to meet privately on Monday evening, May 28, with Mayor Mollman and city councilmen in hopes of pressuring city hall into resolving the Aluminum Ore strike and banning black migration to East St. Louis. On the night of the meeting, CTLU delegates arrived with the men escorting the women representatives from the laundry workers, retail clerks, and waitresses' unions, sending a racist message that white women feared to venture out after dark because black rapists stalked the streets. They arrived at what they thought was to be a private meeting. CTLU leaders Edward Mason and Michael Whalen wondered, however, who had opened the meeting to the public when the delegates entered a city hall auditorium overflowing with nearly 1,000 people, including an estimated 200 women. They noticed that a significant number of those gathered were not union members and some were not even East St. Louisans. One such nonunion attendee was Belleville resident Ferdinand Schwartz, a white paperhanger and painter who had come to the meeting to "protest to the Mayor about the influx of the negro" and demand action.[44]

Mason, Whalen, and others in the CTLU failed to understand that their anti–black migration rhetoric had convinced some white people that the labor group's strategy of working with city hall to end the migration had proved ineffective. The affiliation knew that white residents were concerned not about the influx of black migrants but about black southern migrants not knowing their proper place in East St. Louis. The CTLU did not envision that its anti–black migrant rhetoric, intended to galvanize the mayor's office into action, would create an atmosphere that made mass social violence a possibility. By allowing the meeting to continue, the labor affiliation's officials provided a platform for nonlabor white factions that opposed the expansion of black political influence to mobilize for antiblack violence.

CTLU leaders gave the impression, observers later commented, that they had called the meeting to recruit shock troops to conduct the mass antiblack assaults of May 28 and 29. But the CTLU actually lost control of the gathering to uninvited speakers who railed against black migrants, the companies that hired them, and other perceived problems related to the migration. While unionists considered peaceful solutions, some nonunion people in the audience advocated violent action. Brewery salesman Jerry Kane and others used the meeting as a platform to launch an attack on African Americans. Alexander Flannigan of Belleville, a popular attorney, orator, and politician, argued that black people had to be prevented from moving into white neighborhoods. He called for vigilantism. According to Albertson, Kerr, and others, Flannigan said there was "no law or rule or anything else to curb mob violence." During the meeting two white city police detectives spread the word that patrolmen had just arrested a black man for shooting a white man. At about 10:00 PM, as if on signal, people rushed from the auditorium and joined others waiting outside, where the crowd swelled to 1,200 people. Jeering men stood in front of city hall as policemen escorted the alleged black gunman into the jail. Shouting "Lynch him," some in the throng tried to seize the man, but city and CTLU leaders prevented them from doing so by blocking the entrance to the police station.[45]

City and CTLU officials, fearing violence, attempted to disperse the mob. Mayor Mollman faced the assemblage and implored the hecklers to go home, but people refused to leave. Some, accusing the mayor of having bought the black vote during his reelection, yelled, "To Hell with Mollman; hang him." Meanwhile, CTLU men searched the gathering for union members, whom they ordered to leave. Earl Jimerson and Philip Wolf received beatings from white attackers for assisting black passersby. Mollman, learning of assaults on black commuters at nearby streetcar stops, telephoned Governor Lowden and requested that he send the National Guard for riot duty.[46]

Only a small number of white men and a smaller number of white women among the hundreds on the streets assaulted African Americans. The vast majority of people congregated as bystanders, cheerleaders, and opportunists ready to reap the spoils from the destruction of black people's property. The actual assailants knew exactly what they were doing and operated with the acquiescence or passive support of the police. Those conducting the attacks were primarily artisans, transient laborers, self-employed professionals, nonindustrial workers, businessmen, members of the saloon culture, and prostitutes. Revolver-carrying Ruby Nelson, a well-known prostitute, along with several white teenage prostitutes and some furloughed soldiers from Missouri and Illinois units, led a few groups of street fighters. Contrary to what commentators claimed, industrial workers, especially those from Aluminum Ore and the meatpacking plants, did not constitute a plurality, let alone a majority, of the assailants. This relative absence of industrial workers among the riot participants conforms to a pattern that historian Roberta Senechal points out with respect to the violence that nearly turned Springfield, Illinois, into a sundown town.[47]

Authorities never investigated why white women participated as assailants in East St. Louis when American white women, historically, had not been known to inflict physical punishment on their targets during race riots. Municipal officials and knowledgeable observers noticed that prostitutes predominated among the white women attackers. Scholar McLaughlin conjectures in regard to the July pogrom that the involvement of white women, mostly prostitutes, revolved around issues of gender identities in the workplace, patriotic appeal to women as moral guardians of America, increased social status through antiblack violence, and white racial identity: perhaps the prostitutes sought to win recognition from white society that they, too, were decent white people. If so, one could assume that women attackers had similar reasons for participating in the May event. But the police and reporters never supplied evidence to support such analyses. A more likely explanation for the white prostitutes' participation is that they hoped to eliminate competition from black prostitutes; they lived in a violent world and easily moved from one arena of violence to another to join their male friends in antiblack attacks that occurred in areas adjacent to brothels. The prostitutes, like the male attackers, thought it was safe to assault black men and women because the police had confiscated firearms from many black residents and had shown greater antipathy toward black people than toward white prostitutes, whom some police officers controlled.[48]

From Monday night well into Tuesday, white people assaulted African Americans wherever the former held the numerical advantage. White attackers first descended upon black people waiting for streetcars or walking along Broadway between First and Fourth Streets and along Collinsville Avenue between Broadway and St. Clair Avenue. Around midnight, many attackers coalesced into two large groups and nearly 100 people marched toward the southern end of town. Along the way they damaged Wilkerson's barbershop near Fourth and Broadway, Schreiber's saloon at Fourth and Railroad, Fransen's saloon at Fourth and Trendley, and other establishments that were patronized by African Americans and that, according to assailants, served as black politicians' "headquarters." Mobs threw bricks through windows, ransacked buildings, shot into deserted homes, and set at least one black-occupied dwelling ablaze. A second group, larger in number, headed north to the meatpacking plants, beating black individuals they encountered along Collinsville Avenue and parts of Third Street. Ringleaders and their followers intended to attack black Valley residents but were prevented from doing so by several police officers. They instead continued on to the boundary between East St. Louis and National City, to the "Whiskey Chute" district across from the packinghouses, an area densely packed with saloons, where they engaged in fisticuffs with black workers. Assailants feared entering the predominantly black neighborhoods in the city's South End where, someone said, black residents were "arming themselves and hell would be to pay if [we go] down in the negro settlement."[49]

The forty white patrolmen on the East St. Louis police force, though they prevented black people from being killed, were generally sympathetic to the white throngs and provided opportunities for them to attack African Americans. The police arrested and jailed more than seventy black

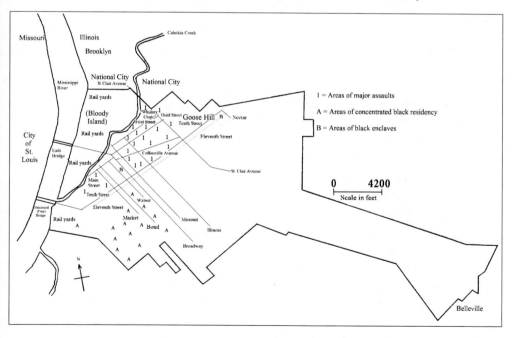

Map 3.1. Area of East St. Louis pogrom, May 28–29, 1917. *Map by author*

men, and far fewer white men, for possession of firearms, conveying the impression that black townspeople were out to kill white people. In one incident, the police stopped six black people in a red Hupmobile as they drove into the city from St. Louis. The officers searched the car and arrested the six for smuggling ammunition and guns into East St. Louis. The police and white people generally knew the significance of black individuals owning or driving a Hupmobile, a high-priced vehicle, when most American car owners possessed relatively inexpensive automobiles like the Model T Ford. A black owner of a Hupmobile or any car, and indeed a black person exhibiting any indicator of material success such as home ownership, violated the common white supremacist image of humble and socially inferior black people. Any degree of black economic achievement signaled to white people that African Americans, by refusing to accept their assigned place at the bottom of the social ladder, threatened the white-dominated hierarchy.[50]

Rumors that Leroy Bundy had been busily arming a black militia received much credence among white residents when the police announced Bundy as the owner of the Hupmobile. Bundy was among the few black East St. Louisans who owned such a vehicle, and he also worked for a St. Louis automobile dealership, selling Hupmobiles to leading black citizens in East St. Louis and Brooklyn. Another rumor identified Bundy as the commander of a mysterious black militia associated with the African American St. George's Lodge of the Odd Fellows that had been practicing military precision drills. But lodge members had been performing military-style drills in uniforms with swords at a playground across from Bundy's house and service station since 1909. Rumors also had spread that Bundy's garage was a recruiting office for the black militia, when in actuality it was a popular place for young black men to repair and service cars and meet their friends. The rumors, nonetheless, prompted the mayor to call upon the state militia to provide troops before the violence spiraled out of control.[51]

State and local authorities organized their forces and, following the arrival of the Illinois National Guard Fourth Regiment on Tuesday evening around seven o'clock, proceeded to restore law and order. Lieutenant Colonel E. P. Clayton commanded guardsmen to man key intersections leading to black neighborhoods to prevent assailants from attacking African Americans. They deterred black retaliation against white people by arresting armed black residents. Soldiers cleared the downtown district, dispersing throngs by threatening deadly force. Authorities effectively suppressed white troublemakers and by nighttime declared the cessation of street violence. Police officers arrested a few leading white agitators, including real estate salesman Steve Proney, on charges of inciting violence. But if any reports were taken of arrestees, they were never found. Furthermore, local officials did not charge attorney Alexander Flannigan and others for encouraging or leading antiblack assaults, presumably either because of their prominence (as in the case of Flannigan) or because of their connections to prominent people in government or business. City leaders treated pogrom instigators with leniency, reflecting an agreement between the two parties that black politicians and residents must either return to their place in the racial hierarchy or risk being run out of town.[52]

June 1917: The Calm before the Storm

The May pogrom was a curious event. The black community remained intact even though an estimated 6,000 African Americans fled to St. Louis following the violence. Although assailants had ample time to wreak havoc between the CTLU meeting and the arrival of the first National Guard units, the uprising did not become a massacre. The May outburst indeed appears benign when compared to other mass upheavals of urban racial conflict that occurred in late nineteenth- and early twentieth-century America, including the attempt in 1908 to cleanse Springfield, Illinois, of black people. According to official count, the mass racial violence of May resulted in seventy-five black people and three white men injured and no reported deaths. Observing that the mass violence had the appearance of a measured, controlled affair, the Reverend George Allison commented that he thought agitators simply had intended to turn the city into a sundown town by intimidating African Americans into leaving East St. Louis.[53]

Industrialists and union leaders denied charges that they had been responsible for the mayhem or had benefited from it in any way. Managers noted that their companies required low-wage black southern migrants to perform work that white laborers shunned. In addition, they lamented the loss of valuable production time during and immediately after the mass violence. Managers adjusted employees' work schedules to enable black laborers to safely commute to and from their jobs. Likewise, CTLU officials stressed that neither they nor Aluminum Ore strikers ignited the mass violence. Labor organizer Philip Wolf said that white Aluminum Ore strikers were not antiblack and pointed out that after a strike meeting on the night of Wednesday, May 30, white strikers, concerned about the safety of their black colleagues, had escorted them home. CTLU leaders invited the Labor Committee of the Illinois State Council of Defense to East St. Louis to hold a hearing to determine the cause of the violence. They trusted the council, which worked with the federal Council of National Defense to ensure harmonious worker-management relations for efficient war production. CTLU men expected Labor Committee chairman John Walker, president of the Illinois Federation of Labor, to corroborate their contention that industrialists and not the CTLU were responsible for encouraging the migration and the mass violence of May.[54]

In early June, the Labor Committee conducted hearings to determine whether the black migration had caused the labor disputes that led to mass racial violence. The committee heard from black migrants like John and Daisy Betts as well as from established African American residents like Leroy Bundy. Both migrants and townspeople testified that black southerners who settled in East St. Louis did so because they thought they had a chance to obtain jobs and a better way of life. The committee also listened to white townspeople's accounts. Attorney Maurice V. Joyce connected the crime wave to the migration. Labor organizer Harry Stanisic and CTLU president Michael Whalen argued that managers had encouraged the migration to drive down white workers' wages and disrupt the labor movement. The committee took testimony from corporate managers, including Charles Fox and American Steel Foundries foreman John Roche. These company officials denied that their firms had dispatched labor agents to the South to entice black laborers to migrate north.[55]

The Labor Committee released its report on June 30 and, admitting that it possessed only circumstantial evidence, charged that corporations had deliberately recruited more black laborers than they had job openings. The committee concluded that "an extensive campaign" existed to "induce negroes in great numbers to come to East St. Louis," and that it "required considerable financing, and its backers took pains to be unknown." In effect, the committee reinforced racist imagery that black southerners, incapable of organizing, leading, and sustaining the migration on their own, needed guidance from white people, in this case industrial employers who treated them as pawns in possible labor disputes. The committee also absolved the CTLU of all wrongdoing. Interestingly, the Labor Committee failed to establish responsibility for the May violence.[56]

In June, CTLU officials temporarily shifted their attention away from the migration to the unionization of black workers when they realized that Mayor Mollman had no intention of meeting their demand to stanch black migration to East St. Louis. Inexplicably, union leaders sent labor organizers to Brooklyn to discuss unionization with black packinghouse workers there. Perhaps they surmised that a strong union presence among the packinghouse workers who lived in that all-black village might spark mass unionization among black workers in the East St. Louis district. But CTLU men discontinued their organizing drive when the Brooklyn police chief threatened to jail union organizers. Most likely, Brooklyn officials made the threat because they were beholden to meatpackers in neighboring National City who provided jobs to Brooklyn residents.[57]

Black leaders involved in talks with the CTLU in June questioned the affiliation's commitment to unionize black workers, especially given its previous reluctance to organize them. Bundy, Bluitt, and other black politicos had to have regarded as preposterous the CTLU's inflammatory argument that black southern migrant workers took jobs away from white East St. Louisans. They knew that migrants settled in Brooklyn as well as in East St. Louis and that African American packinghouse workers commuted to National City just as easily from Brooklyn as they did from East St. Louis, both towns lying adjacent to National City. The black politicians must have speculated that even if African Americans were to be expelled from East St. Louis, the CTLU would still have to contend with Brooklyn's black workers, who presumably would still be taking jobs away from white men. They had to have reached the conclusion that politics underlay the anti–black migrant rhetoric that the CTLU used to assert its leadership among white workers who had initiated militant strikes independent of the labor affiliation.

Several prominent African Americans thought that an alliance with CTLU and mass unionizing of black workers held the potential for improving black people's position in city politics and defusing racial animosities that white working people held toward black laborers. They sought to convince the CTLU to drop its antimigration rhetoric and focus on building a labor movement that could attract large numbers of unskilled white as well as black laborers. Prounion black community activists Lyman Bluitt,

Leroy Bundy, Noah Parden, and Sam Wheat, and lawyer William E. Lilly met with Harry Kerr, Earl Jimerson, and four other CTLU officials to discuss ways to unionize African American workers. The politically astute black leaders did not hold organized labor responsible for the May violence, but they criticized the CTLU's lack of seriousness in organizing black workers. They noted, for example, that Jimerson had said he wanted to "find out who was the mysterious influence" that brought about the migration and the "conditions which existed here, which caused riots." Bluitt and Bundy concluded that the CTLU blamed its failure to organize migrants particularly upon black southern migrants' supposed antiunion attitudes and not on organized labor's historic resistance to accepting skilled and unskilled black workers as union members. In addition, the black politicians had to wonder why the CTLU had tapped them for assistance in organizing black workers rather than any of the many black laborers who had joined white workers in strikes in 1916 and 1917 and those who, like Morris packinghouse worker William Bagley, had led fellow workers in the 1916 walkout. The CTLU's actions reconfirmed for the African American community the organization's lack of interest in unionizing black workers. But the CTLU fit a national pattern, described by historian David Roediger, in which white unionists tended to exaggerate the role of black strikebreakers while ignoring white workers who broke black workers' strikes. Indeed, in the nineteenth and early twentieth centuries black southerners were more labor-conscious and prounion than white southerners.[58]

CTLU leaders experienced problems in building the labor movement because of their choice of rhetoric and their lack of leadership, not because of the Great Migration. They held fast to the idea that managers practiced racial divide-and-conquer tactics in the workplace. Labor officials knew that black workers accepted unions, went on strike, and were no more apt to break strikes than white laborers. Yet the affiliation, committed to antiblack racism, remained unenthused about organizing black workers. Its business union practices, partnership in city governance, and recent anti–black migration rhetoric prevented the organization from reacting to rapidly changing events. The CTLU failed to take a militant stance or exercise leadership during the strike waves that swept the city in 1916 and early 1917. Its chiefs lacked the vision of their counterparts in the Chicago Stockyards Labor Council, who initiated a campaign to unionize black workers.[59]

The role and reaction of city leaders, especially real estate politician-businessmen, in relation to the mass racial violence of May never underwent scrutiny during the Labor Committee investigation. The number of municipal officials and employees who had close personal or business connections with core agitators and perpetrators remains at best speculative. As a group in command of city politics, however, the men contributed greatly to the shaping of antiblack agitation. White politicians who courted the black vote signaled to African American leaders like Bundy their intolerance of a black political organization capable of independent action with the potential to undermine their power. Mollman, Tarlton, and Canavan, who headed one of the Democratic Party machines, had formed a partnership with county Republican Party leaders, including Alexander Flannigan, to prevent reform-minded Democratic and Republican progressives from winning city hall. Progressive reformer James Kirk, owner of the *East St. Louis Daily Journal,* persisted in sensationalizing black crime after the May episode and on occasion predicted future outbreaks of mass racial violence.

White business, civic, and labor leaders continued to blame black southern migrants for generating white people's racial prejudice and aggression toward black people. These individuals issued statements similar to those uttered by their counterparts in Springfield and other towns that had experienced mass racial violence in the previous decades. They denied racism as a contributory factor in the making of antiblack assaults. Kirk, for example, said that white townspeople held no ill will against the "older, law-abiding" black residents. Aluminum Ore manager R. F. Rucker declared that the primary reason for the violence of May 28 and 29 was the threat black people posed to white residents' standard of living and accustomed access to resources.[60]

Black townspeople quickly realized as June progressed that the May event had whetted a thirst for more violence among certain white elements in the city. Alone or in small groups, black East St. Louisans endured physical assaults from white ruffians. African Americans in one neighborhood on June 11 witnessed three drunken white troops curse black women, rob several black men, and wreck a black-owned saloon. But when fifty black men gathered to protect black womanhood by threatening to lynch the three soldiers, policemen arrived and escorted the drunken white men to jail. In general, black inhabitants thought that leaders among the white assailants were planning another round of mass antiblack violence.[61]

After the May pogrom, African Americans experienced an erosion in their formal political rights to equal protection under the law. Black motorists returning from St. Louis frequently encountered police checkpoints where law officers searched their vehicles for firearms. Lyman Bluitt protested when the police stopped and searched his car, telling the officers that they "most assuredly ought to search every man regardless of his color." Noah Parden fell victim to a white political backlash when the St. Clair County Board of Supervisors abolished his seat as county assistant state's attorney. According to white assistant state's attorney L. V. Walcott, the board expressed displeasure "with the arrangement whereby Parden handled the prosecution of all negroes arrested for carrying concealed weapons." Parden's dismissal represented a setback to black people's access to legal redress.[62]

City officials offered no assurance to East St. Louisans that mass racial violence had ended. Black townspeople heard rumors that white residents planned to massacre them on July 4. White people, also hearing rumors, feared that black people schemed to murder them on the same date. Black residents also read in the June 15 issue of the city's main newspaper, the *East St. Louis Daily Journal,* of a call for another "race riot" to bring an end to the purported black crime wave. Black community leaders complained to city officials that police had been disarming black citizens and demanded that their firearms be returned. Mayor Mollman, still mindful of the black vote, ordered the police to return the confiscated guns. No one reported whether or not the police followed through on Mollman's order.[63]

Considering the actions of the mayor's office, the police, the newspaper editor, and thugs with connections to machine politicians, some observers saw tentative preparations by certain authorities or their allies for another round of mass racial violence. Black townspeople redoubled their efforts to obtain weapons after Mollman refused to guarantee African Americans full protection. Black mortician R. M. C. Green, for instance, directed one of his employees, a very light-complexioned African American, to use a hearse to smuggle guns from St. Louis. Mistaken for a white person, the employee successfully passed through police checkpoints. Black residents concluded before the end of June that armed self-defense was their only viable option to protect themselves from additional antiblack violence.

Members of the local unit of the Afro-American Protective League must also have remembered how, nearly twenty years earlier, members of their sister chapter in Decatur, Illinois, resorted to armed self-defense under circumstances similar to those faced by black East St. Louisans in May. Black and white residents worried about a renewal of racial violence when the state withdrew the remaining regular National Guard units on June 25. Federalized militia units, however, remained in place to deter strikes at war production facilities. On June 27, as the last of the Aluminum Ore strikers returned to work without having won their demands, East St. Louisans wondered whether the simmering violence would soon erupt.[64]

Though the historical literature has concentrated on presenting the period from 1915 to July 1917 from the point of view of white townspeople, especially unionists and working people, African Americans occupied center stage in East St. Louis. Black inhabitants continued their push to achieve a substantive presence in the city's political culture. Black voters and community leaders sought greater patronage and representation in municipal and county affairs. In an era of intensified racism and aggressive white supremacy, African Americans in East St. Louis refused to keep their place at the bottom of the white-dominated social hierarchy. They called the notion of a "Negro problem" into question with their insistence on becoming equal partners in city politics and governance. Black leaders like Bundy thought to improve the fortunes of their community by leading an effort to build a black political machine. They realized that as black southern migrants continued to expand the voter base, they would have increasing opportunity to attain political power and alter their relationship with white city leaders.

The Great Migration of African American southerners changed social relations and power dynamics between black and white people in the North. Black migrants saw the opportunity to improve their lives by seeking factory employment, better housing, and full access to political resources in the northern urban industrial economy. Migrants also encountered white, as well as some black, northerners who accused them of creating or exacerbating social and economic tension. But in East St. Louis, migrants found a welcome among some established black residents, especially businessmen and politicians, and among white employers. Black migrants exerted an impact on municipal politics nonetheless. They represented votes to African American politicians who calculated that their community was on the threshold of creating its own independent political machine.

East St. Louis became a site of white northern hostility toward black migrants in particular and African Americans generally. White residents accused migrants of creating tension in the areas of employment and housing and in public spaces. Progressive reform-minded white East St. Louisans condemned black people for, among other things, buying and selling votes to political bosses, swinging local elections, and obtaining patronage. They feared that the migration gave black politicians the impetus to build an African American political machine that would be independent of white political bosses. CTLU officials, ignoring evidence to the contrary, claimed that the arrival of black southern laborers meant fewer jobs for white workers, more difficulties in organizing unions, and a lower standard of living for white working people. White homeowners and renters did not want African Americans residing in their neighborhoods, if for no other reason than the belief that black people depressed property values. White political and business leaders worried about the possibility of black rule as more migrants settled in the city. They had to prevent the rising strength of the black community, whose very presence supported the black drive to acquire political resources and power.

White East St. Louisans responsible for the outbreak of mass racial violence on May 28, 1917, signaled their intolerance of a strong, viable African American political presence in city affairs. They assigned the CTLU, a vociferous opponent of the black migration, responsibility for the mayhem, even though an Illinois state investigation committee absolved the labor affiliation of all responsibility. Among those who sparked the mass violence, persons with ties to influential figures, primarily white real estate politician-businessmen, went unpunished. Schemers launched a pogrom that was neither unplanned nor spontaneous, and the resulting upheaval was similar to other mass antiblack violence that created sundown towns and counties in many regions in the nation. Perpetrators were measured in their use of violence, which perhaps explains the absence of deaths. But they failed to achieve their desired result, the expulsion of all African Americans from the city. Agitators tried throughout June to spark another round of mass violence by conducting random attacks on black people. They found their opportunity to unleash another pogrom on Monday, July 2.

FOUR

The July Massacre

"We'll Have a White Man's Town"

THE MASS racial violence in July 1917 in East St. Louis occurred at the confluence of several historical factors: World War I, the mobilization for the nation's war effort, the wartime Great Migration, the expansion of the national economy, and the continuous intensification of racism. It was the first of the large wartime "race riots" involving mass destruction of property and numerous deaths. This outbreak of mass racial violence signaled a white American reaction to black American aspirations for equality. As black southerners migrated in large numbers to northern industrial cities, white people labeled the migrants a social problem and refused to accept the African American proposition that black people's role in national war mobilization and war production should be connected to the restoration of their civil rights. The July race riot, actually an American pogrom, marked the opening salvo in a broad battle by many white northerners who sought to maintain a rigid racial hierarchy, if necessary through violence.[1]

In East St. Louis, the July massacre stemmed from the same causes as the May riot, also a pogrom. Moreover, the participants were to a large extent the same: the black politicians and white business, civic, labor, and political leaders who had been prominent figures in May were involved again in July. For numerous contemporaries and for later scholars, the July outrage had a direct relationship to labor issues, including white workers' fears that black workers engaged in strikebreaking and antiunion activities. According to the literature, the explosion of violence came about when war mobilization and the Great Migration heightened social, economic, and political tensions that already existed in East St. Louis. But the July massacre is more accurately understood as a profoundly political event that occurred because black East St. Louisans had cracked a rigid racial hierarchy. The dynamics of black politics forced certain white elements either to accept the possibility of equality for African Americans or to respond with violence against them to maintain white domination. Real estate man and political boss Thomas Canavan, for one, stated his awareness of the political dimensions when he said, "Something has got to be done, or the damned niggers will take [over] the town."[2]

The mass racial violence of July accomplished what the May riot had failed to achieve: the elimination of the black community's influential role in local electoral politics. The July massacre had less to do with social tensions revolving around such issues as employment and housing and more to do with black East St. Louisans arriving at the threshold of creating their own independent political organization capable of holding the balance of power in city governance. The July pogrom represented a political solution planned by certain white real estate men, politicians, and businessmen and implemented by their "shock troops," many tied to the city's violent criminal subculture. As political boss and real estate man Locke Tarlton said to a business friend a few days after the pogrom, "[T]his is going to be a white man's town hereafter; the blacks will be run out of here and we'll have a white man's town." Political and social reformers, mainly members of the business community, carried the political solution to completion when they instituted a commission form of municipal government with two of its main objectives being to end independent black political influence and to maintain a racial hierarchy.[3]

Cleansing the City

Those who planned and led the antiblack assaults on July 2 and 3 did not act on behalf of labor unions or out of concern about interracial competition for jobs and housing. They furthered the political agenda of machine boss politicians who wanted to rid the city of black people. White gunmen, including a few city policemen who had been involved in random antiblack attacks in June, conducted their business from the Commercial Hotel. The hotel was owned by real estate men Thomas Canavan and Locke Tarlton, who, according to social worker W. A. Miller and Baptist minister George Allison, maintained their ties to the world of vice and crime there. Instigators carried out a series of ambushes against black residents while the police worked to disarm black residents. White assailants had no fear of being arrested, let alone convicted, because police officers, bondsmen, and politicians protected them.

On the night of Sunday, July 1, agitators escalated their terrorism, driving through black neighborhoods and firing shots at the homes of black inhabitants. Patrolman Harry L. Walker, former patrolman Gus Masserang, and "citizen" John Long were among those carrying out these terrorist attacks. During one episode, a small group of white men killed two black laborers as they returned home from work. In another, a gang of white men, joined by a few uniformed army recruiters on furlough, broke into the downtown office of black community politician and dentist Leroy Bundy, intending to kill him because he had angered white politicians with his attempts to build an independent black political machine. But Bundy, who had been warned of impending trouble by a white business friend, had already left town.[4]

Within the first hour of Monday, July 2, the police department received a phone call from a white grocer who said he had observed black residents with guns gathering in front of an African Methodist Episcopal Church in the city's South End district of Denverside. Apparently black Denversiders had decided to defend themselves in the event of further terrorist attacks. Night chief of police Cornelius Hickey ordered two plainclothes detectives, Sergeant Samuel Coppedge and Frank Wadley, along with two uniformed patrolmen to investigate. The four policemen, joined by reporter Roy Albertson, a frequent visitor to the police station, left for Denverside in an unmarked Ford Model T police car driven by police chauffeur William Hutter. Turning the corner east from Tenth Street onto Bond Avenue, Hutter came face to face with approximately 150 armed black men and abruptly stopped the vehicle. The armed men had been heading west toward the Free Bridge, where they hoped to exact revenge upon several white men who had assaulted two black women earlier that night. When Coppedge shouted, "What is doing here, boys?" the black men hollered, "None of your damned business." Coppedge responded, "We are down here to protect you fellows as well as the whites." The armed black men, thinking the six white men trigger-happy joy riders masquerading as policemen, replied, "We don't need any of your damned protection," and told them to leave. When Coppedge ordered Hutter to drive forward, some of the black men reacted and fired shots, killing Coppedge outright and wounding the two uniformed patrolmen and Wadley. Hutter and Albertson, escaping unharmed, sped the wounded and dying to nearby Deaconess Hospital, where Wadley died on the night of July 3. Ironically, Coppedge and Wadley had protected black residents in the Valley from white mobs during the May violence.[5]

Agitators, hearing that armed black men had killed white police officers, had the excuse they needed to unleash a pogrom. They drew upon a decades-long tradition of aggressive white people's punishments of black people, including lynchings, rapes, and mass violence, which often occurred after individual African Americans had killed, or were presumed to have killed, white agents of the state, including policemen. Antiblack schemers in East St. Louis proceeded with their plans to destroy the city's black community and send a message to African Americans that a price would be paid for refusing to accept their status as social inferiors. Intending to make a dramatic impact on white public opinion, instigators parked Coppedge's blood-soaked, bullet-riddled car in front of police headquarters before sunrise. They succeeded in attracting curious onlookers who gawked at the car and vowed to retaliate against African Americans. Provocateurs counted on little if any official interference, given that, as *St. Louis Times* reporter G. E. Popkess said, policemen demanded vengeance and even attorneys condoned antiblack violence. Unlike the situation on May 28 and 29, agitators this time had the police on their side.[6]

They used the morning hours to prepare for cleansing East St. Louis of African Americans. The aim was to turn East St. Louis into a sundown town, a place devoid of African American residents. Some whites warned black townspeople "to get their women and children away as it was going to be bad in the city." For example, an anonymous person telephoned Lincoln High School's director of music and drawing, Daisy Westbrook, to tell her that she and her family had better leave town immediately. White strangers on the streets advised teamster-businessmen Calvin Cotton and Mack Hearst, physician Thomas Hunter, and other black people to leave downtown before trouble began.

By mid-morning, a group of white men gathered at the Labor Temple, a hall owned by the Smith Brothers real estate firm which rented the space to union locals and other groups wanting to hold meetings. There, the men listened as former railway claims agent Richard Brockway and others directed them to get guns and "return at 3 PM to drive the negroes out of town." An unidentified white man, whom the local newspaper described as having a "pronounced Southern accent," instructed the crowd as to how white southerners "handled negroes" and called upon the throng to "bring their guns." Possibly this unidentified man was a white southern migrant lending his expertise in the use of violence against black people. Or perhaps he was either an agent for southern planters or a planter like the three from Mississippi, Leroy W. Valiant, James Mann, and Henry Crittenden, who, according to what pogrom survivors told Howard University Red Cross official Hallie Queen, came to the city sometime in May or June to convince black southern migrants to return south.[7]

City authorities acted in ways that suggested either gross incompetence or anticipation of another outbreak similar in scale to the one that had occurred in May. Some had connections with those who planned the anti-black pogrom. But whatever their motives, their response left them inadequately prepared to contain and manage the violent assaults that agitators were ready to launch. Chief of police Ransom Payne, for example, instead of ordering white patrolmen to round up suspected white vigilantes in the early morning hours, sent his men home to rest. Perhaps Payne based his decision on information from his brother, Ed Payne, a gangster with connections to figures who operated in the city's illegal economy or who embarked on their terrorist forays from the Commercial Hotel. Chief Payne told W. H. Mills and the department's four other black police detectives not to report for duty, saying that they stood no chance in a confrontation with angry white men. Mayor Fred Mollman failed to countermand the police chief's order to send policemen home, even though reporter Albertson had personally warned the mayor within two hours after the shooting of Coppedge and Wadley that he needed to prepare for trouble. Mollman knew that police response had proved inadequate during the May violence and that the National Guard had been needed to suppress the civil disorder. The mayor first contacted Major W. K. Kavanaugh, commander of the federalized Illinois National Guard units encamped in the city since April 1917, and requested the use of his units. When Kavanaugh told Mollman that his troops had been assigned only to protect war production industry from strikers, the mayor then called the adjutant general of the Illinois National Guard, F. S. Dickson, in Springfield, who agreed to send guardsmen to East St. Louis.[8]

Troops of the Fourth Infantry of the Illinois National Guard, which had suppressed the May pogrom, entered the city on the morning of Monday, July 2, over the course of several hours. Some arrived inexplicably in civilian dress. (More research is needed to explain the low level of troop readiness and to establish how many of the troops had joined the Fourth Infantry after May.) Many of the guardsmen hailed from southern Illinois sundown towns and needed a strong command to carry out their mission. Militia officers initially neither enforced discipline nor took initiative during the morning hours to disperse the gathering crowds. Some soldiers fraternized with the crowds, confiding to them that they carried little or no ammunition and had been ordered not to shoot or charge with fixed bayonets. Reportedly, a few militiamen willingly handed their guns to men who were organizing to assault black people. Lieutenant Colonel E. P. Clayton, who had provided resolute leadership during the May violence, requested additional troops, but his superior, Colonel S. O. Tripp, assistant quartermaster general, overruled him. Tripp, who had neither crowd control nor battlefield experience, took command at 10:00 AM but delayed troop deployment for several hours. Commenting on the situation later, newspaper owner and progressive reformer James Kirk said that well-led soldiers "could have stopped [the violence] in ten minutes." Tripp, as the governor's representative with authority to make decisions, had his own priorities. He opposed, for example, Mollman's demand to impose martial law, considering such action an admission of loss of control. Over all, the National Guard's unprofessional behavior emboldened agitators, who at first were uncertain about how the militia would react, to proceed with their attack against African Americans.[9]

At midday on Monday, July 2, 1917, according to plan, white assailants launched a second round of mass racial violence in East St. Louis, brutally attacking black people, residents and nonresidents alike. The key difference between the May and the July violence was that in July assailants had prepared for action and knew that they could literally get away with murder. The gathering multitudes clustered mainly at intersections of major thoroughfares where black commuters concentrated at streetcar stops. With most of the crowd watching and cheering, a small number of individuals conducted the actual assaults. Sometimes those perpetrating the violence stepped back to rest among the spectators before resuming their murderous deeds. Spectators and killers emotionally needed each other to build and reinforce a sense of community. Their bond turned the violence into a bloodthirsty orgy that gave the East St. Louis massacre its reputation of unspeakable savagery.[10]

The persons who sparked or participated in the mayhem remained, for the most part, officially unknown during the pogrom. Perpetrators, however, did not hide their identity from friends, white residents generally, and business and political leaders. Their anonymity was further ensured when Mayor Mollman's secretary, Maurice Ahearn, ordered police and guardsmen to arrest anyone photographing the beatings or killings or destroy their cameras. (Newsreels and photographs of the pogrom were shown in Belleville, Illinois, and elsewhere, but not in East St. Louis.) The perpetrators became officially anonymous because police either failed to record the names of arrestees or later destroyed arrest records.[11]

Though the identities of many assailants remained unknown, the hundreds, if not thousands, of white spectators and rioters represented a wide cross section of the population. Newspaper accounts reinforced the impression that the July mass racial violence was communal, based on nearly universal white support of such antiblack actions. According to a grand jury investigation in August, a congressional committee in October and November, and criminal trial proceedings in October and November, those who assaulted black men, women, and children included police officers, self-employed and wage-earning working people and professionals, National Guardsmen, politicians, small business owners, and the so-called riffraff or rough element of loafers, saloon bums, saloon loungers, and prostitutes. Perhaps members of the Cahokia Athletic Club and like groups participated in the assaults in the same way that athletic club personnel took part in the Chicago race riot in 1919. The men and women of the saloon culture, concludes scholar McLaughlin, formed a crucial element among the mass murderers. The ringleaders included painter Ralph Hood, middle-aged railroad claims agent Richard Brockway, forty-year-old railroad switchman

Herbert Wood, seventeen-year-old messenger boy Leo Keane, and thirty-two-year-old former National Stockyards Company employee S. L. Schultz, son of a wealthy Mount Carmel, Illinois farmer. Reporters as well as residents noted that workers from Aluminum Ore and from steel, meatpacking, and other large industrial firms—the workers whom CTLU considered most threatened by black migrants—were rarely seen in the crowds, let alone involved in meting out the violence.[12]

The white men and women who conducted the beatings and killings acted in a cavalier fashion, according to reporters and other observers. "Boys of 13, 14, 15 and 16," according to St. Louis Republic reporter Jack Lait, appeared "in the forefront of every felonious butchery, [and] girls and women, wielding bloody knives and clawing at the eyes of dying victims, sprang from the ranks of the mad thousands [announcing that they would] not tolerate a black man." Journalist Carlos F. Hurd observed that white rampagers displayed "a horribly cool deliberateness and a spirit of fun." Ambushers waited near the meatpacking plants and stockyards to chase after and shoot at isolated black workers. In one incident, several white men dragged two black men to an alley, shot them, returned to the street with both victims, and proceeded to hang them. When the rope broke as they hanged one of the helpless men, sending them falling on their backs, the hangmen laughed as several policemen and guardsmen watched. In another incident assailants caught fifty-two-year-old black teamster Scott Clark, and one of the tormentors said, "Let's drag him around a little." Leo Keane and Herbert Wood led at least twelve men in pulling Clark through the streets while others stoned him. They were about to hang Clark from a telephone pole when Colonel Tripp and several guardsmen intervened and rushed Clark to a hospital, where he later died from his wounds. Male assailants also attacked black women and children, mainly in the Valley, a district of primarily low-income black and white working-class homes. According to eyewitness Josie Nixon, a group of white men shot off a black woman's tongue and killed her son before entering a house and murdering a mother and her newborn baby.[13]

Black refugees and white observers reported that white women, mostly teenage and adult prostitutes, frequently targeted black women and children and occasionally assaulted black men. Survivors told Hallie Queen that the women "were far more vile . . . than were the men and far more inventive of cruelty." Some informed Queen that they witnessed women as they killed their victims, "picking out their eyes with [hatpins] before they were quite dead." And others reported watching two white teenage women, after severely pummeling a black woman and staining themselves with her blood, walk away from the scene bragging about their deed. Eyewitnesses also related to Queen that women assailants often tore clothes off black women and beat them with fists, shoes, or beer faucets. The Reverend George Allison recounted how he tried to protect a black woman being chased by seven or eight white prostitutes and three or four drunken pimps. The woman, he continued, escaped, but not before her pursuers had ripped her clothes off to her waist except for her corset. One refugee told Queen of a particularly heartbreaking incident in which a black mother carrying an infant wrapped in a towel was set upon by several white women. She managed to break away, "[c]rossing the Bridge of Mercy [the Free Bridge] . . . crying 'Thank God, I saved my baby.' When she opened the towel, it was empty. In the fight the women had taken the baby. . . . [Upon realizing what had happened,] the mother lost her reason."[14]

More white women participated in physically assaulting African Americans during the July massacre than during the May violence. These women, most identified as prostitutes, seemingly stepped outside of their presumed gender role as cheerleaders or spectators. McLaughlin conjectures that marginalized white individuals like prostitutes sought to increase their social status in the eyes of high-ranking white citizens (see also chapter 3). Their actions confounded many observers, who were at a loss to explain why these women assailants exhibited behavior normally ascribed to men.[15]

But the presence of women, often from the working class, as participants and leaders in mass violence, even in racial conflicts, is nothing remarkable in recent history. Women involved themselves as agitators, attackers, and leaders in various riots during the Civil War. These included, for instance, antidraft riots in New York City, where an antiblack pogrom occurred, and in Boston, Massachusetts, along with food riots in Richmond, Virginia, and other southern cities. Women predominated in and led later food riots, such as the Kosher Meat Boycott in 1902 in New York City. Women also joined in antiblack ethnic cleansing and other acts of racial violence. Even in events where women did not participate, like those in 1898 in Wilmington, North Carolina, and in 1906 in Atlanta, Georgia, they invoked the politics of gender, calling upon white men to protect them from black men whom white supremacists characterized as sexual predators. Some white women, viewing themselves as potential victims of black rapists and as protectors of their families and the white race, had no difficulty in crossing the line from spectator or cheerleader to looter of black homes and businesses and ultimately to assailant. White rioters, both women and men, easily linked notions of womanhood and manhood to racial ideologies, according to Marilynn Johnson and other historians. For example, in the 1908 pogrom in Springfield, Illinois, a forty-two-year-old keeper of a rooming house, Kate Howard, nicknamed "Joan of Arc" by the local press, urged white men to protect white women as she led rioters in destroying a white-owned restaurant that catered to black customers.[16]

White women rioters in East St. Louis possibly possessed similar ideas regarding white womanhood, but they operated under a different dynamic. Prostitutes predominated among the women who attacked black women, children, and men. Like many of the men who participated in the pogrom, they hailed from a violent saloon culture. Perhaps white prostitutes initially thronged into the streets to assault their competitors, black prostitutes. But women and men rioters in the East St. Louis pogroms, particularly the one in July, did not need to elevate the politics of gender as a rallying cry to mobilize white people. Like those who participated in the massacre in 1866 in Memphis, Tennessee, and numerous other conflicts, white assailants sought to destroy black property and lives because they regarded African Americans as a threat to white authority and power. Women— and men—attackers realized that they could injure and murder African Americans at will without fear of retribution from police officers, who expressed little if any concern about protecting black people or arresting and jailing rioters.[17]

European immigrants, particularly the new immigrants, played no noticeable role in the pogrom. Individual immigrants must have assaulted African Americans or looted black homes, as names of obvious eastern or southern European origin do appear among those summoned before the state grand jury in August. But scholars Rudwick and McLaughlin do not identify them as a group that participated in the destruction. The low profile of European immigrants during the July massacre in East St. Louis stood in contrast to the prominent role of immigrants during the mass racial conflict in Chicago in 1919. As historian William Tuttle shows, Chicago's old immigrants, principally Irish Americans, and its new immigrant communities expressed much hostility toward African Americans based on a history of job competition, bitter labor disputes with industrialists, and Chicago politics. But Poles and other Slavic language speakers among the new immigrants only joined the rioting after black strikebreakers threatened their jobs at the meatpacking plants and after white men in blackface set fire to the homes of 948 Polish and Lithuanian working people, a crime blamed on African Americans. In East St. Louis, the absence of measurable immigrant involvement meant that local and state authorities viewed the pogrom through the lens of race and not through the lens of ethnicity.[18]

Some local and county government officials, guardsmen, and policemen acquiesced to or joined antiblack assaults, refusing either to protect African Americans or to arrest rioters. The state's attorney for St. Clair County, Herbert Schaumleffel, for example, watched as attackers beat and killed black people. Schaumleffel even released eighty-nine jailed assailants before police had a chance to book them. Some militiamen looted and then torched black dwellings and businesses and shot at fleeing black occupants, sometimes forcing them back into the burning structures. Several troops and policemen disarmed black men and either handed them over to the mobs to be beaten or killed or attacked the men themselves. Soldiers escorting black men, women, and children to the police station failed to provide them protection from missile-throwing crowds.[19]

African Americans faced assailants whose seemingly pathological racism moved them to be sadistic in the manner of participants in lynching parties who showed no mercy or remorse. Black residents in the Valley and on downtown streets became hunted prey and even a source of entertainment as attackers fulfilled their idea of racial superiority. Black people's lives had no value in the eyes of their tormentors. Mattie House watched as white men shot her husband and hacked his corpse to pieces. A black man who had concealed himself in a box was discovered by ruffians who, after nailing the box shut, "threw it into the flames, remaining until it was burned to ashes." Black clergyman James Taylor observed one group of white men who shot and wounded a black shopkeeper and his family in their store, then torched the shop and incinerated them. According to Josie Nixon, attackers eagerly killed black infants and young children, sometimes throwing them alive into burning structures. Nixon told about one mother who ran from her burning house with her baby in her arms. Once they were outside, said Nixon, the murderers shot "the baby . . . through the head and threw the infant into the fire." In another instance, a black woman and a child who ran from a burning building "were either killed or knocked unconscious . . . and the child was thrown back" into the fire. In yet still another act of cruelty, rioters stood around talking and joking until a black man appeared and someone screamed, "There's a nigger." They all ran after the man, killed him, left the corpse in the street, and then resumed their conversation.[20]

The fact that perpetrators attacked African Americans regardless of gender or age, as well as African Americans who obviously did not even live or work in East St. Louis, suggests that concern about racial competition in local housing and employment was not a principal motivation. Some rioters, knowing that black passengers passed through daily by rail from the South en route to Chicago and elsewhere, converged at the railroad station, intent on beating or at least intimidating black travelers who stepped off trains making routine stops in the station. At times rioters ignored pleas from black people who shouted that they were not from the area. In one notable incident, assailants surrounded a westbound streetcar carrying the Cook family home to St. Louis from a fishing trip and dragged the parents and their two children from the vehicle. Thugs proceeded to torture the parents and son; the daughter somehow escaped. Men tore off Mrs. Lena Cook's clothes and pulled out her hair while she screamed, "We're not from East St. Louis and haven't harmed anyone." These claims of nonresidency were ignored. When Mrs. Cook pleaded for the lives of her husband and seventeen-year-old son, ringleader Charles Hanna, a chauffeur, shot and killed the husband, Edward Cook, while John Gow, a teamster, killed the couple's son. Hanna then punched Lena Cook and threatened to kill her, but she managed to crawl to a nearby drugstore where "a white man interceded for her, telling the mob to 'leave the woman alone.'" Enraged that a white man intervened to help a black woman, a few men clubbed her protector. Ambulance attendants rescued Cook, taking her and the corpses of her husband and son to a hospital.[21]

Ringleaders, for a variety of reasons, allowed some black individuals to pass through the crowds unharmed. They did not, for example, molest barber Mose Lockett, who enjoyed cordial relations with boss politicians. Similarly, leaders of one group of attackers left the popular black saloonkeeper William "Buddy" Bell untouched, perhaps also because of his known connections with boss politicians. One group of rioters spared a Mr. Williamson (no first name given), whom they mistook for his brother, a highly regarded janitor who was most likely a recipient of political patronage. Assailants permitted Captain John Robinson, a longtime black Republican and ward politician held in high esteem by white residents, to walk through the downtown district undisturbed. Sometimes attackers showed mercy. For example, when a group of white men broke into a black family's house intent upon killing its occupants and confronted children, one of the men said, "Let's kill the kids." When one of the children, a little girl, recognized an ice dealer in the mob, she cried out, "Mr. Iceman, don't kill me—please don't." The iceman, moved by the child's plea, led the attackers away.[22]

White assailants most likely justified their destructive assaults on black people's property by invoking the white supremacist idea that African Americans must remain in poverty. Perhaps they ripped clothing off female victims because they envied the economic aspirations that their clothing represented. Their targets were primarily low-income African Americans clustered in majority-white districts in and around the periphery of the downtown and in the Valley along Third Street. Some vandals were simply opportunists, seizing the chance to rob without fear of retribution. Other ransackers, resentful of any African American material advancement, set houses ablaze after carrying off furniture, clothing, and other household contents. White men and women also damaged or destroyed black-owned businesses and several white businesses that employed black people when they found these businesses unprotected by the federalized militia. Mobs set afire railroad cars filled with war munitions and other commodities, railroad freight houses, the Bon-Ton Baking Company, Hill-Thomas Lime and Cement Company, and other firms. Arsonists burned the Broadway Theatre, incinerating several black people who had taken refuge there. Assailants did not attack Armour, Swift, and other large companies that employed black workers because these facilities were protected either by federalized Illinois National Guard units or by private security guards. Aluminum Ore, for example, had a hired defense force and a rifle club that supplied guns to loyal white and black employees; the latter, along with their families, had sought safety on company property.[23]

By late Monday afternoon, Illinois and federal authorities and East St. Louis businessmen concluded that the situation in the city had spiraled out of control. They expressed concerns, mostly having to do with restoring interstate commerce, resuming war production, reestablishing the legitimacy of city hall, and protecting black workers who formed a significant percentage of the workforce in industries supporting federal war effort. The assistant attorney general of Illinois, C. W. Middlekauff, announced that lawlessness reigned in East St. Louis. According to white reporter Paul Anderson of the *St. Louis Post-Dispatch,* the "complete break-down of every [city] agency that preserve[d] order" had given people "a free and unrestricted opportunity to kill." Hill-Thomas Lime and Cement Company secretary Robert Thomas described a police department in a state of mutiny. Kehlor Flour Mills Company president Peyton T. Karr and other businessmen, fearing destruction of their property and a loss of black workers, contacted officials at the War Department in Washington, D.C., requesting armed federal intervention.[24]

Those authorities who performed their duties appropriately faced the daunting task of protecting African Americans from mass murderers, disarming black and white street fighters, and imposing law and order. When Mayor Mollman finally, by late Monday afternoon, convinced Governor Lowden to declare martial law over Colonel Tripp's objections, Tripp handed over command to Lieutenant Colonel Clayton. Though lacking a full complement of units, since troops continued to trickle into the city, Clayton molded his men into a disciplined force that dispersed the throngs by firing shots into the air, charging with fixed bayonets, and jailing at least 500 men and women assailants.[25] Other law enforcement officers rushed to the city with its police department still in disarray. For example, county deputy sheriffs Oscar Roper, Dan O'Connell, and Rufus Shepherd saved several black men and women from a burning house after a policeman gave the excuse that he was guarding a fire hose.[26]

Before Monday ended, rioters had destroyed property and lives across a wide area of central East St. Louis. They stormed through neighborhoods where African Americans were not the majority of residents. Attackers restricted most of their assaults to an area framed by the Free Bridge approach on the south, Eleventh Street on the east, First Street on the west, and on the north, National City and Thirteenth Street and Nectar Avenue in Goose Hill. They centered their rioting on principal streets and intersections, including along Broadway from Collinsville Avenue to Tenth Street, Collinsville at Missouri Avenue, State Street at Collinsville, Third Street at St. Louis, and Third Street at Summit Avenue. Arsonists burned numerous homes in this broad area, many owned or occupied by African Americans. Rampagers surged along Third Street, the main thoroughfare in the Valley. Mobs especially devastated one densely packed district bounded by

Broadway on the north, Walnut Avenue on the south, Fourth Street and Rock Road on the west, and Eleventh Street on the east, where they torched at least 300 houses.[27]

The rampagers showed that white supremacy, though murderous of African Americans, also sought to discipline white people. Assailants injured or killed, or threatened with drawn pistols, white people who attempted to rescue black people or prevent destruction of black homes and shops. Small white businesses that employed significant numbers of black workers were targeted as well. One group of killers ordered a white woman to leave the area when she tried to aid a defenseless black man. Another gang of attackers confronted a Catholic priest who had rushed to rescue an unarmed black man. According to one reporter, "Whenever a white man attempted to drag a negro from the street, intending to give him medical attention, the mob, with drawn pistols, forced him to desist." Assailants with bricks and guns forced ambulance attendants assisting severely injured black people to leave the victims in the street. One mob readied to kill the men of a St. Louis fire engine company attempting to hose down a blazing structure, forcing the firefighters to pack up and return to their station across the river.[28]

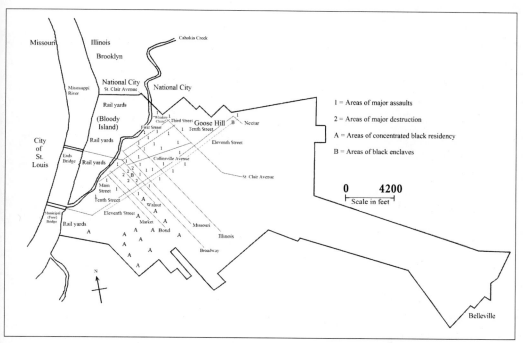

Map 4.1. Area of East St. Louis pogrom, July 2–3, 1917. *Map by author*

Most black residents in the destroyed districts, however, escaped the wrath of the attackers, whose main intention was to cleanse the city of African Americans, not to kill every black person they saw. For instance, Mary Lewis ran unharmed after a mob set fire to her home, though her sister was wounded and Mary's husband was shot to death. Daisy and Cora Westbrook and their mother hid in the basement when rioters entered their home intending to kill them. But the men fled the house upon hearing the thunderous collapse of what turned out to be the burning Broadway Theatre. Mrs. Michael Carey was fortunate that white steamfitter Edward Otto did not kill her when he demanded that she tell him the whereabouts of several black persons. Rosie Augustus said that Otto broke into her house with an ax while his cohorts shot out her windows. Ada White hid in her closet while coal and ice dealer Mike Evanhoff and several other rioters ransacked her house. Witnessing a mob killing two black men, Emma Ballard and her four children grabbed their best clothes, feather beds, and pillows, and after storing these items at the house of a friendly white neighbor, fled to St. Louis. On Tuesday night, packinghouse worker Clarissa Lockett fled when a mob set fire to her house at 48 Third Street. She ran to a nearby saloon owned by a Polish immigrant couple, who sheltered her until she left the next morning for St. Louis.[29]

The percentage and number of black refugees cannot be accurately determined, largely because officials had not taken a reasonable enumeration in spring 1917 and also because the African American population included some people in the process of migration to other locales. The city's black population by June 1917 was estimated at 10,617 by Rudwick, who used school enrollment and federal census figures for 1910 and 1920 for his arithmetic progression method of estimation. On the other hand, authorities and private citizens, estimating the black resident population to fall between 15,000 and 23,000 by June 1917, agreed that more than half the black population left East St. Louis permanently after the uprising. Most refugees, including Daisy Westbrook and her family, streamed across the Eads and Free bridges into St. Louis. According to a National Urban League report, 7,200 refugees entered St. Louis during the pogrom. At least 6,466 people stayed for several days at the St. Louis municipal lodging house, where black and white church and civic groups provided them with food and other assistance and eventually directed them to housing. Hundreds of refugees, including infants and children who "bore marks of the mob's violence," received medical care for their injuries.[30]

Black townspeople untouched by assailants lived in either predominantly black or all-black districts in the city's South End, where residents resorted to armed self-defense. Though Rudwick surmised that black inhabitants' use of firearms was at best sporadic, he concurs with McLaughlin that black East St. Louisans, relying upon a tradition of using firearms to protect their persons and property, made widespread and effective use of guns. Black residents must have heard about earlier instances of antiblack violence in which African Americans had engaged in gun battles to keep white intruders from entering their neighborhoods, for example, in 1906 in Atlanta. On July 2, city leaders like Thomas Canavan and white assailants knew that armed African Americans had wounded or killed an unknown number of white people who ventured into black districts during the mayhem. At one location, according to Major K. Causer of the Fourth Company, Illinois National Guard, black homeowners who observed a gang readying to attack their homes fired "a fearful volley and [left] many white men . . . dead." Survivors retrieved their dead comrades and "either buried them secretly or threw them into the Mississippi." Some attackers clearly did not want word to spread that African Americans had organized an effective defense against white invaders, if for no other reason than that white people would have a more difficult time mounting future assaults against black communities. But black shooters refrained from attacking white people whom they knew to be friendly. One group of black gunmen, for example, spared Aluminum Ore Company staff physician Albert B. McQuillan and his wife when one of the gunmen recognized the company doctor who had been kind to him.[31]

The mass violence subsided on Tuesday, July 3, as guardsmen regained control of the city. But even on Tuesday a few agitators, vengeful policemen, and rogue guardsmen continued their attacks on isolated groups of black people. In one incident in the city's Bloody Island district, three police officers and six soldiers without provocation attacked John Avant and twenty-five black railroad workers as they broke for lunch at a restaurant, killing two of the men and wounding several others, including Avant. One soldier shot off the right arm of black bystander Mineola Magee. According to Allison, arsonists sporadically torched property into Tuesday evening. But for all practical purposes, Clayton had suppressed the riot by that time, allowing East St. Louisans, many of whom had been on the streets on Monday either as observers or participants in mass anti-black violence, to tour the scenes of destruction and death. Some remarked that the charred cityscape reminded them of photographs they had seen of battle-ruined cities in war-torn Europe. Others noted similarities between locations where murderers had hanged black people from telephone poles or trees or incinerated them and depictions of lynching scenes elsewhere. Hallie Queen, however, thought assailants outdid typical lynching parties because they left so many signs of their rampage, such as shells of houses and cremated corpses, when the pogrom finally ended on Tuesday night.[32]

Immediate Aftermath of the July Pogrom

Upon cessation of the violence, officials and civilians assessed the damage and the effects of the pogrom. As they observed the destruction, they could only compare the July massacre to events that had occurred outside the North. Black people, and many white people as well, thought such mass antiblack violence peculiar to the South, unthinkable in a northern industrial city. White people had invaded urban black neighborhoods, killing, wounding, or displacing large numbers of African Americans, in various southern cities, for example, in Wilmington, North Carolina, in 1898. Observers searching for similar occurrences in the North could only recall the racist violence in 1908 in Springfield, Illinois, but they thought that the East St. Louis riot went beyond even that mass antiblack assault. Some scholars have considered the East St. Louis massacre the worst episode of urban mass racial violence to occur in twentieth-century America until the urban uprisings of the 1960s. However, recent scholarship shows that the racial violence in 1921 in Tulsa, Oklahoma, surpassed that of East St. Louis in terms of property damage and deaths.

In East St. Louis, assailants had terrorized at least 7,000 African Americans into fleeing across the river to St. Louis, many with only the clothes on their backs and small bundles in their arms. In addition, unknown numbers had fled to neighboring towns north, east, and south of East St. Louis. White attackers had wounded hundreds of African Americans and had killed thirty-nine, according to the official tally; unofficial death estimates were much higher. Some observers said that as many as 500 black men, women, and children had been massacred. News that nine white men had been killed unsettled white people, especially as some reports hinted that black people in majority-black neighborhoods had retaliated with firearms. Contradicting the official account of nine white deaths, one black policeman told *Chicago Defender* reporter J. M. Batchman that he had seen thirty-eight slain white people lying in a morgue. African Americans probably would have shot and killed even more white attackers if the police had not disarmed a number of black residents in June. But enough black townspeople did engage in armed self-defense to prevent agitators from turning East St. Louis into an all-white, or sundown, town.[33]

Some African Americans across the nation drew lessons about the value of armed self-defense in holding down death tolls during mass assaults on black people, especially when government at all levels failed to protect them. Socialist Hubert H. Harrison, president of the Liberty League of Negro Americans, urged black people to "supply themselves with rifles and fight, if necessary, to defend their property and lives." Harrison argued that as long as white vigilantes murdered defenseless African Americans and authorities stood by indifferently, then black people must be ready to "kill rather than submit to be killed."[34]

Authorities and most news reports labeled the July massacre a race riot, preferring to minimize or ignore the political dimension of the event. But others saw it as a pogrom, a planned attack that targeted a specific population with the intent of disrupting, if not destroying, a community. The superintendent of the Jewish Educational and Charitable Association of St. Louis, Oscar Leonard, for instance, used the term pogrom, "the name by which Russian massacres of Jews [had] become known," to describe the July riot. Leonard quoted a Russian Jewish immigrant who told him that "the Russian 'Black Hundreds' could take lessons in pogrom-making from the whites of East St. Louis." These observers saw official involvement, most blatantly of the police, and politics as the chief causes of the massacre. Later even some civic and business leaders openly agreed that "the source of the trouble was political." They noted that local authorities had quickly apprehended several leading black politicians on charges of inciting the mass racial violence and had used the massacre as an excuse to remove black elected and appointed officials from various political positions. For example, dentist Leroy Bundy, physician Thomas Hunter, American Steel Foundries laborer Fayette Parker, and three others were dismissed from their seats on the St. Clair County Board of Supervisors shortly after the massacre. In addition, the board abolished the office of Negro county physician that had been occupied by Lyman Bluitt at an annual salary of $1,100. African American journalist and activist Ida B. Wells-Barnett reported that the killers had the support "of the civil authorities, the police and the state militia, in . . . murdering over two hundred Negroes and destroying three million dollars worth of property."[35]

Some refugees returned in hopes of starting over, only to learn that white people had looted their homes, carrying away furniture, clothing, and other contents, and in some cases had set ransacked homes ablaze. The newly destitute and homeless thus became victims of a long-standing pattern of theft and wanton destruction of black people's property that occurred in numerous mass racial assaults in nineteenth- and early twentieth-century America. Many of those who lost their homes lived in the Valley, including Daisy Westbrook, who discovered that looters had burned her house to ashes. Emma Ballard saw her house still standing, but with its windows broken; furnishings, clothing, and other items had been stolen or destroyed. Mrs. Willie Flake said that she had been "able to pack one trunk with some clothing and quilts for herself and her children," but she could not find the insurance books she needed to claim her losses. Lulu Thomas was one of a number of pogrom survivors who spotted their good clothes being worn by their white neighbors who obviously had obtained the items through looting.[36]

In the aftermath of the destruction, black East St. Louisans cared for survivors, buried the dead, and began rebuilding their shattered lives. Some black townspeople, concerned about future outbreaks of mass racial violence, left the city permanently. "Respectable" property-owning black families, lamented the local newspaper, fled, never to return. But some long-time black residents stayed and worked to restore the community. They included Afro-American Protective League activist and Republican politician Captain John Robinson; Democratic Party politician Harvey T. Bowman; sisters Lucy Mae and Fannie Turner, schoolteachers and descendants of Virginian slave revolt leader Nat Turner; rolling mill laborer Ephiriam Thomas and his spouse Jennie Thomas, both founders of Mount Zion Missionary Baptist Church; and the Hawkins, Eubanks, and DeShields families who were active in the community. The homeless relied upon Mary Martin and her Colored Old Folks' Home Association that supplied clothing and other items. Black townspeople also received aid from individuals and private groups across the nation, including assistance from two Chicago-based organizations, the Negro Fellowship League and the Bethel African Methodist Episcopal Church. Ida B. Wells-Barnett led Chicagoans in successfully lobbying Governor Lowden to have Illinois relieve St. Louis of the burden of caring for refugees and to provide for community and refugee aid.[37]

Several hundred black people gathered in September for the annual observance of the Emancipation Proclamation, demonstrating by their presence that mass racial violence had not destroyed their community or dimmed the meaning of the yearly commemoration of abolition and freedom. Attendees listened as Captain John Robinson and Fannie Jones, president and secretary, respectively, of the East St. Louis chapter of the Afro-American Protective League of Illinois, educators Martin V. Lucas and John W. Hughes, and other black speakers linked the proclamation and African American patriotism to demands that the federal government make America safe for democracy. Black East St. Louisans expected the federal government to respond to their loyalty to the nation by bringing the leaders of the July violence to justice. African Americans generally lent patriotic support to the president, and young black men enlisted in the military in hopes that their service to country would restore constitutional rights for black citizens.[38]

Some white East St. Louisans and government officials understood the adverse effect of the July pogrom on the local economy. More than 100 white housewives besieged the local state employment office demanding replacements when their black domestics and washerwomen stopped working for them. Business leaders painfully realized both their dependency upon black laborers and the need to protect them from mass assaults. Corporate managers whose operations required low-wage labor sought assistance from Illinois and federal agencies to entice black workers back to their jobs. Representatives of the Terminal Railroad Association and other local businesses met with the federal National War Board to adopt measures to ensure the safety of black workers. They dropped their plans, however, as African American laborers, often at the urging of black ministers like the Reverend J. R. Tunstell, pastor of Beth-Eden Church, began returning to work. City politicians and business leaders soon learned that the interest of the federal government took precedence over local concerns. Industrialists and state and federal officials marshaled their resources to make the city safe for African Americans, if only for the sake of profits, undisrupted interstate commerce, and wartime economic production.[39]

Nationwide, black and white Americans expressed shock, anger, and outrage upon learning about the July atrocities, labeling white East St. Louisans bloodthirsty and barbaric. They argued that the killings mocked notions of American democracy and citizenship rights. Black Howard University professor Kelly Miller, for one, denounced President Woodrow Wilson's failure to condemn the massacre as he conducted a war to make the world safe for democracy. But not everyone condemned the violence. Senators Benjamin Tillman, of South Carolina, and James Kimble Vardaman, of Mississippi, for example, praised white northerners for taking a lesson from white southerners in teaching black people to know their place.[40]

Many Americans were taken aback by the disinterest of East St. Louis political and business leaders in bringing pogrom leaders and participants to justice. Some demanded that the federal government intervene. The National Association of Colored Women, through its Department for Suppression of Lynching and Mob Violence, the National Association for the Advancement of Colored People, and other organizations pressured Congress and the White House to investigate the massacre. The NAACP publicized the horrors of the July uprising nationwide through its magazine the *Crisis*. The association held a "Silent March" on July 28, 1917, in New York City to protest racial violence and joined black civic groups in raising funds for the relief of black refugees. The NAACP also assisted government investigators, submitting to them its findings on the causes of the July bloodletting.[41]

Federal and state officials, deluged with letters from private citizens demanding that lawbreakers be brought to justice, moved to investigate. They quickly disproved rumors that German war saboteurs or political leftists with the Industrial Workers of the World had instigated the July violence. Investigators also debunked a story that unnamed white agitators had funded Leroy Bundy and other black leaders to build a black militia. With such distractions rendered moot, federal and state authorities turned their attention to ferreting out the people responsible for the carnage and destruction and assisting local progressive reformers in reconstructing city government.[42]

Power Struggle for City Hall

City and county officials said they thought it was too risky to bring only white assailants to justice. These leaders argued that African Americans, especially black southern migrants, had provoked white anger and thus brought the violence upon themselves. They created a rationale for punishing the victims of the pogrom as well as the participants. County coroner C. P. Renner of Belleville, carrying the thought further, called for absolving the city of all financial responsibility for the destruction of homes and businesses. Renner did form a coroner's jury to assess the value of damaged property and establish the number of people killed. The jury, reflecting mainly real estate interests, included school board secretary and real estate man Joseph Keys, insurance agent and real estate man Theodore Smith, hardware businessman Charles House, mortician Alonzo Brichler, (city) clerk and former member of the county board of supervisors Charles Scherrer, and building and loan association member and real estate man C. R. Hisrich. The coroner's jury issued estimates that were lower than earlier figures, much to the approval of city boosters.[43]

Real estate men resumed their economic growth policies after the Renner jury's pronouncement signaled to industrialists and financiers that East St. Louis was again safe for capital investment. Thomas Canavan, Leo Scherrer, Fred Harding, Stephen D. Sexton, John W. Renshaw, and other members of the Real Estate Exchange of East St. Louis called upon employers to give preferential treatment to white workers in the hiring process. They took steps to placate white residents by asking white landlords to make tenements available for white newcomers to ensure that white neighborhoods would remain white. But the real estate politician-businessmen who ran city hall knew that a political struggle with progressive reformers still lay ahead.[44]

White faction leaders intensified their decades-long political battle for control of East St. Louis once the nascent black political machine had been removed from city politics. Broadly speaking, their political battles before, during, and after the July mayhem paralleled, albeit on a much smaller scale, the power struggles of black and white populists against white Democratic Party leaders in the South during the late 1880s and early 1890s. Much as southern white political factions eliminated African Americans from the electoral process, white city leaders in East St. Louis had found a way to strip black residents of a decision-making role in local government by minimizing their voting strength.[45]

White businessmen, city officials, and their allies grouped around two poles, machine boss politicians at one end and a loose coalition of progressive reformers at the other. Boss politicians occupied a weaker position relative to reformers after the July pogrom because many East St. Louisans associated the bosses with the massacre, with decades of criminal violence, and with fiscal mismanagement of the city. Reformers convinced many white townspeople that the July violence had resulted from years of rule by boss politicians who coddled black people, drove the city into debt, and relied upon saloons and vice for city revenues.[46]

Progressives, especially those in the Chamber of Commerce of East St. Louis, blasted Mayor Mollman and his political bosses for lax law enforcement and social problems that had beset the city for years. They announced that the chamber was ready "to assist the mayor in handling the reins of the government." Chamber members gained support for their plans to reorganize municipal government from various antisaloon individuals and organizations, including assistant Illinois attorney general C. W. Middlekauff and the Women's Christian Temperance Association. The chamber had its arguments enhanced when its supporters claimed saloons as the foundation of machine politicians' power and denounced saloon owners and liquor companies, along with county and city administrators and the police, for allowing the massacre to happen.[47]

As the Chamber of Commerce embarked upon reconstructing city government, its top priority was reorganization of the Board of Fire and Police Commissioners, which the chamber planned to staff with loyalists. On July 6, the chamber vice president, attorney Maurice V. Joyce, criticized the police for incompetence, and on the next day the Reverend George Allison led more than 300 white businessmen and professionals in demanding a reorganization of the police department. The chamber president, Southern Illinois National Bank director Conrad Reeb, called upon interested, reform-minded white citizens to form a Committee of One Hundred to guide the practical work of reorganizing the police.[48]

Formed three or four days after the July massacre, the Committee of One Hundred had to improve conditions, if for no other reason than to restore the confidence of insurance and industrial firms that the city was safe for their investment. Reeb had consulted lawyers Clarence Eugene

Pope, Daniel McGlynn, Maurice V. Joyce, and a few others about selecting potential members for the committee. They agreed to choose white
men representing a wide range of occupations and interests. Reeb initially
appointed seventy-five white men from real estate, industry, small business, and organized labor to the committee that was to work under the
guidance of the Chamber of Commerce. The committee's tasks involved
finding ways to prevent future outbreaks of mass racial violence and ferreting out those responsible for the July assaults.[49]

Progressives representing industry, civic organizations, and the local retail business community, working mainly through the Chamber of Commerce and the Committee of One Hundred, called upon state and federal
authorities to reconstruct the city. They required the power of the state
and federal government to diminish the influence of their opponents, who
held the reins of local government. Reformers and state and federal authorities realized that it was in their best interests to cooperate with one
another, assigning blame for the mass violence to boss politicians and
quickly restoring law and order. The state had spent time and money in
suppressing two outbreaks of mayhem and wanted to break the will of entrenched antiblack elements keen on furthering a cycle of racist violence.
Federal and state officials encouraged reformers and their allies to assist
in enforcing national priorities at the local level and bringing perpetrators
of the July violence to justice. On July 11, the Illinois General Assembly
awarded $27,500 to be divided among forty-five individual and corporate
members of the chamber to cover expenses incurred in gathering data that
state officials needed to bring pogrom participants to justice. The largest
recipients were Aluminum Ore Company, which received $2,500; Armour,
Morris, Swift, and St. Louis National Stockyards, each given $1,875; and
Missouri Malleable Iron Company, awarded $1,500. The chamber raised
at least $100,000 and deposited the money in Conrad Reeb's Southern
Illinois National Bank in preparation for the campaign to reorganize the
police department.[50]

From mid-July into August, the Chamber of Commerce and the Committee of One Hundred and their allies battled Mayor Mollman over the
restructuring of the Board of Fire and Police Commissioners and other issues. They demanded that he dismiss from the board three of his friends:
real estate man Nelson Schein, Swift employee and city school board president Wallace Watkins, and Heim Brewery manager William Schmidt. The

chamber further insisted that Mollman install its choices for new commissioners: horse dealer J. F. Reed, Southern Railway freight agent E. J. Coffey, and hardware businessman and Southern Illinois National Bank director Fred Giesing. After consulting with Thomas Canavan and Locke Tarlton, Mollman agreed to the chamber's choices for fire and police commissioners but rejected its demand to accept Watkins's resignation. Mollman also refused other chamber demands, including one for his own resignation. He instead instructed Watkins to suspend chief of police Ransom Payne and night chief of police Cornelius Hickey and promote two police sergeants to the chiefs' positions. In August, the Ministerial Alliance of East St. Louis, a civic group composed of leading white Protestant clergymen, exercising its moral authority and acting on the chamber's behalf, criticized Mollman for failing to purge the city of corruption, vice, and crime and called for his resignation. Under pressure, Mollman relented somewhat: while not submitting his own resignation, he installed the chamber's choice, granitoid contractor Frank Keating, as the new chief of police and agreed to wage an antiprostitution campaign as well.[51]

The progressive coalition began unraveling from mid-July onward as class interests split the Committee of One Hundred into labor and business factions. The committee agreed with the suggestion of one labor leader that it fund an East St. Louis United Labor Defense League, a home guard, to operate until a new police department could begin functioning, but members disagreed as to the home guard's duties. Businessmen in the chamber argued that the league should defend employers who hired strikebreakers, but this met with bitter objection from unionists on the committee. In response, the committee's business faction, constituting the majority of the assembly, voted to dissolve the committee. One union member noted that in dissolving the committee, businessmen had severely weakened organized labor's forty-year partnership with reformist elements in the business community. For their part, businessmen assigned primary responsibility for the mass violence to organized labor, saying that the latter had placed its own interests before those of the city.[52]

Many in the Chamber of Commerce and the Committee of One Hundred refused to take action against members of either organization or their friends who had been charged with involvement in the July violence for fear of unraveling the city's political culture of dense and overlapping networks. Chamber member Daniel McGlynn, an attorney, represented two friends, policemen Meehan and O'Brien, accused of shooting and killing two black railroad workers and wounding Mineola Magee on July 3. McGlynn welcomed the police raising funds to defray Meehan's and O'Brien's legal expenses. In another example, the president of the State Bar Association of Illinois, E. C. Kramer, and other legal professionals ignored calls for the disbarment of Alexander Flannigan and other attorneys for their roles in the violence. The corporation counsel for the City of East St. Louis, Jerry Sullivan, typified local lawyers in his lack of interest in impeaching or disbarring St. Clair County state's attorney Herbert Schaumleffel for his failure to enforce the law during the July pogrom. Maurice Ahearn retained his position as clerk of the Board of Fire and Police Commissioners until the state grand jury indicted him for ordering the police to arrest anyone taking photographs during the mass antiblack violence. Particularly illustrative of the networks involved, Ahearn and county Republicans Flannigan and Schaumleffel all had strong ties to Mollman's political machine, headed by the director of the East Side Levee and Sanitary District Locke Tarlton and political boss Thomas Canavan. In turn, Tarlton and Canavan controlled the district and its interests in the Southern Illinois National Bank managed by Chamber of Commerce president Conrad Reeb, who had called for the reorganization of the police department.[53]

In August, the state grand jury, investigating the July violence, took testimony from 33 black men, 25 white women, and 482 white men. Black witnesses who testified included Lyman Bluitt, druggist Matt Hayes, and Othaniel (or O'Faniel) Peoples, along with others who had been arrested on charges ranging from organizing armed black resistance to the murder of police officers Samuel Coppedge and Frank Wadley. Interestingly, employees from Aluminum Ore, the meatpacking plants, and other manufacturers were not prominent among those testifiers who could be positively identified by matching their names from the grand jury list to names in a 1916 city directory of East St. Louis. Twenty-one of the black men who gave statements were laborers. The white people summoned before the grand jury included real estate men and political bosses Thomas Canavan and Locke Tarlton and politicians Fred Mollman and Maurice Ahearn. Philip Wolf was the only prominent unionist called to the stand. Other white testifiers included thirteen railroad workers, eleven National Stockyards employees, ten laborers, eight policemen, seven carpenters, six clerks, six saloonkeepers, five lawyers, four meatpacking workers, four Aluminum Ore Company employees, three brewery employees, three streetcar motormen, two bartenders, two boilermakers, two drivers, two painters, two prostitutes, and two railroad switchmen. In other words, some of those most active in beating and killing African Americans during the pogrom may have been working people, but they were not the industrial employees who had the greatest contact with black laborers.[54]

The state grand jury reported that the mass racial violence of July 2 had been "deliberately plotted" with encouragement or feigned indifference from city and county officials. Those white persons initially brought before the grand jury on accusations of involvement with the massacre did not include any leading city or county politicians or businessmen. On August 16, the grand jury indicted for inciting "strife and ill feeling" 143 white people, including eight policemen, two switchmen, a baker, a blacksmith, a coal dealer, a stationary fireman, a mechanic, a saloonkeeper, a timekeeper, a newsboy, and a nonresident whose father was a wealthy Indiana farmer. In September, according to the *East St. Louis Daily Journal*, the grand jury indicted Mollman, Ahearn, and "thirty-seven East St. Louisans, including many prominent business men" for their role in the July violence. But for reasons never made public, authorities dropped all charges that were brought against these city leaders. No eminent white businessmen, managers, or politicians even faced trial, let alone were convicted of any wrongdoing. Class bias in favor of city political and economic leaders became even more evident when the state took to trial 112 white men, fifteen black men, and five white women who were mainly working people.[55]

By October, Illinois prosecutors had formulated "the doctrine that all persons, black and white, who participated in the race riots in any way [were] responsible for all things that occurred in the outbreak." They officially obfuscated the blame for the violence, erased the boundaries between black targets and white perpetrators, and absolved the state and its agents of complicity in the mass racial violence. Officials knew that white people were reluctant to sit in judgment of accused white assailants, especially those with connections to state or federal government, fearing retribution from the defendants or their friends and relatives. Prosecutors secured the cooperation of white residents by bringing to trial a greater proportion of black than white defendants. Government lawyers succeeded in selecting a jury that consisted mainly of white nonresidents to try the white accused. Defense attorneys, however, did seat Edward Sims, an African American resident of Belleville, saying that his light complexion would not upset white people.[56]

State and local authorities sought to reinforce the impression that black laborers, not all of them having recently migrated to East St. Louis, provoked the massacre. They also wanted to weaken and discredit leading members of the black community, including Noah Parden, Leroy Bundy, Pearl Abernathy, R. M. C. Green, Matt Hayes, Sam Wheat, politician-saloonkeepers William "Buddy" Bell and George Kyle, and physician I. H. King, by claiming that these community leaders had organized, armed, and led black laborers. In the murder of policemen Coppedge and Wadley, they charged Lester Fowler, Othaniel Peoples, Harry Robertson, Bud Townsend, and Herbert S. Wood; laborers Marshall Alexander, Charles Foster, William Palmer, and "Slim" Tackett; Missouri Malleable Iron Company laborer Albert Hughes; Kehlor Flour Mills laborer Dee Smotherman; and American Steel Foundries laborers Guy Moore, Fayette Parker, George Roberts, and Horace Thomas. Later, Robertson and Wood were cleared of all charges. On October 7, the state acquitted Fowler, Moore, and Tackett but convicted the others of the murder of detective Wadley. On October 30, for reasons not made public, Judge George Crow denied all of the convicted any trials on appeal and sentenced each to fourteen years at Southern Illinois Penitentiary in Menard. This action by Judge Crow placated white townspeople and also sent the message that black people who engaged in armed self-defense against white policemen and citizens did not deserve equal treatment before the law. The judge's pronouncement provoked nationally famous black journalist and activist Ida B. Wells-Barnett to say that state and federal officials had defined black armed self-defense as criminal and proceeded to punish black people accordingly.[57]

State prosecutors worked desperately to bring Bundy to trial to punish him for allegedly provoking mass violence and also, perhaps especially, to discredit him as a political leader. The state charged him with ordering the attack that killed white policemen Coppedge and Wadley. The state wanted Bundy in its custody, not in the hands of local authorities, because, according to Allison, city officials had a political reason for apprehending Bundy before the state did. The black activist had much inside knowledge of the city's white political machines, which political bosses feared he was more than willing to share with state and federal investigators. Congressional investigators learned from Allison that other leading black politicians, along with Bundy, risked revealing their own involvement in political networks if they exposed the machine. The minister stressed that any of these leaders would have testified against white politicians but for the fear of machine retribution. When state leaders found that Bundy had fled to his family home in Cleveland, they convinced Ohio governor J. M. Cox to extradite Bundy to East St. Louis to stand trial.[58]

The NAACP conducted a vigorous defense of Bundy from 1917 until 1918, when its relations with him deteriorated. NAACP legal counsel, conducting his affairs, rose in anger when Bundy, against the counsel's advice, talked with state prosecutors about his previous dealings with boss politicians. In 1918, financial issues and personality differences between the two parties reached a crescendo. The dentist argued in a letter he made public that he was not obligated to report his expenditures to the organization. Charging the NAACP with making false statements about him, Bundy declared that the association had failed him at his moment of crisis and promised a full exposé when he settled his case. When Bundy refused to be held accountable for his receipt of NAACP funds, the association parted company with him.[59]

African Americans raising funds for Bundy's defense independently of the NAACP immediately criticized the organization for severing its ties with the community leader. The *Chicago Defender*, an influential black newspaper, stated that the NAACP blundered in not placing the "interests of the Race before personal views." According to the *St. Louis Argus*, the association "was not justified in dropping the interest of the people because of a personal difference as to methods in reaching the desired end." The organization lost prestige with black residents who disapproved of its treatment of Bundy. The city's NAACP chapter folded in early 1919, leaving the St. Louis branch to cover East St. Louis.[60]

Convicted in the killing of Coppedge and Wadley, Bundy began serving a life sentence but was released when the Illinois Supreme Court declared a mistrial on a technicality. He spent the next few years putting his life back in order, not in East St. Louis but in Cleveland, his hometown. The former community leader had become persona non grata in East St. Louis and perhaps a tempting target for some white East St. Louisans. In Cleveland, Bundy became involved in Marcus Garvey's mass-based organization, the Universal Negro Improvement Association (UNIA), which advocated a territorial-separatist black nationalism and promotion of black-owned capitalist enterprises. In 1922, Bundy served as president of the Cleveland UNIA chapter, but he quit the organization in the late 1920s over a salary dispute. He joined the Republican Party and was elected several times in the late 1920s and the 1930s to the Cleveland city council. He remained a militant advocate of equal rights and continued, according to historian Kenneth Kusmer, to work with other black council members to use "their voting leverage to wring concessions from city hall and to enhance their own power within the party."[61]

Reconstruction of City Government

Now that Bundy and similar-minded black politicians had been rendered ineffective, progressive reformers seized the opportunity to establish their version of honest government by ousting machine boss politicians from city hall and removing the black community from its pivotal position so it no longer held the balance of power. The July mass violence directly benefited the reformers. They held the notion that African Americans had been responsible for several decades of rampant patronage, inefficient government, political machines, corruption, lawlessness, and vice. Reformers campaigned for a commission form of municipal government as key to their objectives of greater accountability and efficiency. Their plan called for electing the mayor, who would also function as commissioner of public relations, and four other commissioners with responsibility for police, buildings and fire protection, streets, and finance. This citywide election scheme would nullify voting influence based on election wards, where African Americans had concentrated their strength to vote for black candidates for city council. In addition, reformers charged that the machine had created the political conditions that made possible the antiblack violence of May and July. The progressives' ballot initiative for a commission form of government won approval from voters in the election of November 1917.[62]

Reform-oriented business and political leaders, with wide support from white residents and private organizations, advocated housing segregation as a way to ensure racial harmony. Some real estate men argued that segregation safeguarded the value of white homeowners' properties from black renters and homebuyers, stimulated the housing market, and guaranteed a prosperous future for the city. They stressed that because of Illinois civil rights laws, white homeowners had to rely upon customary residential segregation. Many houses had been abandoned by black tenants during the July massacre; the Real Estate Exchange insisted that white owners rent them out only to white tenants. They also demanded that black people residing in predominantly white neighborhoods move to black districts. The Central Park Improvement Association of East St. Louis and similar white residents' organizations warned African Americans against buying or renting homes in white areas. Fire insurance agents boosted the likelihood of segregated districts by canceling coverage on properties occupied by black people in white neighborhoods. Armour and Company manager Robert Conway, for one, saw the containment of black people to segregated neighborhoods as a way to lessen the migration's impact on white people. He viewed black districts as reservoirs of low-wage black labor that could be tapped during times of labor shortage. Missouri Malleable manager John Pero thought that segregation provided black people, clustered in their own wards, the opportunity to elect their own to city council. But his argument angered black residents who saw citywide elections backed by residential segregation as a ploy to render them voiceless at city hall.[63]

Reformers gained in popularity with white residents as Mayor Mollman's machine lost its political effectiveness. Their criticism of the mayor's inept and corrupt rule gained credibility when the grand jury indicted him for his role in the July violence and congressional investigation revealed the extent of boss corruption, criminal activities, and social violence. The progressive argument that certain politician-businessmen had rendered East St. Louis insolvent resounded with townspeople when the already indebted city issued a bond in order to pay claims for damages resulting from the July violence. In January 1918, officials expected outstanding liabilities to climb to $1 million. Reformers savored victory in 1919 when voters overwhelmingly rejected Mayor Mollman, connecting him with rampant corruption and the mass racial violence of 1917. They also saw the new commission form of municipal government begin its first year of operation, bringing to an end the mayor-council form that had begun under Mayor John Bowman. Leading reformers persuaded Melbern M. Stephens, who had built a good reputation—by East St. Louis standards—when he was mayor in the 1880s and 1890s, to come out of retirement and head the transition to a commission government. But purists among the reformers had to wonder whether the newly elected commission, made up of Melbern M. Stephens as mayor along with Maurice V. Joyce, John McLean, Richard McCarty, and Daniel McGlynn, was capable of achieving the progressive dream of clean, honest government. When these men had presided over the city during the mayor-council years, they had tolerated, if not encouraged, the very problems that progressives railed against.[64]

———

The East St. Louis pogrom of July 1917 has been considered the first major explosion of mass racial violence during the World War I era. It far overshadowed the smaller episode of antiblack mayhem that occurred without any reported deaths in the city in May. It was also larger than the disturbances that followed in August 1917 in Houston, Texas, and in July 1918 in Philadelphia, where several people were killed. The Houston uprising began when African American soldiers retaliated against the police for their massive abuse of black civilians and soldiers. The few days of violence in Philadelphia started when a "respectable" black woman who had moved into a white neighborhood shot at a white mob intent on forcing her to move away. All of these events had little if anything to do with the Great Migration itself, but much to do with the fluidity of race relations and the refusal of African Americans to remain at the bottom of the racial hierarchy.

New outbreaks of mass racial violence occurred after the war, in 1919, in Chicago and other locales. But the July 1917 massacre in East St. Louis was the only pogrom occurring between Reconstruction and the 1943 racial conflict in Detroit during World War II that became the subject of a federal investigation. It riveted Americans' attention with news reports of horrific mayhem and sadistic killings and disrupted interstate commerce and war production. Until recent reconsiderations of other World War I–era episodes of mass racial violence, the official death toll of thirty-nine black and nine white people made the East St. Louis July pogrom the bloodiest of the racial conflicts that occurred in the first half of the twentieth century. Recent reexamination of other events, however, shows that the numbers of deaths resulting from the mass killings of African Americans in 1919 in Phillips County, Arkansas, and in 1921 in Tulsa, Oklahoma, exceeded those in East St. Louis.[65]

The mass antiblack violence of July 1917 took place at the confluence of several historical phenomena that intersected with factors peculiar to East St. Louis. The national context featured fluid social relationships brought about by World War I, wartime production that triggered migrations of workers in search of jobs, and African Americans' efforts to restore and extend their civil rights and resist Jim Crow. These phenomena played out in a broad context of nationalism, industrialization, and modernization, long-term historical forces also present in other societies that have experienced ethnic or racial violence—the anti-Jewish pogroms in czarist Russia, for example, or the anti-Armenian pogroms in Ottoman Turkey. Local political relations in East St. Louis provided the immediate context and the proximate cause of the July massacre. African Americans were intent upon securing patronage, swinging elections, and, most importantly, building a political machine that would lead to a share of political power.[66]

As the immediate aftermath of the July pogrom made clear, black residents' chief antagonists in this quest were not white workers and union leaders but certain elements among real estate machine boss politicians and progressive reformers within business and civic organizations. Leading white citizens decided that black townspeople had to be disciplined or else driven out of town. The riot's shock troops included white police officers and other individuals, mainly nonindustrial workers, some associated with the world of crime and violence that characterized the saloon culture. But as the state grand jury reported, though it suppressed the names of prominent people involved with the violence, city and county officials bore responsibility for planning, encouraging, and executing the riot. A common thread uniting the two outbreaks of mass racial violence in East St. Louis with those in Houston and Philadelphia and with the numerous antiblack clashes in 1919 was that the local black drive for social and economic empowerment, in the context of black people's nationwide demands to make American democracy safe for African Americans, threatened white entitlement to resources and white social dominance.[67]

FIVE

Return to the Political Arena, 1917–1929

AFRICAN AMERICANS were not completely driven out of East St. Louis after the July pogrom. They understood in 1917 what many black Americans learned later, during the waves of race riots and pogroms in the Red Summer of 1919 and over the next three years, namely that white Americans would violently resist the black drive to achieve equality. Worldwide, in the postwar period, people who launched reformist, nationalist, or revolutionary challenges to the status quo of class, gender, racial, ethnic, or colonial hierarchies met with both official and vigilante repression. African Americans saw white attacks on black enclaves in East St. Louis, Chicago, Washington, D.C., Tulsa, and Rosewood, Florida, among other places, as part of this pattern. Black East St. Louisans realized that their enemies—and even their white friends—used the memory of the July pogrom as a cautionary lesson: African Americans had nothing to fear as long as they remained dependent upon white political factions and reconciled themselves to a life of segregation, discrimination, and inequality.

Undeterred, black East St. Louisans joined other African Americans in the postwar period in fashioning movements to advance themselves as a people materially, culturally, and politically. They pushed ahead—making new lives, rebuilding shattered communities, expanding their institutions, and returning to the political arena to strive for power and equality. Like other urban locales of the border region and the North, East St. Louis became more segregated after World War I. Black East St. Louisans therefore shaped their neighborhoods into a black metropolis with a vibrant culture within a white city. They contended with white political and civic leaders who sought to marginalize black political influence, and they found ways to assert their interests in city affairs while operating within the parameters of residential segregation and the precinct system, the foundation of the commission form of government that progressive reformers instituted after the pogrom.[1]

African Americans in East St. Louis made a dramatic political rebirth in the decade after the July pogrom, in part because black southern migrants continued to boost the city's black population. The 1910 federal census counted 5,882 black people among 58,547 inhabitants, and the 1920 census enumerated 7,437 black people among 66,767 residents. In percentage terms, the city's black population grew only marginally during the decade, from 10.0 percent to 11.1 percent of the total. But given the events of 1917 and the ensuing exodus, it is remarkable that there was any growth at all. According to estimates by local authorities, the wartime black population of East St. Louis was at least twice as large as the 1920 enumeration, but the July pogrom sent at least 7,000 black townspeople seeking permanent residency elsewhere. Had the violence not occurred, East St. Louis might have experienced the same rate of growth in its African American population as Chicago, which had 44,103 black people out of 2.1 million residents in 1910 and 109,458 out of 2.7 million in 1920, almost doubling the black proportion of the city from 2.1 to 4.1 percent.

During the 1920s, the African American population of both East St. Louis and Chicago continued to receive a boost from the migration of black southerners. By 1930, East St. Louis counted 11,536 black people in a resident population of 74,347, increasing the black proportion to 15.5 percent. In the same period, Chicago's black population rose to 233,903 in a total population of 3.4 million, or from 4.1 percent to 6.9 percent. Black East St. Louisans, however, were limited by immediate post-pogrom political dynamics from capitalizing on the implicit political strength in their numbers, while black Chicagoans, who did not experience a similar setback from the racial conflict in their city in 1919, forged ahead to make significant political gains. East St. Louis authorities truly feared their city becoming black-influenced, if not black-dominated, in the political arena. Politicians and civic leaders relied heavily upon the reorganized system of citywide elections to minimize black politics and upon various organizations, like the National Urban League, to channel black aspirations in nonpolitical directions.

Though an increase in numbers proved important, black East St. Louisans also developed new strategies and tactics to gain access to city hall and patronage. Like black Chicagoans, African Americans in East St. Louis remained involved with electoral politics after the mass racial violence of the World War I era. But black Chicagoans had a powerful white political boss, Republican William Hale Thompson, as a friend in the mayor's office from 1915 to 1925, and they benefited from his patronage to the black community. Black East St. Louisans lacked generous friends at city hall. They never achieved what black Chicagoans accomplished: sending African American representatives to the city council, the Illinois General Assembly, and the U.S. Congress.

African Americans in East St. Louis and elsewhere began the immediate post–World War I years debating which strategies would be most effective in maneuvering politically in the postwar world of intensified racial hostility and segregation. Black veterans, returning home from Europe, and black civilians connected President Woodrow Wilson's war aim of saving the world for democracy to their struggle to make America safe for democracy. They developed political movements of breadth and depth, spanning the ideological spectrum. Their agitation through all-black and mixed-race labor and political organizations rose as black urban enclaves expanded in population and became more diverse in occupation, class, religious affiliation, and political perspective. Those involved in social actions sought ways to achieve independent control of their community institutions without incurring a violent response from white politician-businessmen and their allies.

Black residents in East St. Louis generally appeared to give short shrift to socialists, communists, and black separatists who showed an inability to deliver practical results to improve the lives of African Americans. Those most interested in extracting resources from city government and attaining their share of local political power expended little if any time with political currents that sought either to transform or to separate from the established structures of political control. Black East St. Louisans acknowledged the presence of the most significant international black separatist movement of the early 1920s, the Universal Negro Improvement Association, led by its founder Marcus Garvey, a Jamaican who established his headquarters in the Harlem section of New York City. But townspeople remained unenthusiastic about the UNIA, with its ideological distance from the local political culture, and most rejected its separatist message.

Some black East St. Louisans found opportunity for involvement in the political arena by working with politically moderate white-dominated or interracial organizations, including trade unions. They realized, however, that cooperation with white people often blunted black people's collective interests in ending racial discrimination. Black workers who joined unions, for example, made little progress as these organizations showed great reluctance to fight antiblack racism. In addition, black working people found the union road to social betterment less fruitful after unions suffered a massive decline in membership during the immediate postwar years, a period marked by economic recession, waves of strikes, and massive antiunion actions by employers.

In the 1920s, black East St. Louisans launched various community protests and other actions and entered formal politics by swinging elections and by fielding African American candidates, both men and women, for precinct committee positions or local offices. Townspeople who were committed to advancing black community interests had to work around not only white politician-businessmen but also black political operatives who used the patronage system solely for their own personal gain. Toward the end of the 1920s, a group of African American activists won the allegiance of black East St. Louisans when they forged a new black political organization, a pro–Democratic Party political submachine. Though the black community never regained its pre–July 1917 level of influence, with its possibility of establishing an independent black political machine, the new organization restored some of the leverage that the black community once had in pre-pogrom East St. Louis.[2]

Economic Reshaping of Post–World War I East St. Louis

White progressive reformers among white businessmen and civic figures emerged after the mass racial violence of July 1917 and the World War I years in control of East St. Louis. They reconstructed the city by installing a commission form of municipal government after defeating various political factions. Reformers successfully diminished for at least several years the political influence of boss machine politicians and blocked the Central Trades and Labor Union's attempt to regain its hand in city affairs. Progressives put an end to the black community's status as a swing voting bloc, while real estate men, landlords, and homeowners segregated African Americans to specific residential enclaves. Progressive reformers anticipated freeing city hall from its decades-long dependency on revenues from saloon licensing fees with the ratification of the Eighteenth Amendment of the U.S. Constitution in 1919, which prohibited the production, sale, and transportation of intoxicating beverages. Business, political, and civic leaders thought the elimination of taverns would also lead to the demise of gambling dens, dance halls, and brothels, and an end to the criminal violence that accompanied such establishments. Some reformers, like white Baptist minister George Allison, welcomed the federal law because they saw saloons as the core of a complex political culture that African American politicians exploited to further black people's interests in opposition to those of the business community. Local progressives thought that the city had finally turned the corner after decades of political battles. They anticipated governing East St. Louis with fiscal responsibility and managerial efficiency.

Leading real estate men continued directing economic development and recruiting industry to the city they liked to call the "Central Industrial Center" of America. They hoped the new commission form of municipal government would provide the political stability that East St. Louis needed if economic expansion was to resume after the war. In 1918, a lumberyard entrepreneur with interests in home construction, Edmund Goedde, president of the Chamber of Commerce, spoke for local businessmen when he said that with a new government in place and a beautification program in the planning stages, the city was ready for civic improvement. He predicted that this would bring increased industrial production that would lead in turn to more jobs and prosperity and better living and working conditions for East St. Louisans. Joseph N. Fining, secretary-manager of the Chamber of Commerce, wanted to attract firms that relied upon skilled workers and that were willing to employ women. Fining did not specify race, but his coded language meant that the chamber wanted to attract white men and women to work and live in East St. Louis. The Chamber of Commerce hired the nationally acclaimed urban planner Harland

Bartholomew, a former member of the U.S. Army Corps of Engineers from St. Louis, to develop a blueprint to transform East St. Louis into a "beautiful city, with model factories and . . . a live, strong community spirit."[3]

Advocates for urban beautification and industrial expansion knew that the presence of railroads constituted a major obstacle to the achievement of their objectives. In 1921, Goedde, real estate man Nathaniel McLean, and others publicly acknowledged what Bartholomew had reported, namely that the railroads, especially the Terminal Railroad Association, had adversely affected the local economy. Railroads owned much land, crisscrossed the city with rail lines, paid low taxes, and maintained a freight rate structure designed to rise and fall according to the fluctuating costs of shipping goods. With a postwar recession still in full swing, railroads were unwilling to ship materials and supplies farther than 50 to 100 miles without charging exorbitant rates. They expressed an interest in lowering rates if wages and prices of commodities were reduced. Chamber of Commerce members realized that the problem was how to maintain the town's self-proclaimed reputation as "the foremost industrial center of the world" when the mainstay of the local economy, railroads, had ceased to expand.[4]

Boosters noticed, as the 1920s progressed, that the city's rate of economic growth had failed to reach pre–World War I levels, but they were unaware that the city had begun its long-term decline. They slowly understood that World War I had ushered in a new economic order that tied urbanites of all social classes to mass consumerism and bureaucratic corporations and national and international markets to fluctuating business cycles. Managers and corporate owners involved in manufacturing, real estate, housing construction, and retail merchandizing fell upon hard times in a postwar recession as their customers, thousands of industrial workers, lost their jobs.[5]

Business owners' outlook returned to one of optimism by mid-1922, however, when the postwar recession ended. Business leaders thought the city's diversified economy provided the means to achieve greater levels of prosperity. They gave little thought to abandoning the generous tax breaks to industrial corporations and other proindustry policies that since the late nineteenth century had catapulted their small town into an industrial city of national importance. For example, in 1922 R. Vernon Clark of Clark Realty Company directed city hall to give a five-year tax exemption to Missouri Car Company, an electric street car manufacturer that planned to employ 500 men within five years. The business community, unconcerned about the city's increasing debt, enjoyed the booming economy that marked the rest of the 1920s.[6]

Politician-businessmen knew that their economic growth policies had contributed to the deepening of the city's systemic problems and limited its ability to achieve fiscal responsibility. Still, they considered industrial output the true indicator of prosperity. They celebrated the low per capita cost of municipal government and continued to attract industry by allowing firms to avoid paying their fair share of municipal taxes. For decades, local officials had relied upon revenue sources such as bonds to cover city expenses, driving the city deeper into debt. In 1926, they hoped to reallocate financial resources to furthering economic growth after city comptroller Walter Flannigen announced that the bonds that the city had procured to pay for damages resulting from the July violence had matured.[7]

Business leaders disagreed on how to showcase East St. Louis as an industrial center with an attractive future. Wholesale produce merchant and landlord E. E. Jett and physician Conrad Vonnahane, for example, proposed disassociating East St. Louis from its past by changing the city's name. Some local businessmen saw regional planning as a way to increase the rate of economic growth or at the very least manage disputes with St. Louis over issues such as the distribution of revenues collected from the Free (or Municipal) and Eads bridge tolls and from railroad freight fees. Leading members of the Chamber of Commerce and the Real Estate Exchange, including its president, William H. Horner, advocated careful planning to solve interurban problems, direct future industrial development, and bring prosperity to East St. Louis. Other members of the Real Estate Exchange, fearful that their city would lose its competitiveness with St. Louis, opposed regional planning. Downtown Business Men's Association president Frank J. Klapp and Louis Riechmann of the Retail Merchants' Association, for example, balked at too close a relationship with St. Louis, fearing that a proposed incorporation into a Saint Louis Standard Metropolitan Statistical Area would open opportunities for the Missourian metropolis to gain the lion's share of industrial growth. But by the end of the 1920s, political and business leaders, for whatever reason, tabled initiatives for regional planning.[8]

During the 1920s, civic-minded politician-businessmen with land interests considered how to improve the quality of life of city inhabitants, realizing that corporate managers living outside of town had no interest in such projects. Real estate men decided to encourage civic pride by improving residential dwellings. They bemoaned the high cost of building materials and labor during the war years that had led to a significant shortage and deterioration of housing stock. They decried the building trades' resistance to adjusting wages down in order to stimulate a home construction boom. The Real Estate Exchange and the construction industry worked closely to keep the construction of new houses in pace with population growth. But city building commissioner Charles E. Guenther admitted in 1929 that the supply of new houses actually continued to lag behind homebuyers' demands.[9]

Real estate interests took a consumerist approach to the housing problem, arguing that East St. Louis had the potential to become a model city of homes attractive to both middle-class and working-class white families. Knowing that housing was contested terrain, developers worried about the possibility of racial conflict as the city continued to attract both white southerners, mainly from western Tennessee, Mississippi, Kentucky, and Georgia, and black southerners primarily from Mississippi and Tennessee. Though they aimed to accommodate industry's need for black labor, city leaders saw no need to construct housing for black people. Furthermore, they regarded residential segregation as a cornerstone of urban growth policy, as a way to minimize racial violence and stabilize social relations in order to recruit industry.[10]

Some black East St. Louisans took initiatives to remedy the lack of adequate housing. A few black entrepreneurs built single-family housing tracts, like the Kenwood subdivision. But not enough of these developments were built to satisfy black townspeople's demand. Some African Americans, like the father of longtime black resident Jeanne Faulkner, had the means to construct their own homes and did so. These black residents demonstrated that, though their community faced numerous problems in the immediate years after the pogroms of 1917, they still considered East St. Louis home.[11]

The Structure of Black East St. Louis after July 1917

The July pogrom did not totally destroy the black community in East St. Louis. Residents in predominantly black neighborhoods in the city's South End escaped unscathed. Even the small black enclave in the North End district known as Goose Hill emerged intact from the mayhem. Perhaps the hundreds of black laborers entering or leaving the meatpacking plants and stockyards of nearby National City during shift changes proved a more tempting target than the Goose Hill settlement. Untouched areas of black neighborhoods formed the nucleus of the African American community that survived the July 1917 massacre.[12]

The July outrage did not deter new waves of black southern migrants from coming to East St. Louis, with its still-booming wartime economy. According to one report, by 1919 the black community had increased to an estimated 18,000 in a city of 100,000. But this figure, supplied by city boosters, represented not much more than a wild guess. That the population dropped in 1919 with cessation of war-related work and the start of a postwar recession was to be expected. The 1920 federal census listed 7,437 African Americans out of a total of 66,767 residents. The number of black townspeople would have been higher if the mass racial violence of 1917 had not taken place. And the legacy of the wartime migration, which the July violence did not reverse, was that the proportion of African Americans from former slave states had increased in black East St. Louis. Based on what black respondents reported to census enumerators in 1920, 66 percent of black East St. Louisans of non-Illinoisan origin were born in Alabama, Kentucky, Mississippi, Missouri, or Tennessee. Most of the rest came from Arkansas, Georgia, Indiana, Louisiana, Texas, and Virginia.[13]

African American southerners continued to find employment in the North, but they had difficulties retaining industrial jobs when massive demobilization of military personnel occurred in 1919. From 1919 to 1922 a postwar recession gripped the nation. The railroading, meatpacking, iron and steel milling, glass manufacturing and other industries that employed most black East St. Louisans decreased their workforce after the rapid wartime expansion. Of the 1,551 employed black East St. Louisan men in 1920, at least 66 percent were laborers. Many of the rest occupied service or nonindustrial positions, working as barbers, bartenders, carpenters, clergymen, domestics, drivers, janitors, laundresses, porters, restaurateurs, schoolteachers, and teamsters. Though government officials did not issue unemployment statistics broken down by race for East St. Louis, the city's experience probably paralleled that of Chicago, where significant numbers of black employees, in particular the men, became unemployed during the economic slump. Industrialists responded to the deepening recession by laying off workers and cutting wages. Of the 17,435 white and black men and 1,869 white and black women employed in East St. Louis–area industrial firms near the end of the war, only 7,895 men and 1,106 women remained on payrolls by June 1921. Proportionately more men than women lost jobs because aluminum, iron, and steel manufacturing, the industries that contracted most rapidly during the postwar slump, employed for the most part only males.[14]

Black workers retained a presence in the industrial workforce and increased their numbers after the recession, most in low-paying, unskilled factory jobs. They constituted a key element in the postwar workforce, functioning as a reservoir of low-wage laborers for employers who continued to divide workers by race. Black workers also substituted for low-paid immigrants after the government enacted immigration quotas in 1924 that drastically reduced the supply of European workers. By that year, of the 2,014 employed black male residents, 1,581 or 78 percent classed themselves as laborers. The remaining 22 percent included 30 butchers, 20 porters, 19 ironworkers, 17 carpenters and janitors, 16 barbers and teamsters, 15 chauffeurs, and 11 chippers.[15]

African American women had less success in obtaining factory employment than black men, but their numbers as industrial wage earners increased nevertheless. They secured jobs primarily in meatpacking and glass manufacturing plants. In 1919, according to the Colored Work Committee of the Young Women's Christian Association, 54 black East St. Louisan women worked in packinghouses, most likely in unskilled positions. Of the 398 black women listed as employed in the 1920 census, 72 worked as laborers. By 1924, black women attained a high profile in laundering, glass manufacturing, and meatpacking.[16]

African American women preferred industrial employment because it offered higher wages and a greater sense of freedom than the more oppressive domestic labor that many wage-earning black women had no choice but to accept. Black women generally washed and ironed clients' clothes in their own homes or at laundries, toiled as servants in white people's houses, or worked as dishwashers, cooks, and waitresses in restaurants. Cooks, who had certain leeway for inventiveness, and laundresses, who brought their work home, had some degree of independence from their employers. But like many other domestics they abhorred the low wages, long working days, constant supervision or other form of intrusion, and sexual abuse from male employers that they endured in white people's homes. A few black women found jobs as farm laborers on the outskirts of the city. Of the 398 wage-earning black women listed in 1920, 147 or 37 percent worked as laundresses or washerwomen for white families, and 53 or 13 percent labored as servants in white homes.[17]

The number of African American business owners and professionals remained static for several years in post–July 1917 East St. Louis, never climbing above the 120 listed in the 1912 city directory. No one knew how many entrepreneurs had left town after the July massacre destroyed their businesses or dispersed their clients. Those remaining, like Charles T. Nash, whose mortuary had been reduced to ashes, rebuilt their establishments and customer base. In 1920, ministers, physicians, schoolteachers, retailers, restaurateurs, and hairdressers were among the city's 111 self-employed black professionals and businessmen. The number of such individuals stood at 110 in 1924, but their ranks included grocers and drink shop owners, a euphemism for saloonkeepers during Prohibition. Black business owners and service providers in East St. Louis relied more than ever on an African American clientele that faced an uncertain welcome from white establishments as segregation tightened its grip.[18]

By the early 1920s, black urban dwellers across the North lived in increasingly segregated neighborhoods, sent their children to segregated schools, and were restricted to segregated places of public accommodation and recreation. White northerners rigorously maintained these exclusions through zoning laws, ordinances, and custom. Longtime black residents of East St. Louis, like their counterparts in other border region cities, had tolerated a haphazard pattern of segregation since the 1870s, sending their children to segregated public schools. They began to experience more widespread segregation after the mass racial violence of July 1917, when white people extended the practice to include housing, theaters, and public accommodations. Black southern migrants had lived under systematic, legalized segregation from the 1890s to the eve of the wartime Great Migration. But after arriving in the North, they had to adjust to the northern version of segregation with, for example, zoning laws that in some ways operated as effectively as the outright segregation laws of the South.[19]

African Americans in East St. Louis nurtured an institutional culture that lessened the adverse impact of residential segregation that turned their neighborhoods into ghettoes. They used their resources to aid one another and to help newly arriving rural black southerners adjust to the rigors of life in an industrial city. They continued to make segregated public schools serve their children's needs and provide employment for black teachers, administrators, and nonprofessional staff. Members of the Young Men's Christian Association and the Young Women's Christian Association redirected their segregated local branches to run training programs that informed black southern migrants about health care practices and the rhythms of factory work. Residents made use of their segregated institutions to celebrate themes and events in their history without undue interference from white people. They continued, for example, to observe Emancipation Proclamation Day, a celebration of the abolition of slavery. Newspaper accounts do not reveal participants' interpretations of such events, but black celebrants' thoughts had to include the hope of extending American democracy to African Americans.[20]

African Americans connected black involvement in World War I to the meaning of freedom and democracy, seeking to make the ideas raised by the Emancipation Proclamation commemorations a daily reality. For example, 1,500 black East St. Louisans gathered in April 1919 to celebrate the return of African American army veterans from the battlefields in France. Local black educators Martin Lucas and Benjamin Bowles praised black veterans and civilians for their unwavering trust and service to the nation and called for this service to be repaid by government concessions to the demand for equality. As the demand remained unanswered, African Americans increased their political agitation for social and economic advancement. For black East St. Louisans, their community served as a springboard for residents to mobilize to reassert their interests.[21]

Actions Outside of Electoral Politics

The July massacre had crushed the independent black political machine. Over the next few years, African Americans gave voice to their concerns by working through their own community institutions as well as with black political movements and with white organizations. As black leaders and activists strove to regain a position of influence in city politics, they continued to rely upon the support of the black community. Those who advocated paths to black social and economic advancement that did not rely upon electoral politics had little competition within the black community, largely because the July violence and subsequent trials of alleged black assailants had either removed from office, discredited, imprisoned, or driven from town the community leaders and activists who had sought to establish an independent black presence.

One way that black people tried to regain their voice after July 1917 was through participation in black political movements, primarily the multifaceted New Negro movement. This movement emerged during World War I, the Great Migration, and the Red Summer of 1919, a period in which the nation's African American population experienced complex shifts, notably migration and urbanization, and faced repression that slowed their advancement toward democratic rights. As articulated by African American philosopher Alain Locke, the "New Negro" was a member of the race who emerged, as the "Old Negro" declined, militantly ready to fight for full citizenship rights through political activism and economic self-help, racial solidarity and pride, and new cultural and aesthetic expressions. The movement embraced diverse political currents, ranging from conservative organizations like Marcus Garvey's Universal Negro Improvement Association to the revolutionary Marxist African Blood Brotherhood to the culturally oriented Harlem Renaissance. While the movement emphasized militant self-defense, New Negro advocates divided over strategies and tactics in the fight against segregation and injustice. Those within the movement who called upon African Americans to look outside of, if not overthrow, the American political system became targets of federal repression.[22]

Black separatist tendencies dominated the New Negro movement. Among these, the UNIA was the most controversial and had the largest number of adherents. Founded in 1916, the UNIA called for stronger ties between Africans and people of African descent in the Americas and for black repatriation to Africa. Its strident anticolonialism irritated Britain and France, both staunch allies of the United States with colonial possessions in Africa, prompting increased federal surveillance of the organization. Garvey became a victim of federal harassment and was convicted and imprisoned on charges of mail fraud; later he was deported. As the result of such actions the UNIA rapidly declined before the decade ended.[23]

The East St. Louis UNIA chapter maintained a low profile and did not attract—at least not obviously—the mass following that UNIA branches did elsewhere, especially in New York City, the organization's headquarters.

The East St. Louis chapter may have recruited its members from among black southern migrants, especially those from the Mississippi Delta who already had a degree of familiarity with the UNIA before migrating north. Members expended their energy primarily on fundraising for the national UNIA and sponsoring lectures about potential opportunities in Africa for entrepreneurial black Americans. The lackluster nature of the East St. Louis chapter had to do both with the presence of a determined anti-UNIA coalition of antiseparatist black people and with the actions taken against the chapter by local and federal authorities.[24]

Antiseparatist black factions, at times with the assistance of white authorities, marginalized or suppressed separatists in East St. Louis. The Interdenominational Ministerial Alliance, an organization of black East St. Louisan clergymen, opposed Dr. M. M. Madden, a separatist who had arrived in town in 1920 hoping to raise funds for a proposed independent black nation-state to straddle the Rio Grande between Mexico and the United States. Ministers A. F. Avant, C. W. Thompson, and Arthur Randall, leaders of the alliance, accused Madden of being an agitator and confidence man or a huckster soliciting money from unsuspecting black people. In 1921, clergymen told Madden to leave town before they had the police arrest him, and Madden, heeding the warning, departed. In another instance of separatist suppression in the city, black residents did not protest in 1925 when police, for reasons not publicized, disrupted a meeting of the APA (its full name was not identified in the local newspaper), a local separatist organization that reportedly planned pilgrimages to Africa; thirty-five APA members were arrested on charges of disturbing the peace. The reception given organizations like the APA and UNIA showed that separatists made little headway among African Americans in East St. Louis.[25]

Other New Negro activists of various social classes gravitated to the NAACP and its program for integration and equality. They knew that the drive for equality under the law, depending upon location, had been tempered by antiblack mass violence between 1917 and 1922 that dramatized the determination of some white antagonists to limit the extent of black activism. NAACP activists walked a tightrope between the black separatist sentiments of the UNIA and the program of accommodation of the National Urban League. In East St. Louis, after a hiatus of several years since 1918 when Leroy Bundy went to prison, at least fifty African American men and women revived a chapter of the NAACP in 1924. They represented a cross section of middle- and working-class people, including teachers, physicians, and other professionals, proprietors, realtors, and other businesspeople, and janitors, laborers, and various wage workers. As with a number of urban chapters, individuals of middle-class status staffed leadership positions in the East St. Louis NAACP. The first to serve as officers once the chapter received its charter from the association's national office were salesman Clarence J. McLinn as chapter president, school principal John M. D. Brown as vice president, schoolteacher Bessie King as secretary, and mortician R. M. C. Green as treasurer. They reflected the anti-Garveyism of the NAACP national office, which regarded the UNIA as a roadblock to any advancement toward equality. But only black people composed the chapter, since the NAACP's goals of integration and racial equality appeared too radical to attract potential white members in a city where a critical mass of white residents vigilantly maintained residential and other forms of segregation.[26]

The East St. Louis branch of the NAACP never encountered disruptions from white opponents as did some of its sister chapters in the South, where white authorities banned the organization. The association's national office worked with the National Urban League and other black groups to help local and federal agents suppress the UNIA and other separatist groups, and this may have been one reason that East St. Louis NAACP members avoided government harassment. More broadly, the chapter experienced no official persecution because it did not demand an end to segregation in housing, employment, education, and public accommodations. Its challenges did not strike at the racial segregation and discrimination that buttressed the city's political culture; if anything, black East St. Louisan NAACP members reinforced the concept of "separate but equal" when they engaged in public protests. Their approach was similar to that of the NAACP chapter in Chicago, relying upon the goodwill of local political and business leaders to defuse tension between black and white citizens. Chapter members, rather than forging an independent path, worked with politicians and businessmen who preferred that the racial hierarchy remained intact. With the chapter accepting the status quo of racial inequality, it slid into a state of dormancy, its members involving themselves in electoral politics and other activities unrelated to the NAACP.[27]

Another way that African Americans asserted their political voice and pursued social and economic advancement was by working under the direction of or in conjunction with white groups. Some black people in East St. Louis chose this route in the immediate aftermath of the July massacre, when African American politics was in disarray. They worked with white or white-directed organizations that seized the opportunity to impose programs that attempted to reorient African Americans to life in a majority-white city.

Black workers, often with support of their community, participated in the labor movement, yet another avenue toward economic advancement outside the electoral political arena. They were aware that their increase in numbers had forced some white union organizers to recognize the urgency to unionize black workers. Leaders of the packinghouse workers' union in East St. Louis and Chicago, for example, announced a nondiscrimination policy toward black laborers in hopes of organizing them. In 1919 in East St. Louis, 300 African American packinghouse laborers pledged to unionize. In sharp contrast to black Chicagoan packinghouse workers, whose interest in unions met stiff opposition from other members of their community, including clergymen, black East St. Louisan meatpacking laborers received encouragement from their community. Black ministers in East St. Louis, for example, exhorted African American packinghouse workers to "cooperate with their white working brethren" and join unions. This display of union interest among black East St. Louisans showed that the memories of the July pogrom had not caused them to reject unions. One black packinghouse worker favoring unionization, Philip Weightman, who had learned the butchering trade in his native Vicksburg, Mississippi, arrived in East St. Louis in 1917 after the July massacre. He found work as a butcher in the hog-killing department at Armour, where he thought black and white workers enjoyed some degree of camaraderie. The East St. Louis labor movement lost and Chicago's gained when Weightman, a valuable union activist, moved to Chicago in 1920. In the 1930s he joined the Communist Party and became a packinghouse union organizer for the Congress of Industrial Organizations.[28]

In the North, however, black workers' increasing interest in unions came up against two roadblocks that stalled their mass unionization: organized labor's reluctance to attack racism within the labor movement and the determination of corporations to destroy unions. The massive strike wave of 1919 that shut down steel, meatpacking, coal mining, and other industries ended in defeat partly because of industrialist and government repression and partly because of divisions between black and white workers. The extremely bitter packinghouse workers' strike in the summer of 1919 in Chicago, the center of the meatpacking industry, and the union drive among packinghouse workers represented the confluence of organized labor's haphazard efforts to address racism and employers' union-busting activities. The packinghouse workers' strike occurred around the time of the worst mass racial violence in Chicago's history. The animosities that generated the Chicago race riot also influenced the strike, further dividing workers and hastening the defeat of the labor movement among packinghouse workers nationally.[29]

The Central Trades and Labor Union of East St. Louis accepted discriminatory practices at workplaces, failing to condemn, for example, segregated locker rooms, lunchrooms, and restrooms at the Aluminum Ore Company and other factories. Labor leaders lacked interest in resolving racial disputes among workers such as the one that occurred in 1920 in neighboring Fairmont City at the Granby Mining and Milling Company, where Mexican and Mexican American strikers fired shots at five black laborers who they claimed were strikebreakers. Mexican and Mexican American workers had migrated during the war and postwar years to the Midwest and other regions where industrialists required additional sources of low-wage labor. The CTLU failed to mediate in another racial incident in 1921 when three white custodians, a man and two women, quit their positions rather than work under the supervision of a new boss, head janitor Lawrence Edward, a black man.[30]

Some unionists who pursued racist policies at the workplace also promoted segregation in the community. When the CTLU raised the issue of equal pay for equal work among black and white workers, they did so not in pursuit of racial equality but as a ploy to decrease the number of black industrial workers. They thought that if managers were forced to hire black people at the same wages they paid white employees, then managers would cease hiring and begin to fire black laborers. In 1918, the CTLU president and city commissioner of public safety, Michael J. Whalen, joined with the city parks department to install a segregated neighborhood park for black working people living in Denverside.[31]

The CTLU did not advance a positive program to address racial disparities during the post–World War I recession when black laborers faced a higher rate of unemployment than white workers. The organization instead adopted an antimigrant stance as a solution to black workers' problems. In 1921, the CTLU joined with relief organizations, United Charities and the East St. Louis Overseer of the Poor, in calling upon employers to hire local white help.[32] The labor affiliation did little to dispel the fear of racial discord that the July violence had engendered when they urged black migrants to avoid East St. Louis or risk attacks by jobless, presumably white, townspeople. In 1924 the CTLU, once again with a sense of urgency, voiced concern through Mayor Melbern M. Stephens's office that the number of migrants, specifically black migrants, exceeded the number of available jobs. Both union officials and NAACP chapter leaders trusted Mayor Stephens with his reputation for honesty to handle the migrant issue judiciously. In a letter to the NAACP national office in March 1924, chapter officials Clarence J. McLinn and Bessie King said that though they considered leading white citizens, like Stephens, friendly to black people, they viewed organized labor as a potential enemy capable of inciting mass racial violence. In language reminiscent of that used in spring 1917, union leaders accused labor agents of enticing black southerners to the city. The CTLU claimed that unemployed black southern migrant laborers held the potential of causing great suffering (presumably more to white than to black workers) in the coming winter months. With labor's backing, Mayor Stephens in a terse communiqué urged the East St. Louis NAACP chapter to announce in black southern newspapers that East St. Louis did not want migrants. The chapter, at the mayor's behest, urged migrants to continue to other destinations, but it did provide these unemployed people some form of assistance.[33]

Labor leaders' poor relationship with black workers became evident during the packinghouse workers' strike that occurred in 1921 and 1922 in East St. Louis as well as in other cities, including Chicago. The Amalgamated Meat Cutters and Butcher Workmen union, hoping to reverse wage cuts, had entered into intense negotiations with meatpackers that lasted several months. In December 1921, workers went on strike after employers withdrew from arbitration. In East St. Louis, at least 2,000 black and white packinghouse employees downed their tools. Managers H. W. Waddell of Armour and Frank A. Hunter of Swift hired strikebreakers who included blacks and whites, men and women. The police maintained a presence around the factories to protect the strikebreakers and prevent fisticuffs between strikers and strikebreakers from disrupting industrial production. However, some white strikers or their supporters shot at black strikebreakers, killing a woman and a man. During the 1921–22 strike, in contrast to 1917, the police remained disciplined and prevented further trouble from erupting, suggesting that the actions of state agents are key in determining whether violence escalates in such situations.

Employers held firm and broke the strike nationwide in February 1922, in part because unionists had failed to build a viable interracial strike campaign. The strike collapsed first in Chicago, the center of the meatpacking industry, because workers in that city had not overcome the legacy of the 1919 race riot that led to the demise of the workers' Stockyards Labor Council and an entrenchment of racial divisions within the labor movement. In October, CTLU officials admitted that their inability to develop and maintain interracial unity was the chief reason for losing the strike. In the absence of viable unions, black workers concerned about improving their conditions had to explore other avenues.[34]

Another way that African Americans sought to reassert their voice in city affairs was by working under the direction of or in conjunction with white-led or white-dominated civic organizations. For example, in 1918 the federal government instituted the War Civics Committee program to improve the living conditions of defense industry workers and their families in selected industrial cities, including East St. Louis. Secretary of War Newton D. Baker, tasked with administering the committee, reasoned that higher worker morale would translate into greater industrial productivity for the war effort. When the war ended abruptly, Baker redirected the committee to integrate veterans into civilian life and peacetime employment. The East St. Louis War Civics Committee, wrote committee executive director Arlyn Wilbur Coffin, comprised at least fifty townspeople drawn "from among the best representatives of all interests—white and black, Protestant and Catholic, labor and capital, Republican and Democrat, men and women, leaders in the various civic, commercial, and philanthropic organizations." The committee's black members, including John W. Hughes, served as committee liaisons to an estimated 18,000 black residents. The War Civics Committee received financial support from Armour, Swift, Aluminum Ore Company, and thirty-nine other corporations. The organization founded the War Camp Community Service of East St. Louis, enabling black residents to establish a club that functioned as a social work agency, employment office, and recreational facility for black veterans.[35]

Some organizations interested in improving race relations reoriented black interests to fit within a white-dominated framework. The National Urban League, for instance, working closely with the War Civics Committee, sought to assimilate black southern migrants into an urban industrial culture by shaping black people into what the organizations defined as responsible citizens and workers. Founded in 1910, the Urban League emphasized the expansion of job opportunities, the improvement of living conditions for low-income African Americans, and the provision of professional social work services to migrants. The organization cultivated cordial relations with industrialists so that black workers would identify their interests with those of managers. The league's efforts in East St. Louis represented a response to the July massacre and its aftermath and also reflected trends in industrial relations that valued cordial relations between employees and paternalistic employers.[36]

The National Urban League formed a chapter in 1918 in East St. Louis with the aim of fostering a working partnership between the black community and industrialists. It emphasized job training, job mediation between black workers and white employers, and health care, housing, and education for black residents. The Reverend G. H. Haines, who had arrived from California in mid-1917 to serve as pastor of St. John's African Methodist Episcopal Zion Church, became an enthusiastic organizer of the league. Black executive secretary Eugene Hinckle Jones visited East St. Louis in March 1918 to seek support for the league from white businessmen willing to assist black professionals in organizing a chapter. In July 1918, black and white civic-minded townspeople formed a committee to oversee the establishment of an East St. Louis chapter of the Urban League. The committee elected George Allison, a white Baptist minister, as chapter chairman, and John Pero, a white Missouri Malleable Iron Company official, as vice chairman. African Americans who staffed other positions in the league chapter included John W. Hughes as second vice chairman, Minnie G. Scott as secretary, and St. Louisan league member George W. Buckner as executive secretary. Black women chapter members—Louise White, Maggie Freeman, Maude Haynes, social worker Mary Martin, and schoolteachers Fanny and Lucy Turner and Gertrude Creath—directed membership campaigns.[37]

The East St. Louis Urban League ran programs that encouraged not integration but black accommodation to segregation. Its Women's Department worked to ameliorate living conditions in low-income neighborhoods and conducted noonday meetings for black workers where they learned the virtues of "regularity, sobriety, punctuality, and thrift." With assistance from the War Civics Committee, the league aided black people by forming a food canning center for women, offering free night schools for adults, and organizing other community-oriented activities.[38]

In 1920, black East St. Louisans disbanded their Urban League chapter, and the St. Louis chapter took responsibility for Urban League work in East St. Louis. The reasons for the chapter's demise remain unclear, but perhaps the chapter's dissenting black members saw no possibility of striking a path independent from white progressive members who wanted to assist them but within a segregated context. Some black East St. Louisans sought the league's direct engagement in electoral politics, perhaps even an endorsement of Illinois governor Len Small and other politicians who pledged support for black economic and social advancement. Perhaps dissidents had wanted a league more involved in politics than mainstream members wished it to be.[39]

Some African Americans preferred to voice black concerns by working through their own clubs, churches, and other community-based institutions that allowed them to exercise high levels of control and independent action. Like their counterparts in other cities, black people in East St. Louis at times acted as a community in advancing their interests on certain issues. Some black East St. Louisans expressed New Negro sensibilities when they extricated themselves from organizations like the War Civics Committee and the local chapter of the National Urban League that sought to make the black community responsive to various groups of white people, especially employers.

African American townspeople greatly increased the likelihood of achieving their objectives when they worked through their own community institutions rather than under the direction of white or biracial organizations. Residents mobilized their clubs, churches, and other establishments to gain access to goods and services otherwise denied them because of segregation. One such community group, the Colored Welfare Association, founded in 1920, practiced social work among less affluent black families. The Reverend John DeShields, pastor of St. Paul's Baptist Church, and former members of the disbanded East St. Louis chapter of the National Urban League tasked the association to continue the work of the chapter.

Matt Hayes and other African American businessmen and businesswomen formed the Gold Bank Boosters' Club, a black equivalent of the East St. Louis Chamber of Commerce, to assist black businesses and provide charity to needy residents. Black residents set up facilities and organized entertainment and cultural events when the city or white organizations prohibited them from accessing cultural activities offered to white citizens. For example, some black townspeople became involved in the local black YWCA and worked with the meatpacking companies to offer recreational services for African American women employed in the packinghouses; this effort gave rise to the Progressive Girls Club of Morris and Company, the Wohelo Club of Swift and Company, and the O. T. C. (full name not given) of Armour and Company. Black women employees made use of the very corporate welfare programs that large businesses had originally implemented to thwart workers' efforts at unionizing and collective bargaining. Other black East St. Louisans, knowing that black girls and women had been denied city social services, created the Girls' Reserves in 1924 and the Colored Mothers' Craft Club in 1928 that sponsored social events for children and women.[40]

Black women continued the clubwomen tradition as key grassroots organizers and leaders in community activism. They, like black women elsewhere, used their segregated institutions to improve conditions for African Americans. Women predominated in their community's affairs largely because social problems such as those relating to public health had a direct impact on the well-being of women and their families and by extension on neighborhoods. They used their clubs and other organizations as pressure groups to obtain resources from white citizens who preferred to assist black people without integrating them into citywide institutions and services. Mary Martin and other women officers at the Colored Old Folks' Home and Orphans' Association turned that institution into the most important African American social work agency servicing black orphans and the elderly. Martin and her colleagues consistently received funding for their work from black organizations and, more significantly, from city hall and the Community Chest, a coordinating body for mainly white community groups.[41]

African American women frequently organized and led campaigns to improve the health and living conditions of low-income black East St. Louisans. They argued that overcrowded and substandard housing, improperly enforced housing codes, and lack of proper sewerage exacerbated public health problems in certain districts. The women won material assistance from city hall, the Real Estate Exchange, and other white organizations that hoped to contain, if not eliminate, public health problems in black areas before they affected white residents.[42]

Like black women health care activists elsewhere, those in East St. Louis pushed public health care to the forefront of community concerns through National Negro Health Week programs and other activities. They publicized discrimination in public health and sought ways to remedy the situation. Black people had access to professional health care in a segregated ward at St. Mary's Hospital, situated between the downtown district and the black ghetto in Denverside. But some, according to longtime resident Jeanne Faulkner, chose to be treated at a segregated hospital that employed black health care providers in St. Louis. Black women led protests to demand African American control of medical services in their districts. Social worker Annette Officer and other women organized the Colored Citizens' Community Committee of the Bond Avenue YMCA and black parent-teacher associations to promote public health care. They also assisted health practitioners in distributing smallpox vaccinations to children, sometimes administering the medicine. In 1928, during an annual Health Day program, black townspeople debated the need for black control of health care services. Annette Officer's husband, mortician William E. Officer Jr., demanded that the Visiting Nurse Association replace departing black nurse Minnie Yieges with another black nurse rather than with the white nurse who had taken Yieges's place. The assembly also called for improved care for black people at St. Mary's Hospital.[43]

Black protesters also mobilized the community around non–health care issues to extract concessions from the authorities. They had the independence to assert their demands without offending white sensibilities as long as they pursued their activities through all-black organizations. In 1924, political activists Harvey T. Bowman, Harry Dunlap, and Robert Miller led 600 residents to form the East St. Louis Welfare League to raise funds to cover the legal expenses of Arnold Rupert, who they thought had been wrongfully convicted and sentenced to hang for the murder of a white man. Rupert's supporters celebrated the success of their protests when Governor Small granted Rupert a reprieve.[44]

The East St. Louis chapter of the NAACP was formed at the time the Rupert affair erupted in the news. Chapter officers and rank and filers, like their colleagues in Chicago, mobilized around New Negro sentiments that made the association at the chapter level appear to be a "moderately 'nationalist' institution." They organized protests and rallies, even though the NAACP had a reputation for using court litigation and legislative lobbying. In 1925, the Reverend Farley Fisher and Bessie King, chapter president and secretary, respectively, led their organization to its first victory when it pressured city hall to reinstate a black police officer who had been dismissed for slapping a white man who had resisted arrest. But the national office insisted that the association was not a legal aid society. It reminded local chapter members that the NAACP only considered legal cases when race was clearly a factor in discriminatory treatment and that the ongoing *Illinois v. Rupert* affair involved salient issues other than racism. With such rebuffs, members got the message: their chapter only existed to carry out the program of the national office. Black townspeople also had to question their support of the NAACP when chapter leaders failed to demand an end to segregation—for example, in the public school system—that violated Illinois civil rights law. After a number of people left the association, Bessie King informed the national office in 1929 that Fisher had been unsuccessful as president and that the chapter had ceased its operations.[45]

Black organizations also agitated around issues such as neighborhood improvement and patronage. In 1926 and 1928, the Denverside Improvement Association, an African American neighborhood group, convinced white city councilmen of the need to improve streets in black areas. In 1927, the black Home Protective Association of East St. Louis organized to obtain city jobs for black residents. Home Protective Association chairman A. S. Moore and secretary Leroy King, demanding that black patronage appointees serve community interests and not their own, informed city councilmen that city hall must consult the association before awarding patronage to black politicos. In 1928, neighborhood people successfully pressured Mayor Frank Doyle to agree to construct a fire station to be staffed solely by black firefighters. The fire station never materialized because in 1929 the city reallocated funds to other projects at the onset of the Great Depression.[46]

The Return to Bloc Voting Status in Electoral Politics

In addition to working through black political movements and white organizations, Black East St. Louisans reentered electoral politics, reestablishing formal political influence on city government. A revived African American voting bloc by the early 1920s provided a successful demonstration of how black townspeople, with encouragement from self-interested white political factions, could circumvent the commission form of municipal government. Black voters knew that the architects of the commission plan had succeeded in preventing the possibility of an African American being elected to city council when they substituted citywide for ward-based elections. But proponents of this newly reconstructed city government failed to eliminate machine politics, which reasserted itself when some of the old guard, including Melbern M. Stephens, Maurice V. Joyce, John McLean, and Daniel McGlynn, returned to power in the 1919 city election and took command as the first commissioners and other officials of the new government. Like other townspeople, black residents quickly learned that each commissioner had exclusive authority over a specific area of city government and was therefore in a position to dispense much patronage. Now that power was invested in each commissioner rather than solely in the mayor, black East St. Louisans discovered that the most effective way to influence politicians was through the precinct system. Black women as well as men saw opportunities for involvement in city politics, working as precinct committee politicians and operatives. They used the system to monitor potential voters' attitudes and behavior, educate the electorate, and reward their precinct workers.[47]

African American women in East St. Louis quickly projected black political strength as they entered formal politics after 1920, when women won the right to vote in national elections under the Nineteenth Amendment. They formed political clubs that served women and the black community generally. Their organizations, independent of the Republican and Democratic parties, educated women in the arts of organizing and leadership, encouraged them to seek political office, and provided campaign workers for political candidates. Laura Thomas, Ida Thornton, and Pinkie B. Reeves organized the influential Colored Women's Republican Club in 1922. Reeves, Melissa Basfield, Mary Martin, and others expanded it in 1924 to include non–East St. Louisans, renaming it the Colored Women's Republican Club of St. Clair County. Reeves, Pearl Chatters, and other clubwomen also educated and mobilized black voters through the Central Colored Women's Republican Club, the Hoover-Curtis Club, and other groups. As a result of their efforts, in 1928 Democrat Eliza Hart and Republican

Nevada Hamilton became the first two black East St. Louisan women to be elected precinct committee leaders.[48]

A dramatic postwar upswing in black voting began when African Americans once again started running for city, county, and state government seats. In 1920, members of the Colored Welfare Association and other black civic and political organizations encouraged African Americans to vote. In September, soft drink parlor operator Charles Henderson ran in the Republican Party primary as the only black politician among six candidates for representative to the Illinois General Assembly, but he lost the election. In April 1922, William Hayes, laborer Walter Nichols, and tailor Douglas Howard, all Republicans, campaigned for the positions of assistant county supervisor, and mortician Charles T. Nash ran for representative to the General Assembly. None of these men, however, won his election. In 1924, black precinct committeepersons and civic and political club members, led by Matt Hayes, mortician William E. Officer Jr., Noah Parden, and others, mobilized to reelect Republican governor Len Small, who had appointed African Americans to state offices and had supported civil rights legislation. Governor Small, mindful that the black vote in Chicago and East St. Louis had aided his reelection, granted clemency to seven black East St. Louisan men—Albert Hughes, William Palmer, Fayette Parker, Othaniel Peoples, George Roberts, Dee Smotherman, and Horace Thomas—who had been convicted for their role in the July pogrom. Black townspeople regarded Small's gesture as a demonstration that their vote had gained significance.[49]

African American candidates sometimes failed to win office in the early 1920s because of antiblack agitation by white racist groups, including the Ku Klux Klan. In 1925, four African American Republicans—Matt Hayes, Calvin Cotton, and Thomas Huddleston, running for county assistant supervisor, and S. Smith, running for constable—protested when the white racist Citizens' Welfare Committee, race-baiting them, accused black people of controlling city politics. The candidates lost their elections, but they successfully pressured city officials to arrest a member of the Citizens' Welfare Committee for distributing antiblack handbills. Black people worried about the East St. Louis klavern of the Invisible Empire, Knights of the Ku Klux Klan, which had announced its establishment within two weeks of the July massacre.[50]

The Ku Klux Klan originated in 1865 and flourished until the federal government suppressed it in the early 1870s. But the Klan reemerged in

1915 in Georgia and quickly mushroomed into a nationwide organization after World War I. The post–World War I Klan provided an ideological framework for white Protestant Americans who perceived that they were losing their supremacy over nonwhite and non-Protestant Americans. The Klan engaged in the postwar repression of immigrants, Catholics, Jews, left-wing political activists, and nonwhite Americans. It also made the restoration of a purported small-town morality part of its mission to maintain white Protestant supremacy. Indeed, Klan members flogged or otherwise punished white Protestant men and women who obtained divorces, violated Prohibition, engaged in premarital or extramarital sex, or strayed from the path of righteousness and 100 percent Americanism as defined by the Klan. The Ku Klux Klan reached its height of popularity in the 1920s, drawing its members mainly from the ranks of native-born white Protestant Americans of the middle and working classes. It promoted segregation, Protestant Christianity, and Prohibition, railed against vice, and ran its own candidates or supported pro-Klan candidates for political office. The Klan in the East St. Louis district rose with the fortunes of the national Klan: its membership totaled 4,000 in 1922 and peaked at 8,000 in 1925.[51]

Black townspeople allied with those white residents who detested the Ku Klux Klan to defeat the Klan's candidates in municipal elections. Sources do not explain why some white East St. Louisans rejected the white supremacist organization, but most likely these white anti-Klan townspeople belonged to one of the groups despised by the Klan—white Catholics, Jews, and eastern and southern European immigrants. These black and white East St. Louisans, including some white machine politicians, opposed the Klan's attempt to capture the reins of city government as Klan chapters elsewhere, in both the North and South, had done. White city boosters remembered how the pogrom of July 1917 had shaken the economic foundation of the city and sought ways to minimize the possibility of Klan-inspired racial violence. The biracial alliance defeated Klan and pro-Klan candidates in municipal elections, hastening the demise of Klan influence in East St. Louis. But the formation of such an alliance did not mean that white residents were ready to vote black politicians into office. For example, in 1926, African American mortician Julius L. Marshall ran second among six Republican candidates for state legislative representative on the strength of the black vote. Marshall would have been on his way to the state legislature if he had secured even a handful of white votes.[52]

African Americans who sought to build a political machine for their community had to contend with two oppositional groups. The first consisted of white Democratic and Republican bosses who controlled much of the black vote through loyal black operatives, and the second consisted of African American party loyalists who placed acquisition of personal power above the needs of black townspeople. Politician-saloonkeeper William "Buddy" Bell represented this coterie of pro–white machine black politicians who retained control over black residents by acting as philanthropists for the needy and as bondsmen for those who ran afoul of the law. Democratic Party operatives and street inspectors Joe Chunn and Harvey T. Bowman kept the fruits of patronage to themselves rather than distribute them when the two padded the city payroll with the names of fictitious black laborers and pocketed the wages allocated for these positions.[53]

Some black Republican and Democratic Party members realized the need to take steps to free their community from the hold of white machine boss politicians. They mobilized for action in 1925 when the commissioner of health and public buildings, John T. Connors, fired Robert J. Miller, an African American janitor who had been a Democratic Party ward boss since 1915, for improperly issuing a city license to a white carnival proprietor. Upon learning of the Miller incident, black Republicans mobilized against party bosses, beginning with Fred Gerold, who had boasted of having the black vote in his pocket. In 1926, William E. Officer Jr. and other black Republicans founded political clubs, including the Republican Central Organization of St. Clair County, to counteract Gerold's power. With assistance from the Methodist Ministers' Alliance and other black groups, the Republican Central Organization worked to elect friendly white precinct candidates, increase black representation in local and state offices, and bring an end to Gerold's reign. In 1928, after a two-year battle, black Republicans scored a victory when they and their allies dethroned Gerold.[54]

Black Democratic activists, operating from a weaker position than their Republican colleagues, learned from the trouncing they suffered at the hands of black Republicans in the April 1926 municipal election. They failed to win the African American vote when black Republicans had extolled the GOP as a friend of black people and attacked local Democrats, connecting them to the national Democratic Party's support for the disfranchisement of black southerners. Black Democratic politicians saw their bargaining position strengthen after their party bosses were weakened in the April election. In 1928, black Democratic Party workers increased their party's presence in the black community by informing voters that a Ku Klux Klan member held a prominent campaign position at the city's Republican headquarters. Black Democratic candidates used the news of a Klan–Republican Party relationship as a club over black Republicans and succeeded in making inroads into the traditionally Republican black vote in the 1928 election.[55]

Black Democratic success in increasing the black vote for the party between 1926 and 1928 also had much to do with the Paramount Democratic Organization (PDO), an all-black political machine organizationally independent of Democratic Party bosses. The PDO proved pivotal in tilting the dynamics of black East St. Louis's political culture toward the Democratic Party. The organization combined party loyalty with independent operations within the black community. Horace Adams, founder and leader of the PDO, who had migrated in 1920 from Corinth, Mississippi, to East St. Louis, switched his allegiance from the Republican to the Democratic Party and embarked upon building a black Democratic organization. Adams criticized the local Republican Party for ignoring its black constituency and failing to fulfill its promises to black partisans. He saw an opening, perhaps when the Democratic Party took a trouncing in 1926, to increase black political strength by working with local Democratic bosses willing to exchange patronage for black votes. Adams, a staunch advocate of racial equality, worked with friends to shape the PDO into a black political machine that retained its organizational independence even as it allied with the Democratic Party to end Republican Party dominance among black voters. The PDO also expanded its terrain of operation from its base in East St. Louis across southern Illinois, welding black people into a voting bloc in statewide elections.[56]

In 1928, black voters in East St. Louis joined those in Chicago and other locales in casting their ballots for the Democratic Party in the national election. They displayed a readiness to bid "farewell to the party of Lincoln" in presidential elections before African Americans elsewhere, largely because of the dynamics of local politics. For example, black Chicagoans voted for Al Smith, the Democratic presidential candidate, in part because former mayor and local Republican Party boss William Hale Thompson opposed Herbert Hoover, the Republican candidate for the

White House. Black Chicagoans, recalling Thompson's generous disbursement of patronage to their community, cast their vote in support of Thompson in hopes of returning him to the mayor's office. But in East St. Louis, black Democratic operatives garnered the African American vote for the national Democratic Party largely because of the callousness of local Republican Party leaders who took the black vote for granted. The Paramount Democratic Organization in East St. Louis received an unexpected boost when the detested Republican boss Fred Gerold strode through black precincts, demanding that residents vote Republican. Black Republicans voted Democratic as a rebuke to Gerold, bringing his political career to an abrupt end in 1929. Similarly, the United Colored Democracy in New York City succeeded in swinging the black vote toward the Democratic Party in the 1932 election when the Republican Party showed indifference to loyal constituents. Black Democratic East St. Louisans emerged from the 1928 national election with their position strengthened in local Democratic politics, enabling them to secure the black vote for the national Democratic Party in future elections.[57]

The PDO faced retribution from Republican bosses who saw an opportunity to disrupt the organization by raising the possibility that its founder, Horace Adams, had engaged in illegal activities. Adams was found guilty of perjury and sentenced to a year at the federal penitentiary in Leavenworth, Kansas. Adams was released early from prison and returned to East St. Louis in 1930, convinced that the Republicans had framed him and determined to reduce the Republican Party to insignificance among black voters.[58]

———

African Americans in East St. Louis and indeed in numerous locales where mass racial violence had taken place between 1917 and 1922 struggled to overcome the fear that was the legacy of these murderous antiblack assaults. They responded to such repression through various manifestations of the New Negro movement, including the conservative UNIA with its separatist vision, the racial egalitarian NAACP with its aggressive program of integration, and black Marxist groups with their call for militant action and armed self-defense of black people against mass antiblack attacks. African Americans formed civic and political organizations and engaged in numerous projects that reflected differences of class, gender, and other social identities within their communities. In the political realm, black

Americans stressed New Negro movement ideals such as control and a degree of independence in their relationships with sympathetic organizations that were dominated or directed by white people or operated in a framework that did not solely emphasize black people's special interests.

African Americans in East St. Louis showed a determination after the July massacre to rebuild their organizations, but they had limited options. Workers were unable to advance after the labor movement collapsed in 1922, and residents, cut off by segregation, remained isolated from white townspeople who shared similar interests in improving community life. Black people made use of protests, political clubs, and the precinct committee system to extract concessions and patronage from city leaders. They minimized or rejected white attempts to dominate or channel black actions, directly or through loyal African American operatives; at the same time, they took care not to provide white townspeople an excuse to renew mass antiblack violence. Black East St. Louisans succeeded in reasserting black interests in electoral politics through a new black political machine, the Paramount Democratic Organization, reorienting the black community toward support of the Democratic Party. As the 1920s drew to a close, black residents realized that further social and political advancement and avoidance of a future pogrom depended upon forming interracial coalitions with sympathetic white organizations.

Breaking the Deadlock, 1930–1945

AFRICAN AMERICAN politics in East St. Louis fragmented during the national crises of the Great Depression and World War II. Black townspeople during the 1930s had undergone further social differentiation and engaged in a range of political actions. Nevertheless, they opposed their status under segregation by using their community institutions, local and national political organizations, New Deal programs, and labor unions as vehicles to attain a share of city resources and to advance African American interests. Black residents remained aware of the legacy of the July 1917 massacre and avoided any semblance of political independence. But Black East St. Louisans, regardless of political perspective, reached an impasse as they involved themselves in local politics: they could be active in city affairs to improve their living conditions, but only within the confines of segregation and white dominance.

The Great Depression, an unprecedented economic catastrophe that brought misery to millions of Americans, paradoxically created the conditions that allowed African Americans to achieve some gains in urban settings, including East St. Louis. It forced the federal government to provide relief for many people. In East St. Louis, the Depression weakened the influence of local politician-businessmen, especially those in the real estate faction who used segregation to control the city, as black and white citizens bypassed them and looked to the federal government to ameliorate their circumstances.

In their efforts to mitigate the harshness of segregation, particularly in housing, black East St. Louisans, like African Americans in Detroit and other urban areas, engaged in a wide range of social and political actions. They formed alliances with regional and national organizations that offered at least the possibility of restoring economic prosperity. Some thought equality could be attained by working with the Communist Party and other organizations on the political left. Workers cooperated with unions, particularly those affiliated with the recently founded Congress of Industrial Organizations, to establish new integrated locals. Many saw in New Deal programs opportunities for social advancement as well as economic relief. Black residents, by allying with the Democratic New Deal coalition, national labor unions, and other forces outside the city, succeeded in winning concessions that they had been unable to secure from local officials.[1]

Black East St. Louisans, like African Americans generally, realized that their alliances with white-dominated institutions and the federal government yielded mixed results. Black workers, for instance, found that even when they were included in labor unions they had to confront workplace segregation and discrimination and organized labor's general reluctance to challenge racism aggressively. And while African Americans often benefited from New Deal programs, these programs simultaneously reinforced patterns of racial disparity.[2]

African Americans, often backed by white allies in politics and organized labor, entered the World War II years determined to challenge the white-dominated racial hierarchy in the name of equality and democracy. They connected grassroots struggles against segregation and discrimination to the national agenda of protecting democracy worldwide from fascism. Black civilians and military personnel, including those in East St. Louis, chafed at the injustices they experienced. As they tenaciously pressed forward with antiracist grievances, observers expected East St. Louis to explode in racial violence.[3]

But East St. Louis, well known as the site of one of the most horrific racial massacres of the World War I era, did not explode in racial violence as did other cities, most notably New York (Harlem) and Detroit. The city did not descend into violence during World War II largely because of changes since the July massacre in the outlook of black and white leaders in political, business, labor, and civic organizations. City officials realized that their town would not survive as a functioning municipality if racial conflict occurred. Black and white citizens in East St. Louis, like those in Pittsburgh, Cincinnati, and other cities, had hammered out an informal accord that maintained white domination while allowing for white-guided black participation in city management. Though black East St. Louisans benefited to some degree from these accords, as did African Americans elsewhere, most knew that such arrangements did not advance them toward equality. They therefore focused their attention on building what was to become the post–World War II civil rights movement.[4]

Hard Times and Government Relief

Like millions of American wage earners and their families across the United States, workers in Illinois sought ways to survive after losing their jobs as industrial production plummeted during the Great Depression. Many whose livelihoods depended upon railroads and industry endured economic hard times. As the Great Depression worsened in 1931, working people in Illinois turned to state agencies for economic assistance after city, county, and private agencies had depleted their resources for the unemployed and the destitute. Laid-off workers relied more heavily upon the Illinois Relief Commission's work programs for the unemployed. At least 700,000 Illinoisans on state food assistance in September 1932, hoping to avoid starvation, looked to the General Assembly for new sources of relief.[5]

African Americans across the nation, many of whom had lived in depressed conditions even before the Great Depression, faced diminishing job opportunities and worsening employment discrimination in a job market that privileged white wage earners. Their efforts to secure jobs became more difficult as African American southerners, escaping from rural areas in hopes of finding employment, continued to move to the cities. In East St. Louis, African Americans, who formed nearly 16 percent of the city's population of 74,347 in 1930, suffered more than did white residents. By 1932, 11,000 out of 16,000 black residents, the latter figure representing 20 percent of the city's population, sought state relief. Mattie Malone, a black high school graduate, tersely described the Depression as an extremely difficult, precarious time when her family's ability to survive depended solely upon public relief. William Nash, who worked at a packinghouse after leaving high school, recalled that black laborers encountered more difficulty in finding jobs than white workers, even in the iron, steel, and meatpacking industries that had traditionally hired African Americans. The jobless continued to expand the city's relief rolls in 1933, though the federal government, under the newly installed administration of President Franklin Delano Roosevelt, provided massive economic assistance.[6]

As the Great Depression deepened, people across the nation tapped into new sources of relief when President Roosevelt committed the federal government to an active role in solving the economic crisis. Working people, preferring jobs to welfare relief, welcomed Roosevelt's New Deal programs. In 1933, a few thousand unemployed black and white people of East St. Louis and St. Clair County obtained public works jobs sponsored by the Civil Works Administration (CWA), one of the first of Roosevelt's New Deal relief agencies. In November, 2,205 men gained full-time employment with the CWA in the city and county, most in road and levee maintenance. Still, the CWA failed to employ all who sought work. For example, in 1934, jobless black men and women formed at least 30 percent of the area's public welfare cases. The anticipated number of unemployed workers seeking CWA jobs increased to 4,000 even after eligibility requirements restricted applicants to those who qualified as "relief cases" based upon family need. The number on work relief in the city and county increased in April to 7,000 men, who supported their families on the average CWA wage of $23 a month. By January 1935, nearly 35 percent of the city's population required economic assistance. The unemployed rushed to secure positions in work projects administered directly by the Works Progress Administration (WPA), which was established in 1935 to continue the functions of the CWA (the WPA's name changed to Work Projects Administration in 1939).[7]

The WPA proved to be a beacon of hope for African Americans on the edge of starvation and desperate for work. Black men formed part of the initial 7,000-man workforce in the local WPA district, which encompassed the counties of St. Clair, Madison, and Macoupin. They obtained jobs digging ditches, grading and paving streets, improving sidewalks and parks, and maintaining levees and drainage canals. In 1936, 800 black women sewing comforters and remodeling old clothes constituted the East St. Louis WPA project, the nation's second-largest program for black women after the one in New Orleans that employed 1,000 black women workers. The WPA remained a major source of relief for black people in the East St. Louis district. In 1936, for example, 852 out of a total of 1,992 families on public relief were African American. The number of unemployed men and women who found work through the WPA in the East St. Louis district increased to a new high in 1938, the year known as the Roosevelt recession, with 11,575 people laboring in a variety of projects in the WPA district.[8]

The nation's youth also were hit hard by the Depression, and many feared that their future careers had been jeopardized by the economic catastrophe. Tens of thousands of American youths, especially the young black people among them, found their only opportunity for obtaining jobs through the federal National Youth Administration (NYA), established in 1935. The NYA trained young women and men in traditional gender jobs, such as needlework and sewing for women and woodcarving and handicrafts for men. Black teenagers, however, experienced a higher rate of unemployment than their white counterparts, largely because of discrimination and segregation. At times, proportionately more black youths than white were enrolled in NYA programs, underscoring the fact that African American young people had a more difficult time than white youngsters in getting jobs. In East St. Louis in August 1937, for example, 150 of the 294 NYA workers were African Americans. In 1941, in anticipation of America's entry into World War II, the NYA expanded its program for black high school students to include more skills training, for example, power sewing for women and cabinet making, sheet metal work, machine shop practice, welding, and forging for men.[9]

The New Deal gave millions a chance to survive and retain a sense of dignity. Black resident Mattie Malone said that many families expressed gratitude after receiving federal relief in the form of jobs and welfare assistance. Another black East St. Louisan, Lee Annie (Adams) Bonner, daughter of Horace Adams, the founder and leader of the mass-based Paramount Democratic Organization, remembered how families saw New Deal programs as offering hope for ordinary working people, restoring their faith in the possibility of making an honest living. WPA bricklayer Joe Ragland, for example, found renewed dignity in his work in 1937 when he set a new one-day record, laying nearly 3,500 bricks an hour as he repaved a section of a street nine feet wide and 700 feet long.[10]

African Americans, however, disapproved of New Deal policies that reinforced patterns of discrimination and segregation. They protested race-based wage disparities and local administrators who engaged in such discriminatory practices, whether in southern locales like Atlanta or northern communities like New York City. In 1936, black East St. Louisans criticized the WPA and the NYA for maintaining segregated programs such as the one that employed 565 black and 131 white women, working on the same type of sewing projects but in separate facilities. Black WPA workers objected in 1938 when a local white WPA official proposed that they take private sector jobs that paid less than WPA jobs, a plan the workers considered detrimental to African American economic advancement. In 1939, black WPA laborers demanded that an administrator protect their jobs from white politicians who wanted to place their own friends in WPA positions.[11]

Black youths in East St. Louis protested segregation within the NYA, setting a pattern of militancy. From 1937 to 1941, they charged that their white counterparts received better training and enjoyed more job placement opportunities. They pressured the agency to convince employers to hire them for skilled industrial and clerical work, not unskilled jobs. As late as 1942, black youths continued to press their grievances against the NYA's discriminatory practices such as the maintenance of segregated facilities. Young East St. Louisans, like their counterparts in Cleveland and other locales, feared that a segregated NYA meant for African Americans "job categories below those which [black working people] had filled in the private sector of the economy before the Depression began."[12]

Upsurge in Community Protests

In addition to pressuring the federal government to eliminate discriminatory practices, African Americans mobilized their community to protest seemingly intractable issues, including unemployment, substandard housing, inadequate education, and discriminatory health care. They agitated for a variety of reasons, mostly for the chance to make life better in their communities, but sometimes to build political awareness and hone leadership skills for a challenge to segregation. African Americans involved in community protests rarely found common ground with white people either as individuals or as members of sympathetic organizations. Those who used community institutions as a vehicle for change contemplated black independence from white control.

Community actions included boycott campaigns—"don't buy where you can't work or shop in dignity"—intended to force small business owners, particularly white entrepreneurs who operated within black communities, to hire unemployed African Americans. Those who joined mass boycotts had numerous reasons for doing so besides seeking to obtain for black residents what the black community considered high-status, skilled, and white-collar employment. Historian Cheryl Greenberg notes, for instance, that in Harlem, unskilled black protestors "also hoped to receive jobs from middle-class blacks once the latter had won white-collar employment and opened businesses." Some black nationalists, including former UNIA members, viewed these "don't buy" campaigns as a step toward the formation of a black state. In September 1932, black East St. Louisans, most likely through the local NAACP chapter and other organizations, launched a boycott similar to those conducted in Baltimore, Harlem, and other locales. One of the actions they engaged in involved picketing white storekeeper Harry Soffer, who had beaten a black man who allegedly had stolen green butter beans. Such campaigns continued sporadically throughout the rest of the decade. In 1940, social worker Annette Officer and other NAACP members led black residents in a "don't buy where you can't work" boycott, picketing white store owners who refused to hire black people. Weldon Phillips, founder and leader of the Young Men's Civic Club, joined the NAACP in demanding that white store owners hire black youths, boycotting one establishment that rejected protesters' demands. Activists succeeded in getting employers to hire qualified black job seekers in five white-owned stores. But according to longtime black resident Olga Wayne, most "don't buy" boycotts failed. The East St. Louis experience approximated that in Harlem, where, according to Greenberg, conflicting agendas of participating protest organizations limited the success of most "don't buy" campaigns. Such actions were of value, however, in that they laid the foundation for future protests, including those involving civil rights.[13]

Many African Americans in the politically charged 1930s connected community protests to improve life in black neighborhoods to notions of making American democracy work for black people. Black housewives, for instance, mobilized to support black businesses and to increase their families' economic clout by organizing housewives' associations, like the Housewives League of Detroit and the Harlem Housewives League. These organizations sought to increase opportunities for black employment through "don't buy where you can't work" drives and also promoted economic self-help. In 1933, some black Illinoisan women founded the Original Illinois Housewives Association, a nonprofit entity headquartered in Chicago, to equip black housewives of all social classes with better household skills to "serve as power for an increased economic independence that makes for better living." They declared their faith "in the democratic form of society" and regarded "equality of opportunity as the sacred guarantee of the democratic society to each and all of its members." Pinkie B. Reeves, state central committeewoman for black Republicans in the Twenty-second Congressional District, led a group of women in establishing an East St. Louis chapter of the Original Illinois Housewives in 1934. The association pursued primarily social work and philanthropic activities, sponsoring, for example, lectures by representatives of the YWCA, the Red Cross, and other groups. The Original Illinois Housewives Association effected little social change in the economic arena as the Great Depression forced many of its members into unemployment. But the organization, like its counterparts in Detroit and elsewhere, served as a training ground for women to become political activists and community leaders interested in advancing African American civil rights.[14]

Black East St. Louisan women allied with black health care professionals and others to reverse the decline in the quality of health care as the Depression depleted city funds for public health programs. Women activists made "their struggle for improved health conditions . . . part of a political agenda for black rights, especially the right to equal access to government resources." They related public health to issues of housing, education, and employment and worked to secure moral and, where possible, financial commitments from local, state, and federal officials for their cause. The women concentrated their efforts on lowering mortality and morbidity rates in those black neighborhoods where a CWA survey revealed a high correlation between contagious diseases and substandard, unsanitary housing. Black women demanded that the East St. Louis health department close black schools hit by outbreaks of smallpox and meningitis. The department complied, but only because of its concern about the possible spread of communicable diseases to white residents. In 1934, Elizabeth T. Nash, spouse of mortician Charles T. Nash, and others in the Colored Women's Welfare League started a free medical examination campaign for black children. Leaguers sponsored their first "Better Babies" conference, similar to those held in other locales across the nation, to promote improved health care for infants and young children. In addition, the Colored Women's Welfare League along with the Visiting Nurse Association administered ongoing vaccination programs for black children. In 1935, African Americans in the Visiting Nurse Association organized weekly clinics that dispensed nutritional advice to black mothers and children. In September 1936, women activists convinced the school board to appoint an African American physician to serve black schools. Mary Martin and her Old Folks' Home Association began providing, in 1937, educational programs on health, communicable diseases, and sanitation to parents and children. In 1938, educator Maude Haynes and dietitian Annie Mae DeShields and others from various black civic and church groups offered free health clinics for children with the assistance of the WPA.[15]

While women worked to bring health care to neighborhoods, local African American physicians, all men, pushed to improve access for black residents to medical services in white hospitals. Doctors knew of the indignities that expectant black mothers faced in having to travel to St. Louis for prenatal and postnatal care because the two East St. Louis hospitals, St. Mary's and Christian Welfare, refused to serve black maternity patients. In 1937, black physician Robert H. Beverly, a Governor Horner appointee for St. Clair County, reported that black residents of the county suffered from a "prevalence of tuberculosis [and a] lack of hospitalization and even adequate medical care." Beverly noted that an estimated two-thirds of the county's African Americans were on relief while political and medical officials remained "in the financial throes of extreme stringency," making "ordinary hospitalization . . . a luxury to the St. Clair County Negro." Beverly's candid assessment galvanized black physicians to pressure local hospitals to provide comprehensive health care for African Americans.[16]

In 1939, eight black physicians, including Nathaniel G. Hagler, W. H. A. Barrett, H. H. Weathers, Silas S. Wood, and Edgar F. Woodson, concerned about the absence of African American doctors in local hospitals, called upon the St. Clair County Medical Society to amend its constitution. They wanted the society to remove its provision restricting membership to "persons of the white race residing in St. Clair County." The doctors needed membership in the society in order to belong to state and national physicians' associations and obtain employment in state and federal facilities.[17]

In 1940, some African American medical professionals, including Nathaniel Hagler, formed an association "to support construction and maintenance of a hospital" for African Americans. But previously supportive city councilmen withdrew their backing of the hospital the following year following a disagreement among the black doctors. Apparently, physicians Barrett, Weathers, Wood, and Woodson had convinced councilmen and the mayor that the black hospital was unnecessary and did not meet "the standards maintained by St. Mary's and Christian Welfare hospitals." But Hagler persevered with his plans and in 1944 opened within his home a fifteen-bed hospital to provide maternity care for African American women.[18]

The feud between Hagler and Barrett over the feasibility of a black hospital reflected local and national debates in the 1930s about whether African Americans needed to carve out separate facilities to serve their interests within a segregated system or fight for inclusion in mainstream institutions. Hagler, in proposing a black-owned hospital, advanced the separatist notion that black people needed to rely upon their own initiative, while Barrett took the integrationist view that African Americans received better care in white medical facilities. These local debates over black medical care echoed the wider themes of politicized health care activism nationwide as black citizens struggled for their fair share of medical resources in face of segregation and scarce funding.[19]

African Americans continued to agitate to improve living conditions within their segregated ghettoes. Black East St. Louisans, noted white township relief officer John Rogers, connected their need for better medical care to the dilapidated conditions of black residences. Social worker John Clark of the St. Louis branch of the National Urban League, echoing a common refrain, said that a lack of adequate housing was a major issue for black East St. Louisans. According to white registered electrician and building inspector C. E. McCarns, black tenants lived in the city's worst housing, often owned by absentee landlords in St. Louis, Chicago, and Texas. A group of visiting European housing experts saw in East St. Louis "the worst living conditions . . . in [the United States] or abroad." During the 1930s, very few families possessed the means to make improvements to their dwellings, let alone construct new ones. In 1931, Cora Hughes, spouse of Lincoln High School principal John W. Hughes, led a local campaign of the Better Homes in America, a predominantly white national organization based in Washington, D.C., and dedicated to the beautification of residences. As chairperson of the Better Homes department of the state association of clubs, Hughes enlisted civic-minded black townspeople in beautifying their neighborhoods. Home improvement projects, however, stalled as the Great Depression deepened.[20]

Housing became a major political issue in 1934, when the East St. Louis Housing Board, the U.S. Public Housing Administration, and the Federal Emergency Relief Administration (FERA), clearly intending to maintain residential segregation, unveiled a proposal for the construction of two low-rise housing projects, one for black people and one for white people. The federal government essentially acquiesced to powerful, local pro-segregation interest groups. These agencies labeled many districts where black townspeople resided as slums, and they planned to replace existing black housing but not to build additional units for black residents. Their plan had the potential to reduce further the already severely limited housing options for African Americans, especially as segregation restricted them to certain areas. In October 1934, the chairman of the East St. Louis Housing Board, C. E. Jenks, informed the director of housing of FERA, Colonel Horatio B. Hackett, that the board opposed the black housing project. Jenks tried to persuade Hackett to drop plans for the black project, arguing that such housing attracted more black southern migrants to the city, rapidly boosted the black population, drained city and county relief funds, and increased black political strength. Perhaps not wanting to alienate African Americans in the New Deal coalition, Hackett rejected the board's arguments.[21]

In 1935, the East St. Louis NAACP chapter mobilized to pressure federal agencies to continue with plans for the construction of two housing projects. Though the NAACP stood for integration, the organization thought new segregated housing preferable to no housing for black people. A local black attorney for the chapter, Louis Orr, informed the director of the Public Works Administration's Housing Department, Angelo R. Class, that African Americans faced special hardships in a racially segregated housing market. Orr had heard that local planners, under the guise of slum clearance, wanted to build the white housing project in a black district, displacing black homeowners without providing alternative housing for them. For five years, the NAACP relentlessly reminded federal officials of their responsibility to provide housing for African Americans. The chapter considered its efforts successful when the U.S. Public Housing Administration announced in 1940 that funding was available for the construction of a housing project for black people as well as one for white people, each project in its appropriately segregated district.[22]

Federally sponsored housing thus emerged as a racially contested affair in East St. Louis, as well as in other segregated cities such as Milwaukee, where black and white people bitterly debated the locations of housing projects. East St. Louis residents did not realize the extent to which the federal Home Owners' Loan Corporation reinforced segregation in the housing market, though politician-businessmen in the local Real Estate Exchange must have known. The loan corporation had written off large sections of East St. Louis that consisted mainly of low-income black and white working-class residences, refusing to extend loans to improve homes in those districts. Since the agency rated housing in low-income white districts slightly higher than housing in black areas, white residents vigilantly maintained segregated neighborhoods. Fearing lower property values, they reacted negatively to one plan for the placement of a black housing project in a white district. Perhaps the experience of East St. Louis paralleled that of other cities. The government agencies showed more concern about finding land than about the location of the building site. It appears that the authorities saw a housing project separate from its surroundings. For example, in 1942, in Detroit, the government constructed the Sojourner Truth housing project in a white neighborhood. The project was for black tenants, but residents of the white neighborhood thought the project should be for white tenants.

In early 1941, a committee made up of white homeowners living next to the site of the proposed black housing project protested. City leaders rushed to calm committee members and white townspeople generally. Unlike, for example, in Detroit, where officials vacillated on siting and constructing housing projects for either black or white families, East St. Louis planners avoided racial violence by adamantly demanding that the government locate each housing project deep within its appropriate segregated zone. In 1943, after eight years of controversy and protests, 153 black and 264 white families moved into the John Robinson Homes and Samuel Gompers Homes for black and white residents, respectively.

But the federal government never committed itself to provide housing to all who needed it, and it assigned housing a low priority during World War II. For most black East St. Louisans and a significant number of white townspeople, segregated, overcrowded substandard housing remained the norm.[23]

In another form of community action, black East St. Louisans continued their long tradition of agitation around the issue of public schools. The city's schools had been segregated since the 1870s, when black children were first permitted to attend. Most black residents did not challenge the segregated school system, considering black public schools to be community institutions that affirmed African American culture and history and provided jobs for black people. Instead, residents mobilized to force the school board to allocate resources and funding equally between black and white schools and to correct problems such as overcrowding in black schools.[24]

In 1931, parents and education professionals contacted an outside agency, the Illinois State Committee of the North Central Association of Colleges and Secondary Schools, seeking support for their demands that the school board address inadequacies at the black Lincoln High School, particularly in its library, laboratory, and instructional equipment. The state committee criticized the city's Board of Education for allowing substandard conditions to persist at the school and for threatening to revoke the school's accreditation, a move that could have left black students without a high school. In September, at least 200 African American parents besieged the board during one of its meetings and denounced school officials' proposal to save Lincoln by sending the overflow of students to a Lincoln School Annex that the board had established to avoid state penalties. Calling the annex a firetrap, protesters demanded physical improvements in all of the city's black schools. The record is silent as to whether they got them, but it is unlikely that any such improvements were made to black schools during the Great Depression.

Five years later, black parents decided that further action was needed when they—and white townspeople—learned that the accrediting association, in its April 1936 reevaluation, had described both black and white high schools as dirty, crowded, and deficient. African American residents again demanded action, knowing the school board's history of first serving the needs of its white constituency. The board planned to send at least seventy-eight students to the high school in neighboring Brooklyn;

black parents rejected this plan because of the distance that schoolchildren would have to travel and because Brooklyn High School itself lacked state accreditation.[25]

By 1940, black residents began debating the value of maintaining segregated schools, where black students lacked access to the vocational and technical training programs they needed to secure employment in industrial firms retooling for war production. The assessment that the school board treated black people as second-class citizens was confirmed when white school superintendent D. Walter Potts admitted that segregation prevented black students from enrolling in special courses that were offered only at the white schools. In addition, local administrators' prioritization of National Defense Program funding to white schools offered proof that city officials maintained unequal education for black students through segregation, with federal acquiescence. Black townspeople decided that if they wanted better schools, they needed to agitate for educational equality through desegregation.[26]

Forging Alliances with the Political Left and Organized Labor

The national crisis created by the Great Depression opened up new possibilities for challenging the inequities brought about by segregation, if not segregation itself. African Americans knew that community protests alone did not ameliorate economic hard times and so they often engaged in other forms of action simultaneously. Some, for example, worked with the political left, either because they thought that the Great Depression indicated a failed capitalist economy or because they agreed with communists and socialists that economic relief, full employment, improved working and living conditions, and an end to racism were attainable. Perhaps some African Americans thought that the political left offered the possibility of independent black political action. Others, mainly black workers, used the labor movement not only to win job security but also to advance their interests in the political arena. This was particularly the case in East St. Louis, given labor's historical voice in city affairs.[27]

The Communist Party of the United States of America (CPUSA), a predominantly white organization, regarded African Americans as the most exploited and oppressed people within the American working class and therefore as the most capable of advancing workers' interests. Black people noted the CPUSA's militant antiracist stance, particularly evident in its successful legal defense of the Scottsboro Boys, nine black Alabaman teenagers accused of raping two white women. African Americans saw the party's zeal for racial equality when the organization placed black members in the leadership of interracial unemployment councils. In 1934, for example, black laborer Walidad Wilson became a leader of unemployment councils in the industrial Tri-Cities area, comprising the small towns of Granite City (a sundown town where black people had been forbidden to remain overnight, let alone reside), Madison, and Venice, all located several miles north of East St. Louis.[28]

As early as 1930, politician-businessmen and city authorities had made clear their loathing of the Communist Party, which they regarded as an enemy of industrial capitalism. City officials harassed Communists for distributing literature, holding rallies, and demanding that city hall increase its relief program for laid-off workers. Local leaders, worried by the Communist Party's frequent calls for interracial working-class solidarity and equality, seized every opportunity to disrupt Communist rallies and meetings where black and white people assembled. For example, in February 1931, police and park officials broke up an unemployment rally that had attracted a "large crowd of Negroes, interspersed with whites" at Lincoln Park, located deep within the city's main black district. The police continued to arrest white Communists who delivered speeches in black neighborhoods through November.[29]

City hall's harassment of Communists reached a crescendo in December 1931 when police arrestees included for the first time local black Communists. A police raid on a private residence netted sixteen people, including five black men and four black women. Using tear gas for the first time, the police earned much bad publicity when several officers required medical attention after inhaling the gas and one died from a heart attack during the raid. The event caught the attention of one national publication, the *Nation,* which condemned the police for violating "the constitutional right of . . . fellow-citizens peaceably to assemble." Undeterred, Mayor Frank Doyle, police chief James Leahy, and other officials vowed to end Communist agitation, using violence if necessary. In a show of force, policemen armed with riot guns patrolled the street in front of the courthouse where the sixteen arrestees stood trial. Clearly, city officials and the police wanted to prevent any "attempt to organize Communism among the Negro residents." But authorities failed to intimidate the crowd of primarily black people from holding rallies and packing the courtroom in support of the Communist Party members and supporters.[30]

African American laborers worked with Communists, accepting their support in labor disputes. In May 1933, black women workers, who made up the majority of the 200 nut pickers at the East St. Louis branch of the Funsten Nut Company, welcomed Communist endorsement when they struck for higher wages. Twenty people, including nine Communists, marched outside the factory in support of the women strikers, encouraging the nut pickers in their "strike against starvation wages." The workers won a pay increase from two to three dollars a week. Authorities worried about the possibility of a strong alliance between black workers and Communists taking root in East St. Louis, like the one that had developed at Funsten factories in St. Louis. They arrested nine demonstrators, including African American domestics Rose Palmer and Addie Carum and black laborer Mack Sheppard. Nonetheless, in 1934 a black worker–Communist Party alliance did emerge at the East St. Louis Funsten factory. Two hundred nut pickers, now members of the Trade Union Unity League (TUUL), a Communist-organized labor union, struck over the issue of open shop versus union shop when managers refused to collect money from several black TUUL members who, for unknown reasons, had not paid their union dues. The nut pickers remained on strike for two weeks before returning to work without a settlement. The workers lost their jobs, however, when Funsten decided to close its East St. Louis operations in 1935. African Americans drew from the Funsten incident the lesson that a black worker–Communist Party alliance yielded few gains and that black people had better opportunities for success working with mainstream unions.[31]

Black workers in East St. Louis, at least to a certain extent, had long regarded labor unions as a vehicle for improving their working conditions and, given labor's participation in local government, for bolstering their political voice. In the 1930s, the impact of the Great Depression, the prounion administration of President Roosevelt, and a series of militantly aggressive unionizing campaigns increased their interest in joining the labor movement. Black as well as white workers began unionizing in earnest in 1933 when the Roosevelt administration implemented the National Industrial Recovery Act (NIRA), which in section 7(a) acknowledged workers' right to bargain collectively to gain higher wages and better working conditions. They had the support of the administration, which calculated that a unionized workforce with the means of obtaining higher wages had the potential of reviving a lagging consumer-based national economy. Workers remained hopeful about union recognition, even though they knew that the NIRA lacked provisions to enforce the right to collective bargaining. They realized that managers at Aluminum Ore (by now renamed Aluminum Company of America, or Alcoa), East St. Louis Casting Company, Southern Malleable Iron Company, Lewin Metals Company (renamed Lewin-Mathes Company by 1940 or 1941), and other factories refused to recognize unions and fired employees who agitated for them. Workers responded to managers' intransigence in 1934 with waves of strikes that rocked Obear-Nestor Glass Company, Aluminum Ore Company, and other East St. Louis–area industrial firms. In 1936, working people lost section 7(a) support when the U.S. Supreme Court ruled the NIRA and National Recovery Administration unconstitutional because they delegated legislative power to the executive branch. But by then workers were committed to forming labor unions.[32]

American workers in the mid- to late 1930s unionized in large numbers, especially in mass production industries. They received encouragement when President Roosevelt and his congressional allies passed the National Labor Relations Act of 1935 that established the National Labor Relations Board and provided for the protection of workers' right to unionize. From 1936 to 1940, black and white workers in the East St. Louis area struck for union recognition, among other demands. The Congress of Industrial Organizations (CIO) led unionizing drives in a number of occupations, most notably in steel manufacturing and meatpacking. Even the American Federation of Labor, which preferred organizing skilled craft workers, threw its energy into unionizing mass production industries. By 1941, unionists representing the AFL, the CIO, and a few independent unions had organized at least forty-nine of the fifty-five large industrial firms in and around East St. Louis, including Aluminum Ore, Armour, Morris, Obear-Nestor Glass, and St. Louis National Stockyards. The AFL unionized thirty-six of these companies and split jurisdiction with the CIO at three others. CIO unions became exclusive bargaining agents at seven plants, including the major meatpackers, except for Swift and Company, where the majority of workers had voted in the AFL. By 1944, the AFL through its local affiliation, the Central Trades and Labor Union of East St. Louis, counted 18,000 members in seventy-one locals. The CIO represented 6,000 workers organized through its local affiliate, the Industrial Union Council.[33]

Black wage earners proved instrumental in organizing CIO and AFL unions, participating in strikes as leaders as well as rank and filers. They favored the CIO over the AFL, according to packinghouse worker William Nash, because the former practiced industrial unionism, organized all workers at a worksite, and called upon workers to overcome racial divisions. African American workers applauded the CIO's special efforts to win their confidence. Black workers often succeeded in organizing under the CIO where they constituted a significant percentage of the workforce. For example, at Armour and Company they formed the United Packinghouse Workers union and at Lewin-Mathes Company they formed the International Mine, Mill and Smelter Workers union. According to black packinghouse worker Rusha Durr, union representative of Local 42 of the CIO packinghouse workers' union, African Americans composed 60 percent of the Packinghouse Workers' Organizing Committee membership. Black workers joined AFL unions in plants where they did not constitute a critical mass, for instance, the United Brick and Clay Workers of America at the Hill Brick Company of East St. Louis and the Chemical Workers Union at Monsanto Chemical.[34]

Black wage earners realized, however, that their involvement with the labor movement delivered limited results. They gained opportunities for material advancement, won union protection, held leadership positions in interracial locals, increased their numbers within the mass production industries, and received strong commitments for civil rights from militant, particularly socialist and Communist, union organizers and officials. But in some union locals black workers faced antagonistic white workers who regarded African American moves toward racial equality at the workplace as a threat to white entitlement to the best jobs and the highest pay. Moreover, some unions, especially AFL affiliates, continued to bar black workers from membership. Carpenters Joseph B. Preston and Ben Halpert, for example, attempted several times to join an AFL union, only to be rebuffed. In response, Preston and Halpert, along with some others, founded the Illinois Craftsmen's Association to protect their interests as skilled black workers.[35]

Joining the National Democratic Party Coalition

Many African American northerners who were reluctant to work with the political left and disillusioned with organized labor turned to mainstream party politics, where they threw their support to the Democratic Party. Most black voters, for historical reasons, had backed the Republican Party, especially in national elections. But urban black support for the Democratic Party increased slowly but steadily, becoming significant by the late 1920s when African Americans voted Democratic in a number of cities, including New York. African Americans showed greater interest in the Democratic alternative once the Republican Party proved incapable of ending the Great Depression. Both black Republican and Democratic politicos in East St. Louis saw the need to turn out the black vote in the contested presidential election of 1932, as President Herbert Hoover and Democratic challenger Franklin Roosevelt debated the extent of federal involvement in managing the national economy and providing work relief.

African Americans allied with the Republican Party reminded black voters that any support for the Democratic Party, which had a significant base among white southern segregationists, meant an endorsement of continued oppression of African Americans in the Jim Crow South. Black Republicans often raised the specter of white southern Democrats, who had disproportionate influence in the Democratic Party, to deflect African American criticism of President Hoover's dismal economic policy, considered by many as an impediment to working people's efforts to survive the Depression.[36]

But black Democratic operatives reminded potential voters that Hoover's strategy to woo white southerners away from the Democratic Party meant that he did not have black people's interests at heart. They cited the Hoover administration's glaring insults toward African Americans in two symbolic incidents. The first involved Hoover's insensitivity to black Gold Star Mothers who were segregated from white Gold Star Mothers when both groups traveled together on an ocean liner to France for events commemorating their sons who had died in World War I battles. The second Hoover insult occurred when the first lady, Lou Henry Hoover, did not invite the wife of Oscar De Priest, a black congressman from Chicago, to a White House function for lawmakers' wives because she feared upsetting the wives of white southern senators and representatives. Black Democrats used these incidents to claim that President Hoover took the traditionally Republican black vote for granted. They were confident that a majority of black East St. Louisans would vote Democratic, especially as the black political machine, the Paramount Democratic Organization (PDO), had been patiently building a base for the Democratic Party since the mid-1920s. The PDO saw its efforts come to fruition in the early 1930s when black voters pushed Democrats to victory in all contested offices. The black organization won accolades from Democratic Party bosses, who rewarded the PDO by appointing an African American, attorney Frank E. Summers, as assistant state's attorney.[37]

The Paramount Democratic Organization's continued expansion and solidification of its power in black precincts did not sit well with white politicians. The PDO showed its independence from Democratic Party bosses in the primary election in April 1934 by placing Aubrey H. Smith, an African American dentist and former member of the St. Clair County Board of Supervisors, on the ballot as one of the Democratic nominees for representative in the Illinois General Assembly. Smith, a Virginia native who had settled in East St. Louis in 1927, won by a slim margin, mostly because of a large black turnout. Smith's victory upset some white politicos who sent a "message" to PDO leader Horace Adams by having him arrested, beaten, and briefly jailed for his involvement with a black gambling den operator. In July, the police board dropped all charges against Adams but warned him to stay out of trouble. Undeterred, Adams's PDO scored a political triumph in the election of November 1934 when Smith became the first black politician and the first black Democrat to represent East St. Louis—a majority-white city—in the Illinois General Assembly. But Smith had served only one term when white political leaders united to defeat him in his bid for reelection in 1936. Perhaps had the energetic wheeler-dealer Horace Adams not been killed in an auto accident, Smith might have seen a second term.[38]

The PDO and its sister organization, the Paramount Negro Women's Democratic Organization, continued to strengthen their political positions within the black community while supporting the Democratic Party. Through the efforts of these two groups, black East St. Louisans entered the national Democratic Party coalition several years before 1936, when African Americans nationwide made their historic swing to the Democratic Party. The African American–Democratic Party alliance made possible black influence on the national level through electoral politics. African Americans harnessed the Democratic New Deal coalition to press for the restoration of civil rights, particularly for black southerners, and for the attainment of equality.[39]

First Challenges to Segregation and Inequality during World War II

By 1940, increasing numbers of black people placed civil rights and equality high on their agenda as they realized that labor organizations and New Deal programs reinforced patterns of segregation in employment, housing, health care, education, and other areas. At the same time, they had not recovered from the Great Depression as had many white Americans who had access to occupations in industries retooling for war production. African Americans were approximately 16 percent of East St. Louis's population but constituted 60 percent of the total caseload of federal and state government relief programs. Since the 1930s, black residents had engaged in a wide range of activities, including community protests, union organizing drives, and other forms of grassroots politics, in an effort to end racial discrimination. But they found equality elusive, notwithstanding President Roosevelt's rhetoric of saving democracy from fascism. Black people, more than ever, made a concerted effort to win state and federal commitment to racial equality as the nation prepared to enter World War II to fight fascism. One community leader, the Reverend G. T. Allen, an employee in a machine operators' training program, wrote to the National Labor Relations Board in 1944, asking, "How can we as leaders encourage our people to . . . go all out for victory while these [racist] practices . . . exist? . . . After all, winning Victory on the battle fronts [and losing] it [at] home, we will have accomplished nothing."[40]

Black East St. Louisans endured, after the racial massacre of July 1917, an expanded, rigorous customary segregation that violated long-standing Illinois civil rights laws. Social worker Annette Officer, a city resident since 1917, assisted people in finding jobs in 1932 and 1934. She reported, "Sears, Roebuck . . . told me outright that they didn't hire negroes." Officer also recalled that in 1938 she "tried once or twice to go to the Majestic [Theatre] . . . the young lady at the window frankly told me she was sorry but could not sell me a ticket." Officer and other black people could not eat purchased meals at lunch counters in many white-owned establishments.

Black attorney Louie Orr, aware of only six civil rights cases filed during his seven years of practicing law in St. Clair County, attributed black people's reluctance to file complaints to the legacy of fear created by the July mass racial violence. Orr said that "if a negro attempts to raise a question about his rights or . . . is sponsoring some progressive movement to tear down some prejudice, there's always a bunch of white people that the first thing they will say is 'this young man is trying to start a race riot.'"[41]

By the end of the 1930s, African Americans hoped to enlist the state government in their fight against segregation. In 1940, the Illinois General Assembly created the Commission on the Condition of the Urban Colored Population to investigate the impact of segregation and discrimination on African Americans and recommend legislation to correct social problems found in areas such as employment. State government planners hoped, through the commission's findings, to prevent mass racial violence as the United States anticipated entry into World War II. The commission held hearings in Chicago, Springfield, and East St. Louis to learn about the persistence of racial disparities.[42]

Several white managers, testifying before the commission, denied that their companies had policies against hiring black people. They blamed trade unions for keeping workplaces white, implying that the unions had control over who applied for jobs. Illinois-Iowa Power Company district manager F. R. Noack said that his enterprise had closed-shop contracts with three AFL unions, the International Union of Operating Engineers, Gas Fitters and Helpers Union, and Hod Carriers and Common Laborers Union, whose business agents sent him only white job applicants. A manager at Union Electric Company, G. W. Welsh, claimed that his company had only one black employee, a janitor-watchman, because it secured its workers through the business agent of the AFL International Brotherhood of Electrical Workers Union, who only sent white job seekers to the company. Noack and Welsh, when asked why their companies did not hire black workers for positions not covered by union contracts, simply reiterated that their companies did not have policies of discrimination.[43]

African Americans testified before the commission about the nature of the segregation and discrimination they experienced. Unity Mutual Insurance Company district manager W. K. Allen, a resident of East St. Louis for twenty-one years, said that "Negroes . . . scarcely get any service at . . . white places, such as restaurants, cafeterias, lunch counters, theatres, and what not." Allen informed the commissioners that white employers denied black people their civil rights "in the economic field." He cited in particular Hormel Packing Company and Lubrite Refining Company for their blatant refusal to hire black workers. The industrial secretary of the National Urban League chapter in St. Louis, Sidney Williams, thought that inclusion of black workers in the industrial workforce "had not increased in the past five years." Williams blamed managers for applying technological innovations that resulted in "[b]lack workers [getting] hit harder than white workers 'because of their unskilled ability.'" He also said that Hunter Packing Company, in reaction to the unionization of packinghouse workers, had begun to fire black employees and replace them with white workers. In addition, Williams reported that several labor unions, mainly AFL affiliates in the building trades, impeded integration by refusing to accept black members.[44]

African Americans informed the commissioners that they wanted jobs, not relief, and they wanted equality and not discrimination from the WPA. Some said that they had been forced to go on relief to become eligible for WPA jobs. Pauline Lewis of the Original Illinois Housewives Association had worked for the city recreation department for several years before 1940, when the WPA became the sole source of funding for that department. Lewis said that she had to declare herself a "pauper" and "go through the Relief channel" if she wanted to work for the department. She also found that the WPA practiced wage discrimination. When the department "was tax-supported" by the city, Lewis noted, all instructors "made an equal salary except the supervisor [but] now [as WPA-funded employees], negro instructors are paid at the lowest white rate. They are paid," said Lewis, "on average $68.00 a month and the white workers who do identically the same work . . . [have] the same experience and training in similar positions . . . make as much as $20.00 more per month."[45]

On the eve of America's entry into World War II, black people had no intention of setting aside their grievances as they had done during World War I. They planned campaigns to bring the fight for equality into the workplace as well as into the political arena. In 1941, African Americans gained a federal commitment to civil rights after black union leader A. Philip Randolph's proposed march on Washington convinced President Roosevelt to issue Executive Order 8802, establishing the Fair Employment Practice Committee (FEPC) to end discrimination at companies holding federal defense contracts. Black people supported the Double V campaign: victory for democracy overseas and victory for democracy at home. Double V dramatized the irony that the government wanted African Americans to fight for democracy in Europe and Asia, but not in the United States.[46]

Arguing for the notion of equal rights of citizenship, African Americans expected employers holding defense contracts from the federal government to hire them for technical, skilled, managerial, and clerical positions. In 1941, black workers in East St. Louis saw job prospects improve slightly at ten firms that employed 2,850 of the 3,199 black men and women working for the area's fifty-five largest corporations. But in 1942, African Americans reported cases of exclusion and underemployment at area corporations awarded defense contracts. They remained overwhelmingly restricted to unskilled jobs or excluded from defense jobs altogether, even though significant reserves of qualified black workers were available. Black workers were well aware that some firms, ignoring the executive order, flatly refused to employ African Americans.[47]

Some black Americans concluded that they had no reason to support the government in a time of war when African Americans remained, at best, second-class citizens in a nation hostile to their aspirations for equality. Many of these dissenters—perhaps a few tens of thousands nationwide—belonged to pro-Japanese black organizations that advocated separatism. One such group, which gained notoriety for East St. Louis, was the Pacific Movement of the Eastern World (PMEW). It had several thousand members in chapters scattered mainly across the Mississippi River states, from Illinois and Missouri to Mississippi and Louisiana. The PMEW, founded in 1933, drew most of its members and much of its philosophy from the defunct UNIA. Pacific Movement advocated, among other things, black pride, black-owned enterprises, and a black nation-state, ideally to be carved from the United States. In addition, PMEW leaders advised African Americans to avoid military service. The organization looked to Japan, the sole nonwhite world power, to challenge global white supremacy, defeat the United States, Great Britain, and France through warfare, and reward black people by establishing an African American nation-state. PMEW, and apparently some white Americans, including novelist Pearl S. Buck and Secretary of War Henry Stimson, thought that the next conflict would be a race war between Japan and the Western powers. The organization's fervent hope for an African American–Japanese alliance to defeat white supremacy blinded it to Japanese racism against the Asians whom Japan had conquered. Such was the depth of desire to end white supremacy among many PMEW members who hoped for Japanese victory over the United States.[48]

Pacific Movement of the Eastern World, with its pro-Japanese stance and contacts with Japanese agents, fell under the surveillance of police departments and the Federal Bureau of Investigation, which regarded the PMEW as capable of igniting a race war or engaging in subversion across the nation in a future war against Japan. The organization's headquarters, which moved in 1940 from St. Louis to East St. Louis, largely because most of its national leaders by that time were East St. Louisans, became the subject of intense FBI scrutiny. Originally composed of former members of the local UNIA chapter, the East St. Louis chapter of the PMEW, which at one point during the 1930s had as many as 950 members, only counted a few dozen activists as members in 1941. PMEW abruptly folded after the Japanese bombing of Pearl Harbor when federal agents, deciding that the pro-Japanese organization posed a serious threat to national security, raided PMEW headquarters. They arrested leaders David Erwin and General (his first name) Lee Butler, both laborers, and others, later convicting them on charges of sedition. For the authorities, Erwin's former association with Marcus Garvey marked him as a dangerous man who hated white people and opposed the United States.[49]

The significance of the Pacific Movement of the Eastern World and other antiwar black organizations such as the Nation of Islam rested with their potential to mobilize African Americans to protest federal foot-dragging in resolving issues of racial inequality and white Americans' intransigent refusal to regard black citizens as equals. The Pacific Movement had sought to expand its presence as African Americans nationwide furiously debated the extent to which black people should be involved with a federal government that showed more concern about America as an "arsenal for democracy" than about democracy for nonwhite Americans, particularly black southerners. But across the nation, the PMEW and similar organizations encountered strenuous opposition from most black people, even from those in accord with its view of the United States as a white supremacist nation. According to residents Lee Annie (Adams) Bonner and Lillian (Adams) Parks, daughters of PDO leader Horace Adams, most black East St. Louisans opposed the PMEW and favored the Double V campaign. Some black Americans, including the national leaders of the NAACP, actively assisted the government in suppressing the Pacific Movement of the Eastern World and other pro-Japanese black organizations in exchange for stronger federal support for civil rights.[50]

The federal government was keenly aware of African American criticism with respect to the nation's lack of will to acknowledge black demands for equality. Officials who were not supportive of black people's efforts to attain civil rights sought to blunt black criticism of America's shortcomings by harassing African American newspaper editors, activists, and others whom they thought capable of turning black people against the war effort. But others, favoring civil rights, urged the Roosevelt administration to quiet African American criticism by promoting black social and economic advancement. U.S. Employment Service field director George A. Scott, for one, encouraged employers to hire more black workers so as to avoid mass racial violence that could disrupt industrial war production. Scott informed the employment agency's director for Illinois, Chester Hepler, that the most serious race problem in Illinois existed in East St. Louis. Noting that black southerners and white "hillbillies," mainly from Tennessee and Arkansas, were streaming into the city in search of jobs, Scott worried that mass racial violence loomed if black and white migrants failed to obtain employment. Scott praised corporations such as American Steel Foundries, Sterling Steel Castings Company, Armour and Company, and Aluminum Ore Company for hiring black workers. He faulted companies like Socony Vacuum Oil Company, which refused to hire black laborers, and Hunter Packing Company, which specifically refused to hire black women, for contributing to racial tension.[51]

African Americans neither waited for the federal government to resolve civil rights issues at the workplace nor slowed down their grassroots campaigns for employment equality after the March on Washington in 1941. They turned the Fair Employment Practice Committee and other government agencies into useful tools to advance their Double V campaign, claiming that their contributions to the war effort entitled them to full rights of citizenship and freedom from segregation and discrimination. Black workers, insisting upon equality of treatment and an end to workplace discrimination, used the FEPC as a battering ram against recalcitrant employers and local union officials. They demanded access to job training programs and war production jobs. Black laborers urged A. H. R. Atwood,

East St. Louis district director of the Committee on Industrial Relations of the Illinois State Employment Service, to place additional trained field workers in "employer relations" to encourage managers to hire from an expanding pool of black workers who had completed job training programs. In 1942, the unofficial branch of the National Urban League in East St. Louis, the all-black Citizens Defense and Urban League Organizing Committee, which was led by its president, mortician William E. Officer Jr., with assistance from government agencies and a local CIO union, tirelessly worked to convince managers to hire African Americans.[52]

Black workers in war production industries forced the federal government to address their grievances, which it did, if for no other reason than to keep production running. In 1944, African Americans filed with the FEPC numerous grievances regarding employment discrimination. Black employees at Monsanto Chemical Company complained over a period of several months about wage discrimination and mistreatment from managers and white co-workers. James Overton stated that he received eighty-five and a quarter cents an hour while a white worker earned ninety-one and a quarter cents an hour for performing the same work. Carey Jones, employed as a skilled rigger, said that he had been paid common laborer wages. In March 1944, 380 out of 386 black Monsanto workers struck in protest over a company ruling made in consultation with an officer of the AFL union local that revoked a twenty-year customary right of black helpers to ride in the cabs of trucks with white drivers. Their work stoppage suspended vital operations at the plant until the FEPC negotiated terms of agreement and strikers returned to work on March 21. According to FEPC worker Harry H. C. Gibson, strikers had based their grievances on "the desire . . . to receive equal opportunities for upgrading along with the white employees." Black workers won a moral victory when FEPC regional director Elmer Henderson and other government and military officials directed the company and the union to resolve black workers' grievances.[53]

Many black women in East St. Louis made the transition from nonindustrial to industrial employment, though a number continued to labor as domestic workers. While war mobilization demanded full utilization of able-bodied workers, African American women continued encountering discrimination in 1942 as employers hired only white and black men and white women. By 1944, black women, working with the FEPC and other federal agencies, saw their job prospects improve, particularly at the feed mills, railroad freight depots, and newly established worksites such as the Indian Lake Egg Company. But black women remained underrepresented in industrial work. They still had to rely upon black community organizations and the government to urge reluctant employers to hire and promote them.[54]

Black working women and men realized that the FEPC and other state and federal agencies, lacking the means to enforce antidiscrimination rulings, were largely ineffective in resolving grievances of workplace segregation and discrimination. They saw the FEPC in particular dismissing many of their cases on grounds of insufficient evidence. For example, in 1943, the FEPC rejected a complaint filed by fifteen black women who charged that Walworth Company had refused to hire them. The company claimed that it preferred to hire women who lived close to the plant, and since the company was located in a white area, it hired only white women. The company also noted that it did not have separate restrooms for black women.

Black workers flooded the regional FEPC office with grievances pertaining to issues of discrimination, far surpassing the number of complaints filed by Jewish American and Mexican American workers, or even Japanese Americans who had been released from War Relocation Centers. By 1944, African Americans saw favorable results as the office focused more on the problems of hiring black women and upgrading the jobs of black men and women workers. They also recognized that the office agreed with them that certain employers, such as Western Cartridge Company, a munitions maker in East Alton, Illinois, that refused to hire a single black worker in its workforce of 15,000 men, and certain labor unions, like the railroad brotherhoods, perpetuated racial discrimination.[55]

———

African Americans engaged in a range of grassroots and electoral politics in East St. Louis that paralleled, and was foundational to, black people's actions at the national level. They agitated to increase their chances of remaining employed during the Great Depression, but also to gain access to skilled industrial occupations and to achieve job security through membership in labor unions and participation in the Democratic Party–led New Deal coalition. But black Americans acknowledged on the eve of America's entry into World War II that their engagements in community actions, social movements, and political parties had yielded mixed results.

They earned a place as decision makers in local and national affairs but not as equal partners. As long as white Americans maintained segregation, black people had to continue to push to attain their goal of equality.

An informal racial accord, a shared understanding between black and white leaders, manifested itself in East St. Louis with the realization among white officials that they had to include African Americans in their plans for modernization of the area's industry, job creation, and improvement of housing stock after the war. As early as 1943, economic boosters knew that East St. Louis's expansion as an industrial city had come to an end during the interwar years. They learned the value of, and became dependent upon, federal economic assistance during the Great Depression and the war. White political and economic leaders looked forward to the continuance of federal support into the postwar years. These city planners understood that any attempts, including through the use of mass racial violence, to prevent black residents' social and economic advancement risked the city's economic future. East St. Louis was never an industrial giant like Chicago or Detroit, and it did not have the same ability to absorb the shock of racial violence. Mayor John T. Connors of East St. Louis, knowing his city's vulnerability to the possibility of racial violence, praised residents for remaining united, regardless of race, in winning the war. Local officials hoped that with the accord in place, peaceful race relations, within a context of segregation, would pave the way for a prosperous postwar future.[56]

African American residents, however, demanded an equal voice in the postwar era. Lincoln High School principal O. V. Quinn, in describing black political assertiveness, stated that black workers in particular had forged "a good strategic position" from which to demand inclusion in the city's postwar planning. Quinn especially held high hopes for further cooperation between black labor and the CIO, which had "given Negro workers greater opportunity." According to Quinn, if black labor were to be "ignored in post-war planning, [then] Negro labor can be expected to protest."[57]

Black East St. Louisans' optimism for the postwar future was tempered, however, by the legacy of the mass violence of July 1917: persistent white intolerance of African Americans' determination to pursue their special interests and their independence in city affairs. For instance, local AFL representative Fred Olds, voicing the sentiments of many white East St.

Louisans, told black townspeople to "[l]eave things alone, as they now are," adding, "don't ask for trouble." Black residents knew that Olds, in using the word "trouble," referred to the July pogrom. But after fighting for twelve years for economic survival during the Great Depression and an additional four years for democracy's survival during World War II, black women and men would not be denied. They resolved to mobilize their institutions and form interracial alliances to bring to an end segregation and discrimination in postwar East St. Louis.[58]

Postscript

IMMEDIATELY AFTER World War II, African Americans in East St. Louis launched campaigns to gain civil rights and dismantle segregated institutions. Their determination to achieve equality had been strengthened by a wide array of factors. First, black townspeople framed their protests with the rhetoric of democracy articulated by the government to defeat fascism and by the Double V campaign to assault racism. Civilians and returning veterans vowed to fight for democracy as they battled against workplace discrimination. Finally, black East St. Louisans received support for their struggle for justice from the NAACP, the Illinois Human Rights Commission, and white allies in organized labor and the government.

Black residents of the city first employed mass civil disobedience in 1949 to desegregate the public school system. In the process, they ignored segregationists' threats of mass antiblack assaults, overcoming the legacy of fear engendered by the July 1917 massacre. Threats notwithstanding, as long as black East St. Louisans remained under the oversight of white political machines and refrained from seeking political independence from these machines, they had little to fear in terms of antiblack violence. The school desegregation campaign in East St. Louis was the harbinger of mass civil rights actions that occurred from the mid-1950s to the mid-1960s in Montgomery, Alabama, and other locations.[1]

Black people anticipated a bright future in East St. Louis as the civil rights movement of the 1950s and 1960s desegregated parks and recreational facilities, places of public accommodation, and other public spaces. Like the black population in cities such as Chicago and Detroit, the African American community in East St. Louis expanded significantly with a post–World War II migration of black southerners that surpassed that of the Great Migration. Migrants came from across the rural South to East St. Louis and other cities in the North, Midwest, and Pacific West in search of employment and a better way of life. African Americans often repeated the saying, "If you can't get a job in East St. Louis, then you can't get one anywhere."

Black townspeople saw increasing numbers of African Americans, with the approval of white political machine bosses, appointed and elected to political office. The fact that black politicians in East St. Louis tied their fortunes to white machines reduced the prospects of building an independent African American political machine in the city, but it also helped prevent a violent backlash by white residents who perceived a threat to their entitlement to resources and power. Black residents furthered their opportunities for patronage and power during the late 1960s, when East St. Louis became a majority-black city through black in-migration and white flight to the suburbs. In 1971, James Williams became the city's first black mayor.[2]

Black machine politics became entrenched in the 1970s in the nearly all-black East St. Louis. But by then, the city had undergone massive deindustrialization that wreaked havoc on its economy. Machine politicians and reformers and their respective supporters, the men and women who ran the precinct committee system, divided over how to govern the municipality and respond to constituencies that expected services from a city that by now lacked a viable economy. While some cities in such circumstances, Pittsburgh, for example, recovered from the loss of their major industries, East St. Louis, despite financial assistance from the state, never did. East St. Louis found itself in the same situation as Gary, Indiana, and other deindustrialized cities that experienced a continuous decline in population and per capita wealth and income and an expansion of a low-income black citizenry.

Black East St. Louisan struggles for social advancement and political power must be seen within the context of historical transformations: urbanization, industrialization, progressive-era reforms, black migrations, the Great Depression and the world wars, and the historic African American quest for equality. These efforts need to be viewed in relation to the local white business community that ran this border region industrial city for many decades. The economic and social problems that beset black East St. Louis today have their roots in the latter third of the nineteenth century, when real estate politician-businessmen fashioned a town to create profits for themselves and for industrialists, not to provide a high quality of life for residents. Municipal mismanagement became entrenched during the interwar years after several generations of economic boosters locked the city to the fate of railroads and intermediary industries. This dependence impaired the ability of post–World War I politician-businessmen to apply regional planning or recruit industries based on new technologies.

City leaders ignored the signs of economic decline that were apparent as early as 1920, when a nationally renowned urban planner pointed out that East St. Louis's economic growth had been strangled by the railroads. White politicians and businessmen, including those involved in real estate, knew before the end of World War II that the economy of East St. Louis had ceased to expand. But post–World War II city boosters, wedded to a political machine culture, did not see the need to change decades-old economic policies. Politician-businessmen failed to pull the city out of an economic decline that had become brutally obvious by the 1960s. Black city leaders in the 1970s inherited many of the city's long-term problems from white politician-businessmen who had developed the economy and commanded politics in East St. Louis for nearly a century. But worse, they also inherited from these white politician-businessmen a machine mentality and mode of operation. In East St. Louis, both white and black machine and reformist political leaders lacked the means and the will to recruit different types of industry and institute economic and political innovation that might have meant prosperity for black and white residents in the years ahead.

NOTES

Preface

1. Elliott M. Rudwick, *Race Riot at East St. Louis, July 2, 1917* (Carbondale: Southern Illinois University Press, 1964); Roberta Senechal, *Sociogenesis of a Race Riot: Springfield, Illinois, in 1908* (Urbana: University of Illinois Press, 1990).

2. James Loewen, *Sundown Towns: A Hidden Dimension of American Racism* (New York: New Press, 2005); Elliot Jaspin, *Buried in the Bitter Waters: The Hidden History of Racial Cleansing in America* (New York: Basic Books, 2007).

Introduction

1. Jack Lait's article for the *St. Louis Republic* was reprinted as "Described and Analyzed by a . . . Relible [*sic*] Journalist," *East St. Louis Daily Journal* (hereafter cited as *ESLDJ*), July 5, 1917, 4, section 2; "As the *Journal* Views It," *ESLDJ*, July 6, 1917, 4. Eyewitness Lulu Suggs is quoted in "The Massacre of East St. Louis," *Crisis* 14 (September 1917): 219–38, reprinted in *The Black Worker: A Documentary History from Colonial Times to the Present,* ed. Philip S. Foner and Ronald L. Lewis (Philadelphia: Temple University Press, 1980), 5:318–32. On property damage, city fire marshal John H. Richards stated that the approximate loss on buildings and railroad cars was $373,605, not $3 million as initially estimated, in U.S. Congress, House, Special Committee to Investigate the East St. Louis Riots, *Transcripts of the Hearings of the House Select Committee That Investigated the Race Riots in East St. Louis, Illinois, 1917* (Washington, D.C.: Government Printing Office, 1918), 1745 (hereafter cited as *House Transcripts*). On more white than black people killed during the fighting, as stated by residents: "Interview with Dr. Oliver W. H. Tyler: Interviewed by George Peters," September 25, 1972, Oral History T-276, Black Community Leaders Project, Western Historical Manuscript Collection, University of Missouri–St. Louis; Olga Wayne, interview by author, September 21, 1999, East St. Louis. On many dozens or a few hundred black deaths, see, for example, "12 Negroes on Trial for Riot Murders," *ESLDJ*, October 1, 1917, 1; U.S. Congress, House, Committee on Rules, *Riot at East St. Louis, Illinois* (Washington, D.C.: Government Printing Office, 1917), 5; "East St. Louis Riots," 65th Cong., 2d. sess., *Congressional Record,* February 4, 1918, vol. 56, pt. 2, 1654.

2. Elliott M. Rudwick, *Race Riot at East St. Louis, July 2, 1917* (Carbondale: Southern Illinois University Press, 1964), ix–x, 3–6, 217–33; Malcolm McLaughlin, *Power, Community, and Racial Killing in East St. Louis* (New York: Palgrave Macmillan, 2005), 2–4, 178–81. Rudwick employs social strain theory advanced in Allen D. Grimshaw, "A Study in Social Violence: Urban Race Riots in the U.S."

(Ph.D. diss., University of Pennsylvania, 1959). Grimshaw's dissertation and his *Racial Violence in the United States* (Chicago: Aldine, 1969) influenced subsequent scholars analyzing race riots and rioters. Rudwick and McLaughlin, of course, also utilize other sources, including local newspapers, court reports, and Illinois state documents, for example, Illinois State Council of Defense (World War I), *Report of the Labor Committee of the State Council of Defense of Illinois upon the Inquiry into the Recent Influx of Southern Negro Laborers into East St. Louis and Race Riot in Connection Therewith: At a Meeting . . . Held at Chicago, June 2, 1917*, RS 517.020, roll 30-873, Illinois State Archives, Springfield (hereafter cited as *Labor Committee Report*). On one hand, Rudwick had the fortune to interview residents who witnessed the riots and subsequent events. On the other hand, researchers after Rudwick have had access to collections that were unavailable to him, for example, the Lawrence Y. Sherman Papers in the Abraham Lincoln Presidential Library in Springfield. Black East St. Louisan newspapers whose issues unfortunately are no longer extant include *Messenger* (late 1890s), *Southern Illinois Press* (early 1920s), *Advance Citizen* (1920s), *East St. Louis Globe* (early 1930s), *East St. Louis Citizen* (1930s), *Spotlight* (1930s), *East St. Louis Gazette* (late 1930s), and the *Crusader* (1940s). These titles are briefly described in "East St. Louis Newspapers," folder 14, box 42, Negro in Illinois Papers, Illinois Writers' Project, Chicago Public Library (hereafter cited as Negro in Illinois Papers). Since pre-1945 black East St. Louisan sources no longer exist, evidence for black community institutions, culture, and politics comes mostly from local white sources like the *East St. Louis Daily Journal* as well as a few black publications from other cities, for example, the *St. Louis Argus*.

3. That major primary source is the voluminous *House Transcripts*.

4. Quoted passage in Richard W. Thomas, *Life for Us Is What We Make It: Building Black Community in Detroit, 1915–1945* (Bloomington: Indiana University Press, 1992), xi. A growing literature documents the ways in which black (and other) working people connected workplace or other noncommunity affairs to their communities, which reinforced their noncommunity struggles. Examples include Joe William Trotter Jr., *Coal, Class, and Color: Blacks in Southern West Virginia, 1915–1932* (Urbana: University of Illinois Press, 1990); Earl Lewis, *In Their Own Interests: Race, Class, and Power in Twentieth-Century Norfolk, Virginia* (Berkeley: University of California Press, 1991); Robin D. G. Kelley, *Race Rebels: Culture, Politics, and the Black Working Class* (New York: Free Press, 1994); Tera W. Hunter, *To 'Joy My Freedom: Southern Black Women's Lives and Labors after the Civil War* (Cambridge, Mass.: Harvard University Press, 1997).

5. On social strain, see, for example, William M. Tuttle Jr., *Race Riot: Chicago in the Red Summer of 1919* (New York: Atheneum, 1970), quoted passage at 65; Dominic J. Capeci Jr. and Martha Wilkerson, *Layered Violence: The Detroit Rioters of 1943* (Jackson: University of Mississippi Press, 1991), xii, 174; Dominic J. Capeci Jr., "Race Riot Redux: William M. Tuttle, Jr., and the Study of Racial Violence," *Reviews in American History* 29, no. 1 (2001): 165–81. Quoted passage on Grimshaw in Roberta Senechal, *Sociogenesis of a Race Riot: Springfield, Illinois,*

in 1908 (Urbana: University of Illinois Press, 1990), 3. Critique of social strain theory in Senechal, *Sociogenesis of a Race Riot*, 3–10. In agreement with Senechal's core argument is Brian Butler, *An Undergrowth of Folly: Public Order, Race Anxiety, and the 1903 Evansville, Indiana Riot* (New York: Garland, 2000), 11.

6. On patronage as a sign of white willingness to treat black people with representation and empowerment, see William J. Grimshaw, *Bitter Fruit: Black Politics and the Chicago Machine, 1931–1991* (Chicago: University of Chicago Press, 1992), 8, 48–49. On the importance of real estate interests in developing and turning cities into economic growth machines, see, for example, John R. Logan and Harvey L. Molotch, *Urban Fortunes: The Political Economy of Place* (Berkeley: University of California Press, 1987), 13–15, 52–57. On conflicts between black and white urban dwellers and real estate boards over private property rights, homeownership, neighborhoods, and related concerns, see David M. P. Freund, *Colored Property: State Policy and White Racial Politics in Suburban America* (Chicago: University of Chicago Press, 2007), 15–18. On the expulsion, often by force, of African Americans and other racial or ethnic minorities to create sundown, or all-white, towns, see James W. Loewen, *Sundown Towns: A Hidden Dimension of American Racism* (New York: New Press, 2005), 9–12, 90–115.

7. Quoted passage on border towns in Kenneth Kusmer, *A Ghetto Takes Shape: Black Cleveland, 1870–1930* (Urbana: University of Illinois Press, 1976), 55. On border cities in the Ohio River valley, see Joe William Trotter Jr., *River Jordan: African American Urban Life in the Ohio Valley* (Lexington: University Press of Kentucky, 1998), xiii–xv. On the mix of black-white interactions in midwestern cities, see, for example, Allan H. Spear, *Black Chicago: The Making of a Negro Ghetto, 1890–1920* (Chicago: University of Chicago Press, 1967), 5–7; David M. Katzman, *Before the Ghetto: Black Detroit in the Nineteenth Century* (Urbana: University of Illinois Press, 1973), 22–25, 82–83, 120–26; Kusmer, *Ghetto Takes Shape*, 3–65.

8. For succinct coverage of East St. Louis's political and industrial developments, see Andrew J. Theising, *Made in USA: East St. Louis, the Rise and Fall of an Industrial River Town* (St. Louis, Mo.: Virginia Publishing, 2003), 59–119. On East St. Louis as an industrial suburb, see Graham Romeyn Taylor, *Satellite Cities: A Study of Industrial Suburbs* (reprint, New York: Arno Press, 1970), 127–38. On industrial satellites or industrial suburbs, see, for example, Raymond A. Mohl and Neil Betten, *Steel City: Urban and Ethnic Patterns in Gary, Indiana, 1906–1950* (New York: Holmes and Meier, 1986), 11–12; Howard Gillette, *Camden after the Fall: Decline and Renewal in a Post-Industrial City* (Philadelphia: University of Pennsylvania Press, 2005), 18–20. On businessmen as a powerful class of local political actors, see Edward Greer, *Big Steel: Black Politics and Corporate Power in Gary, Indiana* (New York: Monthly Review Press, 1979), 20; Herbert G. Gutman, "Class, Status, and Community Power in Nineteenth-Century American Industrial Cities: Paterson, New Jersey: A Case Study," in *Work, Culture, and Society in Industrializing America: Essays in American Working-Class and Social History* (New York: Vintage, 1977), 236–37.

9. On the nadir, see Rayford W. Logan, *The Negro in American Life and Thought: The Nadir, 1877–1901* (New York: Dial Press, 1954). On the late nineteenth and early twentieth centuries as a period of intellectual ferment in African American life, see, for example, August Meier, *Negro Thought in America, 1880–1915* (Ann Arbor: University of Michigan Press, 1963), 82, 121–22, 138, 161–70.

10. On the "tragic sameness" theme, see, for example, Spear, *Black Chicago,* 224–29; Katzman, *Before the Ghetto,* 208–11. For the view that the tragic sameness perspective is overworked, see, for example, Joe William Trotter Jr., *Black Milwaukee: The Making of an Industrial Proletariat, 1915–45* (Urbana: University of Illinois Press, 1985), 272–77. On pre–World War I urban black politicians' diminishing opportunities because of citywide direct elections, see Katzman, *Before the Ghetto,* 203; Kusmer, *Ghetto Takes Shape,* 143–47. On white progressive reformers and African Americans, see, for example, William A. Link, *The Paradox of Southern Progressivism, 1880–1930* (Chapel Hill: University of North Carolina Press, 1992), 125–42; Steven J. Diner, *A Very Different Age: Americans of the Progressive Era* (New York: Hill and Wang, 1998), 9, 125–26; Heather Cox Richardson, *The Death of Reconstruction: Race, Labor, and Politics in the Post–Civil War North, 1865–1901* (Cambridge, Mass.: Harvard University Press, 2001), 59, 210–24, 244–45.

11. On black southerners as their own agents in the making of the Great Migration, see, for example, James R. Grossman, *Land of Hope: Chicago, Black Southerners, and the Great Migration* (Chicago: University of Chicago Press, 1989), 5–6; Joe William Trotter Jr., *The Great Migration in Historical Perspective: New Dimensions of Race, Class, and Gender* (Bloomington: Indiana University Press, 1991), ix–x, xi. On the political impact of migrants, see Tuttle, *Race Riot,* 88; Grossman, *Land of Hope,* 6, 19, 38–40, 57, 161. On black machine and submachine politics, see Harold F. Gosnell, *Negro Politicians: The Rise of Negro Politics in Chicago* (Chicago: University of Chicago Press, 1935), 136–52; Martin Kilson, "Political Change in the Negro Ghetto, 1900–1940s," in *Key Issues in the Afro-American Experience,* ed. Nathan I. Huggins, Martin Kilson, and Daniel M. Fox (New York: Harcourt Brace Jovanovich, 1971), 2:167–92; Roger Biles, "Black Mayors: A Historical Assessment," *Journal of Negro History* 77, no. 3 (Summer 1992): 110, 111.

12. On reformers controlling black politicians and political and social activism, see, for example, John Dittmer, *Black Georgia in the Progressive Era, 1900–1920* (Urbana: University of Illinois Press, 1977), 129–30. H. Leon Prather Sr. discusses the need to employ precise terms other than the umbrella descriptor "race riot" when referring to specific forms of mass racial violence; see Prather, *We Have Taken a City: Wilmington Racial Massacre and Coup of 1898* (Cranbury, N.J.: Associated University Presses, 1984), 11, 173. This author uses the term pogrom, agreeing with Jewish immigrant and Jewish American sources that the July race riot was a pogrom. The concept of pogrom is discussed further in chapters 3 and 4 of this volume. On the Wilmington massacre as a white response to black political strength, see David S. Cecelski and Timothy B. Tyson, eds., *Democracy Betrayed: The Wilmington Race Riot of 1898 and Its Legacy* (Chapel Hill: University of North Carolina Press, 1998), 4–6. On events in Houston, where black soldiers

retaliated against brutal police harassment of African American civilians, see Robert V. Haynes, *A Night of Violence: The Houston Riot of 1917* (Baton Rouge: Louisiana State University Press, 1976), 16, 140–70 passim. On events in Philadelphia, where white residents attacked black people who moved into white neighborhoods and police were reluctant to protect African Americans, see Vincent P. Franklin, "The Philadelphia Race Riot of 1918," *Pennsylvania Magazine of History and Biography* 99, no. 3 (July 1975): 336–50. On black agriculturalists' labor and freedom struggles against violent planter-led white reaction in Elaine, Arkansas, and the surrounding Arkansas-Mississippi delta region, see Nan Elizabeth Woodruff, *American Congo: The African American Freedom Struggle in the Delta* (Cambridge, Mass.: Harvard University Press, 2003), 74–109. On a concerted, massive white attack that destroyed the black community and its prosperous businesses in Tulsa, Oklahoma, see Scott Ellsworth, *Death in a Promised Land: The Tulsa Race Riot of 1921* (Baton Rouge: Louisiana State University, 1982), 3–7. On numerous occurrences of ethnic cleansing between 1890 and 1968 in U.S. villages and small towns, as well as in larger towns and cities, see Loewen, *Sundown Towns*, 4–5.

13. On the civil rights militancy of African American veterans of World War I, see, for example, Steven A. Reich, "Soldiers of Democracy: Black Texans and the Fight for Citizenship, 1917–1921," *Journal of American History* 82 (March 1996): 1478–1504. On various "New Negro" expressions in new or existing organizations, see Judith Stein, *The World of Marcus Garvey: Race and Class in Modern Society* (Baton Rouge: Louisiana State University Press, 1986), 38–60 passim; Winston James, *Holding Aloft the Banner of Ethiopia: Caribbean Radicalism in Early Twentieth-Century America* (New York: Verso, 1998); Christopher Robert Reed, *The Chicago NAACP and the Rise of Black Professional Leadership, 1910–1966* (Bloomington: Indiana University Press, 1997), 44–65. On ghettoization, see Gilbert Osofsky, *Harlem: The Making of a Ghetto, 1890–1903* (New York: Harper and Row, 1966), 71–123; Spear, *Black Chicago*, 6–8, 26–27. On ghettos as a base to mobilize for social and political actions, sometimes along lines of class and gender in the 1920s, see Lewis, *In Their Own Interests;* Trotter, *Black Milwaukee*, 116–39; Thomas, *Life for Us Is What We Make It*, 228–29.

14. On black workers and the labor movement of the 1930s and 1940s, see Trotter, *Black Milwaukee*, 158–60; Rick Halpern, "Organized Labor, Black Workers, and the Twentieth Century South: The Emerging Revision," in *Race and Class in the American South since 1890*, ed. M. Stokes and R. Halpern (New York: Oxford University Press, 1994), 43–76; Robert J. Norrell, "Caste in Steel: Jim Crow Careers in Birmingham, Alabama," *Journal of American History* 73, no. 3 (1986): 669–94; Robert Korstad and Nelson Lichtenstein, "Opportunities Found and Lost: Labor, Radicals, and the Early Civil Rights Movement," *Journal of American History* 75, no. 3 (1988): 786–811; Michael Goldfield, "Race and the CIO: The Possibilities for Racial Egalitarianism during the 1930s and 1940s," *International Labor and Working-Class History* 44, no. 1 (1993): 1–32. On the federal government's nominal commitment to antidiscrimination in employment, see Andrew Edmund Kersten, *Race, Jobs, and the War: The FEPC in the Midwest, 1941–46*

(Urbana: University of Illinois Press, 2000), 2, 11–20. On World War II race riots in Detroit and Harlem, see Capeci and Wilkerson, *Layered Violence*, 3–31; Cheryl Lynn Greenberg, *"Or Does It Explode?" Black Harlem in the Great Depression* (New York: Oxford University Press, 1991), 211–14.

15. On the 1949 school desegregation campaign in East St. Louis, see Elliott M. Rudwick, "Fifty Years of Race Relations in East St. Louis: The Breaking Down of White Supremacy," *Midcontinent American Studies Journal* 6 (Spring 1965): 3–15. On grassroots involvement and leadership in the civil rights movement before the 1950s, see John Dittmer, *Local People: The Struggle for Civil Rights in Mississippi* (Urbana: University of Illinois Press, 1994), 1–40.

Chapter 1: Historical Roots of an African American Community, 1800–1898

1. On the importance of working people's community and workplace culture, see John T. Cumbler, *Working-Class Community: Work, Leisure, and Conflict in Two Industrial Cities, 1880–1930* (Westport, Conn.: Greenwood, 1979); James R. Barrett, *Work and Community in the Jungle: Chicago's Packinghouse Workers, 1894–1922* (Urbana: University of Illinois Press, 1987); David Montgomery, *The Fall of the House of Labor: The Workplace, the State, and American Labor Activism, 1865–1925* (New York: Cambridge University Press, 1987), 1–2. On the African American community nurturing political or social action, see Steven Hahn, *A Nation under Our Feet: Black Political Struggles in the Rural South from Slavery to the Great Migration* (Cambridge, Mass.: Harvard University Press, 2003), 163–313; Allan H. Spear, *Black Chicago: The Making of a Negro Ghetto, 1890–1920* (Chicago: University of Chicago Press, 1967), 7–8. On black working people shaping urban life, see Joe William Trotter Jr., *Black Milwaukee: The Making of an Industrial Proletariat, 1915–45* (Urbana: University of Illinois Press, 1985), xi–xii; Richard W. Thomas, *Life for Us Is What We Make It: Building Black Community in Detroit, 1915–1945* (Bloomington: Indiana University Press, 1992), 2–14; Tera W. Hunter, *To 'Joy My Freedom: Southern Black Women's Lives and Labors after the Civil War* (Cambridge, Mass.: Harvard University Press, 1997), viii.

2. For histories that focus on the mass racial violence in 1917 in East St. Louis, see Elliott M. Rudwick, *Race Riot at East St. Louis, July 2, 1917* (Carbondale: Southern Illinois University Press, 1964); Malcolm McLaughlin, *Power, Community, and Racial Killing in East St. Louis* (New York: Palgrave Macmillan, 2005). Quoted passage in William M. Tuttle Jr., *Race Riot: Chicago in the Red Summer of 1919* (New York: Atheneum, 1970), 65–66.

3. On mass violence as a tool of repression, see Robert L. Zangrando, *The NAACP Crusade against Lynching, 1909–1950* (Philadelphia: Temple University Press, 1980), 5, 8, 12–17; James W. Loewen, *Sundown Towns: A Hidden Dimension of American Racism* (New York: New Press, 2005), 4–5, 9, 26–38. On brief period of racial egalitarianism, see Kenneth Kusmer, *A Ghetto Takes Shape: Black Cleveland, 1870–1930* (Urbana: University of Illinois Press, 1976), 9–10.

4. Urban African American historiography, which overlaps discussion of black labor, looks at white real estate men in the context of residential segregation and

the development of ghettoes; see Spear, *Black Chicago*, 6–7, 11–12, 21, 23–24; Gilbert Osofsky, *Harlem: The Making of a Ghetto: Negro New York, 1890–1930* (New York: Harper and Row, 1968), 13, 112. On land as commodity in shaping the development of cities and social relationships, see John R. Logan and Harvey L. Molotch, *Urban Fortunes: The Political Economy of Place* (Berkeley: University of California Press, 1987), 17–37. On land entrepreneurs in a small industrializing city, see Herbert G. Gutman, "Class, Status, and Community Power in Nineteenth-Century American Industrial Cities: Paterson, New Jersey: A Case Study," in *Work, Culture, and Society in Industrializing America: Essays in American Working-Class and Social History* (New York: Vintage, 1977), 234–60. On cities built fundamentally by capital-labor conflicts, see David Harvey, "Labor, Capital and Class Struggle around the Built Environment in Advanced Capitalist Societies," *Politics and Society* 6, no. 3 (1976): 265–95, and *The Limits to Capital* (Chicago: University of Chicago Press, 1982). On African American urban electoral political actions, see Martin Kilson, "Political Change in the Negro Ghetto, 1900–1940s," in *Key Issues in the Afro-American Experience,* ed. Nathan I. Huggins, Martin Kilson, Daniel M. Fox (New York: Harcourt Brace Jovanovich, 1971), 2:171–72.

5. A significant proportion of African American historiography on postbellum urban African American life and rural-to-urban migrations focuses on black people as laborers and on their political and social relationships with black middle-class people, white workers, and employers. For an overview, see Joe William Trotter Jr., "The African American Worker in Slavery and Freedom," in *The African American Experience: An Historiographical and Bibliographical Guide,* ed. Arvarh E. Strickland and Robert E. Weems Jr. (Westport, Conn.: Greenwood, 2001), 33–43. On skill and wage disparities structuring a split labor market, see David M. Gordon, Richard Edwards, and Michael Reich, *Segmented Work, Divided Workers: The Historical Transformation of Labor in the United States* (New York: Cambridge University Press, 1982); Richard Edwards, *Contested Terrain: The Transformation of the Workplace in the Twentieth Century* (New York: Basic Books, 1979). On antiblack hostility and white identity in the labor movement, see David R. Roediger, *The Wages of Whiteness: Race and the Making of the American Working Class* (London: Verso, 1991). On workers' interracial unity, see Eric Arnesen, *Waterfront Workers of New Orleans: Race, Class and Politics, 1863–1923* (New York: Oxford University Press, 1991), viii–ix.

6. "'Old Hog Hide' Is Oldest Existing Civil Record in Entire Northwest," *ESLDJ,* August 8, 1926, 2-A; "Slavery in Illinois First Existed at Old Town of St. Philip," *ESLDJ,* September 8, 1918, section 2, 1; Mason McCloud Fishback, "Illinois Legislation on Slavery and Free Negroes, 1818–1865," *Transactions of the Illinois State Historical Society* 9 (1904): 417. On "Black Laws," see Helen Cox Tregillis, *River Roads to Freedom: Fugitive Slave Notices and Sheriff Notices Found in Illinois Sources* (Bowie, Md.: Heritage Books, 1988). On slavery in the Northwest Ordinance, see Paul Finkelman, *Slavery and the Founders: Race and Liberty in the Age of Jefferson* (Armonk, N.Y.: M. E. Sharpe, 1996). On slavery in preplantation or non-plantation colonial economies, see Daniel H. Usner Jr., *Indians, Settlers, & Slaves*

in a Frontier Exchange Economy: The Lower Mississippi Valley before 1783 (Chapel Hill: University of North Carolina Press, 1992), 6–9, 276–86; Peter H. Wood, *Black Majority: Negroes in Colonial South Carolina from 1670 through the Stono Rebellion* (New York: Knopf, 1974), 13–34.

7. "Negroes, a Political Issue in Early Southern Illinois History," folder 7, box 29, Negro in Illinois Papers; Finkelman, *Slavery and the Founders*, passim; Fishback, "Illinois Legislation on Slavery and Free Negroes," 417–19; Elmer Gertz, "The Black Laws of Illinois," *Journal of the Illinois State Historical Society* 56, no. 3 (Autumn 1963): 454–73; Tregillis, *River Roads to Freedom*, 2–13; Sylvestre C. Watkins Sr., "Some of Early Illinois' Free Negroes," *Journal of the Illinois State Historical Society* 56, no. 3 (Autumn 1963): 495–507; Juliet E. K. Walker, *Free Frank: A Black Pioneer on the Antebellum Frontier* (Lexington: University Press of Kentucky, 1983), 98–101. On opposing kidnappers, see "Slaves Sold to Illinois Landholders," *ESLDJ*, September 6, 1925, 2-A.

8. U.S. Bureau of the Census, *Seventh Census of the United States, 1850, Population Schedules, Illinois*, reel 20, "St. Clair County," and *Eighth Census of the United States, 1860, Population Schedules, Illinois*, M653, reel 224, "St. Clair County" (all population schedules hereafter cited are from the U.S. Census Bureau's decennial national census for the year stated). All calculations are by the author. Benjamin G. Merkel, "The Underground Railroad and the Missouri Borders, 1840–1860," *Missouri Historical Review* 37 (April 1943): 271–85; Robert P. Howard, *Illinois: A History of the Prairie State* (Grand Rapids, MI: Eerdmans, 1972).

9. Sundiata Keita Cha-Jua, *America's First Black Town: Brooklyn, Illinois, 1830–1915* (Urbana: University of Illinois Press, 2000), 1–3, 11–23.

10. "The Colored Immigrants," *East St. Louis Gazette*, April 1, 1876, folder 43, "Notes on African-Americans in East St. Louis," box 10, Negro in Illinois Papers. *1880 Population Schedules, Illinois*, T9, reel 246, "St. Clair County"; *1900 Population Schedules, Illinois*, T623, reels 340, 341, "St. Clair County"; all calculations are by the author. On black people in the Ohio River border region, see Joe William Trotter Jr., *River Jordan: African American Urban Life in the Ohio Valley* (Lexington: University Press of Kentucky, 1998), xiii–xv, 44–51. On black southerners' politicized actions connecting labor issues to democracy during Reconstruction and in the Populist and other social movements, see W. E. B. Du Bois, *Black Reconstruction in America, 1860–1880* (reprint, New York: Vintage Books, 1995), 15–16; Eric Foner, *Reconstruction: America's Unfinished Revolution, 1863–1877* (New York: Harper and Row, 1988), 289–91; Hahn, *Nation under Our Feet*, 163–313. On postbellum black migrations to Kansas, Oklahoma, and elsewhere, see Nell Irvin Painter, *Exodusters: Black Migration to Kansas after Reconstruction* (Kansas: University Press of Kansas, 1976), 156–59. On black migrations to achieve prosperity, see Kenneth M. Hamilton, *Black Towns and Profit: Promotion and Development in the Trans-Appalachian West, 1877–1915* (Urbana: University of Illinois Press, 1991).

11. *Directory of East St. Louis, Fairmont, National City, Washington Park, Illinois* (East St. Louis, Ill.: J. Lethem, printer, 1924, hereafter cited as *1924 City Directory*). All calculations are by the author. R. F. Rucker in *House Transcripts*, 1849–50.

12. Robert A. Tyson, *History of East St. Louis: Its Resources, Statistics, Railroads, Physical Features, Business and Advantages* (East St. Louis, Ill.: John Haps, 1875), 94. "Directory of 1887," *East St. Louis Journal,* January 2, 1944, 5 (hereafter cited as *ESLJ*); *1906 City Directory,* City Directories of the United States, segment IV, 1902–35 (Woodbridge, Conn.: Research Publications, 1970–), microform, reel 1.; Clementine R. Hamilton, *The Ebony Tree* (East St. Louis, Ill.: privately printed, [1971?]), 50, 52, 54; St. Paul Baptist Church, *1999 Annual Reports,* 91. *1880 Population Schedules, Illinois,* listed Timothy Peacock's first wife, Kentucky-born Sarah, "keeping house"; Illinois-born Mary Chism (or Chisum), "keeping house"; and her husband John, a laborer. *1900 Population Schedules, Illinois,* listed Peacock, teamster; Zelphia Williams's Georgia-born husband, plasterer; Peacock's second wife, Charity, and Zelphia Williams without occupations; widowed Mary Chism, washerwoman. The 1900 census listed Chism born in Missouri as Chiseau. Lampley listed in *1920 Population Schedules, Illinois,* T625, reel 404, "St. Clair County." "First Negro Catholic Church Recently Occupied Gets Name from African Bishop, A.D. 343," *ESLDJ,* January 4, 1925, section 4, 1-C, 6-C.

13. "To Stall Officers," *ESLDJ,* January 23, 1906, 2; "Deaths and Funerals," *ESLDJ,* May 8, 1907, 3; "Negro Veteran Dies," *ESLJ,* February 5, 1934, 1; "The Colored Folks from the Other Side of the River," *East St. Louis Gazette,* August 14, 1869, 3; "The Corner Stone of the New Building of the G.U.O.F. (Colored)," *East St. Louis Gazette,* April 15, 1876; "City and County News," *East St. Louis Gazette,* August 31, 1878, 3, folder 22, "Notes on African American Social Life in East St. Louis, Illinois," box 38, Negro in Illinois Papers; "Negro Prominent in Lodge Circles Taken by Death," *ESLDJ,* May 27, 1927, 5; "25 Years Ago in East St. Louis," *ESLJ,* July 31, 1934, 4. Henry Jones's and John Woods's occupations in *City Directory of East St. Louis and a Street Directory* (East St. Louis, Ill.: East St. Louis Publishing, 1912, hereafter cited as *1912 City Directory*). "Convention Closed," *ESLDJ,* July 21, 1901, 2; "Mrs. Pyron's Funeral," *ESLDJ,* August 27, 1906, 4. In *1900 Population Schedules, Illinois,* Maggie Pyron's husband, Albert, was a machinist. On Grand Army of the Republic's significance for African American Civil War veterans in all-black and integrated GAR posts, see Barbara A. Gannon, "The Won Cause: Black and White Comradeship in the Grand Army of the Republic" (Ph.D. diss., Pennsylvania State University, 2005).

14. *1850 Population Schedules, Illinois,* reel 20, "St. Clair County"; *1860 Population Schedules, Illinois,* M653, reel 224, "St. Clair County"; *1870 Population Schedules, Illinois,* M593, reel 279, "St. Clair County"; *1880 Population Schedules, Illinois,* T9, reel 246, "St. Clair County"; *1900 Population Schedules, Illinois,* T623, reels 340, 341, "St. Clair County"; *1912 City Directory.* All calculations are by the author.

15. *Population Schedules, Illinois,* for 1850 through 1900; *1912 City Directory.* All calculations are by the author. On late nineteenth-century Atlanta and urban black women in nonindustrial occupations, see Hunter, *To 'Joy My Freedom,* 26–27, 56–59, 74–82.

16. Andrew J. Theising, *Made in USA: East St. Louis, the Rise and Fall of an Industrial River Town* (St. Louis, Mo.: Virginia Publishing, 2003), 9–11; Richard

Wade, *The Urban Frontier: Pioneer Life in Early Pittsburgh, Cincinnati, Lexington, Louisville, and St. Louis* (Chicago: University of Chicago Press, 1959), 39–42; Paul W. Gates, *Landlords and Tenants on the Prairie Frontier* (Ithaca, N.Y.: Cornell University Press, 1973); Wyatt Winton Belcher, *The Economic Rivalry Between St. Louis and Chicago, 1850–1880* (New York: Columbia University Press, 1947); Eric H. Monkkonen, *America Becomes Urban: The Development of U.S. Cities and Towns, 1780–1980* (Berkeley: University of California Press, 1988).

17. "The Great Ferry Monopoly" and "The Wooden Railroad," *ESLJ*, Jubilee Edition, May 26, 1940, 12-C, 8-D, 10-D; Carl R. Baldwin, "East St. Louis," *St. Louis Commerce*, November 1982, 69–70; Tyson, *History of East St. Louis*, 24; Theising, *Made in USA*, 63; Zane L. Miller and Patricia M. Melvin, *The Urbanization of Modern America: A Brief History*, 2d ed. (San Diego, Calif.: Harcourt, Brace, Jovanovich, 1987); "The Wooden Railroad," *ESLJ*, Jubilee Edition, May 26, 1940, 8-D, 10-D.

18. "High Lights," in *East St. Louis Centennial Program, 1861–1961* (East St. Louis, Ill.: Centennial Committee, 1961). On railroads in Atlanta, see Hunter, *To 'Joy My Freedom*, 44–45; *1912 City Directory*, 1415. The Mobile & Ohio, Illinois Central, Louisville & Nashville, Chicago, Burlington & Quincy, and Great Northern railroads were among those that operated equipment repair facilities and freight houses in East St. Louis.

19. "East St. Louis: Manifesting Determination to Hold Enviable Station Won among Important Cities of the Union," *ESLDJ*, May 22, 1901, 2. On the city as an economic growth machine, see Logan and Molotch, *Urban Fortunes*, 13, 32–37, 52–57.

20. "A Cowardly Assassin," *St. Louis Globe Democrat*, November 21, 1885, 7; "City Celebrated When First Building Was Erected above Level Reached by 1844 Flood," *ESLDJ*, August 24, 1924, 1-C; "Stock Yards Horse and Mule Market 25 Years Old," *ESLDJ*, April 8, 1920, 1; "National Stock Yards," *ESLDJ*, January 23, 1923, 10; Tyson, *History of East St. Louis*, 122–25; Ellen Nore, *St. Louis National Stockyards Company: East Side Story, 125 Years* (St. Louis: St. Louis National Stockyards Company, 1998), 2.

21. Belcher, *Economic Rivalry Between St. Louis and Chicago*; Jeffrey S. Adler, *Yankee Merchants and the Making of the Urban West: The Rise and Fall of Antebellum St. Louis* (New York: Cambridge University Press, 1991); James Neal Primm, *Lion of the Valley: St. Louis, Missouri, 1764–1980*, 3d ed. (St. Louis: Missouri Historical Society Press, 1998), 188–226; J. L. Pennifill, Vice President, Springfield, Jerseyville & St. Louis Railway, to T. J. Potter, Assistant General Manager, CB&Q RR, October 1, 1880, Burlington Archives, Newberry Library, Chicago.

22. "Early Realtor Boosted City," *ESLJ*, Jubilee Edition, May 26, 1940, 12-D; "About the New Bridge," *ESLDJ*, February 24, 1901, 4; "Present Name of E. St. Louis Adopted before Civil War," *ESLDJ*, June 15, 1924, 1-C, 3-C; Theising, *Made in USA*, 68. On renaming towns after culturally advanced cities, see Kenneth T. Jackson, *Crabgrass Frontier: The Suburbanization of the United States* (New York: Oxford University Press, 1985), 272; "Semi-Centennial of East St. Louis," *ESLDJ*,

April 11, 1915, 4, 5. Names of prominent landowners and subdivisions on East St. Louis plat maps in *Standard Atlas of St. Clair County, Illinois, Including a Plat Book* (Chicago: Geo. A. Ogle, 1901).

23. "No More Floods," *ESLJ*, Jubilee Edition, May 26, 1940, 10-E, 14-E; Theising, *Made in USA*, 72–73.

24. "Semi-Centennial of East St. Louis," *ESLDJ*, April 11, 1915, 4–5; *1912 City Directory*, 1325, 1335; "Eads Bridge, Wonder Span," *ESLJ*, Jubilee Edition, May 26, 1940, 1-D; Baldwin, "East St. Louis," 70; Tyson, *History of East St. Louis*, 46–51; Theising, *Made in USA*, 64, 72–83, 134–35; "'English' McCarthy Settled in East St. Louis in 1765," *ESLDJ*, February 10, 1929, 1-A, 2-A; "The Great Charter Battle," *ESLJ*, Jubilee Edition, May 26, 1940, 10-F; G. Ishmael Williams, Marlesa A. Gray, W. Kevin Pope, *Gateway to the Past: Cultural Resources Investigations in East St. Louis, Illinois* (Springfield: Illinois Department of Transportation, 1982), 1:95–97; "Present Name of E. St. Louis Adopted before Civil War," *ESLDJ*, June 15, 1924, 1-C, 3-C.; "East St. Louis," *St. Louis Evening Post*, July 19, 1878, [2]; "The Bloody City," *St. Louis Evening Post*, July 24, 1878, 1; "A Cowardly Assassin," *St. Louis Globe Democrat*, November 21, 1885, 7; "Mayor Bowman Murder Still Unsolved Crime," *ESLJ*, Jubilee Edition, May 26, 1940, 10-F, 12-F, 14-F; untitled document on Melbern Stephens, Allen Papers, privately owned by Andrew Theising; *Illinois and Its Builders* (N.p.: Illinois Biographical Association, 1925), 314; "Moving West Side Dirt to Raise Levels," *ESLDJ*, January 24, 1926, 1-C; Melbern Stephens in real estate in *1912 City Directory*, 1471.

25. On industrial suburbs, see Graham Romeyn Taylor, *Satellite Cities: A Study of Industrial Suburbs* (New York: Appleton, 1915; reprint, New York: Arno Press, New York Times, 1970), 2–27, 127–135; Edward Greer, *Big Steel: Black Politics and Corporate Power in Gary, Indiana* (New York: Monthly Review Press, 1979), 51–71; Mohl and Betten, *Steel City: Urban and Ethnic Patterns in Gary, Indiana, 1906–1950* (New York: Holmes & Meier, 1986), 10–25; Cumbler, A Social History of Economic Decline; John T. Cumbler, *A Social History of Economic Decline: Business, Politics, and Work in Trenton* (New Brunswick, N.J.: Rutgers University Press, 1989); Spencer R. Crew, *Black Life in Secondary Cities: A Comparative Analysis of the Black Communities of Camden and Elizabeth, N.J., 1860–1920* (New York: Garland, 1993), 87–88; Peter Gottlieb, *Making Their Own Way: Southern Blacks' Migration to Pittsburgh, 1916–30* (Urbana: University of Illinois Press, 1987).

26. "East St. Louis: A Short Review of Its History," *ESLDJ*, June 14, 1902, 2–8.

27. Theising, *Made in USA*, 95–97, 99, 122.

28. "Stock Yards Horse and Mule Market 25 Years Old," *ESLDJ*, April 8, 1920, 1; "National Stock Yards," *ESLDJ*, January 23, 1923, 10; Tyson, *History of East St. Louis*, 122–25; Nore, *St. Louis National Stockyards Company*, 2, 4, 6–11,14. The Stockyards rapidly expanded its capacity: in 1874 it handled 234,002 cattle, 498,840 hogs, 41,407 sheep, and 2,335 horses and mules, and in 1906, 1,121,380 cattle, 1,923,209 hogs, 578,652 sheep, and 166,393 horses and mules, as reported in "East St. Louis: A Short Review of Its History," *ESLDJ*, June 14, 1902, 2–8; "Armour's East St. Louis Packing Plant Now Ready for Business," *ESLDJ*, February

22, 1903, 8; *East St. Louis Retail Merchants Association Commercial Profile, 1907* (n.p.: n.p., 1907), 11; *1912 City Directory,* 1355–56.

29. Paul Y. Anderson in *House Transcripts,* 275; "East St. Louis: A Short Review of Its History," *ESLDJ,* June 14, 1902, 2–8; American Steel Foundries in "Iron and Steel Industry," *ESLDJ,* October 25, 1909, 6.

30. Robert P. Howard, *Illinois: A History of the Prairie State* (Grand Rapids, Mich.: Eerdmans, 1972), 444; Joseph N. Fining, *Economic and Other Facts Regarding East St. Louis* (East St. Louis, Ill.: Chamber of Commerce, 1920), 28–30, 32–35, 39–41, 43–45; "East St. Louis: A Short Review of Its History," *ESLDJ,* June 14, 1902, 2–8; Duncan C. Smith, "Know Your East St. Louis: Aluminum, an Interesting Story about an East St. Louis Industry," *East St. Louis Today,* no. 4 (April 1936): 7–8; *Aluminum Ore Co.: East St. Louis Works* (company pamphlet, 1948), 4–7.

31. U.S. Bureau of the Census, *Thirteenth Census of the United States, 1910: Bulletin: Population: Illinois* (1913), 30. According to census figures, in 1900 white East St. Louis was 85.9 percent native-born and 14.0 percent foreign-born, and in 1910, 81.9 percent of whites were native-born and 17.8 percent were foreign-born; "East St. Louis," *ESLDJ,* June 14, 1902, 2–8. No published census tabulations correlating place of origin and occupation with gender and race or nationality exist.

32. John P. Pero and Alois Towers in *House Transcripts,* 695, 703, and 2387.

33. John P. Pero, Philip Wolf, and Alois Towers in *House Transcripts,* 695, 703, 2265, and 2387. On certain European immigrant groups first seen as "not white," see Noel Ignatiev, *How the Irish Became White* (New York: Routledge, 1995); Matthew Frye Jacobson, *Whiteness of a Different Color: European Immigration and the Alchemy of Race* (Cambridge, Mass.: Harvard University Press, 1998); James R. Grossman, "'Amiable Peasantry' or 'Social Burden': Constructing a Place for Black Southerners," in *American Exceptionalism? U.S. Working-Class Formation in an International Context,* ed. Rick Halpern and Jonathan Morris (New York: St. Martin's Press, 1997), 230; Barbara J. Fields, "Whiteness, Racism, and Identity," *International Labor and Working-Class History* 60 (Fall 2001): 48–60, and "Of Rogues and Geldings," *American Historical Review* 108 (December 2003): 1397–1405; "25 Years Ago in East St. Louis," *ESLJ,* April 16, 1933, 4.

34. McLaughlin, *Power, Community, and Racial Killing in East St. Louis,* 14–17.

35. Trotter, *Black Milwaukee,* xii.

36. Montgomery, *Fall of the House of Labor,* 44–57 passim; "A New Concept for Labor," *ESLJ,* May 26, 1940, 10-E; mention of Stephens as a real estate man in McLaughlin, *Power, Community, and Racial Killing in East St. Louis,* 206n89.

37. "The '77 Rail Strike," *ESLJ,* May 26, 1940, 9-D, 14-D; Williams, Gray, and Pope, *Gateway to the Past,* 118.

38. "The '77 Rail Strike," *ESLJ,* May 26, 1940, 9-D, 14-D; Williams, Gray, and Pope, *Gateway to the Past,* 118–20; David T. Burbank, *Reign of the Rabble: The St. Louis General Strike of 1877* (New York: A. M. Kelley, 1966), 2–3, 6–12 passim. Available sources do not specify whether black workers participated as Workingmen's Party strike leaders.

39. "The '77 Rail Strike," *ESLJ*, May 26, 1940, 9-D, 14-D. Unfortunately, sources did not reveal the names of black labor activists. On the Knights, see Leon Fink, *Workingmen's Democracy: The Knights of Labor and American Politics* (Urbana: University of Illinois Press, 1983). On the Knights' interracial unity, see Peter Rachleff, *Black Labor in the South: Richmond, Virginia, 1865–1890* (Philadelphia: Temple University Press, 1984), 117–20, 169–76. The Knights' interracial unity excluded Chinese American workers. See Alexander Saxton, *The Indispensable Enemy: Labor and the Anti-Chinese Movement in California* (Berkeley: University of California Press, 1971); Jehu Baker, "To the Voters of the 18th Congressional District: Election Frauds That Endanger the Integrity of Elections in St. Clair County and in the 18th Congressional District: Hon. Jehu Baker's Exposure of Ballot Corruption in East St. Louis, and Appeal to the Voters of the 18th Congressional District" [1886?]; "A Cowardly Assassin," *St. Louis Globe Democrat*, November 21, 1885, 7; "Semi-Centennial of East St. Louis," *ESLDJ*, April 11, 1915, 4–5; "A New Concept for Labor," *ESLJ*, May 26, 1940, 10-E; Williams, Gray, and Pope, *Gateway to the Past*, 121.

40. Baker, "To the Voters of the 18th Congressional District; "East St. Louis Parties," *ESLDJ*, March 29, 1900, 2.

41. On progressives imposing order, see Robert H. Wiebe, *The Search for Order, 1877–1920* (New York: Hill and Wang, 1967); Zane Miller, *Boss Cox's Cincinnati: Urban Politics in the Progressive Era* (New York: Oxford University Press, 1968); "The So-Called Republican Ticket," *ESLDJ*, February 25, 1901, 2; "What the Citizens' Party Has Done," *ESLDJ*, March 24, 1901, 4; "Citizens Convention," *ESLDJ*, March 17, 1901, 4; "The Friend of Organized Labor," *ESLDJ*, March 24, 1901, 4; "A New Concept for Labor," *ESLJ*, May 26, 1940, 10-E.

42. "Trades and Labor Union," *ESLDJ*, January 12, 1892, 1; "A New Concept for Labor," *ESLJ*, May 26, 1940, 10-E.

43. Ira Berlin et al., *Slaves No More: Three Essays on Emancipation and the Civil War* (New York: Cambridge University Press, 1992), 4–5, 15–50; Lloyd A. Hunter, "Slavery in St. Louis, 1804–1860," *Bulletin of the Missouri Historical Society* 30 (July 1974): 233–65; Edward A. Miller Jr., *The Black Civil War Soldiers of Illinois: The Story of the Twenty-ninth U.S. Colored Infantry* (Columbia: University of South Carolina Press, 1998), 5–36; "Negro Veteran Dies," *ESLJ*, February 5, 1934, 1.

44. On the North, see, for example, Loewen, *Sundown Towns*; on the South, see Foner, *Reconstruction*, xxv–xxvi.

45. Irving Dilliard, "Civil Liberties of Negroes in Illinois since 1865," *Journal of the Illinois State Historical Society* 56, no. 3 (Autumn 1963): 593–94; Illinois State Convention of Colored Men, *Proceedings of the Illinois State Convention of Colored Men Assembled at Galesburg . . .* (Chicago: Church, Goodman and Donnelley, 1867).

46. On the postbellum South, see C. Vann Woodward, *Origins of the New South, 1877–1913* (Baton Rouge: Louisiana State University Press, 1951), 107–395; John W. Cell, *The Highest Stage of White Supremacy: The Origins of Segregation in South Africa and the American South* (New York: Cambridge University Press,

1982), 82–102. On the postbellum North, see David M. Katzman, *Before the Ghetto: Black Detroit in the Nineteenth Century* (Urbana: University of Illinois Press, 1973), 50, 175–206. On discriminatory laws not labeled as antiblack legislation, see David Delaney, *Race, Place, and the Law, 1836–1948* (Austin: University of Texas Press, 1998). On decades of antiblack mass social violence that also occurred in the North, see Zangrando, *NAACP Crusade against Lynching*. On black women in politics, see Elsa Barkley Brown, "Negotiating and Transforming the Public Sphere: African American Political Life in the Transition from Slavery to Freedom," *Public Culture* 7 (1994): 107–46; "To the Colored Voters of St. Clair County," folder 14, "Notes on African-Americans in East St. Louis, 1865–1916," box 29, Negro in Illinois Papers. On Union League chapters elsewhere, see Michael W. Fitzgerald, *The Union League Movement in the Deep South: Politics and Agricultural Change during Reconstruction* (Baton Rouge: Louisiana State University Press, 1989), 127–35; Dilliard, "Civil Liberties of Negroes in Illinois since 1865," 594; Helen Horney and William E. Keller, "The Negro's Two Hundred Forty Years in Illinois: A Chronology," *Journal of the Illinois State Historical Society* 56, no. 3 (Autumn 1963): 435–36.

47. Trotter, *River Jordan*, 78, 86. On battles over public schools in Alton, Illinois, see Shirley J. Portwood, "'We Lifted Our Voices in Thunder Tones': African American Race Men and Race Women and Community Agency in Southern Illinois, 1895–1910," *Journal of Urban History* 26 (2000): 740–58; Adam Fairclough, "'Being in the Field of Education and also Being a Negro . . . Seems . . . Tragic': Black Teachers in the Jim Crow South," *Journal of American History* 87 (June 2000): 65; *Proceedings of the Illinois State Convention of Colored Men*, 7. On exclusionism, see, for example, Howard N. Rabinowitz, *Race Relations in the Urban South, 1865–1890* (Urbana: University of Illinois Press, 1980), 164–65; "Schools and Education in East St. Louis," folder 27, "Notes on African Americans in East St. Louis Schools, 1867–1940," box 14, Negro in Illinois Papers; "Captain Robinson, Most Colorful Negro Character of City," *ESLDJ*, February 28, 1926, 3-A; "Will Erect a Memorial to Ex-Slave," *St. Louis Argus*, February 26, 1926, 1; Tyson, *History of East St. Louis*, 94; Hamilton, *Ebony Tree*, 33; Edward English, *The Good Things of East St. Louis* (Mascoutah, Ill.: Top's Books, 1992), 2. On de facto racial segregation, see Joel Williamson, *The Crucible of Race: Black-White Relations in the American South since Emancipation* (New York: Oxford University Press, 1984), 50–61. On de jure segregation before the 1890s, see Leon F. Litwack, *Trouble in Mind: Black Southerners in the Age of Jim Crow* (New York: Vintage Books, 1998), xiii–xvii. On de jure segregation forming in the 1890s as a system enforcing physical, not social, distance, see C. Vann Woodward, *The Strange Career of Jim Crow*, 2d ed. rev. (New York: Oxford University Press, 1966), vii, ix; Illinois General Assembly, *Journal of the House of Representatives of the Twenty-ninth General Assembly of the State of Illinois* (Springfield: State Journal Steam Printer, 1875), 37, 119; "Schools and Education in East St. Louis."

48. "Notes on African-Americans in East St. Louis Schools, 1867–1940," folder 27, box 14, Negro in Illinois Papers. Fifty-six-year-old Virginia-born Hutchinson

was also a laborer. Other ad hoc committee members were forty-six-year-old Mississippi-born laborer John Browning, twenty-five-year-old Missouri-born teamster John Campbell, thirty-three-year-old Missouri-born teamster Henry Ellington, Jack Ferguson, Edwin Hayes, forty-year-old Virginia-born laborer Edward Henry, John Henry, James Hightower, thirty-six-year-old Illinois-born laborer Hagan Jarrett, Alexander Johnson, thirty-one-year-old Mississippi-born laborer Eli Morrison, Elizabeth Pittman, Jake Scott, Joseph Smith, Sarah Stevenson, Charles Wilson, and Molly Wilson. Data for Edward Henry and Hutchinson in *1870 Population Schedules, Illinois;* for Browning, Campbell, Ellington, Jarrett, and Morrison, in *1880 Population Schedules, Illinois.* The 1880 census does not make clear which of the two men named Charles Wilson, the twenty-four-year-old Missouri-born steamboat deck hand or the thirty-year-old Mississippi-born laborer, was on the committee. "Schools and Education in East St. Louis," folder 27, "Notes on African-Americans in East St. Louis Schools, 1867–1940," box 14, Negro in Illinois Papers. Robinson's title of Captain was an honorary one, according to "'Cap'n' Robinson Most Colorful Negro Character of City," *ESLDJ,* February 28, 1926, 3A.

49. James D. Anderson, *The Education of Blacks in the South, 1860–1935* (Chapel Hill: University of North Carolina Press, 1988). Quoted passage in Adam Fairclough, *Teaching Equality: Black Schools in the Age of Jim Crow* (Athens: University of Georgia Press, 2001), 5–10, 14–19.

50. "A New Concept for Labor," *ESLJ,* May 26, 1940, 10-E. On African Americans voting for the Democratic Party in the late nineteenth century, see August Meier, *Negro Thought in America, 1880–1915: Racial Ideologies in the Age of Booker T. Washington* (Ann Arbor: University of Michigan Press, 1963), 26–33.

51. "At a Mass Meeting of Colored Voters," *ESLDJ,* March 27, 1894, 3; "Colored People Want Municipal Jobs," *ESLDJ,* July 25, 1894, 3, evidence of black firefighters has not been found; "Republican League Club," *ESLDJ,* August 25, 1894; *1880 Population Schedules, Illinois,* listed Tennessee-born Daniel Jenkins at age nine, his Mississippi-born father, a laborer, and his mother, an Alabaman. "Colored Mass Meeting," *ESLDJ,* July 18, 1895, 3; "The Colored Vote Changed," *ESLDJ,* March 5, 1896, 2, denouncing the People's Party were Harvey T. Bowman, Isaac Bryant, Rev. W. G. Colby, A. Collier, C. B. Jones, Missouri-born laborer James Reese, F. M. Smith, and Thomas Wiley; *1990 Population Schedules, Illinois,* listed Missouri-born Bowman as an editor. In the population schedules, C. B. Jones was either Illinois-born Charles Jones, a teamster, Mississippi-born Clem Jones, a barber, or Missouri-born Columbus Jones, a packinghouse hog scrapper. Bowman as editor of the *Advance Citizen* in "Cook Charges Negro Padded City Payroll," *ESLDJ,* September 24, 1926, 1A, 10A.

52. "The Colored Voters Return to the Citizens' Party," *ESLDJ,* March 28, 1897, 4; "East St. Louis Politics," *ESLDJ,* March 27, 1902, 2; "Unofficial Vote Cast in East St. Louis at Election, April 1, 1902," *ESLDJ,* April 2, 1902, 2.

53. On local chapters of the Afro-American Protective League of Illinois, see Sundiata Keita Cha-Jua, "'A Warlike Demonstration'": Legalism, Armed Resistance,

and Black Political Mobilization in Decatur, Illinois, 1894–1898," *Journal of Negro History* 83, no. 1 (Winter 1998): 52–72; "Notes on the Peoria Local of the Afro-American Protection League, 1895," folder 15, box 38, Negro in Illinois Papers; "A Successful Convention," *Illinois Record,* November 27, 1897, 1; "A Successful Convention of the Afro-Am. League, Jas. H. Porter Elected President," *Illinois Record,* October 1, 1898, 1, 3. On the National Afro-American League, see Emma Lou Thornbrough, "The National Afro-American League, 1887–1908," *Journal of Southern History* 27 (November 1961): 494–512. Chavis quoted in "The Afro-American League," *Illinois Record,* November 13, 1897, 1.

54. William Cohen, *At Freedom's Edge: Black Mobility and the Southern White Quest for Racial Control, 1861–1915* (Baton Rouge: Louisiana State University Press, 1991), xiv–xvi.

55. Dewey W. Grantham, *Southern Progressivism: The Reconciliation of Progress and Tradition* (Knoxville: University of Tennessee Press, 1983), 240–41; Meier, *Negro Thought in America,* 100–18, 161–206; Louis R. Harlan, *Booker T. Washington: The Wizard of Tuskegee, 1901–1915* (New York: Oxford University Press, 1985), 224–28; Linda O. McMurry, *To Keep the Waters Troubled: The Life of Ida B. Wells* (New York: Oxford University Press, 1999), 255–57; David Levering Lewis, *W. E. B. Du Bois: Biography of a Race, 1868–1919* (New York: Holt, 1993), 243–45.

56. Meier, *Negro Thought in America,* 118. On Washington and the radicals' perspectives, see Christopher Robert Reed, *The Chicago NAACP and the Rise of Black Professional Leadership, 1910–1966* (Bloomington: Indiana University Press, 1997), 11; National Negro Business League, *Twentieth Annual Meeting: Held at St. Louis, Missouri, August 13, 14, 15, 1919,* in Records of the National Negro Business League, Part I: Annual Conference Proceedings and Organizational Records, 1900–1919 (Bethesda, Md.: University Publications of America, 1994), microfilm, 3:00669–00670; "Notes on the Peoria Local of the Afro-American Protection League, 1895," folder 15, box 38, Negro in Illinois Papers; "To President McKinley," *ESLDJ,* December 7, 1898, 3. Committee members were clergymen D. J. Donohue, William M. Collins, John DeShields, Orlando H. Banks, and Gran A. Duncan and laypersons Joseph Cooksey, Sarah H. Banks, John Gibbs, and schoolteacher Minnie C. Scott; *1900 Population Schedules, Illinois,* listed Sarah Banks as wife of Orlando Banks. Minnie Scott's job in "Board of Education Eliminates Supervisors," *ESLDJ,* May 13, 1913, 1, 4. On the Fortune-Washington relationship, see Louis R. Harlan, ed., *The Booker T. Washington Papers* (Urbana: University of Illinois Press, 1972), 2:327–28, 357–58.

57. "Politics in East St. Louis" and "East St. Louis Politics," *Illinois Record,* September 3, 1898, 1 and 2; "East St. Louis," *Illinois Record,* February 11, 1899, 3; "Illinois Negroes Organize," *Illinois Record,* April 9, 1898, 1; "Colored Recruits," *ESLDJ,* July 5, 1898, 3; "The State Convention," *Illinois Record,* September 17, 1918, 2; "East St. Louis," *Illinois Record,* February 11, 1899, 3.

58. "Col. John Robinson's Reception," *ESLDJ,* January 11, 1897, 3; "Col. John Robinson Gets Job," *ESLDJ,* January 15, 1905, 8; "East St. Louis, Ill.," *Illinois Record,* May 28, 1898, 3; Hamilton, *Ebony Tree,* 4; *1900 Population Schedules, Illi-*

nois; "Colored Citizens," *ESLDJ,* March 25, 1903, 3; "East St. Louis ILL.," *Illinois Record,* May 7, 1898, 3; "Negro Council Club," *ESLDJ,* February 24, 1901, 5. Negro Council Club leading members in 1901 included Daniel Adams, T. Barefield, W. W. Buchanan, Mississippi-born Madison Crosby (i.e., Cosby), Mississippi-born Thomas Green, Kentucky-born S. W. Hawkins, George Kyle, Arkansas-born William H. H. Pitts, and James Reese. *1900 Population Schedules, Illinois,* listed Cosby, Green, and Hawkins as self-employed teamsters and Pitts as city hall janitor; "The Colored Citizens of the Second Ward," *ESLDJ,* March 23, 1900, 3; "Negro Council Club," *ESLDJ,* March 30, 1900, 3; "The Colored Voters," *ESLDJ,* April 5, 1900, 2.

59. On the nadir, see Rayford W. Logan, *The Negro in American Life and Thought: The Nadir, 1877–1901* (New York: Dial Press, 1954), 15–22. On ferment, see Meier, *Negro Thought in America,* 19–25, 161–70.

Chapter 2: The African American Political Experience, 1898–1915

1. Three works discuss African Americans, but not as significant political actors in pre-1915 East St. Louis: Elliott M. Rudwick, *Race Riot at East St. Louis, July 2, 1917* (Carbondale: Southern Illinois University Press, 1964), 17 passim; Andrew J. Theising, *Made in USA: East St. Louis, The Rise and Fall of an Industrial River Town* (St. Louis, Mo.: Virginia Publishing, 2003), 144 passim; and Malcolm McLaughlin, *Power, Community, and Racial Killing in East St. Louis* (New York: Palgrave Macmillan, 2005), 23 passim. On Wilmington, North Carolina, see David S. Cecelski and Timothy B. Tyson, *Democracy Betrayed: The Wilmington Race Riot and Its Legacy* (Chapel Hill: University of North Carolina Press, 1998), 5–6. On mass antiblack violence arising from decades of racism, discrimination, and legal and extralegal assaults on black people's citizenship, see, for example, William Ivy Hair, *Carnival of Fury: Robert Charles and the New Orleans Race Riot of 1900* (Baton Rouge: Louisiana State University Press, 1976); Roberta Senechal, *Sociogenesis of a Race Riot: Springfield, Illinois, in 1908* (Urbana: University of Illinois Press, 1990), 2, 5, 159–60, 175–77; Brian Butler, *An Undergrowth of Folly: Public Order, Race Anxiety, and the 1903 Evansville, Indiana Riot* (New York: Garland, 2000), 11–13; David Fort Godshalk, *Veiled Visions: The 1906 Atlanta Race Riot and the Reshaping of American Race Relations* (Chapel Hill: University of North Carolina Press, 2005).

2. "City's Population Trebled since Realtors Formed Board," *ESLDJ,* January 30, 1927, 2-E, 6-E, 10-E; "High Lights," in *East St. Louis Centennial Program, 1861–1961* (East St. Louis, Ill.: Centennial Committee, 1961); Theising, *Made in USA,* 135–38.

3. "Our Great Levee and Sanitary Project as It Was Organized and as It Stands," *ESLDJ,* November 4, 1923, 1-B, 2-B; *1912 City Directory,* 1459; "High Lights," in *East St. Louis Centennial Program, 1861–1961;* G. Ishmael Williams, Marlesa A. Gray, W. Kevin Pope, *Gateway to the Past: Cultural Resources Investigations in East St. Louis, Illinois* (Springfield: Illinois Department of Transportation, 1982), 113–15; Paul Y. Anderson, and E. J. Verlie, and Robert W. Sikking in *House*

Transcripts, 3812–24, and 4596–4617, and 4647–51; Theising, *Made in USA,* 139, 140, 142, 184.

4. *1912 City Directory,* 1339; "City's Population Trebled since Realtors Formed Board," *ESLDJ,* January 30, 1927, 2-E, 6-E, 10-E; Zane L. Miller and Patricia M. Melvin, *The Urbanization of Modern America: A Brief History,* 2d ed. (San Diego, Calif.: Harcourt, Brace, Jovanovich, 1987); John R. Logan and Harvey L. Molotch, *Urban Fortunes: The Political Economy of Place* (Berkeley: University of California Press, 1987) 20, 100–10; Theising, *Made in USA,* 7, 9–11.

5. Eric H. Monkkonen, *America Becomes Urban: The Development of U.S. Cities & Towns, 1780–1980* (Berkeley: University of California Press, 1988); Lura Mary Gard, "East St. Louis and the Railroads to 1875" (master's thesis, Washington University in St. Louis, 1947), 2, 12, 22, 176–80; W. R. Crompton to T. J. Potter, General Superintendent, CB&Q RR, November 24, 1879, "East St. Louis Papers, 1858, 1864, 1878–79," 33 1870 5.6, Burlington Archives; James Neal Primm, *Lion of the Valley: St. Louis, Missouri, 1764–1980,* 3d ed. (St. Louis: Missouri Historical Society Press, 1998), 200–25; Godshalk, *Veiled Visions,* 13–14, 17; "East St. Louis," *ESLDJ,* June 14, 1902, 2–8; "Coming of First Railroad Brought Rapid Growth Here," *ESLDJ,* July 13, 1924, 1-C, 6-C; Harland Bartholomew, *A Comprehensive City Plan for East St. Louis, Illinois: Prepared for the War Civics Committee* (East St. Louis, Ill.: Daily Journal, 1920), 1; Williams, Gray, and Pope, *Gateway to the Past,* 127; Kenneth M. Reardon, "State and Local Revitalization Efforts in East St. Louis, Illinois," in "Globalization and the Changing U.S. City," ed. David Wilson, special issue, *Annals of the American Academy of Political and Social Science* 551 (May 1997): 236; National and Union Live Stock Yards, Joint Rate Committee, J. W. Midgeley, Commissioner, Southwestern Railway Association, September 13, 1886, and W. L. Tamblyn, Chairman, National and Union Live Stock Yards, Joint Rate Committee, October 12, 1886, to Charles E. Perkins, Director, CB&Q RR, "Rates: Correspondence, Papers, Agreements, 1882–89," 33 1880 7.3, Burlington Archives.

6. Theising, *Made in USA,* 64–65, 95; Harry Dadisman Holmes, "Socio-Economic Patterns of Non-Partisan Political Behavior in the Industrial Metropolis: St. Louis, 1895–1916" (Ph.D. diss., University of Missouri, Columbia, 1973), 55–61; "Guaranty Agreement," 9 T3.2, "Terminal Railroad Association of St. Louis," Illinois Central Archives; W. W. Baldwin, *Corporate History of the Chicago, Burlington & Quincy Railroad Company and Affiliated Companies* (Chicago: The Railroad, 1917); "C. of C. Asks Rate Equality in New Plan," *ESLDJ,* April 12, 1928, 1, 2; "Terminal Held as Only Foe to Use of Bridge," *ESLDJ,* August 14, 1928, 1, 2.

7. Paul Y. Anderson in *House Transcripts,* 3798–3800, 3803–6.

8. On various cities' annexation campaigns, see Kenneth T. Jackson, *Crabgrass Frontier: The Suburbanization of the United States* (New York: Oxford University Press, 1985), 144–48; "Greater East St. Louis," *ESLDJ,* March 18, 1902, 2; "Annexation Questions," *ESLDJ,* March 20, 1902, 2; "Annexation of Winstanley Park, Alta Sita and Denverside," *ESLDJ,* March 21, 1902, 2; "Unofficial Vote Cast in East St. Louis," *ESLDJ,* April 2, 1902, 2.

9. "East St. Louis," [1918], [1], part I, series VI, E:87, National Urban League Records, Manuscript Division, Library of Congress, Washington, D.C.; "Incorporation Causes Fight," *ESLDJ*, August 15, 1906, 3; "25 Years Ago in East St. Louis," *ESLJ*, June 23, 1933, [4]; Robert E. Conway in *House Transcripts*, 143–44. "National City, Population of 465," *ESLDJ*, January 16, 1921, 3; "25 Years Ago in East St. Louis," *ESLJ*, November 24, 1933, 6; "25 Years Ago in East St. Louis," *ESLJ*, April 29, 1934, 4.

10. On social history of saloons, particularly working-class ones, see Madelon Powers, *Faces along the Bar: Lore and Order in the Workingman's Saloon, 1870–1920* (Chicago: University of Chicago Press, 1998). On saloons as working-class institutions that performed many functions, see James R. Barrett, *Work and Community in the Jungle: Chicago's Packinghouse Workers, 1894–1922* (Urbana: University of Illinois Press, 1987), 81–86. On middle- and upper-class people's saloons, see Mark Edward Lender and James Kirby Martin, *Drinking in America: A History*, rev. ed. (New York: Free Press, 1987). On social aspects of East St. Louis saloons, see McLaughlin, *Power, Community, and Racial Killing in East St. Louis*, 75–78, 80–82.

11. Rudwick, *Race Riot at East St. Louis*, 197–216; Alois Towers, and George W. Allison, and Robert E. Johns, and Anderson in *House Transcripts*, 2589, and 3548–52, and 4320–21, and 4421–22; Dennis R. Judd and Robert S. Mendelson, *The Politics of Urban Planning: The East St. Louis Experience* (Urbana: University of Illinois, 1973), 7; Towers, and W. A. Miller in *House Transcripts*, 2593, and 4064–87; Allison, and W. A. Miller in *House Transcripts*, 3554–55, and 4079–80; Mark Thomas Connelly, *The Response to Prostitution in the Progressive Era* (Chapel Hill: University of North Carolina Press, 1980); Philip Jenkins, "'A Wide-Open City': Prostitution in Progressive Era Lancaster," *Pennsylvania History* 65 (Autumn 1998): 509–26; Joel Best, *Controlling Vice: Regulating Brothel Prostitution in St. Paul, 1865–1883* (Columbus: Ohio State University Press, 1998).

12. Nulsen in *House Transcripts*, 1052. On East St. Louis saloons as incubators of criminal violence and havens for criminals, see McLaughlin, *Power, Community, and Racial Killing in East St. Louis*, 78–82.

13. On interracial sex districts in other cities, see, for example, Kevin J. Mumford, *Interzones: Black/White Sex Districts in Chicago and New York in the Early Twentieth Century* (New York: Columbia University Press, 1997), xii–xiii, 47; Allison, and H. H. Hunsaker in *House Transcripts*, 3502–6, and 4587–92; Myrtle Gardner quoted in "Exhibit G," *House Transcripts*, in *The East St. Louis Race Riot of 1917*, ed. Elliott Rudwick, reel 6 (Frederick, Md.: University Publications of America, 1985); Bevington in *House Transcripts*, 4388–93; Allison in *House Transcripts*, 3554–55; Theising, *Made in USA*, 141.

14. On progressives in Atlanta, see, for example, Gregory Mixon, *The Atlanta Riot: Race, Class, and Violence in a New South City* (Gainesville: University Press of Florida, 2005), 57–58; Anderson, and Towers, and Allison, and W. A. Miller, and Johns in *House Transcripts*, 280–81, 3835, and 2589, 2592–93, and 3500, and 4080–81, and 4320–21. During the Chicago race riot of July 1919, Ragen Colts, a

Chicago athletic club, was a group of antiblack assailants with political connections; see William M. Tuttle Jr., *Race Riot: Chicago in the Red Summer of 1919* (New York: Atheneum, 1970), 32–33; Miller and Melvin, *Urbanization of Modern America,* 54–55.

15. Robert Wiebe, *The Search for Order, 1877–1920* (New York: Hill and Wang, 1967).

16. Robert L. Allen, *Reluctant Reformers: Racism and Social Reform Movements in the United States* (Washington, D.C.: Howard University Press, 1974), 92–119; Dewey W. Grantham, *Southern Progressivism: The Reconciliation of Progress and Tradition* (Knoxville: University of Tennessee Press, 1983), 117–18, 123–27, 230–45; Christopher Robert Reed, *The Chicago NAACP and the Rise of Black Professional Leadership, 1910–1966* (Bloomington: Indiana University Press, 1997), 8–10. On white progressives generally and Jane Addams in particular, see, for example, Elisabeth Lasch-Quinn, *Black Neighbors: Race and the Limits of Reform in the American Settlement House Movement, 1890–1945* (Chapel Hill: University of North Carolina Press, 1993), 13–16; Valerie Babb, *Whiteness Visible: The Meaning of Whiteness in American Literature and Culture* (New York: New York University Press, 1998), 139–42. On racism in the first two decades of the twentieth century, see George M. Fredrickson, *The Black Image in the White Mind: The Debate on Afro-American Character and Destiny, 1817–1914* (New York: Harper and Row, 1971); I. A. Newby, *The Development of Segregationist Thought* (Homewood, Ill.: Dorsey Press, 1968).

17. On racism, hard work, and free labor, see Heather Cox Richardson, *The Death of Reconstruction: Race, Labor, and Politics in the Post–Civil War North, 1865–1901* (Cambridge, Mass.: Harvard University Press, 2001), xiv–xv, 243–45; Quincy Ewing, "The Heart of the Race Problem," *Atlantic Monthly* 103 (1909): 389–97. On progressive reformers' advocacy of time, patience, discipline, and education as a solution to the "Negro problem," see Ray Stannard Baker, *Following the Color Line: An Account of Negro Citizenship in the American Democracy* (New York: Doubleday, Page, 1908), 292–307. Grantham, *Southern Progressivism,* xvii, xix; "Negroes as Voters," *ESLDJ,* April 24, 1900, 4; J. Morgan Kousser, *The Shaping of Southern Politics: Suffrage Restriction and the Establishment of the One-Party South, 1880–1910* (New Haven, Conn.: Yale University Press, 1974); Philip A. Klinkner with Rogers M. Smith, *The Unsteady March: The Rise and Decline of Racial Equality in America* (Chicago: University of Chicago Press, 1999), 72–105; Alexander Keyssar, *The Right to Vote: The Contested History of Democracy in the United States* (New York: Basic Books, 2000).

18. On Jack Johnson symbolizing one aspect of white northerners' commitment to white supremacy, see Mumford, *Interzones,* 12, 17.

19. Joe William Trotter Jr., *River Jordan: African American Urban Life in the Ohio Valley* (Lexington: University Press of Kentucky, 1998), 64–65; Earl Lewis, *In Their Own Interests: Race, Class, and Power in Twentieth-Century Norfolk, Virginia* (Berkeley: University of California Press, 1991), 13–17; Walter A. Fogel, *The Negro in the Meat Industry* (Philadelphia: University of Pennsylvania Press, 1970), 18,

24–25, 27; *1912 City Directory.* All calculations are by the author. Alois Towers in *House Transcripts,* 2372.

20. John P. Pero in *House Transcripts,* 709–10. David Lee Lightner, "Labor on the Illinois Central Railroad, 1852–1900" (Ph.D. diss., Cornell University, 1969), 227–29; Frank A. Hunter and Robert E. Conway in *House Transcripts,* 93–94, and 125–26, 129, 181–82; Conway and Hunter in *Labor Committee Report,* 15–16, 22–23. On racism in the meatpacking industry, see Rick Halpern, *Down on the Killing Floor: Black and White Workers in Chicago's Packinghouses, 1904–54* (Urbana: University of Illinois Press, 1997); Charles B. Fox in *House Transcripts,* 1507, 1641, 1683–90; "25 Years Ago in East St. Louis," *ESLJ,* April 16, 1933, 4; Gordon Crook in *1912 City Directory;* Elijah Smith, a laborer, in "Chamber of Commerce Plans Forum Meeting in Honor of Late Inventor of Aluminum," *ESLJ,* February 24, 1936, 2.

21. Tuttle, *Race Riot,* 113–14, 144; Trotter, *River Jordan,* 67–68; Harry Kerr and Alois Towers in *House Transcripts,* 1901, 1911, 1913, 2010–11, and 2372, 2512–22, and 3195. On white working-class Americans and "whiteness," see, for example, David R. Roediger, *The Wages of Whiteness: Race and the Making of the American Working Class* (London: Verso, 1991).

22. Herbert G. Gutman, "The Negro and the United Mine Workers of America: The Career and Letters of Richard L. Davis and Something of Their Meaning, 1890–1900," in *Work, Culture, and Society in Industrializing America: Essays in American Working-Class and Social History* (New York: Vintage Books, 1977), 121–208; Peter Rachleff, *Black Labor in the South: Richmond, Virginia, 1865–1890* (Philadelphia: Temple University Press, 1984), 72–73; Eric Arnesen, *Waterfront Workers of New Orleans: Race, Class, and Politics, 1863–1923* (New York: Oxford University Press, 1998); Daniel Letwin, *The Challenge of Interracial Unionism: Alabama Coal Miners, 1878–1921* (Chapel Hill: University of North Carolina Press, 1998); Brian Kelly, *Race, Class, and Power in the Alabama Coalfields, 1908–21* (Urbana: University of Illinois Press, 2001); Towers and Edward F. Mason in *House Transcripts,* 2515, and 3195; "Organized Porters Union," *ESLDJ,* August 11, 1903, 3; "Colored Porters Organize," *ESLDJ,* August 13, 1903, 3; "Union Labor's Big Day," *ESLDJ,* September 8, 1903, 3. Wilson and Jones's age and birthplace in *1900 Population Schedules, Illinois.*

23. *1900 Population Schedules, Illinois.* All calculations are by the author. Trotter, *River Jordan,* 38–41; *1912 City Directory,* 1484; *Labor Committee Report,* 69; "Threats Fail to Halt Clarence Darrow of Negro Race," *ESLDJ,* July 4, 1926, 3-A; "N. W. Parden Gets Appointment," *ESLJ,* January 6, 1935, 3; "Champion of Negroes Dies at 80," *ESLJ,* March 2, 1944, 1, 16. Parden's mother was a slave and his father a white slaveholder. On Noah Parden and the U.S. Supreme Court, see Mark Curriden and Leroy Phillips Jr., *Contempt of Court: The Turn-of-the-Century Lynching That Launched 100 Years of Federalism* (New York: Faber and Faber, 1999); "East St. Louis," *Illinois Record,* February 11, 1899, 3. Robinson is listed as a laborer in *1880 Population Schedules, Illinois.*

24. Quotes on "better classes" and "middle-class ways" in Glenda Elizabeth Gilmore, *Gender and Jim Crow: Women and the Politics of White Supremacy in*

North Carolina, 1896–1920 (Chapel Hill: University of North Carolina Press, 1996), xix; Kevin K. Gaines, *Uplifting the Race: Black Leadership, Politics, and Culture in the Twentieth Century* (Chapel Hill: University of North Carolina Press, 1996), 3–4.

25. Grantham, *Southern Progressivism*, 244–45. On black clubwomen and their relations to working-class black women, see, for example, Paula Giddings, *When and Where I Enter: The Impact of Black Women on Race and Sex in America* (New York: Morrow, 1984); Evelyn Brooks Higginbotham, *Righteous Discontent: The Women's Movement in the Black Baptist Church, 1880–1920* (Cambridge, Mass.: Harvard University Press, 1993); Mumford, *Interzones,* 47; Elizabeth Lindsey Davis, *The Story of the Illinois Federation of Colored Women's Clubs* (Chicago, 1922; reprint, New York: G. K. Hall, 1977), xvii–xix, 2, 22, 24, 113, 139. The *1912 City Directory* listed Sarah Jones without an occupation, her husband S. B. Jones as pastor at St. Luke's AME Church, Mary Martin with no occupation, her husband Armstead as a stockyard worker, Alberta McKenzie with no occupation, her husband Thomas as a laborer, Mary Paris with no occupation, and her husband Coleman as a laborer. Clementine R. Hamilton, *The Ebony Tree* (East St. Louis, Ill.: privately printed, [1971?]), 74–75. *1900 Population Schedules, Illinois* listed Sarah Flood with no occupation and her husband Richard as a laborer; Rachel Ingram with no occupation lived with brother-in-law B. Gates, a laborer. "Colored Home to Widen Scope of Aid to Orphans," *ESLJ,* November 1, 1934; "Anniversary of Negro Old Folks Home on Sunday," *ESLJ,* June 16, 1939, 13.

26. Rudwick, *Race Riot at East St. Louis,* 198, 200–5, 211–13; McLaughlin, *Power, Community, and Racial Killing in East St. Louis,* 56–57. On black prostitution and vice in other cities, see, for example, Tera W. Hunter, *To 'Joy My Freedom: Southern Black Women's Lives and Labors after the Civil War* (Cambridge, Mass.: Harvard University Press, 1997), 112–14.

27. Allison in *House Transcripts,* 3762. Images and life of gritty wide-open industrial East St. Louis in Sherwood Anderson, "Nobody's Home," *Today: An Independent National Weekly,* March 30, 1935, 6–7, 20–21.

28. "Notes on African American nationalist movements . . . ," folder 4, box 44, Negro in Illinois Papers; James W. Loewen, *Sundown Towns: A Hidden Dimension of American Racism* (New York: New Press, 2005); "The Negro Lynched," *ESLDJ,* June 8, 1903, 3. On black Illinoisan response to lynchings in their state, see Cha-Jua, "A Warlike Demonstration"; Senechal, *Sociogenesis of a Race Riot,* 28–46. On black Springfielders' resistance, see Anthony M. Landis, "They Refused to Stay in Their Place: African American Organized Resistance During the Springfield, Illinois, Race Riot of 1908" (master's thesis, Southern Illinois University, Edwardsville, 2002); Alois Towers in *House Transcripts,* 2376. Towers said that the murder had occurred six years before 1917, but he actually meant 1909. "Twenty-Five Years Ago Today in East St. Louis," *ESLJ,* December 23, 1934, 6. On lynching generally, see, for example, Ida B. Wells-Barnett, *Southern Horrors: Lynch Law in All Its Phases* (New York: New York Age Print, 1892); W. Fitzhugh Brundage, *Lynching in the New South: Georgia and Virginia, 1880–1930* (Urbana: University of Illinois Press, 1993); Jacquelyn Dowd Hall, *Revolt against Chivalry: Jessie Daniel*

Ames and the Women's Campaign against Lynching, rev. ed. (New York: Columbia University Press, 1993); Philip Dray, *At the Hands of Persons Unknown: The Lynching of Black America* (New York: Random House, 2002), ix–xi.

29. "Negro Club Organized," *ESLDJ,* December 11, 1903, 3. Club officers were M. C. Johnson, president; Fred T. Morrison, vice president; saloonkeeper George Kyle, treasurer; James Richmond, secretary; Alabama-born barber James Kyle and bartender William Kyle, captain and assistant secretary, respectively, and Perry Wilson, business agent. James and William Kyle listed in the *1900 Population Schedules,* George and William Kyle in *1912 City Directory.* National Association for the Advancement of Colored People, *Branch Bulletin,* February 1919. Branch officers Fred Halsey, president; William S. Baldwin, vice president; H. T. Bolden, secretary; and Russell M. C. Green in "Negroes Organize for Advancement," *ESLDJ,* May 23, 1915, 4. Chapter officers physician W. H. A. Barrett, president; Mary V. Campbell, secretary; and executive committee persons B. F. Bowles, Pearl Abernathy, physician J. E. Ellis, and the Reverend I. S. Stone in "Completing the Work of the Emancipator: Six Years of Struggle Toward Democracy in Race Relations: Being the Sixth Annual Report of the National Association for the Advancement of Colored People, 1915," in *Pamphlets and Leaflets by W. E. B. Du Bois,* ed. Herbert Aptheker (White Plains, N.Y.: Kraus-Thomson, 1986), 179. Halsey's occupation in "Negro Teacher Sues for $12,000 Damages," *ESLJ,* March 9, 1936, 6. Occupations of others listed in *1912 City Directory.*

30. "Representative Colored Meeting," *ESLDJ,* February 26, 1901, 3; notices of General Maceo meetings in *ESLDJ,* February 28, 1901, 3, and March 8, 1901, 2. On black Americans linking antiwhite supremacy with anti-imperialist politics, see, for example, Willard B. Gatewood Jr., *"Smoked Yankees" and the Struggle for Empire: Letters from Negro Soldiers, 1898–1902* (Urbana: University of Illinois Press, 1971); Scot Ngozi-Brown, "African-American Soldiers and Filipinos: Racial Imperialism, Jim Crow and Social Relations," *Journal of Negro History* 82, no. 1 (Winter 1997): 42–53.

31. Dilliard, "Civil Liberties of Negroes in Illinois since 1865," *Journal of the Illinois State Historical Society* 56, no. 3 (Autumn 1963): 595; "Colored Voters Club Reorganized," *ESLDJ,* March 10, 1901, 3.

32. "Address to the Public by the Negro National Democratic League," *Chicago Broad-Ax,* July 21, 1900; "Presidential Candidate Arrested," *ESLDJ,* July 13, 1904, 3. Brief biographies of Scott in "Wm. T. Scott Dies," *ESLDJ,* January 25, 1917, 5; "The Only Negro Ever a Candidate for President," *St. Louis Argus,* June 16, 1916, 1; William Newton Hartshorn, ed., *Era of Progress and Promise, 1863–1910: The Religious, Moral, and Educational Development of the American Negro since His Emancipation* (Boston: Priscilla Publishing, 1910), 471–72; Monroe N. Work, ed., *Negro Year Book: An Annual Encyclopedia of the Negro, 1918–1919,* 5th ed. (Tuskegee, AL: Negro Year Book Publishing, 1919), 427.

33. "East St. Louis Parties," *ESLDJ,* March 29, 1900, 2.

34. "Railroad Employees at East St. Louis," *Times* (Washington, D.C.), October 30, 1900, clipping attached to letter of J. T. Harahan, Second Vice President,

to Stuyvesant Fish, President [of Illinois Central], November 10, 1900, "Fish, Stuyvesant, In-Letters: President's Office, Jan. 1883–Nov. 1906," 1 F 2.2, Newberry Library, Chicago. Adlai E. Stevenson was the grandfather of Adlai E. Stevenson II, the unsuccessful Democratic Party candidate for president in 1952 and 1956. *1912 City Directory,* 1526.

35. On racism in the railroad unions, see Eric Arnesen, "'Like Banquo's Ghost, It Will Not Down': The Race Question and the American Railroad Brotherhoods, 1880–1920," *American Historical Review* 99, no. 5 (December 1994): 1601–33; "Labor Unions and Lodges," *ESLDJ,* October 25, 1909, 5, section 1.

36. "The So-Called Republican Ticket," *ESLDJ,* February 25, 1901, 2. Background information on J. B. Sikking in *East St. Louis Retail Merchants Association Commercial Profile,* 2. "Important to East St. Louis," *ESLDJ,* March 13, 1901, 2.

37. "To-Morrow," *ESLDJ,* April 4, 1910, 4; "News You Read in Your Journal of 25 Years Ago Today," *ESLJ,* March 1, 1935, 6. Former Progressive Party members included Charles S. Lambert, Fred Gerold, William Roach, John Kickhan, Joseph Nester, Louis Draggon, C. G. Derleth, and Eugene S. Coddington. Former Citizens' Party members were M. M. Stephens, Frank Keating, George W. Brichler, Henry J. Eckert, A. G. Schlveter, Fred Glessing, Thomas J. Canavan, and John E. Garvey. For a general history of the progressive era in urban America, see Steven J. Diner, *A Very Different Age: Americans of the Progressive Era* (New York: Hill and Wang, 1998); Miller and Melvin, *Urbanization of Modern America;* Raymond A. Mohl, *The New City: Urban America in the Industrial Age, 1860–1920* (Arlington Heights, Ill.: Harlan Davidson, 1985), 85–88; Monkkonen, *America Becomes Urban.* On progressives' concerns about moral responsibility and the changing urban environment, see Paul Boyer, *Urban Masses and Moral Order in America, 1820–1920* (Cambridge, Mass.: Harvard University Press, 1978).

38. "Colored Voters Organized," *ESLDJ,* March 7, 1901, 3; "Colored Voters All Right," *ESLDJ,* October 27, 1902, 3. Burkhalter and Gibbs's places of birth and occupations are listed in *1900 Population Schedules, Illinois.*

39. "Colored Recognition," *ESLDJ,* May 14, 1903, 2; "Colored Citizens," *ESLDJ,* March 25, 1903, 3; "Unofficial Vote Cast in East St. Louis at Election April 7, 1903," *ESLDJ,* April 8, 1903, 2; "Colored Voters to Demand Commensurate Recognition," *ESLDJ,* November 9, 1908, 4. No evidence was found to determine whether the Independent Municipal Party awarded patronage to black voters.

40. "Elect Officers," *ESLDJ,* September 2, 1906, 8. Other major figures in the league were Missouri-born laborer Henry Clay and Georgia-born steamboat hand Stephen Craft (occupations and birthplaces from *1900 Population Schedules, Illinois*), as well as laborers George Brockman and Gran A. Duncan, glass factory worker William Freeman, and hotel cook Fred Howard (occupations from the *1912 City Directory*).

41. "A Diabolical Deed," *ESLDJ,* April 7, 1907, 5; "State's Attorney," *ESLDJ,* 2 September 1908, 3.

42. "Progressive Citizens Candidates," *ESLDJ,* March 20, 1910, 10. The Progressive Citizens' Party arose after the demise of the Citizens' Party, roughly ap-

proximating the split in the national Republican Party between the regulars who supported President William Howard Taft and the progressives who supported former President Theodore Roosevelt. See "To-morrow," *ESLDJ*, April 4, 1910, 4; "Progressive Citizens Candidates," *ESLDJ*, March 20, 1910, 10; "Progressive Citizens Party Makes Practical Clean Sweep," *ESLDJ*, April 6, 1910, 1, 4. The Progressive Citizens, emphasizing class harmony, fielded candidates with ties to both labor and business. Those with connections to labor included Illinois Central Railroad machinist John C. Malinee; packinghouse butcher, recently turned businessman, Daniel O'Brien; former Big Four Railroad clerk, now fire department chief, Edward F. Dowling; and former Elliot Frog and Switch Works employee, now proprietor of the Soellinger Bakery, Theodore Soellinger. Candidates with ties to the business community included Claus E. Tieje of the Tieje Grocer Company, brick contractor Andrew Rouge, Peerless Baking Company manager Michael Mackin, and the proprietor of Summers Sheet Metal Works, Neil Summers.

43. "Negroes in Mass Meeting Repudiate Rodenberg," *ESLDJ*, November 4, 1910, 1, 2; "Colored Voters Organized Club," *ESLDJ*, September 20, 1912, 2.

44. On African American freedom festivals keeping alive the memory of milestones in African American history, see, for example, Mitch Kachun, *Festivals of Freedom: Memory and Meaning in African American Emancipation Celebrations, 1808–1915* (Amherst: University of Massachusetts Press, 2003); Thavolia Glymph, "'Liberty Dearly Bought': The Making of Civil War Memory in Afro-American Communities in the South," in *Time Longer Than Rope: A Century of African American Activism, 1850–1950,* ed. Charles M. Payne and Adam Green (New York: New York University Press, 2003), 111–39. "Grand United Emancipation Day," *ESLDJ*, September 22, 1912, section 3, 3. Local black leaders at the celebration in 1912 included John Robinson, president of the Illinois Afro-American Protective League; Clara Bates and her husband, a saloonkeeper; barber James E. Bland, secretary of the Progressive Citizens' League; school administrator Benjamin Franklin Bowles; driver Henry Brown; schoolteacher John M. D. Brown; laborer William M. Chambers; Rev. Sidney Cheers of Mt. Olive Baptist Church; General Cooper, a cook; Rev. John DeShields of St. Paul Baptist Church; Dora Easterly and her husband, grocer William M. Easterly, president of the Progressive Citizens' League; bartender William Garrett; Rev. M. L. Jackson; Illinois Central Railroad employee Henry McGill; Ella Prince and her husband, a Tudor Iron Works employee; hod carrier Walter Rankins; laborer Samuel R. Wheat; and Morris packinghouse laborer Robert William (all occupations listed in *1912 City Directory*).

45. "Colonizing Voters," *ESLDJ*, August 1, 1912, 3; "A Rodenberg Trick," *ESLDJ*, November 8, 1912, 6; "The Public Pulse: Rodenberg Rush Colonizing Negroes for Voting Purposes," *ESLDJ*, September 18, 1912, 2; "Board of Education Eliminates Supervisors," *ESLDJ*, May 13, 1913, 1, 4. On Bowles's professional background, see "Was Elected Vice-President," *ESLDJ*, July 6, 1905, 3; "B. F. Bowles Honored," *ESLDJ*, July 31, 1912, 8; Hamilton, *Ebony Tree,* 34. Among the

seven of the eleven board members not rehiring Bowles were S. J. Cashel, whose brother, county sheriff Charles Cashel, prevented a lynching in Belleville in 1909, and Canavan protégée Fred Mollman, who ran for mayor in 1915. "The Public Pulse: A Plea for Statesmanship Instead of Politics," *ESLDJ,* November 2, 1914, section 2, 1.

46. "Gerold's Office Now Mollman Headquarters," *ESLDJ,* March 30, 1915, 1; "Lambert's Self-Arraignment and Self-Condemnation," *ESLDJ,* April 4, 1915, section 2, 4; Theising, *Made in USA,* 137–40.

47. "Gerold's Office Now Mollman Headquarters," *ESLDJ,* March 30, 1915, 1.

48. "Gerold's Office Now Mollman Headquarters," *ESLDJ,* March 30, 1915, 1; "Mollman Admits He Should Be Defeated" and "A Challenge to Mollman and Managers" and "Their Double-Dealing Tactics" and "Would Tax the Angels and Saints" and "The Municipal Campaign," *ESLDJ,* April 2, 1915, 4; "Mollman Success Would Strangle Money Market," *ESLDJ,* April 5, 1915, 1.

49. "'Kid' Amos Will Come Back if Mollman Wins," *ESLDJ,* April 2, 1915, section 1, 1; "Police Put Lid on Black Crook," *ESLDJ,* April 4, 1915, section 2, 1. On the use of racism in progressives' campaigns to rid cities of brothels and other adult entertainment establishments where intimate interracial exchanges frequently occurred, see, for example, Mumford, *Interzones,* 20, 21.

50. U.S. Bureau of the Census, *Thirteenth Census of the United States, 1910.* On Illinoisan women's voting in local elections, see Wanda A. Hendricks, *Gender, Race, and Politics in the Midwest: Black Club Women in Illinois* (Bloomington: Indiana University Press, 1998), xvi.

51. "Women Voters Out for Chamberlin," *ESLDJ,* April 5, 1915, 1. On Vella Bundy, see Allison in *House Transcripts,* 3761.

52. "Chamberlin Wins Most of Ticket," *ESLDJ,* April 7, 1915, 4.

53. On the South, see especially C. Vann Woodward, *Origins of the New South, 1877–1913* (Baton Rouge: Louisiana State University Press, 1951), 107–395; Trotter, *Black Milwaukee,* xii; Kimberley Phillips, *Alabama North: African-American Migrants, Community, and Working-Class Activism in Cleveland, 1915–45* (Urbana: University of Illinois Press, 1999); Joe William Trotter Jr., ed., *The Great Migration in Historical Perspective: New Dimensions of Race, Class, and Gender* (Bloomington: Indiana University Press, 1991), x.

54. Conway in *House Transcripts,* 169.

Chapter 3: The May Uprising: An End to Expanding Black Power

1. The argument that the Great Migration created or contributed to social tension, especially in the housing market, is set forth in, for example, Elliott M. Rudwick, *Race Riot at East St. Louis, July 2, 1917* (Carbondale: Southern Illinois University Press, 1964), 173; William M. Tuttle Jr., *Race Riot: Chicago in the Red Summer of 1919* (New York: Atheneum, 1970), 21, 66, 106–7; Malcolm McLaughlin, *Power, Community, and Racial Killing in East St. Louis* (New York: Palgrave Macmillan, 2005), 110–11. On social strain as an inadequate explanation for early twentieth-century race riots, see a critique in Roberta Senechal, *Sociogenesis of a*

Race Riot: Springfield, Illinois, in 1908 (Urbana: University of Illinois Press, 1990), 3–10.

2. On white southern migrants during the World War I years, see James N. Gregory, *The Southern Diaspora: How the Great Migrations of Black and White Southerners Transformed America* (Chapel Hill: University of North Carolina Press, 2005), 45, 59–60.

3. Lyman B. Bluitt in *House Transcripts,* 1362–66; Maurice V. Joyce and Leroy N. Bundy in *Labor Committee Report,* 19, 69. For the argument that tensions between old settlers and migrants were not serious, see, for example, Gregory, *Southern Diaspora,* 117–99. Rudwick, *Race Riot at East St. Louis,* 4–6, 174–96; Robert E. Conway, and Thomas J. Canavan, and Edward Mason, and James W. Kirk, and H. F. Bader, and Russell E. Townsend, in *House Transcripts,* 170, and 1413–14, 1476, and 3122, and 3202, and 3447, and 4470–71.

4. Rudwick, *Race Riot at East St. Louis,* 27–40; McLaughlin, *Power, Community, and Racial Killing in East St. Louis,* 106–8, 118, 122.

5. Evidence found thus far shows that from 1915 to 1917 black migrants to East St. Louis talked solely about jobs. But what Leroy Bundy in *Labor Committee Report,* 69–72, and Lyman Bluitt in *House Transcripts,* 1363, learned from migrants is similar to migrants' responses in Emmett Scott, "Documents: Letters of Negro Migrants of 1916–1918," *Journal of Negro History* 4, no. 3 (July 1919): 290–340, and "Additional Letters of Negro Migrants of 1916–1918," *Journal of Negro History* 4, no. 4 (October 1919): 412–65; Carole Marks, *Farewell—We're Good and Gone* (Bloomington: Indiana University Press, 1992), 3; Nan Elizabeth Woodruff, *American Congo: The African American Freedom Struggle in the Delta* (Cambridge, Mass.: Harvard University Press, 2003), 4–5, 21–46; Steven Hahn, *A Nation under Our Feet: Black Political Struggles in the Rural South from Slavery to the Great Migration* (Cambridge, Mass.: Harvard University Press, 2003), 465–68; Milton C. Sernett, *Bound for the Promised Land: African American Religion and the Great Migration* (Durham, NC: Duke University Press, 1997), 11–12. On the Great Migration as black agency, see Tuttle, *Race Riot,* 88; Peter Gottlieb, *Making Their Own Way: Southern Blacks' Migration to Pittsburgh, 1916–1930* (Urbana: University of Illinois Press, 1987), 7; James R. Grossman, *Land of Hope: Chicago, Black Southerners, and the Great Migration* (Chicago: University of Chicago Press, 1989), 6, 19, 38–40, 57, 161; Joe William Trotter Jr., ed., *The Great Migration in Historical Perspective: New Dimensions of Race, Class, and Gender* (Bloomington: Indiana University Press, 1991), xi, 15; Robert Gregg, *Sparks from the Anvil of Oppression: Philadelphia's African Methodists and Southern Migrants, 1890–1940* (Philadelphia: Temple University Press, 1993), 147; Kimberley Phillips, *Alabama North: African-American Migrants, Community, and Working-Class Activism in Cleveland, 1915–45* (Urbana: University of Illinois Press, 1999), 48–52.

6. Leroy Bundy in *Labor Committee Report,* 74–75.

7. Frank A. Hunter, and Robert E. Conway, and Frank G. Cunningham, and John P. Pero, and Clarence Eugene Pope in *House Transcripts,* 71, and 140–41, and 200–201, and 692–94, and 2771.

8. William Kings, and Warren King, and Andrew Avery in *Labor Committee Report*, 149–50, and 151–56, and 160–66; Marks, *Farewell*, 3; Gregg, *Sparks from the Anvil of Oppression*, 13–15. On activities of black industrial laborers in various workers' organizations in the South from the 1870s into the 1890s, see Hahn, *Nation under Our Feet*, 414–25; Gottlieb, *Making Their Own Way*, 12–33; Grossman, *Land of Hope*, 30–31; Beverly A. Bunch-Lyons, *Contested Terrain: African-American Women Migrate from the South to Cincinnati, Ohio, 1900–1950* (New York: Routledge, 2002); Elizabeth Clark-Lewis, *Living In, Living Out: American Domestics and the Great Migration* (Washington, D.C.: Smithsonian Institution, 1994); Darlene Clark Hine, "Black Migration to the Urban Midwest: The Gender Dimension, 1915–1945," in Trotter, *Great Migration in Historical Perspective*, 130–42; Woodruff, *American Congo*, 29.

9. John and Daisy Betts, and William Kings, and George Lewis, and Sam Pettis in *Labor Committee Report*, 135–45, and 149–51, and 157–60, and 167–71. For one official account of black women industrial workers, see Emma L. Shields, "Negro Women in Industry," *Bulletin of the Women's Bureau*, no. 20 (Women's Bureau, U.S. Department of Labor, Washington, D.C.: Government Printing Office, 1922), 6–7. On networks of kin and friends, see Gottlieb, *Making Their Own Way*, 8, 49–51; Hahn, *Nation under Our Feet*, 466–68; Sernett, *Bound for the Promised Land*; Gregg, *Sparks from the Anvil of Oppression*. Earl Jimerson in *House Transcripts*, 2090. Rev. Thomas W. Wallace's background in "East St. Louisans Want Riot Inquiry by Judge Landis," *St. Louis Post-Dispatch*, July 8, 1917, in *Tuskegee Institute News Clippings File* (hereafter cited as *TINCF*), 7:0146.

10. Tuttle, *Race Riot*, 184–86; Bluitt and Kirk in *House Transcripts*, 1364, and 3213–14, 3380.

11. "Democrats Object to Negro Registration," *ESLDJ*, October 8, 1916, 1; "Prevent Registration of Imported Negroes," *ESLDJ*, October 9, 1916, 1; "Register Today," *ESLDJ*, October 17, 1916, 1; "Big Negro Colonization Scheme," *ESLDJ*, October 19, 1916, 4; "Negroes Arrive Too Late to Register," *ESLDJ*, October 20, 1916, 1; "May Make Appeal to Federal Authorities," *ESLDJ*, October 22, 1916, 1; "Perjury Cases Are Continued," *ESLDJ*, October 31, 1916, 1; "Government Agents Investigate Reported Colonization of Arrivals from South," *St. Louis Star*, date unreadable, in *TINCF*, 5:0515; "Mr. Trautman's Answer in Regard to Colonization Charge," *ESLDJ*, November 1, 1916, [6]; "Import Negroes," *ESLDJ*, November 5, 1916, 1; Roy Albertson, and Robert J. Boylan, and W. Green, and Jimerson, and Kane in *House Transcripts*, 471, and 579, and 1127, and 2024, and 4194–4208; "Democrats Will Have Checkers on the Job at Next Registration," *ESLDJ*, October 11, 1916, 1; "Honest Voters Are Resenting Corrupt Election Practices," *ESLDJ*, November 1, 1916, 1; "Honest Voters Victorious in Election Board Scandal," *ESLDJ*, November 3, 1916, 1.

12. "Bundy Involves Mayor in Open Confession," *ESLDJ*, November 26, 1917, 1, 5; "Negro Elected Alderman of East St. Louis," *St. Louis Argus*, April 7, 1916, 1. The newspaper failed to list Reverend Duncan's first name and misspelled Huddleston (the spelling used in the *1912 City Directory*) as Hutterson. Occupations of

Eubanks, Green, Hayes (or Matt Hays), Huddleston, and Lilly in the *1912 City Directory;* Wallace's occupation in "East St. Louisans Want Riot Inquiry by Judge Landis," *St. Louis Post-Dispatch,* July 8, 1917, in *TINCF,* 7:0146.

13. "East St. Louis Negroes to File Protest," *ESLDJ,* October 12, 1916, 1.

14. "Colored Voters Meet, Form Democratic League," *ESLDJ,* October 15, 1916, section 2, 2; "Negroes Hold Meeting," *ESLDJ,* October 26, 1916, 1; "Bundy Involves Mayor in Open Confession," *ESLDJ,* November 26, 1917, 1, 5; Rudwick, *Race Riot at East St. Louis,* 186.

15. "Democrats Are Confident of Victorious Election," *ESLDJ,* November 6, 1916, 1; "Unofficial Vote Cast at Election November 7, 1916," *ESLDJ,* November 12, 1916, 4; "Negro Lawyer Is Appointed Assistant State's Attorney," periodical title unreadable, November 17, 1916, in *TINCF,* 5:0712; "Negro Dentist Is Held in Chicago," *ESLDJ,* October 19, 1916, 1; "Vote Fraud Inquiry Halts Dr. Bundy," *ESLDJ,* October 20, 1916, 1; "Record Vote Being Cast," *ESLDJ,* November 7, 1916, 1.

16. Paul Y. Anderson in *House Transcripts,* 3787–89.

17. W. Green, and Allison, and Anderson in *House Transcripts,* 1128–32, and 3747–52, 3761, and 3801–2; "The Real Cause of [East] St. Louis Riot," *Indianapolis* (second word of title unreadable), July 14, 1917, in *TINCF,* 6:1022–23.

18. Michael Whalen in *Labor Committee Report,* 56; Jimerson and Towers in *House Transcripts,* 2017, and 2395–2396. On the CTLU using the politics of racism and fear, see Rudwick, *Race Riot at East St. Louis,* 16–17; McLaughlin, *Power, Community, and Racial Killing in East St. Louis,* 114.

19. Towers in *House Transcripts,* 2414–21; Peter Ward in *Labor Committee Report,* 183.

20. On white workers in a state of fear and near powerlessness in face of employers seeking to render them docile while black migrants searched for employment, see McLaughlin, *Power, Community, and Racial Killing in East St. Louis,* 88–109 passim.

21. Towers in *House Transcripts,* 2414–21.

22. Towers in *House Transcripts,* 2424, 2427; McLaughlin, *Power, Community, and Racial Killing in East St. Louis,* 90.

23. Hunter, and Kerr, and Jimerson in *House Transcripts,* 75, and 1863–64, and 2018, 2020, 2022, 2123; Rudwick, *Race Riot at East St. Louis,* 20–22, 147; Conway in *Labor Committee Report,* 9; McLaughlin, *Power, Community, and Racial Killing in East St. Louis,* 90–91.

24. Frank E. Nulsen, and Harry Kerr, and Jimerson, and Alois Towers in *House Transcripts,* 1043–46, and 1865, and 2056, 2068, 2089–90, and 2414, 2432–35.

25. Charles B. Fox and Philip Wolf in *House Transcripts,* 1511–18, and 2137, 2139–51; Rudwick, *Race Riot at East St. Louis,* 16–17; McLaughlin, *Power, Community, and Racial Killing in East St. Louis,* 98–109. J. R. Gibbons to C. B. Fox, August 3, 1916; R. F. Rucker to Gibbons, October 21, 1916; Gibbons to Rucker, October 21, 1916; Gibbons to Rucker, December 11, 1916; Aluminum Company of America Records, 1888–1990, MSS no. 280, series IV: Employees Records,

Subseries 1: General (1905–1990), Historical Society of Western Pennsylvania Archives, Pittsburgh, PA.

26. Fox in *House Transcripts,* 1528–29; Fox in *Labor Committee Report,* 26 [33].

27. Conway, and Fox, and R. F. Rucker, and Kerr, and Wolf in *House Transcripts,* 128, 151, and 1519–20, 1546, 1683–90, and 1812–14, 1818–19, 1831, and 1956–57, 1966, 1968–70, and 2137–42, 2151–54, 2180–83; Chancery Case File 1218, "Aluminum Ore Company vs. G. Tebeau et al., Answer of Defendants, May 2, 1917," Law and Chancery Case Files, 1911–1922, Law and Equity Records, 1908–1939, Records of the United States District Court for the Eastern District of Illinois at East St. Louis, RG21, National Archives–Great Lakes Region, Chicago.

28. Chancery Case File 1218, "Aluminum Ore Company vs. George A. Lehman et al., Motion of Complainant for Issuance of Preliminary Injunction, and Affidavits, May 2, 1917," Law and Chancery Case Files, 1911–1922, Law and Equity Records, 1908–1939, Records of the United States District Court for the Eastern District of Illinois at East St. Louis, RG21, National Archives–Great Lakes Region, Chicago; Fox, and Rucker, and Wolf in *House Transcripts,* 1558–85, and 1818–19, and 2197–98, 2212; "Strike Called at Ore Company Plant," *ESLDJ,* April 19, 1917, 1; "War Declared by Aluminum Ore Company on Its Employes," *ESLDJ,* May 25, 1917, 1; "German Plot Scented in Aluminum Ore Explosions," *ESLDJ,* May 27, 1917, section 2, 1.

29. Rudwick, *Race Riot at East St. Louis,* 16–20, 27–29; Hunter, and Conway, and Wolf, and Towers, and Mason in *House Transcripts,* 73, and 154, and 2316, and 2512–13, and 3133–35, quoted passage from Towers. On white workers' racial identity, see McLaughlin, *Power, Community, and Racial Killing in East St. Louis,* 38–40, 114–15.

30. Patrick F. Gill, Conciliator, to William B. Wilson, Secretary of the Department of Labor, October 16, 1917, Case File 33–378, Dispute Case Files, 1913–48, Records of the Federal Mediation and Conciliation Service, RG280, entry 14, National Archives, College Park, Md.; Bundy, and Andrew Avery in *Labor Committee Report,* 82–83, and 164; Conway, Boylan, and Canavan, and Fox, and Kerr, and Wolf, and Alois Towers in *House Transcripts,* 128–29, and 580, and 1482–83, and 1528–29, and 1863–64, 1867–68, 1945, and 2157, 2309–20, and 2437, 2495–99; McLaughlin, *Power, Community, and Racial Killing in East St. Louis,* 37, 97–98.

31. Jimerson and Wolf in *House Transcripts,* 2078, and 2244–45. Quotes from Henry Louis Taylor Jr. and Walter Hill, eds., *Historical Roots of the Urban Crisis: African Americans in the Industrial City, 1900–1950* (New York: Garland Publishing, 2000), 4–5.

32. Joe William Trotter Jr., *Black Milwaukee: The Making of an Industrial Proletariat, 1915–45* (Urbana: University of Illinois Press, 1985), 66–67; Canavan, and Albert B. McQuillan, and Pope in *House Transcripts,* 1471–78, and 1709–10, and 2751–52. On Chicago, see Tuttle, *Race Riot,* 161–64, 171–75; Allan Spear, *Black Chicago: The Making of a Negro Ghetto, 1890–1920* (Chicago: University of Chicago Press, 1967), 210–12; "Citizens Would Keep Negroes from Alta Sita," *ESLDJ,* September 10, 1916, 1. The newspaper never reported what happened to

the three black families in Alta Sita. McQuillan in *House Transcripts,* 1709–10. On neighborhoods and housing segregation, see Stephen Grant Meyer, *As Long as They Don't Move Next Door: Segregation and Racial Conflict in American Neighborhoods* (Lanham, Md.: Rowman and Littlefield, 2000).

33. "400 Men Debate on Negro Segregation," *ESLDJ,* February 27, 1916, 1; Daniel T. Kelleher, "St. Louis' 1916 Residential Segregation Ordinance," *Bulletin of the Missouri Historical Society* 26 (April 1970): 239–48; Elizabeth Noel Schmidt, "Civic Pride and Prejudice: St. Louis Progressive Reform, 1900–1916" (Ph.D. diss., University of Missouri–St. Louis, 1986), 122–27, 129–33; "Don't Submit to Segregation," *St. Louis Argus,* March 17, 1916, in *TINCF,* 5:0849; Allison in "Delivers Sermon on Race Problem," *ESLDJ,* June 4, 1917, 1, 2.

34. "Provide Settlement for Negro Influx," *ESLDJ,* May 22, 1917, 4. Author determined black housing patterns in East St. Louis from *1912 City Directory* and 1880, 1900, and 1910 census manuscripts. On Denverside, see McLaughlin, *Power, Community, and Racial Killing in East St. Louis,* 23–24. On black ghettos, see, for example, Spear, *Black Chicago,* 203, 208–10.

35. Canavan, and Albert B. McQuillan, and Kerr, and Pope in *House Transcripts,* 1471–78, and 1710, and 1906, 1908–10, and 2751–52. On health and housing, see Tera W. Hunter, *To 'Joy My Freedom: Southern Black Women's Lives and Labors after the Civil War* (Cambridge, Mass.: Harvard University Press, 1997), 212–18; Susan L. Smith, *Sick and Tired of Being Sick and Tired: Black Women's Health Activism in America, 1890–1950* (Philadelphia: University of Pennsylvania Press, 1995), 40–42.

36. D. E. Parsons in *Labor Committee Report,* 29 (i.e., 36); Frank E. Nulsen and Fox in *House Transcripts,* 1043–44, and 1509; Irwin Raut in *Labor Committee Report,* 126–29, 132–33.

37. Wolf, and Towers, and Mason, and Townsend, and Allison in *House Transcripts,* 2309, and 2376, and 3181–82, and 3432, 3447–49, and 3626; Rudwick, *Race Riot at East St. Louis,* 8–9, 25–26, 212–15; McLaughlin, *Power, Community, and Racial Killing in East St. Louis,* 59–61, 78–82. See also discussion of crime in chapter 2.

38. C. P. Renner and Kerr in *House Transcripts,* 1276–79 and 1869. On jook joints, see Hunter, *To 'Joy My Freedom,* 168–71; "Negroes and Whites Stage Race Riot," *ESLDJ,* May 24, 1917, 1; "Police Watch Many Threatening Negroes," *ESLDJ,* May 28, 1917, 1.

39. W. H. Mills, and W. Green, and Bluitt in *House Transcripts,* 1118, and 1127, and 1363–66.

40. Canavan and McQuillan in *House Transcripts,* 1476–79 and 1710; Glenda Elizabeth Gilmore, *Gender and Jim Crow: Women and the Politics of White Supremacy in North Carolina, 1896–1920* (Chapel Hill: University of North Carolina Press, 1996), 102–5, 108; Hunter, *To 'Joy My Freedom,* 99.

41. Jimerson and Towers in *House Transcripts,* 2061–65 and 2454–56.

42. M. J. Whalen in *Labor Committee Report,* 56; Kerr, and Wolf, and Jimerson, and Mason in *House Transcripts,* 1869, 1907, 1962, 1998–2000, and 2136,

2569, and 2312–17, and 3141–42, 3148. Facsimile of the open letter in "Negro Labor and the Unions," *American Industry in War Time* 1, no. 1 (August 10, 1917): 7, in Rudwick, *East St. Louis Race Riot of 1917* (Frederick, Md.: University Publications of America, 1985), reel 7; Rudwick, *Race Riot at East St. Louis*, 161, 163.

43. "Mollman's Talk in South Taken Up at Riot Inquiry," *St. Louis Post Dispatch*, November 1, 1917, in *TINCF*, 7:0143; "'The Conspiracy of the East St. Louis Riots,' Speech by Marcus Garvey, [July 8, 1917]," in *The Marcus Garvey and UNIA Papers*, vol. 1, *1826–August 1919*, ed. Robert Hill (Berkeley: University of California Press, 1983), 214–15; McLaughlin, *Power, Community, and Racial Killing in East St. Louis*, 88–89, 118–19.

44. M. J. Whalen in *Labor Committee Report*, 57; Kerr, and Jimerson, and Tower, and Mason in *House Transcripts*, 1869–70, 1915, 1948, and 2025–26, and 2472–73, and 3156–57, 3167–68, 3174, 3182; "800 Union Men Protest Importation of Negroes," *ESLDJ*, May 29, 1917, 1; Rudwick, *Race Riot at East St. Louis*, 27.

45. Conway, and Albertson, and Boylan, and Canavan, and Kerr, and Jimerson, and Clarence Pope, and James M. Kelly, and Mason in *House Transcripts*, 156, and 473–75, and 584–85, and 1416, and 1916, 1949, 1964, and 2028–29, and 2599–2600, and 2861, 2875–76, and 3161–62, 3169–73; "Union Laborers Start Race Riots," *St. Louis Argus*, June 1, 1917, 1.

46. Boylan, and Canavan, and Jimerson, and Wolf, and Kelly in *House Transcripts*, 585–86, and 1417, and 2031–32, and 2215–16, 2219, 2302–3, and 2852.

47. "Six Wounded in Street Demonstrations Tues. Night," *ESLDJ*, May 31, 1917, 1; Albertson, and Wolf, and Allison, and Eli Chrisan, and Ruby Nelson, and Grace Yent in *House Transcripts*, 476, and 2219, 2242–44, and 3548–52, 3578, and 4713, 4749, and 4793, and 4801–2. On differences between crowds and mobs, see Malcolm McLaughlin, "Reconsidering the East St. Louis Race Riot of 1917," *International Review of Social History* 47 (2002): 187–212; see also Senechal, *Sociogenesis of a Race Riot*, 98.

48. McLaughlin, *Power, Community, and Racial Killing in East St. Louis*, 152–59.

49. "Six Wounded in Street Demonstrations Tues. Night," *ESLDJ*, May 31, 1917, 1; "Union Laborers Start Race Riots," *St. Louis Argus*, June 1, 1917, 1; Albertson and Allison in *House Transcripts*, 474, 476–77 and 3629–30; "Presence of Foreign and Lawless Negro Element Injures City," *ESLDJ*, May 29, 1917, 1, 5. Police detectives Samuel Coppedge and Frank Wadley, who deterred mobs from the Valley, died facing armed black men on July 2 in an incident that sparked the murderous massacre of July 2, 1917. "Riot Situation Is Now under Control," *ESLDJ*, May 31, 1917, 1. On black-owned saloons and businesses as political headquarters, see also Senechal, *Sociogenesis of a Race Riot*, 81, 132–34.

50. "Presence of Foreign and Lawless Negro Element Injures City," *ESLDJ*, May 29, 1917, 1, 5. On white policemen's reluctance to protect black people, especially during episodes of mass racial violence, see, for example, Tuttle, *Race Riot*, 231–35.

51. "The People of the State of Illinois v. Leroy Bundy et al., March term, 1919," in Rudwick, *East St. Louis Race Riot of 1917*, reel 7, 765, 796, 825–27. On car

ownership among African Americans in plantation districts undermining white planters' control over black sharecroppers, see Woodruff, *American Congo,* 44.

52. "Six Wounded in Street Demonstrations Tues. Night," *ESLDJ,* May 31, 1917, 1; "Riot Situation Is Now under Control," *ESLDJ,* May 31, 1917, 1; Albertson in *House Transcripts,* 477; "Union Laborers Start Race Riots," *St. Louis Argus,* June 1, 1917, 1.

53. Albertson, and Bluitt, and Allison in *House Transcripts,* 475, and 1349, and 3629–30; "Riot Situation Is Now under Control," *ESLDJ,* May 31, 1917, 1; James W. Loewen, *Sundown Towns: A Hidden Dimension of American Racism* (New York: New Press, 2005), 90–15; "Disorders Abate with Police and Militia in Full Control," *ESLDJ,* June 3, 1917, 1.

54. "Factories Must Close if Cannot Get Negro Help," *St. Louis Argus,* June 8, 1917, 1; "Disorders Abate with Police and Militia in Full Control," *ESLDJ,* June 3, 1917, 1; "Race Riot Aftermath," *St. Louis Argus,* June 8, 1917, 4; C. B. Fox, and Peter Ward in *Labor Committee Report,* 27 (i.e., 34), and 186; Phillip W. Coyle and Wolf in *House Transcripts,* 30 and 2216, 2218–20, 2241; "Defense Council to Investigate Riots," *ESLDJ,* June 4, 1917, 1, 2; Towers in *House Transcripts,* 2367. Brief history and mission of the Illinois State Council of Defense and its Labor Committee in Marguerite Edith Jenison, *The War-Time Organization of Illinois* (Springfield: Illinois State Historical Library, 1923), 284–85.

55. Joyce, and Fox, and Harry Stanisic, and Whalen, and Bundy, and John and Daisy Betts, and Roche in *Labor Committee Report,* 17, and 24–25, and 36 (i.e., 43), and 56–57, 60–61, and 68–83, and 135–45, and 177–78; Towers in *House Transcripts,* 2369–70, 2391, 2504–5.

56. *Labor Committee Report,* 36–38 (i.e., 43–45).

57. Jimerson in *House Transcripts,* 2077. Brooklyn officials' antiunionism was similar to that of some black clergymen and local National Urban League officials in Chicago in 1919, as stated in Tuttle, *Race Riot,* 148–51.

58. John Eubanks, and Bluitt, and Kerr, and Jimerson in *House Transcripts,* 1136–37, and 1355–56, 1366, and 2011–12, and 2035–37, 2046, 2048. On organized labor's partial interest in unionizing black workers on the eve of an episode of mass racial violence, see, for example, Tuttle, *Race Riot,* 109–23, 153–54; David R. Roediger, "What if Labor Were Not White and Male?" in *Colored White: Transcending the Racial Past* (Berkeley: University of California Press, 2002): 179–202. Mention of William Bagley in Rudwick, *Race Riot at East St. Louis,* 147; McLaughlin, *Power, Community, and Racial Killing in East St. Louis,* 91.

59. Tuttle, *Race Riot,* 124–25.

60. "Union Laborers Start Race Riots"; "Factories Must Close if Cannot Get Negro Help," *St. Louis Argus,* June 8, 1917, 1; "Delivers Sermon on Race Problem," *ESLDJ,* June 4, 1917, 1, 2; Senechal, *Sociogenesis of a Race Riot,* 173–78; "Presence of Foreign and Lawless Negro Element Injures City," *ESLDJ,* May 29, 1917, 1, 5; Rucker in *House Transcripts,* 1829–30.

61. McLaughlin, *Power, Community, and Racial Killing in East St. Louis,* 108–9; "Policemen Held Up By Armed Soldiers," *ESLDJ,* June 11, 1917, 1; "Serious

Charges against Three Members of the Militia in E. St. Louis," *The Forum,* June 16, 1917, 1, 3.

62. Bluitt in *House Transcripts,* 1350; "Parden Loses Job as Prosecutor," *ESLDJ,* June 15, 1917, 1.

63. Bluitt, and Kerr, and Allison in *House Transcripts,* 1350, and 1971, and 3630–31; "Negroes in Hold-Up," *ESLDJ,* June 15, 1917, 1.

64. "As the Journal Views It," *ESLDJ,* July 6, 1917, 4, section 2; "Union Laborers Start Race Riots," *St. Louis Argus,* June 1, 1917, 1; "Negroes in Hold-Up," *ESLDJ,* June 15, 1917, 1; Kerr in *House Transcripts,* 1971. R. M. C. Green smuggling weapons is discussed by Mrs. Frances Nash Terrell and Mrs. Claudia Nash Thomas, interview by author, September 24, 1999, East St. Louis. Sundiata Keita Cha-Jua, "'A Warlike Demonstration': Legalism, Armed Resistance, and Black Political Mobilization in Decatur, Illinois, 1894–1898," *Journal of Negro History* 83, no. 1 (Winter 1998): 52–72.

Chapter 4: The July Massacre: "We'll Have a White Man's Town"

1. The July pogrom was the only major episode of mass racial violence during World War I. During the war, two urban clashes occurred, one on August 23, 1917, in Houston, Texas, and the other in July 1918 in Philadelphia. Both were minor when compared with the July 1917 pogrom in East St. Louis. On the "riot" in Houston where black soldiers retaliated against a city police department that habitually abused black civilians and military personnel, see Robert V. Haynes, *A Night of Violence: The Houston Riot of 1917* (Baton Rouge: Louisiana State University Press, 1976), 47–170, 318–22; Garna L. Christian, *Black Soldiers in Jim Crow Texas, 1899–1917* (College Station: Texas A&M University Press, 1995), xv, 145–72, 177. On the violence in July 1918 in Philadelphia, which took place after a middle-class black woman moved into her new home in a white neighborhood and shot at a white mob intent on forcing her to move out, see Vincent P. Franklin, "The Philadelphia Race Riot of 1918," *Pennsylvania Magazine of History and Biography* 99, 3 (1975): 336–50. Other major racial conflicts occurred after the war from 1919 to 1922 in cities like Chicago and Washington, D.C., and in rural locales like Elaine, Arkansas, and Rosewood, Florida. Discussion of social tension abounds in the literature pertaining to race riots during World War I and World War II; see, for example, William M. Tuttle Jr., *Race Riot: Chicago in the Red Summer of 1919* (New York: Atheneum, 1970), 10–30, 243–67; Dominic J. Capeci Jr. and Martha Wilkerson, *Layered Violence: The Detroit Rioters of 1943* (Jackson: University of Mississippi Press, 1991), 175–207.

2. Elliott M. Rudwick, *Race Riot at East St. Louis, July 2, 1917* (Carbondale: Southern Illinois University Press, 1964), 3–6, 218–33; Malcolm McLaughlin, *Power, Community, and Racial Killing in East St. Louis* (New York: Palgrave Macmillan, 2005), 2–3; Thomas Canavan quoted by George W. Allison in *House Transcripts,* 3635.

3. Locke Tarlton quoted by Allison in *House Transcripts,* 3636.

4. Patrick F. Gill, Conciliator, to William B. Wilson, Secretary of the Department of Labor, October 16, 1917, Case File 33–378, Dispute Case Files, 1913–48,

Records of the Federal Mediation and Conciliation Service, RG280, entry 14, National Archives, College Park, Md.; Anderson, and Charles B. Fox, and W. A. Miller in *House Transcripts*, 281–84, 351, and 1652, and 4089, 4101; "Town a Living Hell for Three Days," *Chicago Defender*, July 14, 1917, in *TINCF*, 6:1024; Allison in *House Transcripts*, 3532; Calvin Cotton and Thomas G. Hunter in *House Transcripts*, 673–76 and 1066–67; "Soldiers Arrive to Preserve Order," *ESLDJ*, July 2, 1917, 1. State prosecutors charged Masserang, Long, Walker, and another white man as the gun-carrying joy riders in "The People of the State of Illinois v. Leroy Bundy et al., March Term, 1919," in *The East St. Louis Race Riot of 1917* (University Publications of America, 1985), reel 7. James Taylor in Ida B. Wells-Barnett, "The East St. Louis Massacre: The Greatest Outrage of the Century," Correspondence of the Military Intelligence Division, U.S. War Department, RG165, entry 65, microfilm M1440, roll 1, no. 10218–60, National Archives, Washington, D.C., 11. Taylor's occupation in *1912 City Directory*; Roy Albertson in *House Transcripts*, 482–85; "Soldiers Arrive to Preserve Order, *ESLDJ*, July 2, 1917, 1. On politicians' hatred of Bundy, see "Bundy Involves Mayor in Open Confession," *ESLDJ*, November 26, 1917, 1, 5. On Bundy's whereabouts on Monday morning, see "The People of the State of Illinois v. Leroy Bundy et al."

5. Albertson in *House Transcripts*, 478–83, 498, 501–2. Albertson's story is the only published eyewitness account. One dispute of his account appeared in "Riot a National Disgrace," *St. Louis Argus*, July 6, 1917, which reported that Albertson simply added Coppedge's verbal exchange that occurred a month earlier. Congressional investigators questioned Albertson's investigative skills after learning that he had not interviewed black residents for their version of the confrontation; see *House Transcripts*, 499–503, 542–67. "Soldiers Arrive to Preserve Order," *ESLDJ*, July 2, 1917, 1; "The People of the State of Illinois, Defendant in Error, vs. Leroy N. Bundy, Plaintiff in Error," no. 13366, 1920 Ill. LEXIS 1231, 3–5; "Detective Shot by Negro Dies," *St. Louis Republic*, July 4, 1917, in *TINCF*, 7:0098; "Presence of Foreign and Lawless Negro Element Injures City," *ESLDJ*, May 29, 1917, 1, 5. See also chapter 3.

6. Albert B. McQuillan and Allison in *House Transcripts*, 1712–13 and 3629–30. For an example of white reaction to a black man killing a white police officer, see William Ivy Hair, *Carnival of Fury: Robert Charles and the New Orleans Race Riot of 1900* (Baton Rouge: Louisiana State University Press, 1976). On the systematic, communal nature of lynching and other acts of mass antiblack violence, see, for example, W. Fitzhugh Brundage, *Lynching in the New South: Georgia and Virginia, 1880–1930* (Urbana: University of Illinois Press, 1993); Philip Dray, *At the Hands of Persons Unknown: The Lynching of Black America* (New York: Random House, 2002); Frank G. Cunningham and G. E. Popkess in *House Transcripts*, 223 and 402–4; "As the Journal Views It," *ESLDJ*, July 6, 1917, 4, section 2.

7. "Grand Jury Returns Indictments for 103," *ESLDJ*, August 15, 1917, 1; Hallie E. Queen, "East St. Louis as I Saw It," Lawrence Y. Sherman Papers, Abraham Lincoln Presidential Library, Springfield (hereafter cited as Sherman Papers). In the 1927 issue of *Who's Who in Colored America: A Biographical Dictionary of Notable*

Living Persons of Negro Descent in America, Hallie Elvera Queen served as chairperson of the Howard University chapter of the American Red Cross and was Holder of Service Cross for War Service. Daisy [Westbrook] to Louise [Westbrook?], n.d., folders 6 and 7, box 133, Sherman Papers; Paul Y. Anderson and Cotton in *House Transcripts,* 284 and 682–83; "Brockway Delivered Speeches," *ESLDJ,* November 14, 1917, 1. The census manuscripts show a number of white residents who listed the southern states as their place of nativity. More research in the census manuscripts is needed to gain a clearer picture of white residents from the South and elsewhere.

8. Cunningham and Albertson in *House Transcripts,* 220 and 482, 485–86; "Mayor Mollman Indicted by Race Riot Grand Jury," *St. Louis Post-Dispatch,* September 9, 1917, in *TINCF,* 8:1043; Popkess, and Robert J. Boylan, and W. H. Mills, and W. Green, and Otto Nelson in *House Transcripts,* 405–6, and 590, and 1109–10, and 1122, and 1298; "Soldiers Arrive to Preserve Order, *ESLDJ,* July 2, 1917, 1; "Military Authorities Are in Full Control," *ESLDJ,* July 3, 1917, 1, 2, 5. On Ed Payne, see McLaughlin, *Power, Community, and Racial Killing in East St. Louis,* 61, 76.

9. "Proceedings before Board of Inquiry, East St. Louis, Illinois," in Rudwick, *East St. Louis Race Riot of 1917,* reel 6, 2–3. On Monday, July 2, 30 troops arrived at 8:30 AM, 34 at 10:20 AM, 47 at 12:50 PM, 63 at 4:00 PM, 69 at 7:00 PM, and 44 at 8:00 PM; on Tuesday, 70 troops entered the city at 1:45 AM, 63 at 2:00 AM, 53 at 2:30 AM, 56 at 3:00 AM, and 113 at 4:15 AM. Three additional units appeared on Tuesday, and two more, one numbering 573 troops, on Wednesday. Anderson, and Albertson, and Boylan, and S. O. Tripp, and Jimerson, and Daniel McGlynn, and Kirk, and H. F. Bader in *House Transcripts,* 258–59, 264, and 486–87, 505, and 590–92, 598, and 758, 761, and 2049–50, and 3059–60, and 3386–87, and 4449; "Military Authorities Are in Full Control," *ESLDJ,* July 3, 1917, 1, 2, 5. "Race Mobs Kill 15 to 75 Negroes," *New York City Sun,* July 3, 1917, in *TINCF,* 6:1036–37; "Murder and Arson in High Carnival at East St. Louis for Day and Night," [title unreadable] in *TINCF,* 1006–7; "Town Living Hell for Three Days," *Chicago Defender,* July 14, 1917, *TINCF,* 6:1024; Lindsey Cooper, "The Congressional Investigation of East St. Louis," *Crisis* 15 (January 1818): 116–21, in *The Black Worker: A Documentary History from Colonial Times to the Present,* ed. Philip S. Foner and Ronald L. Lewis (Philadelphia: Temple University Press, 1980), 5:305–6.

10. Rudwick, *Race Riot at East St. Louis,* 44. On differences between mobs and crowds, see Malcolm McLaughlin, "Reconsidering the East St. Louis Race Riot of 1917," *International Review of Social History* 47 (August 2002): 187–212, and McLaughlin, *Power, Community, and Racial Killing in East St. Louis,* 137–52. See also relevant sections in George Rudé, *The Crowd in History: A Study of Popular Disturbances in France and England, 1730–1848* (New York: Wiley, 1964); Brundage, *Lynching in the New South;* Dray, *At the Hands of Persons Unknown.*

11. Rudwick, *Race Riot at East St. Louis,* 88. Like Rudwick and McLaughlin, this author had no success in locating police records. Albertson in *House Tran-*

scripts, 496–97; "Photographers Threatened," *St. Louis Globe Democrat,* July 3, 1917 in *TINCF,* 6:0984; "Grand Jury Holds Him Responsible for Riot," *Chicago Defender,* September 15, 1917, in *TINCF,* 6:1029. Newsreels and photographs of the July violence were shown in other places but not in East St. Louis; see "Belleville Bars Riot Pictures," *ESLDJ,* July 10, 1917, 3; "Moving Pictures of Race Riot," *St. Louis Argus,* July 27, 1917, 1.

12. Cunningham, and Anderson, and Popkess, and Albertson, and Robert J. Boylan, and McGlynn, and Kirk, and Allison in *House Transcripts,* 223, and 280–84, 307, 350–52, 359, and 417–18, and 492, 507, and 604, 619, and 3099, and 3385, and 3657; Carlos F. Hurd in Wells-Barnett, "East St. Louis Massacre," 11; "Race Rioters Fire East St. Louis," *New York Times,* July 3, 1917, in *TINCF,* 6:0989. During the Chicago race riot of July 1919, the Ragen Colts, an athletic club, was a group of antiblack assailants with political connections; see Tuttle, *Race Riot,* 32–33. Reporters who used terms like saloon bums already held negative views of saloon customers, who were mainly workers spending much of their spare time at saloons. See also McLaughlin, "Reconsidering the East St. Louis Race Riot of 1917"; Anderson in *House Transcripts,* 284; "Brockway Delivered Speeches," *ESLDJ,* November 14, 1917, 1; "Described and Analyzed by a . . . Relible [*sic*] Journalist," *ESLDJ,* July 5, 1917, 4; "East St. Louis Rioter Sentenced to Chester," *ESLDJ,* August 19, 1917, 1; "Authorities to Keep Bundy Return Quiet," *ESLDJ,* October 14, 1917, 1; McLaughlin, *Power, Community, and Racial Killing in East St. Louis,* 147–52. On low numbers of industrial workers in mass racial violence, see Senechal, *Sociogenesis of a Race Riot,* 98.

13. Anderson and Kirk in *House Transcripts,* 253, 255–56 and 3384–85; "Military Authorities Are in Full Control," *ESLDJ,* July 3, 1917, 1, 2, 5; "Authorities to Keep Bundy Return Quiet," *ESLDJ,* October 14, 1917, 1; "Mollman Summoned to Rioters' Defense," *ESLDJ,* October 18, 1917, 1, 5; Jack Lait quoted in "Described and Analyzed by a . . . Relible [*sic*] Journalist," *ESLDJ,* July 5, 1917, 4; Hurd in Wells-Barnett, "East St. Louis Massacre," 11; Anderson, and Daniel McGlynn, and George W. Allison in *House Transcripts,* 306, and 3099, and 3657–58; "Complete Probe of Riot Begun," *ESLDJ,* July 5, 1917, 1, 2; "Race Rioters Fire East St. Louis," *New York Times,* July 3, 1917, in *TINCF,* 6:0989; "Race Rioters Fire East St. Louis and Shoot or Hang Many Negroes," *New York Times,* July 3, 1917, in *TINCF,* 6:0989; Rudwick, *Race Riot at East St. Louis,* 99–101; Wells-Barnett, "East St. Louis Massacre," 6.

14. Mrs. Howard and Hurd in Wells-Barnett, "East St. Louis Massacre," 6 and 12; Queen, "East St. Louis as I Saw It"; "Race Rioters Fire East St. Louis," *New York Times,* July 3, 1917, in *TINCF,* 6:0989; Allison in *House Transcripts,* 3657.

15. See discussion of prostitutes in particular and white women generally in chapter 3 of this volume and in McLaughlin, *Power, Community, and Racial Killing in East St. Louis,* 152–59.

16. William F. Hanna, "The Boston Draft Riot," *Civil War History* 36, no. 3 (1990): 262–73; Michael B. Chesson, "Harlots or Heroines? A New Look at the Richmond Bread Riot," *Virginia Magazine of History and Biography* 92, no. 2

(April 1984), 131–75; Paula E. Hyman, "Immigrant Women and Consumer Protests: The New York City Kosher Meat Boycott of 1902," *American Jewish History* 70, no. 1 (September 1980): 91–105; Andrea Meryl Kirshenbaum, "'The Vampire That Hovers over North Carolina': Gender, White Supremacy, and the Wilmington Race Riot of 1898," *Southern Cultures* 4, no. 3 (Fall 1998): 9–14 passim; Marilynn S. Johnson, "Gender, Race, and Rumours: Re-examining the 1943 Race Riots," *Gender & History* 10, no. 2 (August 1998): 252–55, 262; James L. Crouthamel, "The Springfield Race Riot of 1908," *Journal of Negro History* 45, no. 3 (July 1960): 176.

17. See discussion of saloon culture and criminal violence in chapter 2 of this volume and in McLaughlin, *Power, Community, and Racial Killing in East St. Louis,* 59–61, 78–82; Kevin R. Hardick, "'Your Old Father Abe Lincoln Is Dead and Damned': Black Soldiers and the Memphis Race Riot of 1866," *Journal of Social History* 27, no. 1 (Autumn 1993): 109–28; Jack Lait in "Described and Analyzed by a . . . Relible [*sic*] Journalist," *ESLDJ,* July 5, 1917, 4, section 2.

18. Tuttle, *Race Riot,* 61–62 passim.

19. Jimerson, and Allison, and Stewart Campbell in *House Transcripts,* 2049–51, and 3693, and 3978; "As the Journal Views It," *ESLDJ,* July 6, 1917, 4, section 2; "Race Rioters Fire East St. Louis," *New York Times,* July 3, 1917, in *TINCF,* 6:0989; "Town a Living Hell for Three Days," *Chicago Defender,* July 14, 1917, in *TINCF,* 6:1024; Clarissa Lockett and Mr. Buchanan in Wells-Barnett, "East St. Louis Massacre," 6 and 16.

20. Queen, "East St. Louis as I Saw It"; Josie Nixon in Wells-Barnett, "East St. Louis Massacre," 7. Nixon and her husband Samuel, a carpenter and contractor, and daughter Pearl, a packinghouse worker, had lived in East St. Louis since 1904. Popkess and Kirk in *House Transcripts,* 384 and 3385.

21. "Mollman Summoned to Rioters' Defense," *ESLDJ,* October 18, 1917, 1, 5; Rudwick, *Race Riot at East St. Louis,* 103–6; McLaughlin, *Power, Community, and Racial Killing in East St. Louis,* 140–41. See McLaughlin, 248n102, for an explanation as to why Rudwick used Dow instead of Gow. Like McLaughlin, this author uses Gow because this form of his name frequently appeared in the *East St. Louis Daily Journal* and in the list of names of those who appeared before the grand jury.

22. "2 More Identified as Race Rioters," *ESLDJ,* November 15, 1917, 1; "Captain Robinson Most Colorful Negro Character of City," *ESLDJ,* February 28, 1926, 3-A; Joe D. Williamson in *House Transcripts,* 1861–62. In "Widely Known Negro Buried with All Pomp," *ESLDJ,* March 25, 1924, 1, 8, it is stated in a laudatory manner that William Bell "became associated with the liquor industry, and for many years was in the saloon business. . . . One of the outstanding figures in the race riots in 1917 . . . Bell wielded an almost unbelievable power to calm the troubled waters. . . . Those who know say that he was more influential than any other man and did more to end the ruthless killing, than any other one man in East St. Louis." Untitled document signed "K. Causer, Major, 4th Regt., July 3–12," folders 6 and 7, box 133, Sherman Papers.

23. Anderson in *House Transcripts,* 362; Daisy [Westbrook] to Louise [Westbrook?], n.d., folders 6 and 7, box 133, Sherman Papers; "The Following Report Was Made by George Austin," *St. Louis Globe Democrat,* July 3, 1917, in *TINCF,* 6:0985; "Race Rioters Fire East St. Louis," *New York Times,* July 3, 1917, in *TINCF,* 6:0989; "Blacks Shot Down Like Rabbits," *St. Louis Republic,* July 3, 1917, in *TINCF,* 6:0998–99; "Town a Living Hell for Three Days," *Chicago Defender,* July 14, 1917, in *TINCF,* 6:1024; "Military Authorities Are in Full Control," *ESLDJ,* July 3, 1917, 1–3; Gould in Wells-Barnett, "East St. Louis Massacre," 15; Queen, "East St. Louis as I Saw It"; E. M. Sorrells in *House Transcripts,* 3905–71; black employees at Aluminum Ore in Olga Wayne, interview by author, September 21, 1999, East St. Louis.

24. C. W. Middlekauff, State of Illinois Office of the Attorney General, to L. Y. Sherman, July 24, 1917, folder 1, box 133, Sherman Papers; Anderson and Robert R. Thomas in *House Transcripts,* 299, 322–23, 362, 447–48, and 1402–3; Peyton T. Karr, President, Kehlor Flour Mills Co., East St. Louis, to Adjutant General, War Department, Washington, D.C., July 3, 1917, and J. R. Mathews, President, Corno Mills Co., East St. Louis, to Adjutant General, July 3, 1917, Glasser File, ca. 1938, Internal Disturbance (geographical file), Records of the Department of Justice, RG60, entry 126, National Archives, College Park, Md.

25. Anderson, and Robert J. Boylan, and Colonel S. O. Tripp, and Frank E. Nulsen in *House Transcripts,* 263, 272, 322–23, and 592–93, 599–610, and 824–25, 843–44, 852–54, and 1033–34; "Soldiers Arrive to Preserve Order," *ESLDJ,* July 2, 1917, 1; "Complete Probe of Riot Begun," *ESLDJ,* July 5, 1917, 1, 2; "Race Rioters Fire East St. Louis," *New York Times,* July 3 1917, in *TINCF,* 6:0989.

26. Anderson and Stewart Campbell in *House Transcripts,* 322–23 and 3978; "3 Whites on Trial for Keyser Murder," *ESLDJ,* October 15, 1917, 1; "Mollman Summoned to Rioters' Defense," *ESLDJ,* October 18, 1917, 1, 5; "Death Penalty Asked for Three White Men," *ESLDJ,* October 21, 1917, 1; "Rioter Admits Guilt," *ESLDJ,* October 23, 1917, 1.

27. "Military Authorities Are in Full Control," *ESLDJ,* July 3 1917, 1, 2, 5.

28. Untitled document signed "K. Causer, Major, 4th Regt., July 3–12," folders 6 and 7, box 133, Sherman Papers; "Race Rioters Fire East St. Louis," *New York Times,* July 3, 1917, in *TINCF,* 6:0989; "Congress Discusses Ill. Race Massacre," *Guardian,* July 7, 1917, in *TINCF,* 6:1010–11; Anderson in *House Transcripts,* 254, 256. "Riot Promises to Bring Reorganization," *ESLDJ,* July 6, 1917, 1; "Military Authorities Are in Full Control," *ESLDJ,* July 3, 1917, 1, 2, 5.

29. Wells-Barnett, "East St. Louis Massacre," 16; Daisy [Westbrook] to Louise [Westbrook?], n.d., folders 6 and 7, box 133, Sherman Papers; "Two Defendants Deny Riot Accusations," *ESLDJ,* November 28, 1917, 1; Wells-Barnett, "East St. Louis Massacre," 4, 6.

30. "Grand Jury Returns Indictments for 103," *ESLDJ,* August 15, 1917, 1; Rudwick, *Race Riot at East St. Louis,* 162–66, 269n34; Fred W. Mollman, and Maurice Joyce in *Labor Committee Report,* 7, and 19–20; Future research using the city directory that the author recently located, but not in time to include all of the

findings in this work, might yield a higher figure than the one used by Rudwick. "7,000 Blacks Flee East St. Louis as Troops Stop Riot," *New York City Call,* July 6, 1917, in *TINCF,* 7:0014; "Military Authorities Are in Full Control," *ESLDJ,* July 3, 1917, 1, 2, 5; "Riots Cut Attendance in East Side Schools," *TINCF,* 7:0043; "Several Hundred Negroes Brought Across the River," *TINCF,* 6:1018; "Fear-Stricken Negroes Leaving East St. Louis," *TINCF,* 6:0990; Daisy [Westbrook] to Louise [Westbrook?], n.d., folders 6 and 7, box 133, Sherman Papers; "St. Louis," [1918?], box E:87, part I, series VI, National Urban League Records, Manuscript Division, Library of Congress, Washington, D.C.; "Thousands Leave East St. Louis Cared for Here," *St. Louis Argus,* July 6, 1917, in *TINCF,* 6:1001; "3,000 Refugees Cared for Here," *St. Louis Republic,* July 4, 1917, in *TINCF,* 6:1002; Wells-Barnett, "East St. Louis Massacre," 8, 18.

31. Rudwick, *Race Riot at East St. Louis,* 53–57; McLaughlin, *Power, Community, and Racial Killing in East St. Louis,* 163–76. This author agrees with McLaughlin's (164) assessment that "perhaps, in light of the effective use of nonviolent direct action being made [in the civil rights movement] in the Southern states in his own day, Rudwick sought to emphasize the moral supremacy of African Americans in the East St. Louis race riot" by minimizing their armed self-defense. See also David S. Cecelski and Timothy B. Tyson, eds., *Democracy Betrayed: The Wilmington Race Riot of 1898 and Its Legacy* (Chapel Hill: University of North Carolina Press, 1998), 5; David Fort Godshalk, *Veiled Visions: The 1906 Atlanta Race Riot and the Reshaping of American Race Relations* (Chapel Hill: University of North Carolina Press, 2005), 100–114; Gregory Mixon, *The Atlanta Riot: Race, Class, and Violence in a New South City* (Gainesville: University Press of Florida, 2005), 105–10. On the issue of armed self-defense in African American history, see Christopher B. Strain, *Pure Fire: Self-Defense as Activism in the Civil Rights Era* (Athens: University of Georgia Press, 2005); Thomas Canavan, and McQuillan, and Frank Weckermeyer in *House Transcripts,* 1424–26, and 1691–96, and 1785–87; untitled document signed "K. Causer, Major, 4th Regt., July 3–12," folders 6 and 7, box 133, Sherman Papers.

32. Avant in Wells-Barnett, "East St. Louis Massacre," 14–15; Mineola Magee and Allison in *House Transcripts,* 1373–79 and 3634; "Military Authorities Are in Full Control," *ESLDJ,* July 3, 1917, 1, 2, 5; "Mayor Mollman Issues Statement, *ESLDJ,* July 8, 1917, 1, 2; "East St. Louis Looks Like War Zone City," *Chicago News,* July 5, 1917, in *TINCF,* 6:1015; "Seek Bodies, Fire Ruins East St. Louis," *TINCF,* 6:1004; Queen, "East St. Louis as I Saw It."

33. "7,000 Blacks Flee East St. Louis as Troops Stop Riot," *New York City Call,* July 6, 1917, in *TINCF,* 7:0014; "Military Authorities Are in Full Control," *ESLDJ,* July 3, 1917, 1, 2, 5; "Several Hundred Negroes Brought Across the River," *TINCF,* 6:1018; "Fear-Stricken Negroes Leaving East St. Louis," *TINCF,* 6:0990; "Thousands Leave East St. Louis Cared for Here," *St. Louis Argus,* July 6, 1917, in *TINCF,* 6:1001; "3,000 Refugees Cared for Here," *St. Louis Republic,* July 4, 1917, in *TINCF,* 6:1002; Wells-Barnett, "East St. Louis Massacre," 8, 18; "St. Louis," [1918?], box E:87, part I, series VI, National Urban League Records. On ratio of

black refugees to estimated black population, see "Grand Jury Returns Indictments for 103," *ESLDJ*, August 15, 1917, 1; Rudwick, *Race Riot at East St. Louis*, 162–66, 269–70. For official toll of thirty-nine deaths, see Simon Stickgold, "Illinois Race Riots" (Research Memorandum 5, Illinois Interracial Commission, Springfield, 1943). For unofficial reports from a low of fifteen to a high of a few hundred deaths, see "Race Mobs Kill 15 to 75 Negroes," *TINCF*, 6:1036–37; "Two More White Men Die," *St. Louis Globe Democrat*, July 18, 1917, in *TINCF*, 7:0011; "Rioters Kill 350 Negroes in E. St. Louis," *New York City Call*, July 3, 1917, in *TINCF*, 7:0085; "Complete Probe of Riot Begun," *ESLDJ*, July 5, 1917, 1, 2. For a high estimate of 500 killed, see Leonidas C. Dyer in *Riot at East St. Louis, Illinois: Hearings before the Committee on Rules . . . August 3, 1917* (Washington, D.C.: Government Printing Office, 1917), 5; Allison in *House Transcripts*, 3635–36; "Town a Living Hell for Three Days," *Chicago Defender*, July 14, 1917, in *TINCF*, 6:1024–25.

34. "Urged Negroes to Get Arms," *New York* [rest of title unreadable], July 5, 1917, in *TINCF*, 7:0098; Jeffrey B. Perry, ed., *A Hubert Harrison Reader* (Middletown, Conn.: Wesleyan University Press, 2001), 94–95.

35. Oscar Leonard, "The East St. Louis Pogrom," *Survey* 38 (July 14, 1917): 331–33, in Foner and Lewis, *Black Worker*, 5:309–12; "E. St. Louis Wipes Out Disgrace of Race Riots and Plans Better City," *New York Tribune*, February 3, 1918, in *TINCF*, 8:1008; "Lawyer Says Riots Awakened Employers," *St. Louis* [rest of title unreadable], January 17, 1918, in *TINCF*, 8:1014; "Complete Probe of Riot Begun," *ESLDJ*, July 5, 1917, 1, 2; "Riot Promises to Bring Reorganization," *ESLDJ*, July 6, 1917, 1; "12 Negroes on Trial for Riot Murders," *ESLDJ*, October 1, 1917, 1. Black leaders included city detective James Vardaman, Illinois assistant state's attorney for St. Clair County Noah Parden, laborers Marshall Alexander and Sam Wheat, mortician R. M. C. Green, physician Lyman B. Bluitt, Negro Businessmen Association member and realtor Pearl Abernathy, saloonkeepers William "Buddy" Bell and George Kyle. Sources did not name black women among the arrestees. Sam Wheat as alderman in "Negro Elected Alderman of East St. Louis," *St. Louis Argus*, April 7, 1916, 1; Pearl Abernathy in National Negro Business League, *Twentieth Annual Meeting: Held at St. Louis, Missouri, August 13, 14, 15, 1919*, in Records of the National Negro Business League, Part I: Annual Conference Proceedings and Organizational Records, 1900–1919 (Bethesda, Md.: University Publications of America, 1994), microfilm, 3:00669–00670; occupations of Abernathy, Alexander, Bell, Bluitt, Kyle, Parden, and Wheat from the *1912 City Directory*. "Supervisors Hold Lily White Meeting," *ESLDJ*, July 9, 1917, 2; "Four Negroes Attend Supervisors' Meeting," *ESLDJ*, August 6, 1917, 1; Wells-Barnett, "East St. Louis Massacre." Parker's occupation listed in *McCoy's East St. Louis City Directory, 1916* (East St. Louis, Ill.: McCoy, 1916, hereafter cited as *1916 City Directory*); Parker's membership on the Board of Supervisors in "2 Whites on Trial for Negro's Murder," *ESLDJ*, October 8, 1917, 1; "Negro Members of County Board Fail to Attend," *St. Louis Post-Dispatch*, July 8, 1917, in *TINCF*, 6:1021.

36. Anderson in *House Transcripts,* 362; Daisy [Westbrook] to Louise [Westbrook?], n.d., folders 6–7, box 133, Sherman Papers; Emma Ballard and Mrs. Willie Flake in Wells-Barnett, "East St. Louis Massacre," 4 and 5.

37. "Negroes Leaving East Saint Louis," *St. Louis Argus,* July 20, 1917, in *TINCF,* 6:0992; "Red Cross Aid Will Be Given," *ESLDJ,* July 9, 1917, 1; "St. Louis Gets 10,000 Negroes as Riot Result," *ESLDJ,* July 10, 1917, 3; "'Cap'n' Robinson, Most Colorful Negro Character of City," *ESLDJ,* February 28, 1926, 3-A; Bowman in "Cook Charges Negro Padded City Payroll," *ESLDJ,* September 24, 1926, 1, 10-A; Clementine R. Hamilton, *The Ebony Tree* (East St. Louis, Ill.: privately printed, [1971?]), 9; Lucy Mae Turner, "The Family of Nat Turner, 1831 to 1954: Part II—Conclusion," *Negro History Bulletin* 18 (April 1955): 4, 15, 17, 156–57. Occupations listed in *1912 City Directory;* Elizabeth Lindsay Davis, *The Story of the Illinois Federation of Colored Women's Clubs* (Chicago, 1922; reprint, New York: G. K. Hall, 1977), 24; Wells-Barnett, "East St. Louis Massacre," 18; "Citizens Committee Report" attached to letter, Ida B. Wells-Barnett to Senator Lawrence Y. Sherman, July 20, 1917, folder 1, box 133, Sherman Papers.

38. "Negroes Will Observe Their Freedom's Day," *ESLDJ,* September 18, 1917, 1; "Negroes Celebrate Their Freedom," *ESLDJ,* September 23, 1917, 7. Unfortunately, local annual Emancipation Proclamation Day speeches were not recorded. On black East St. Louisan response to the draft, see "10,000 Negroes in East St. Louis Neglect Registration Duties," *ESLDJ,* May 25, 1917, 1; "Anti-Negro Riots Due to Labor Causes," *New York Times,* July 8, 1917, in Hampton University Newspaper Clipping File, 459:37–38; "War Department Will Call First of East St. Louis Drafted Negroes Oct. 3," *ESLDJ,* September 26, 1917, 1; "Many Negroes Left E. St. Louis," *St. Louis Post-Dispatch,* October 9, 1917, in *TINCF,* 7:0010; "11 Negroes Arrested for Evading Draft," *ESLDJ,* October 15, 1917, 1; "East St. Louis Is Expected to Furnish 1,500 Negroes for Crack Eighth Infantry," *ESLDJ,* November 18, 1917, 1, section 2; "Several Hundred Included in Draft Men to Leave in August Calls from This City," *ESLDJ,* July 28, 1918, 10; "108 East St. Louis Youths Registered for Military Duty Aug. 24—Drawing This Week," *ESLDJ,* September 1, 1918, 9.

39. "Complete Probe of Riot Begun," *ESLDJ,* July 5, 1917, 1, 2; "Government Inquiry on in E. St. Louis Riots," *TINCF,* 7:0013; Phillip W. Coyle, and Frank A. Hunter, and Robert E. Conway in *House Transcripts,* 6, 20–21, 29, 31–32, and 61, and 125; "Negro Pastor Urges Colored to Return," *ESLDJ,* October 31, 1917, 1. Local white leaders, even southern planters with powerful connections to the federal government, had to place "patriotism before economic gain"; see Nan Elizabeth Woodruff, *American Congo: The African American Freedom Struggle in the Delta* (Cambridge, Mass.: Harvard University Press, 2003), 39–40.

40. "The East St. Louis Carnage," *New York City Telegram,* July 5, 1917, in *TINCF,* 6:1009; "A Negro's Protest against the White Man's Appalling Savagery," *New York Sun* [n.d.], in *TINCF,* 6:1037; "Negroes of U.S. Stirred by Riot," *St. Louis Republic,* July 4, 1917, in *TINCF,* 6:1040–41; "State, Nation Disgraced by East St. Louis Riots," [n.d.], in *TINCF,* 7:0028–29. J. Silas Harris to . . . Sherman,

July 16, 1937; L. Amasa Knox to . . . Sherman, July 16, 1917; C. S. Dodson to Sherman, July 16, 1917; W. K. Kavanaugh to . . . Sherman; July 16, 1917; J. N. Rarick to . . . Sherman, July 17, 1917; J. R. Ranson [and] E. P. Blakemore, Civic League of Wichita, Kansas, to the President . . . Wilson, [n.d.]; Nannie H. Burroughs to . . . Sherman, July 25, 1917, folder 1, Sherman Papers. Peyton M. Lewis to . . . Sherman, July 20, 1917, folder 2, box 133, Sherman Papers. On white supremacists betraying notions of American democracy, see Cecelski and Tyson, *Democracy Betrayed,* 6. On concerns about democracy, see "The President and the Negro," *New York Evening Post,* August 14, 1917, in *TINCF,* 6:1040; Kelly Miller, "The Disgrace of Democracy," Correspondence of the Military Intelligence Division, United States War Department, RG165, entry 65, microfilm M1440, roll 6, no. 10218, National Archives, Washington, D.C.; Tillman and Vardaman in 65th Cong., 1st sess., *Congressional Record,* July 16, 1917, vol. 55, pt. 5, 5151, and August 16, 1917, vol. 55, pt. 6, 6061–67.

41. Letters from NAACP chapters between July 22 and August 5 to Senator Sherman, and Nannie H. Burroughs, National Association of Colored Women, to Lawrence Y. Sherman, July 25 and July 28, 1917, folder 1, box 133, Sherman Papers; Martha Gruening and W. E. B. Du Bois, "The Massacre of East St. Louis," in Foner and Lewis, *Black Worker,* 5:318–32; "Dr. DuBois Here to Assist the N.A.A.C.P. Branch," *St. Louis Argus,* July 13, 1917, in *TINCF,* 7:0065; "N.A.A.C.P. Riot Fund Growing," *St. Louis Argus,* July 17, 1917, 1; "N.A.A.C.P. Makes Riot Report," *St. Louis Argus,* August 10, 1917, 1; "Minutes of the Meeting of the Board of Directors, September 17, 1917," National Association for the Advancement of Colored People Records, Manuscript Division, Library of Congress, Washington, D.C. (hereafter cited as NAACP Records), 1:0557.

42. Chas. M. Thomas to Lawrence Y. Sherman, January (i.e., July) 11, 1917, folder 1, box 133, Sherman Papers. W. C. Thrasher to Lawrence Y. Sherman, July 14, 1917; Fred Hotes to Sherman, July 16, 1917; A. C. King, Manager, Heller and Livingston Clothing Co., to Sherman, July 17, 1917; and F. J. Klapp, Klapp's Shoe and Hosiery House, to Sherman, July 17, 1917, folder 6–7, box 133, Sherman Papers. "Compete Probe of Riot Begun," *ESLDJ,* July 5, 1917, 1, 2; "Riot Promises to Bring Reorganization," *ESLDJ,* July 6, 1917, 1; "Federal Probe, Re-Organization Urged for Police, *ESLDJ,* July 8, 1917, 1, 6; "Brundage Here" and "Negroes Wait on Lowden," *ESLDJ,* July 11, 1917, 1; "Wants U.S. to Probe East St. Louis Riots," *ESLDJ,* July 17, 1917, 1; "Grand Jury Returns Indictments for 103," *ESLDJ,* August 15, 1917, 1.

43. "Wants U.S. to Probe East St. Louis Riots," *ESLDJ,* July 17, 1917, 1; "Negroes Started, but White Men Finished It," *St. Louis Globe Democrat,* July 4, 1917, in *TINCF,* 6:0988; "Blacks Organized," *ESLDJ,* July 8, 1917, 1; C. P. Renner in *House Transcripts,* 1256–57, 1280.

44. "Real Estate Exchange in Rousing Meet," *ESLDJ,* July 18, 1917, 7.

45. On the South, see Hahn, *Nation under Our Feet,* 431–51.

46. "Post-Dispatch Is Source of Many Riot Report Facts," *St. Louis Post-Dispatch,* July 8, 1918, in *TINCF,* 8:1031–32; Conway, and Anderson, and Boylan,

and Canavan, and Miller in *House Transcripts,* 188, and 368–72, and 630–32, and 1446–49, and 4065–80.

47. Philip W. Coyle and quote by J. W. Paton in *House Transcripts,* 25–26, 447. C. W. Middlekauff, State of Illinois Office of the Attorney General, to L. Y. Sherman, July 24, 1917, folder 1, box 133, Sherman Papers. Rev. E. T. Soper, WCTU, Gillett, WI, to L. Y. Sherman, July 1917, and Mary B. Birkicht, St. Louis, Missouri, to L. Y. Sherman, August 20, 1917, folder 1, box 133, Sherman Papers; Olof Z. Cervin, architect, Rock Island, Ill., to L. Y. Sherman, July 6, 1917, C. C. Warren, insurance agent, Freeport, Ill., to L. Y. Sherman, July 6, A. H. Owens, chairman of Christian County Division of Antisaloon League, to L. Y. Sherman, July 6, 1917, Dr. Cleaves Bennett, Champaign, Ill., to L. Y. Sherman, July 7, 1917, Leslie J. Owen, attorney, LeRoy, Ill., to L. Y. Sherman, July 7, 1917, and J. Fred Ammann to L. Y. Sherman, [n.d.], folder 2, box 133, Sherman Papers.

48. "As the Journal Views It," *ESLDJ,* July 6, 1917, 4, section 2; "Riot Promises to Bring Reorganization," *ESLDJ,* July 6, 1917, 1, 2; "Federal Probe, Re-organization Urged for Police," *ESLDJ,* July 8, 1917, 1, 6; "100-Committee Plans Lasting Organization," *ESLDJ,* July 9, 1917, 1; Clarence Eugene Pope in *House Transcripts,* 2617.

49. "See Bright Future for East St. Louis," *ESLDJ,* July 15, 1917, 4, section 4; "Committee of 100 Meet and Discuss Commission Gov'nt," *ESLDJ,* August 28, 1917, 1; "E. St. Louis Closes Its Greatest Year," *ESLDJ,* December 30, 1917, 1; Pope in *House Transcripts,* 2606–7, 2610–16.

50. "Further Inquiry to Be Held into East St. Louis Riots," *New York Age,* July 20[?], 1918, in *TINCF,* 8:1027–28; Marguerite Edith Jenison, *War Documents and Addresses* (Springfield: Illinois State Historical Library, 1923), 347–50; Frank E. Nulsen and Pope in *House Transcripts,* 1024 and 2625.

51. Anderson and Pope in *House Transcripts,* 375 and 2617–19, 2624; "Mollman Refuses Watkins Resignation," *ESLDJ,* July 13, 1917, 1; "Payne and Hickey Are Suspended by Board," *ESLDJ,* July 16, 1917; "Police Board Members Resignations Refused," *ESLDJ,* July 17, 1917, 1; "Riot Views of Pastors' Alliance," *ESLDJ,* August 16, 1917, 6, 8; "Will Ignore Pastors' Resolution—Mollman," *ESLDJ,* September 11, 1917, 1; "Keating to Enforce the City Ordinances for Sunday Closing," and "Police Backed by Uncle Sam; Begins War on Prostitutes," *ESLDJ,* August 19, 1917, 1.

52. John P. Pero and Robert E. Johns in *House Transcripts,* 735–37 and 4333–38.

53. "George B. Vashon," *Annual Conference Proceedings, 1910–1950,* NAACP Records, 8:0441–46; Pope, and McGlynn, and Allison in *House Transcripts,* 2619–20, and 2986, 3067–68, 3070–71, 3077–80, and 3690–93; "Police Would Raise $500 for Indicted Members Defense," *ESLDJ,* August 21, 1917, 1; "Chief Keating Prohibits Solicitation of Funds for Relief of Indicted Police," *ESLDJ,* August 28, 1917, 1; "Coroner Will Resume Hearing Wednesday," *ESLDJ,* July 10, 1917, 1. See chapter 3 of this volume for details on political alliances between Democrats and Republicans.

54. The author determined occupations of testifiers by cross-referencing their names in "Participants in East St. Louis Race Riot," in Rudwick, *East St. Louis*

Race Riot of 1917, reel 7, to names in "Grand Jury Returns Indictments for 103," *ESLDJ,* August 15, 1917, 1, and *1916 City Directory.* Seventy-five names could not be matched to an occupation because the *1916 City Directory* listed two or more persons of the same name. The names of 306 testifiers were not listed in the *1916 City Directory,* perhaps because directory compilers failed to include these 306 testifiers, the directory was compiled before some of the testifiers became residents, or testifiers were nonresidents.

55. "[Grand Jury of St. Clair County, Report] Belleville, Illinois, August 14, 1917," in Rudwick, *East St. Louis Race Riot of 1917,* reel 7; "Grand Jury Returns Indictments for 103," *ESLDJ,* August 15, 1917, 1; "36 Now under Arrest on Various Rioting Grand Jury Charges," *ESLDJ,* August 17, 1917, 1; "Mollman and Secretary Are Indicted," *ESLDJ,* September 9, 1917, 1; "Political Intriguing Responsible for My Indictment, Mollman," *ESLDJ,* September 11, 1917, 1.

56. "Riot Jurors Chosen from Out in County," *ESLDJ,* October 16, 1917, 1; Anderson in *House Transcripts,* 358–59; "Hard to Get Jurors to Try Two Whites," *ESLDJ,* October 9, 1917, 1; "Riot Jury May Get Case Early To-Night," *ESLDJ,* November 21, 1917, 1.

57. "State Case against Negroes Weak," *St. Louis Argus,* October 5, 1917, 1; Rudwick, *Race Riot at East St. Louis,* 111–20; "Complete Probe of Riot Begun," *ESLDJ,* 5 July 1917, 1, 2; "12 Negroes on Trial for Riot Murders," *ESLDJ,* October 1, 1917, 1; "Negroes Offer Alibis for Accused Blacks," *ESLDJ,* October 5, 1917. Occupations of Albert Hughes, Guy Moore, George Roberts, Dee Smotherman, Slim Tackett, and Horace Thomas listed in *1916 City Directory.* Occupations of Marshall Alexander, Charles Foster, and William Palmer noted in *1912 City Directory;* Othaniel (O'Faniel?) Peoples not listed in either city directory. Parker's membership on the Board of Supervisors in "2 Whites on Trial for Negro's Murder," *ESLDJ,* October 8, 1917, 1; "Jurors Finally Get First Riot Case," *ESLDJ,* October 7, 1917, 1; "2 Whites on Trial for Negro's Murder," October 8, 1917, 1; "Crow Gives Negroes 14 Years Each," *ESLDJ,* October 31, 1917, 1. On history of white people denying black people the right to self-defense while African Americans had built a tradition of armed self-defense, see Strain, *Pure Fire,* 1–32; Patricia A. Schechter, *Ida B. Wells-Barnett and American Reform, 1880–1930* (Chapel Hill: University of North Carolina Press, 2001), 149.

58. Schechter, *Ida B. Wells-Barnett and American Reform,* 152; Allison in *House Transcripts,* 3761–65; "As the Journal Views It," *ESLDJ,* July 6, 1917, 4, section 2; "Witnesses Declare Bundy Was Leader," *ESLDJ,* October 4, 1917, 1, 5; "Attorneys File Habeas Corpus for Release of Dr. Bundy," *ESLDJ,* August 14, 1917, 1; "Bundy Fights Return," *ESLDJ,* August 19, 1917, 1; "Bundy Habeas Corpus Proceedings Up Today," *ESLDJ,* August 21, 1917, 1; "Bundy Extradition Hearing Is Up Today with Ohio Officials," *ESLDJ,* August 29, 1917, 1.

59. "Dr. Bundy Declares It's 'Persecution,'" *ESLDJ,* October 15, 1917, 1; "Minutes of the Meeting of the Board of Directors, December 10, 1917" and "East St. Louis," *Crisis* 15, no. 2 (December 1917): 62; "Dr. Bundy Disclosing Fall Election Frauds," *ESLDJ,* November 19, 1917, 1; "Bundy Involves Mayor in Open

Confession," *ESLDJ*, November 26, 1917, 1, 5; "Bundy Exposes Political Fraud in East St. Louis," *St. Louis Argus*, November 30, 1917, 1; *Minutes of the Meeting of the Board of Directors*, NAACP Records, 1:0578; "East St. Louis Hero Near[s] Trial for Life Ans. NAACP," *New York News*, August 18, 1918, in *TINCF*, 8:1011; "Bundy Deserted by Association Which Helped in Defense," *ESLDJ*, July 27, 1918, 1, 6; "Twelve Attorneys to Clash in Fight to Secure Justice for L. N. Bundy," *ESLDJ*, November 14, 1918, 1.

60. "Dr. Leroy Bundy's Trial Postponed," *Chicago Defender*, September 14, 1918, in *TINCF*, 8:1010; "Review of the Dr. Bundy Case," *St. Louis Argus*, September 27, 1918, in *TINCF*, 8:1025; "The Case of Dr. Bundy," *Crisis* 16, no. 5 (September 1918): 224–25. The last news of the East St. Louis chapter is found in the March 1919 issue of the NAACP *Branch Bulletin*.

61. "Raise $1507 Bundy Fund for Defense," *ESLDJ*, May 16, 1920, 1; "Jury Gives Bundy Life Sentence," *ESLDJ*, March 28, 1919, 1; "Review of the Dr. Bundy Case," *St. Louis Argus*, September 27, 1918, 1; "Bundy Takes Stand," *St. Louis Argus*, March 28, 1919, 1; "The Bundy Verdict Is Said to Be Unjust," *ESLDJ*, April 4, 1919, 1; W. E. B. Du Bois, "Leroy Bundy," *Crisis* 25, no. 1 (November 22, 1922): 16–21; Robert Hill, ed., *The Marcus Garvey and UNIA Papers* (Berkeley: University of California Press, 1983), 4:700–1; "Dr. Leroy N. Bundy Attempts Suicide," *Chicago Defender*, September 22, 1923, 1; David D. Van Tassel and John J. Grabowski, *The Encyclopedia of Cleveland History* (Bloomington: Indiana University Press, 1987), 136–37; "Dr. Le Roy Bundy, Negro Political Leader Is Dead," *Cleveland Press*, May 28, 1943; David D. Van Tassel and John J. Grabowski, *The Dictionary of Cleveland Biography* (Bloomington: Indiana University Press, 1996), 72; Rudwick, *Race Riot at East St. Louis*, 261n108; Kenneth L. Kusmer, *A Ghetto Takes Shape: Black Cleveland, 1870–1930* (Urbana: University of Illinois Press, 1976), 272–73.

62. Albertson in *House Transcripts*, 520–25. "Chamber Endorses Commission Form," *ESLDJ*, October 30, 1917, 3; Pero in *House Transcripts*, 723; Andrew J. Theising, *Made in USA: East St. Louis, The Rise and Fall of an Industrial River Town* (St. Louis, Mo.: Virginia Publishing, 2003), 184. "Maurice V. Joyce Asserts Lax Rule Caused Race Riot," *St. Louis Post-Dispatch*, July 6, 1917, in *TINCF*, 6:1002–3; "Politics Caused Race Riot Mayor Mollman Is Told," *ESLDJ*, September 14, 1917, 1; "Rev. Allison Tells of Conditions Here," *ESLDJ*, November 9, 1917, 1, 5; "Rev. Allison Tells about Politicians," *ESLDJ*, November 11, 1917, 1, 9, 10; "Mollman Warned Blood Would Flow," *ESLDJ*, November 13, 1917, 1; "Congressmen Learn of Political Ring," *ESLDJ*, November 14, 1917, 1, 5; "Dr. Bundy Disclosing Fall Election Fraud," *ESLDJ*, November 19, 1917, 1; "Bundy Involves Many in Open Confession," *ESLDJ*, November 26, 1917, 1, 5; Boylan and McQuillan in *House Transcripts*, 626, 634–35 and 1707–8. Similar claim made for the 1919 Chicago race riot in Tuttle, *Race Riot*, 64–66; "Commission Form for East St. Louis Receives Impetus," *ESLDJ*, September 11, 1917, 1; "Commission Carries by Majority of 2,330," *ESLDJ*, November 7, 1917, 1.

63. Advertisement, *ESLDJ*, July 8, 1917, [8]; "See Bright Future for East St. Louis," *ESLDJ*, July 15, 1917, 4, section 2; "Factories on Way to East St. Louis,"

ESLDJ, July 15, 1917, 1, section 2; "Nothing Can Stop the Growth of Our City," *ESLDJ*, July 15, 1917, 1, section 3; "Real Estate Exchange in Rousing Meet," *ESLDJ*, July 18, 1917, 7; "Black Hand Warnings," *ESLDJ*, July 15, 1917, 1; "E. St. Louis Is Quiet after the Race Massacre," *St. Louis Argus*, July 13, 1917, in *TINCF*, 6:0990; "Negroes Leaving East Saint Louis," *St. Louis Star*, July 20, 1917, in *TINCF*, 6:0992; "East St. Louis," *St. Louis Argus*, July 27, 1917, 4; "Troops Remain in East St. Louis," *St. Louis Argus*, July 27, 1917, 1; Conway in *House Transcripts*, 165–66, 177; "Zones for Negro Homes Proposed in East St. Louis," *St. Louis Star*, January 10, 1918, in *TINCF*, 8:1015; Pero in *House Transcripts*, 722–23 (unfortunately Pero neither provided names of his African American conversationalists nor quoted them verbatim).

64. "East St. Louis Is Sued for $700,000," *Chicago Defender*, January 12, 1918, in *TINCF*, 8:1015; "E. St. Louis Riot Mayor Defeated for Reelection," *St. Louis Argus*, February 27, 1919, in *TINCF*, 10:1034; Theising, *Made in USA*, 184, 186.

65. For Arkansas, see Woodruff, *American Congo*, 86–103. For Tulsa, see, for example, Scott Ellsworth, *Death in a Promised Land: The Tulsa Race Riot of 1921* (Baton Rouge: Louisiana State University Press, 1982), 66–67, 69; Alfred L. Brophy, *Reconstructing the Dreamland: The Tulsa Riot of 1921, Race, Reparations, and Reconciliation* (New York: Oxford University Press, 2002).

66. "George B. Vashon," *Annual Conference Proceedings, 1910–1950*, NAACP Records, 8:0446.

67. W. E. B. Du Bois, "Returning Soldiers," *Crisis* 13 (May 1919); Mark Robert Schneider, *"We Return Fighting": The Civil Rights Movement in the Jazz Age* (Boston: Northeastern University Press, 2002), 7–13.

Chapter 5: Return to the Political Arena, 1917–1929

1. On no worries of another racial conflict, see Mayor Fred H. Mollman to Adjutant General F. S. Dickson, September 5, 1918, no. 10218–60/10, Memorandum, Brigadier General Frank P. Wells, Illinois Reserve Militia to Adjutant General, Chief of Staff, Illinois: "Possible Race Riots in East St. Louis, Illinois," September 9, 1918, no. 10218–60/11, Correspondence of the Military Intelligence Division, U.S. War Department, RG165, entry 65, microfilm M1440 ("Negro Subversion") roll 4, National Archives, Washington, D.C. On black people under control of white political factions, see Martin Kilson, "Political Change in the Negro Ghetto, 1900–1940s," in *Key Issues in the Afro-American Experience,* ed. Nathan I. Huggins, Martin Kilson, Daniel M. Fox (New York: Harcourt Brace Jovanovich, 1971), 2:171–72. On widening segregation in northern cities after World War I, see Allan H. Spear, *Black Chicago: The Making of a Negro Ghetto, 1890–1920* (Chicago: University of Chicago Press, 1967), 72; Kenneth L. Kusmer, *A Ghetto Takes Shape: Black Cleveland, 1870–1930* (Urbana: University of Illinois Press, 1976), 170–73. On using residential segregation to build black-controlled community institutions and a black city within a white city, see Joe William Trotter Jr., *Black Milwaukee: The Making of an Industrial Proletariat, 1915–45* (Urbana: University of Illinois Press, 1985), 81, 93, and Trotter, *River Jordan: African American Urban Life*

in the Ohio Valley (Lexington: University Press of Kentucky, 1998), 95–121; St. Clair Drake and Horace Cayton, *Black Metropolis: A Study of Negro Life in a Northern City* (1944; reprint, University of Chicago Press, 1993), 80–83. On tactics elsewhere to effect a return to the formal political arena, see Paul Ortiz, "'Eat Your Bread without Butter, but Pay Your Poll Tax!' Roots of African American Voter Registration Movement in Florida, 1919–1920," in Charles M. Payne and Adam Green, eds., *Time Longer Than Rope: A Century of African American Activism, 1850–1950* (New York: New York University Press, 2003), 196–229.

2. Articles in East St. Louis newspapers reported in 1917 and 1918 that black men were not signing up for military service because of disruptions caused by the 1917 race riots. Though no documentation has been found to show returning black veterans in East St. Louis engaging in political actions, it can be assumed that they did. Federal agents concluded that socialist and communist activities involved mainly white Americans of eastern European descent and had no influence with black East St. Louisans. "Memorandum, July 8, 1919, Director of Negro Economics to Secretary of Dept. of Labor," folder 8/102-C, box 18, Field Reports of the Division of Negro Economics, 1918–19, General Records, 1907–42, Department of Labor, RG174, entry 1, National Archives, College Park, Md.; "18 Arrested in Raid on Reds Are Held by U.S. Authorities," *ESLDJ,* January 4, 1920, 1, 3; "Members of Slovak Association No. 55 Surrenders," *ESLDJ,* January 8, 1920, 1; "May Day Circulars Litter Down Town Sections," *ESLDJ,* May 2, 1921, 1; report by Emil A. Solanka, St. Louis, Mo., "Radical Activities in the St. Louis District," February 28, 1920, April 10, 1920, and July 10, 1920, no. OG229849, microfilm M1085, General Investigative Records, Records of the Federal Bureau of Investigation, RG65, entry 29, National Archives, College Park, Md.; "Nine Foreigners Refused Citizen Papers, Two Were as Communists," *ESLDJ,* May 13, 1921, 1.

3. "East St. Louis Shows Most Remarkable Growth of Any American Municipality," *ESLDJ,* September 8, 1918, section 3, 1, 4; "City Approaches Expanding Period," *ESLDJ,* October 15, 1919, 2; "Bartholomew to Supervise City Plan Commission in Program Here," *ESLDJ,* December 31, 1918, 1; Harland Bartholomew, *A Comprehensive City Plan for East St. Louis, Illinois: Prepared for the War Civics Committee* (East St. Louis, Ill.: Daily Journal, 1920), 2, 37, 39.

4. "The Status of the Railroads," *ESLDJ,* April 6, 1921, 4; "How Suggested Terminal's Plan Affects East St. Louis," *ESLDJ,* July 2, 1922, 1-A, 2-A; "Our City's Industrial Progress," *ESLDJ,* March 13, 1921, 4.

5. Andrew J. Theising, *Made in USA: East St. Louis, The Rise and Fall of an Industrial River Town* (St. Louis, Mo.: Virginia Publishing, 2003), 7–12. On working people's relations to mass consumerism, see Lizabeth Cohen, *Making a New Deal: Industrial Workers in Chicago, 1919–1939* (New York: Cambridge University Press, 1990), 8; "Industries Reduce Working Force," *ESLDJ,* July 29, 1920, 1; "Plants Slow Up," *ESLDJ,* January 9, 1921, 2.

6. "Industry and Real Estate Healthy," *ESLDJ,* September 24, 1922, 1-C, 3-C; "More Employed in the East Side District Than in St. Louis," *ESLDJ,* August 23, 1923; "East St. Louis Has Passed Through One of the Best Years in Its History,"

ESLDJ, December 30, 1923, 2-B; "Business Depression Vanishing," *ESLDJ*, January 2, 1921, 1, 7; "No 'Lop-Sidedness' Here," *ESLDJ*, January 24, 1922, 4; "City Exempts Manufacturer from City Tax," *ESLDJ*, April 4, 1922, 2; "Prosperity in Employment Is Report Theme," *ESLDJ*, June 15, 1923, 1-A, 6-A; "Unemployment Is Noticeable," *ESLDJ*, December 10, 1923, 9; "Employment Is Better for July," *ESLDJ*, August 24, 1924, 1-C, 2-C; "East St. Louis in Infancy as Factory Center," *ESLDJ*, October 25, 1925, 1-C, 2-C; "Business Leaders See City as Future Steel Center," *ESLDJ*, December 13, 1925, 1-D, 2-D; "City Prosperous," *ESLDJ*, January 24, 1926, section 3, 1; "East St. Louis on Threshold of Expansion," *ESLDJ*, March 7, 1926, 1-C; "C. of C. Opens Drive for Greater City, *ESLDJ*, February 21, 1928, 1, 2; "Come to East St. Louis," *ESLDJ*, February 3, 1929, 4-A; "Industries Owe a Moral Debt," *ESLDJ*, November 14, 1929, 4.

7. Theising, *Made in USA*, 183–87; see also chapter 1 of this volume; "Running Cost in E. St. Louis Shows Gains," *ESLDJ*, January 6, 1928, 1, 2; "Factory Output of Territory Is $400,000,000," *ESLDJ*, January 11, 1928, 5; "East St. Louis Expenses below Other Illinois Cities," *ESLDJ*, November 27, 1925, 1-A, 3-A; "Per Capita Cost of Government Here Second Lowest in Nation," *ESLDJ*, October 31, 1926, 1-C; "East St. Louis Has Favorable Rank in Governmental Cost," *ESLDJ*, November 12, 1926, 1-A; "East St. Louis Has Low Living Cost," *ESLDJ*, January 15, 1928, 1-C; East St. Louis, Illinois, "Proceedings of the City Council, Regular Meeting, April 35, 1921," and "Proceedings of the City Council, Adjourned Meeting, April 30, 1921," microfilm, Illinois State Archives, Springfield; "City under Debt Limit," *ESLDJ*, June 30, 1926, 1.

8. "People Who Think City Is Suburb of St. Louis Are Wrong," *ESLDJ*, May 23, 1928, 5; "Launches Move to Change Name of East St. Louis," *ESLDJ*, November 30, 1924, 1-C, 2-C; "Dr. Vonnahane Recites His 16 Reasons Favoring Move for Changing Name of City," *ESLDJ*, April 12, 1928, 14; "Two Sides Heard on East St. Louis Change of Name, *ESLDJ*, April 20, 1928, 2; Vonnahane listed as Vonnahme in the 1924 and 1926 city directories; "St. Louisans Balk Swap of Eads and Free Bridges," *ESLDJ*, May 17, 1926, 1; "Bridge Exchange Again Confronts City," *ESLDJ*, June 2, 1926, 1, 2; "Miller Submits New Bridge Plan" and "Miller's Plan to Break Terminal R.R. Monopoly," *ESLDJ*, July 15, 1926, 1, 2; "City Council Indorses St. Louis Bridge Plan," *ESLDJ*, July 20, 1926, 1, 2; Organization Formed to Protect City in Bridge 'Change Issue,'" *ESLDJ*, December 12, 1926, 1, 2; "C. of C. Has No Funds to Fight RR Rate Case," *ESLDJ*, February 16, 1928, 1, 2; "Terminal Held as Only Foe to Use of Bridge," *ESLDJ*, August 14, 1928, 1, 2; "Railroad to Use Municipal Bridge," *ESLDJ*, November 20, 1928, 1, 2; "East St. Louis Suffers from Unfair Tariff," *ESLDJ*, January 13, 1929, 1-C; "Local C. of C. to Decide on Industry Plan," *ESLDJ*, January 26, 1927, 1; "C. of C. Reconsiders 'Metropolitan Area' Stand," *ESLDJ*, December 7, 1928, 1, 2; "Realtors Would Exploit Industrial Advantages," *ESLDJ*, March 6, 1927, 1-C, 2-C; "C. of C. Denies Part to Enter 'Metropolitan Area,'" *ESLDJ*, November 11, 1928, 2; "Trying to Annex East St. Louis," *ESLDJ*, November 11, 1928, 4-A; "B.M.A. Opposes 'Metropolitan Area,'" *ESLDJ*, November 25, 1928, 1, 4; "Metropolitan Area Idea May

Jeopardize Prospects," *ESLDJ*, November 30, 1928, 4-A; "Business Men Renew Fight on Area Plan," *ESLDJ*, December 16, 1928, 1-C; "St. Louis Admits Its Mistakes," *ESLDJ*, January 29, 1929, 6; "First Necessity of Attractive City," *ESLDJ*, January 25, 1921, 4; "More Vision Needed," *ESLDJ*, July 29, 1929, 4.

9. Emmett J. Scott, *Negro Migration during the War* (New York: Oxford University Press, 1920; reprint, New York: Arno Press, 1969), 98–99; "Building in East St. Louis Keeps Pace with People," *ESLDJ*, September 27, 1925, 1-D, 2-D; "381 Residences Built Here in Eleven Months," *ESLDJ*, December 8, 1929, 1-C.

10. "East St. Louis Fast Transforming Itself into Model City of Homes with Growing Residence Sections," *ESLDJ*, September 24, 1922, 2-C; "East St. Louis," [1918–1920?], part I, series VI, box E:87, National Urban League Records, Manuscript Division, Library of Congress, Washington, D.C.

11. On black people confronting inadequate housing conditions in other cities, see Richard W. Thomas, *Life for Us Is What We Make It: Building Black Community in Detroit, 1915–1945* (Bloomington: Indiana University Press, 1992), 89–94; Christopher Robert Reed, *The Chicago NAACP and the Rise of Black Professional Leadership, 1910–1966* (Bloomington: Indiana University Press, 1997), 71; Trotter, *Black Milwaukee*, 66–71, and *River Jordan*, 106–9; "$500,000 Subdivision Being Opened Here for Negro Dwellers," *ESLDJ*, November 4, 1928, 1-C; "Negroes to Have Modern Conveniences in Kenwood Development Subdivision," *ESLDJ*, November 11, 1928, 1-C; "Real Estate Deal Marks Negro Growth," *ESLDJ*, September 9, 1923, 2; Jeanne A. Faulkner, interview by author, September 24, 1999, East St. Louis.

12. On black residents facing sharpening segregation and using their communities as a base for political action, see Trotter, *River Jordan*, 103–4, 109–11.

13. 1919 population estimate in V. P. Randall, "Report on East Saint Louis, Illinois, September 24, 1919," in *Black Workers in the Era of the Great Migration, 1916–1929*, ed. James R. Grossman (Frederick, Md.: University Publications of America, 1985), 21:00318, 00320; U.S. Bureau of the Census, *Fourteenth Census of the United States, 1920*, all calculations by the author; "7433 Negroes in City," *ESLDJ* December 1, 1920, 1; "Negro Population of E. St. Louis 7433," *St. Louis Argus* December 3, 1920, 1; Scott, *Negro Migration during the War*, 99.

14. Tuttle, *Race Riot*, 130–32; Scott, *Negro Migration during the War*, 100; *Fourteenth Census of the United States, 1920*, all calculations by the author; "Aluminum Ore Cuts Off 600 Men in Local Plant," *ESLDJ*, October 1, 1920, 1; "Aluminum Ore Cuts Wages of All Employees," *ESLDJ*, December 1920, 9; "Big Plants Report Slight Decreases in Employment as Reaction Sets In," *ESLDJ*, December 16, 1920, 1; "Employment Officials Says 5,000 Are Idle in This Industrial Zone," *ESLDJ*, December 29, 1920, 1; "Central Trades Hears Report on Jobless in City," *ESLDJ*, January 13, 1921, 1; Plants Slow Up," *ESLDJ*, January 9, 1921, 2; "9,001 Employes [*sic*] in 52 Industries as against 19,304 in Normal Periods," *ESLDJ*, June 23, 1921, 1; "Five Men for Every Place Available Now," *ESLDJ*, July 11, 1921, 2.

15. Examples of contemporary articles favorably reporting on black migrants' adjustment to urban life include John B. Abell, "The Negro in Industry," *Trade Winds* (March 1924): 17–20; John W. Barton, "Negro Migration," *Methodist*

Quarterly Review 74 (January 1925): 84–101; P. O. Davis, "The Negro Exodus and Southern Agriculture," *American Review of Reviews* 68 (October 1923): 401–7; Dwight Thompson Farnham, "Negroes, a Source of Industrial Labor," *Factory and Industrial Management* (August 1918): 123–29; George Edmund Haynes, "Effect of War Conditions on Negro Labor," *Proceedings of the Academy of Political Science* 8 (February 1919): 299–312; George Edmund Haynes, "The Negro at Work: A Development of the War and a Problem of Reconstruction," *American Review of Reviews* 59 (April 1919): 389–93; George Edmund Haynes, "Negro Migration—Its Effect on Family and Community Life in the North," *Proceedings of the National Conference of Social Work* (1924): 62–75; George Edmund Haynes, "Negroes Move North," *Survey* 40 (August 9, 1919): 697–99; Joseph A. Hill, "Recent Northward Migration of the Negro," *Monthly Labor Review* 18 (March 1924): 475–89; Charles S. Johnson, "Black Workers and the City," *Survey* 53 (March 1925): 641–43; Charles S. Johnson, "How Much Is the Migration a Flight from Persecution," *Opportunity* 1 (September 1923): 272–74; Charles S. Johnson, "How the Negro Fits in Northern Industries," *Industrial Psychology* 1 (June 1926): 399–412; Charles S. Johnson, "The Negro Migration," *Modern Quarterly* 2 (July 1925): 314–26; *1924 City Directory*, all calculations by the author.

16. Emma L. Shields, "Negro Women in Industry," *Bulletin of the Women's Bureau,* no. 20 (Women's Bureau, U.S. Department of Labor, Washington, D.C.: Government Printing Office, 1922), 11–15, 34–35; Jane Olcott, *The Work of Colored Women* (New York: Colored Work Committee, War Work Council, National Board, Young Women's Christian Associations, [1919]), 113; *Fourteenth Census of the United States, 1920,* all calculations by the author; [Aluminum Ore Co., Swift and Co., East Side Packing Co., Certain-Teed Products Co., Model Laundry Co.] in Grossman, *Black Workers in the Era of the Great Migration,* 18:00715, 00658, 00693, 00719, 00864.

17. Trotter, *River Jordan,* 101. On domestic laborers, see Elizabeth Clark-Lewis, *Living In, Living Out: African American Domestics in Washington, D.C., 1910–1940* (Washington, D.C.: Smithsonian Institution Press, 1994); Tera W. Hunter, *To 'Joy My Freedom: Southern Black Women's Lives and Labors after the Civil War* (Cambridge, Mass.: Harvard University Press, 1997), 52–61, 235. On domestic service as an important occupation for black women, see Elizabeth Ross Haynes, "Negroes in Domestic Service in the United States," *Journal of Negro History* 8 (October 1923): 384–442; *Fourteenth Census of the United States, 1920,* all calculations by the author; "Colored Girls Want Farm Work," *ESLDJ,* July 2, 1920, 8.

18. *1912 City Directory,* all calculations by the author. Charles Nash in "In the District Court of the United States for the Eastern District of Illinois: Transcript of Testimony and Proceedings before the Grand Jury, September 22, 1942 to and including September 29, 1942," folder 146–10–2, sec. 22, class no. 146–10, 441, Classified Subject Files, Records of the Department of Justice, RG60, entry 114BD, National Archives, College Park, Md. Frances Nash Terrell and Claudia Nash Thomas, interview by author, September 24, 1999, East St. Louis, Ill., *Fourteenth Census of the United States, 1920,* all calculations by the author.

19. Trotter, *River Jordan,* 73–74, 77–78, 82. On racial segregation covertly enforced through laws, see David Delaney, *Race, Place, and the Law, 1836–1948* (Austin: University of Texas Press, 1998).

20. "Two Colored Schools Point with Pride to Good Records," *ESLDJ,* October 19, 1924, 10; "Board Defers Move in School Redistricting Dispute in North End," *ESLDJ,* June 15, 1928, 1; "First of New Schools," *ESLDJ,* September 1, 1929, 1-C; "Colored Leader of Note Leads Local 'Y' Work," *ESLDJ,* April 13, 1919, 12; "Establish a Center for Colored 'Y,'" *ESLDJ,* May 16, 1919, 3; "Dedication of East St. Louis YMCA Sunday," *St. Louis Argus,* July 25, 1919, 8; "Y.W.C.A. Recreation Center," *ESLDJ,* February 13, 1920, 1; "Colored Class to Observe Health Work," *ESLDJ,* April 3, 1921, 8; "Large Numbers of Negroes Are Arriving Daily," *ESLDJ,* August 7, 1923, 1, 2; "Shows Importance of Bond "Y" Drive," *ESLDJ,* April 2, 1925, 5. The local newspaper never reported what speakers said at Emancipation Day celebrations; see "Emancipation Day Picnic in Lincoln Park," *ESLDJ,* September 21, 1922, 2; "Emancipation Day Picnic in New Park," *ESLDJ,* September 22, 1922, 2; "Emancipation Day Marked Double Event," *ESLDJ,* September 24, 1922, 5; "Negroes Plan Emancipation Day Convention Here," *ESLDJ,* August 30, 1925, 2-C; "Emancipation Day to See Launching of Ten-Day Event," *ESLDJ,* September 20, 1925, 8; "Negroes Plan to Celebrate Emancipation," *ESLDJ,* August 12, 1928, 6; "Negroes Plan 15-Day Fair in September," *ESLDJ,* August 21, 1928, 10; "Political Days Set Aside for Big Negro Fair," *ESLDJ,* August 29, 1928, 10.

21. On welcoming returning veterans, see "1,500 Colored Citizens Hear Stories of War," *ESLDJ,* April 6, 1919, 10.

22. Alain Locke, ed., *The New Negro: An Interpretation* (New York: Macmillan, 1925); Stanley B. Norvell and William M. Tuttle Jr., "Views of a Negro during 'The Red Summer' of 1919," *Journal of Negro History* 51 (July 1966): 210–11. On federal repression of various African American political formations, see Theodore Kornweibel Jr., *"Seeing Red": Federal Campaigns against Black Militancy, 1919–1925* (Bloomington: Indiana University Press, 1998). On the African Blood Brotherhood, see Winston James, *Holding Aloft the Banner of Ethiopia: Caribbean Radicalism in Early Twentieth-Century America* (London: Verso, 1998), 155–84.

23. Judith Stein, *The World of Marcus Garvey: Race and Class in Modern Society* (Baton Rouge: Louisiana State University Press, 1986), 186–207.

24. "Lecturer Would Populate Liberia," *ESLDJ,* May 12, 1920, 7. On the presence of the UNIA in the South, see Steven Hahn, *A Nation under Our Feet: Black Political Struggles in the Rural South from Slavery to the Great Migration* (Cambridge, Mass.: Harvard University Press, 2003), 471–72; Nan Elizabeth Woodruff, *American Congo: The African American Freedom Struggle in the Delta* (Cambridge, Mass.: Harvard University Press, 2003), 116–17.

25. "Work of Agitator Traced by Local Colored Ministers," *ESLDJ,* January 20, 1920, 1; "Colored 'Moses' Tells of Scheme to Lead Fellows to Promised Land," *ESLDJ,* February 1, 1920, 10; "Lecturer Would Populate Liberia," *ESLDJ,* May 12, 1920, 7; "Negro Colonizer to Speak at City Hall," *ESLDJ,* July 1, 1921, section 2, 3; "Negro Meeting Raided by Cops," *ESLDJ,* January 16, 1925, 1.

26. "Application for Charter, February 3, 1924," and "Membership Reports, Illinois, Danville-Evanston," box C252, group II, NAACP Records. Occupations of the first fifty members: barbers, 2; butchers, 1; contractors, 1; editors, 1; engineers, 1; housekeepers, 1; housewives, 6; insurance agents, 2; insurance collector, 1; janitors, 5; laborers, 7; ministers, 2; physicians, 1; policemen, 3; porters, 1; professors (i.e., schoolteachers), 3; proprietors, 1; realty agents, 1; secretaries, 1; salesmen, 1; shipping clerks, 1; teachers, 2; upholsterers, 1; undertakers, 3; YWCA secretaries, 1.

27. On opposing the UNIA while assisting authorities, see Trotter, *River Jordan*, 119–20. On the Chicago NAACP chapter and its relations to city politics, see Reed, *Chicago NAACP*, 61–65.

28. "Unions Are Beginning to Take Friendly Interest in Negro Workers," *New York City Call*, September 28, 1917, in *TINCF*, 6:0447; "Live Better by Joining Labor Unions," *ESLDJ*, April 4, 1919, 5; Philip Weightman interview, October 7, 1986, tape 284, Illinois Labor History Society, United Packinghouse Workers of America Interviews, 1979–83 (SC 452), State Historical Society of Wisconsin, Madison. For contemporary accounts of black workers' importance to industry and the labor movement, see Abram L. Harris, "Negro Labor's Quarrel with White Workingmen," *Current History Magazine of the New York Times* 24 (September 1926): 903–8; Arnold T. Hill, "The Negro in Industry," *American Federationist* 32 (October 1925): 915–20; Arnold T. Hill, "Negro Labor," *American Federationist* 35 (December 1928): 1452–56. On Chicago's packinghouse workers, see Olcott, *The Work of Colored Women*, 113; Tuttle, *Race Riot*, 108–28; Rick Halpern, *Down on the Killing Floor: Black and White Workers in Chicago's Packinghouses, 1904–54* (Urbana: University of Illinois Press, 1997).

29. On the connections between the labor movement and the Chicago race riot of 1919, see Tuttle, *Race Riot*, 109–12, 153–56.

30. V. P. Randall, "Report on East Saint Louis, Illinois," 21:00318, 21:00320; "Aluminum Ore Company 'Jim Crows' the Race Men," *Chicago Defender*, March 23, 1918, in *TINCF*, 8:0191; "Mexicans Being Questioned after Attempt to Beat Negro Laborers," *ESLDJ*, August 9, 1920, 1; "Quit Jobs under Negro," *St. Louis Star*, August [3], 1921, in *TINCF*, 14:0131.

31. "Labor Men Plan Purchase of Park Site for Negroes," *ESLDJ*, September 13, 1918, 1; Whalen's position as city commissioner listed in 1924 and 1926 city directories.

32. "Labor Union Heads Say Many Facing Want Minus Jobs," *ESLDJ*, August 16, 1921, 4; "Figures on Unemployment Believed High," *ESLDJ*, September 9, 1921, 1; "C. of C. Asked for Support of Jobless Plans," *ESLDJ*, October 9, 1921, 2; "Unemployment Decreased in Last 30 Days," *ESLDJ*, October 14, 1921, 1, 7; "Industry Here over Fifty Per Cent Normal," *ESLDJ*, November 13, 1921, 1, 7.

33. "Urged Jobless to Avoid City," *ESLDJ*, January 30, 1921, 2; "County Overseer Would Give Work to People Living in East St. Louis," *ESLDJ*, May 11, 1921, 1, 2. Clarence McLinn and Bessie King, letter to NAACP National Office, July 21, 1924; "Resolution, Mayor's Office, East St. Louis, July 14, 1924"; M. M. Stephens, Mayor, to C. J. McLinn, President, and Bessie King, Secretary, East St. Louis

NAACP, July 16, 1924; East St. Louis Branch to Mayor, July 21, 1924; East St. Louis Branch to J. Weldon Johnson, July 21, 1924, folder "East St. Louis," box G-56, Branch Files, group I, 1909–1939, NAACP Records.

34. "Strike Vote on New Wage Scale Called," *ESLDJ*, March 15, 1921, 1, 2; "Packing House Employes Will Strike," *ESLDJ*, October 11, 1921, 1; "Plant Boards Meet to Talk Wage Decrease," *ESLDJ*, November 10, 1921, 1; "Over 2,000 Packer Employes Strike in Local Yards," *ESLDJ*, December 5, 1921, 1, 2; "Packers Hiring Men," *ESLDJ*, December 6, 1921, 1, 2; "Packers Pay Off Men on Strike," *ESLDJ*, December 8, 1921, 1, 2; "11 Held after Negro Is Shot at Stock Yards," *ESLDJ*, December 14, 1921, 1, 2; "Striker Held for Assault on Sol. Tartt," *ESLDJ*, December 16, 1921, 10; "Bullet Fired from a Group Strikes Negro," *ESLDJ*, January 4, 1922, 1, 2; "2 Negro Women Shot in Fight in Strike Zone," *ESLDJ*, January 6, 1922, 1, 2; "Strikers to Vote on Return to Work," *ESLDJ*, January 25, 1922, 1, 2; "Strikers Want Old Jobs Back," *ESLDJ*, February 1, 1922, 1, 2; "New Attempt to Form Union in Packing Houses," *ESLDJ*, October 15, 1922, 1, 2. One cannot discount either managers or third-party provocateurs intent on sparking racial violence. On events in Chicago, see Halpern, *Down on the Killing Floor*, 70–72.

35. Arlyn Wilbur Coffin, *Building East St. Louis for Tomorrow: First Annual Report of the War Civics Committee* (East St. Louis, Ill.: War Civics Committee, 1919), 1, 3, 5, 7, 11, 22; "East St. Louis," *Survey* 44 (August 16, 1920): 630; Bartholomew, *A Comprehensive City Plan for East St. Louis, Illinois*, xiii; "War Civics Audit to Disclose Funds Spent during Two Years' Work Here," *ESLDJ*, December 12, 1920, 1; William F. McDermott, "The Rebirth of East St. Louis," *Survey* 42 (May 17, 1919): 274–75; V. P. Randall, "Report on East Saint Louis, Illinois," 21:00318, 00320; "Urban League E. St. Louis," *St. Louis Argus*, April 25, 1919, 1.

36. "League on Urban Conditions among Negroes Founded," *ESLDJ*, July 27, 1918, 9; Nancy J. Weiss, *The National Urban League, 1910–1940* (New York: Oxford University Press, 1974); Jesse Thomas Moore Jr., *A Search for Equality: The National Urban League, 1910–1961* (University Park: Pennsylvania State University Press, 1981).

37. William J. Harrison, *The First 75 Years, 1918–1993* (St. Louis: Urban League of Metropolitan St. Louis, 1993), 10–11; *East St. Louis Urban League: For Social Service among Negroes* 1, no. 2 (February 1919), 1–6, folder on "Chicago Commission on Race Relations, 1919–1920, Press Notices, Pamphlets, Miscellaneous," Frank Orren Lowden Correspondence, 1917–1921, RG101.027, Illinois State Archives, Springfield; "Negroes to Plan Their Betterment," *ESLDJ*, November 9, 1917, 3; "Urban League for St. Louis, Mo. and E. St. Louis," *St. Louis Argus*, March 22, 1918, 1; "Committee Named for Urban League, *ESLDJ*, July 4, 1918, 8; "Urban League Branch in East St. Louis," *St. Louis Argus*, July 26, 1918, 1; "The East St. Louis Urban League," *St. Louis Argus*, March 19, 1920, 3. African American officers included John W. Hughes as second vice chairman, Minnie G. Scott as secretary, and St. Louisan league member George W. Buckner as executive secretary; Louise White, Maggie Freeman, Maude Haynes, Mary Martin, Fanny and Lucy Turner, and Gertrude Creath directed membership campaigns. In the *1924*

City Directory Lucy Turner's husband Charles was listed as a laborer, and Maude Haynes's husband William as a druggist; Creath's occupation in Clementine Hamilton, *The Ebony Tree* (East St. Louis, Ill.: privately printed, [1971?]), 23.

38. "League on Urban Conditions among Negroes Founded," *ESLDJ*, July 27, 1918, 9; "Needy Colored People to Have Xmas Dinners," *ESLDJ*, December 23, 1918, 1; "Urban League Report Shows Lot of Things Accomplished," *ESLDJ*, August 17, 1919, 7; "Urban League to Make Gifts," *ESLDJ*, December 24, 1919, 1; "Urban League Was Benefitted," *ESLDJ*, January 2, 1920, 3; "Urban League Notes," *ESLDJ*, March 2, 1920. "Community Leadership," *Survey* 63 (February 14, 1920): 588; Coffin, *Building East St. Louis for Tomorrow*, 21–24; "Physical Aid to Be Given City, Says War Civics Report," *ESLDJ*, February 15, 1920, 12; "Propose Night School for Negroes," *ESLDJ*, December 28, 1920, 2; "War Civics Expenses Totalled $124,412," *ESLDJ*, December 30, 1920, 1, 2; "Open Night Class for Negro Students," *ESLDJ*, January 12, 1921, 2.

39. Harrison, *The First 75 Years*, 11; "Would Revive Urban League for Negroes," *ESLDJ*, September 20, 1920, 7; "Small Ticket Lauded at Meet," *ESLDJ*, August 23, 1920, 4.

40. "Small Ticket Lauded at Meet," *ESLDJ*, August 23, 1920, 4; "Colored Boosters Donate to Home, *ESLDJ*, May 17, 1920, 3; "$140 Collected for Colored Relief," *ESLDJ*, August 8, 1920, 5; "City News in Brief," *ESLDJ*, December 31, 1920, 1; "Colored Club Is Searching for Man with New Game," *ESLDJ*, March 3, 1921, 2; "Colored 'Y' Notes," *ESLDJ*, April 11, 1920, 12; "YWCA, East St. Louis," *St. Louis Argus*, February 27, 1920, 3. Details on the Progressive Girls, Wohelo, and O.T.C. clubs remain unknown. "80 Colored Girls Taken in Reserves," *ESLDJ*, December 7, 1924, 3-B; "Negro Court of Honor Organized," *ESLDJ*, April 3, 1927, 2-A; "Negro Mothers' Club Holds April Meet," *ESLDJ*, April 23, 1928, 2.

41. Trotter, *River Jordan*, 117–18; "Many Baskets Given to Poor Colored People," *ESLDJ*, January 6, 1920, 5; "Plans Made for a New Nursey," *ESLDJ*, February 15, 1920, 6; "Soliciting Fund to Build Home for Colored Old Folks," *ESLDJ*, November 27, 1921, 10-A; "Distributing Xmas Baskets," *ESLDJ*, December 24, 1924, 3; "Building for Day Nursery Is Bought by Negro Society," *ESLDJ*, March 27, 1927, 3; "Suffering Looms for 4 Percent in East St. Louis," *ESLDJ*, December 11, 1927, 1-A; "85 Children Cared for by Negro Home," *ESLDJ*, March 11, 1928, 5; "Colored Day Nursery Is Formally Opened," *ESLDJ*, October 17, 1927, 7. East St. Louis, Illinois, "Proceedings of the City Council, Regular Meeting, August 18, 1919," microfilm, Illinois State Archives, Springfield; "Colored Old Folks Home Is Defended," *ESLDJ*, August 2, 1925, 5; "Colored Relief Body Shows a Successful Year," *ESLDJ*, January 17, 1926, 7; "300 at Banquet of Negro G.O.P. Club," *ESLDJ*, February 16, 1927, 2; "Year Success for Negro Old Peoples Home," *ESLDJ*, December 25, 1927, 2-C; Hamilton, *Ebony Tree*, 74–75.

42. On centrality of black women's grassroots activism and health care, see Susan L. Smith, *Sick and Tired of Being Sick and Tired: Black Women's Health Activism in America, 1890–1950* (Philadelphia: University of Pennsylvania Press,

1995), 1–3. On white authorities and black health care, see Hunter, *To 'Joy My Freedom*, 187–218.

43. "Hospital Serves, Regardless of Patient's Creed or Color" and "26 Nationalities Are Admitted to Hospital in Year," *ESLDJ*, September 19, 1926, 3-D and 9-D; Jeanne A. Faulkner; "Dunbar School Is Unhealthful, Negroes Infer," *ESLDJ*, February 5, 1925, 2; "Negro P.T.A. Obtains Help for Children," *ESLDJ*, February 20, 1927, 2; "Negro Infant Mortality Rate Here Is High," *ESLDJ*, September 9, 1926, 3; "Negro School P.T.A. Helps Health Work," *ESLDJ*, March 13, 1927, 4; "Dunbar Parent-Teachers Association Begins Drive to Combat Diphtheria," *ESLDJ*, November 21, 1927, 10; "Colored Children Being Vaccinated," *ESLDJ*, February 11, 1921, 2; "Large Numbers of Negroes Are Arriving Daily," *ESLDJ*, August 7, 1923, 1, 2; "Children Jam into City Hall in Droves," *ESLDJ*, January 26, 1925, 1, 2; "4 New Smallpox Cases Reported," *ESLDJ*, February 1, 1925, 1. "Officer Speaks at Negro Health Day Affair Here," *ESLDJ*, February 6, 1928, 10; Smith, *Sick and Tired of Being Sick and Tired*, 47–56.

44. "Raising $350 Fund to Save Negro Slayer," *ESLDJ*, May 18, 1924, 1.

45. Clarence McLinn and Bessie King, letter of July 21, 1924 to NAACP National Office; Rev. Farley Fisher and Mrs. Bessie King to Mr. Robert W. Bagnall, Director of Branches, folder "East St. Louis, Ill., March 10, 1925," NAACP National Office to Reverend Fisher, March 25, 1925, box G:56, group I, 1909–39, Branch Files, NAACP Records; East St. Louis Branch of the NAACP, *Perseverance and Progress: A History of the East St. Louis Branch of the NAACP* (East St. Louis, Ill., 1995), 6; Reed, *Chicago NAACP*, 45–46. Quoted passage, "moderately 'nationalist' institution," in Mark Robert Schneider, *"We Return Fighting": The Civil Rights Movement in the Jazz Age* (Boston: Northeastern University Press, 2002), 5.

46. "Negroes Object When Street Is Not Improved," *ESLDJ*, May 4, 1926, 1; "Negroes Seek Parley with City Council," *ESLDJ*, April 21, 1927, 12; "Negro Section Asks for Water Supply," *ESLDJ*, June 29, 1927, 2; "Improvements Are Planned in Negro Sections," *ESLDJ*, March 28, 1928, 1, 12; "Negroes to Hold Street Dance," *ESLDJ*, July 19, 1928, 10.

47. "'Lowest Office' Runs Politics" and "'Indifference Makes Politics,'" *ESLJ*, February 11, 1934, 4.

48. The following citations are representative of brief news blurbs that are the only sources that glimpse at the richness of black women's political activities: "Colored Women to Organize Clubs," *ESLDJ*, April 27, 1922, 2; "Colored G.O.P. Women Meet," *ESLDJ*, September 18, 1924, 5; "GOP Colored Women of Eighth Precinct Elected," *ESLDJ*, January 20, 1926, 10; "Colored Women of G.O.P. Club Name Campaign Heads," *ESLDJ*, January 24, 1926, 4; "County Colored G.O.P. Women to Have Convention," *ESLDJ*, January 31, 1926, section 2, 4; "Colored G.O.P. Ladies Meet," *ESLDJ*, February 7, 1926, 6-C; "Mrs. Chatters Heads County's Colored G.O.P. Women," *ESLDJ*, May 30, 1926, 3; "Colored G.O.P. Women Meet," *ESLDJ*, February 1, 1927, 2; "Negro Women's G.O.P. Club to Meet Saturday," *ESLDJ*, June 2, 1927, 12; "Negro Republican Women Attend Fair," *ESLDJ*, August 28, 1927, 3; Colored Women's Club Will Meet Wednesday,"

ESLDJ, January 22, 1928, 2-C; "Colored Women of G.O.P. Plan Affair Thursday," *ESLDJ,* February 7, 1928, 10; "Negro Woman, a Democrat, Says She Was 'First,'" *ESLDJ,* April 12, 1928, 14; "Negress Nominated in Precinct over Five Opponents," *ESLDJ,* April 15, 1928, 3; "Republican Negro Women Elect Heads," *ESLDJ,* May 29, 1928, 2; "Hoover-Curtis Club Formed by Negroes," *ESLDJ,* September 30, 1928, 2-C; "Pearl Chatters Is Elected President of Political Club," *ESLDJ,* June 9, 1929, 4. The *1924 City Directory* listed Pearl Chatters, Pinkie ("Pinksey") Reeves, and Ida Thornton's husbands as laborers, Melissa Basfield's husband as a minister, and Nevada Hamilton's occupation as rooming house owner.

49. "Small Ticket Lauded at Meeting," *ESLDJ,* August 23, 1920, 4; "Colored Man Enters Race for Assembly," *ESLDJ,* August 4, 1920, 1; election results, *ESLDJ,* September 16, 1920, 1; "Three Tickets in Field for Tuesday Voters," *ESLDJ,* April 2, 1922, 4; "Three Negroes Lose in Attack by Democrats," *ESLDJ,* April 5, 1922, 1, 2; "Rapid Voting in South End Making Record," *ESLDJ,* April 11, 1922, 1, 2; "Schnipper, Messick, Miller Winners," *ESLDJ,* April 12, 1922, 1, 2; "Prominent Negro Politician Is Buried with Honors," *ESLDJ,* April 26, 1926, 2; "Colored Speaker Addresses Big Crowd," *ESLDJ,* March 16, 1924, 4-B; "Small Has Aided Colored People," *ESLDJ,* April 7, 1924, 2; "City's Voting Strength to Be Near 28,000," *ESLDJ,* August 24, 1924, 1, 3; "Dinner Given to Pardoned Negroes," *ESLDJ,* November 7, 1924, 1-A. The *1924 City Directory* lists occupations for Henderson, Howard, and Nichols.

50. "Anti-Negro Circulars Bring Election Arrest at Polls," *ESLDJ,* April 7, 1925, 1; "East St. Louis Unofficial Vote by Precincts at Yesterday's Election," *ESLDJ,* April 8, 1925, 3. Matching the street address in the newspaper to the *1924 City Directory,* the directory listed S. Smith as Cortec Smith, a laborer; the *East St. Louis, Furmont, National City, Washington Park Directory, 1926* (Alton, Ill.: Huber Directory Co.; reprint, Woodbridge, Conn.: City Directories of the United States, Research Publications, Primary Source Media, 199–) listed C. [Calvin] Cotton as a minister. "Ku Klux Klan Being Formed on East Side," *St. Louis Times,* July 11, 1917, in *TINCF,* 6:0626; "Says Klan Has 4,000 Members in E. St. Louis," *ESLDJ,* August 20, 1922, 2; "Editor of Klux Paper Speaks at Meeting Here," *ESLDJ,* September 11, 1922, 1; "Secrets of Klan May Be Bared in Legal Action," *ESLDJ,* September 17, 1922, 4-A; "Ku Klux Klan Koncilium on Monk's Mound," *ESLDJ,* September 21, 1922, 1; "Charges Violation of Election Laws," *Montgomery Advertiser,* February 27, 1923, in *TINCF,* 18:0203; "Protection for Klantaugua Is Asked of Mayor," *ESLDJ,* June 3, 1924, 1, 2; "Klan Closes Show Blaming Police," *ESLDJ,* June 4, 1924, 1; "Negro Warned in "Klux Klan" Note to Move, *ESLDJ,* September 15, 1922, 1; "Local Ku Klux Chapter Posts Reward Offer," *ESLDJ,* September 18, 1922, 1; "Supposed Klan Candidates Get Names on Ticket," *Atlanta Constitution,* March 1, 1923, in *TINCF,* 18:0200; "Local Klansmen Help Initiate 100 Near Herrin," *ESLDJ,* May 2, 1924, 2.

51. On the second manifestation of Ku Klux Klan generally, see Kenneth T. Jackson, *The Ku Klux Klan in the City, 1915–1930* (New York: Oxford University Press, 1967). On women in the Ku Klux Klan of the 1920s, see Kathleen M. Blee,

Women of the Klan: Racism and Gender in the 1920s (Berkeley: University of California Press, 1991), 2–4. On the second manifestation of the Ku Klux Klan drawing members from a wide cross section of middle- and working-class Protestant white Americans, see David M. Chalmers, *Hooded Americanism: The First Century of the Ku Klux Klan, 1865–1965* (New York: Doubleday, 1965), 40, 41, 60, 121, 135, 152, 177. On middle-class white Protestants constituting a sizeable segment of the Ku Klux Klan, see Nancy MacLean, *Behind the Mask of Chivalry: The Making of the Second Ku Klux Klan* (New York: Oxford University Press, 1994), xi–xii, 53–62 passim; "Says Klan Has 4,000 Members in E. St. Louis," *ESLDJ*, August 20, 1922, 2; "Kounty Klan Gets Charter from Dragon," *ESLDJ*, January 16, 1925, 1.

52. "Primary Vote Will Be Record," *ESLDJ*, February 27, 1923, 1, 2; "City Campaign to Open at Once," *ESLDJ*, February 28, 1923, 1, 2; "Negroes Attend Wake and Hear Mayor in Talk," *ESLDJ*, March 30, 1923, 1, 2; "Veach Repudiates Klan," *ESLDJ*, April 1, 1923, 1, 2; "Clouds Fail to Check Heavy Voting," *ESLDJ*, April 3, 1923, 1, 2; "Ku Klux Klan Defeated in E. St. Louis Election," *St. Louis Argus*, September 10, 1926, 1; "Negro Voters Organize for Coming Election," *ESLDJ*, February 18, 1926, 2; "Colored Ministers' Alliance Endorses Julius L. Marshall," *ESLDJ*, March 18, 1926, 8; "Clean Politics Goal of Negro Body Formed," *ESLDJ*, March 10, 1926, 1; "Negro Body to Fight Political Dictatorship," *ESLDJ*, March 24, 1926, 2; "Tuesday's Unofficial Vote of Republican Primary in East St. Louis," *ESLDJ*, April 14, 1926, 4; Jackson, *Ku Klux Klan in the City*; MacLean, *Behind the Mask of Chivalry*, 17–18.

53. "City's Voting Strength to Be Near 28,000," *ESLDJ*, August 24, 1924, 1, 3. For examples of local activism, see "Widely Known Negro Buried with All Pomp at Command," *ESLDJ*, March 25, 1924, 1, 8; "Kills Negress as Revenge for Turning Him Up," *ESLDJ*, April 17, 1924, 1; "Joe Hunt to Face Trial for Murder," *ESLDJ*, April 18, 1924, 1; "Negro Carnival Going Full," *ESLDJ*, June 28, 1923, 1; "Wife of Negro Politician," *ESLDJ*, January 6, 1925, 1; "Cook Charges Negro Padded City Payroll," *ESLDJ*, September 24, 1926, 1, 10-A.

54. Newspaper did not quote black politician, in "City Discharges Democratic Negro Boss," *ESLDJ*, July 9, 1925, 1; "Dismissal of Negro Boss Is Not Acted On," *ESLDJ*, July 14, 1925, 1; "Janitor Problem Unsolved as Connors Waits 2 Days before Seeking Pay for Ousted Pair," *ESLDJ*, August 4, 1925, 1; "Gerold Is Routed from Payroll," *ESLDJ*, April 15, 1928, 1, 4.

55. "Candidates Are Invited before Negro Club," *ESLDJ*, April 1, 1926, 2; "Negroes of 60th Precinct Form Campaign Club," *ESLDJ*, April 5, 1926, 3; "Candidates Are Present at Rally of G.O.P. Negroes," *ESLDJ*, April 6, 1926, 2, "Democratic Move Initiated to Ban City Hall Control of Party after G.O.P. Win," *ESLDJ*, April 8, 1926, 1, 2; "Negro Democrats to Hear Orator," *ESLDJ*, August 30, 1926, 2; "Democrats to Get Out Vote for Election," *ESLDJ*, September 14, 1926, 10; "Negro G.O.P. Rally Tonight," *ESLDJ*, October 27, 1926, 2; "Negroes Urged to Vote G.O.P. Ticket Nov. 2," *ESLDJ*, October 29, 1926, 1, 2; "Brennan Money Fails to Sway Local Negroes," *ESLDJ*, November 1, 1926, 2; "Results in Vote Here

for Precinct Committee Posts," *ESLDJ*, April 11, 1928, 1, 2; "400 Negroes at Thompson Meet They Sponsor," *ESLDJ*, September 9, 1928, 1, 3; "Republicans to Get Going Full Blast at Once," *ESLDJ*, September 18, 1928, 1; "Negro Orator Is Speaker Here for Hoover and G.O.P.," *ESLDJ*, September 18, 1928, 12; "3,000 Attend Emancipation Day Ceremony," *ESLDJ*, September 23, 1928, 1, 3; "G.O.P. in City and County to Work Together," *ESLDJ*, October 21, 1928, 1, 2; "Negroes Won to G.O.P. at Night Rally," *ESLDJ*, October 25, 1928, 1, 7; "Robinson Appeals to Negroes," *ESLDJ*, October 31, 1928, 1, 2.

56. Lee Annie Bonner and Lillian Parks, interview by author, September 22, 1999, East St. Louis. Bonner and Parks are daughters of Horace Adams.

57. On African American voters deserting the Republican Party in 1936, see Nancy J. Weiss, *Farewell to the Party of Lincoln: Black Politics in the Age of Lincoln* (Princeton, N.J.: Princeton University Press, 1983). On the political realignment of African Americans, see Rita Werner Gordon, "The Change in the Political Alignment of Chicago's Negroes during the New Deal," *Journal of American History* 56 (December 1969): 584–603. On Chicago, see Drake and Cayton, *Black Metropolis*, 343–50; John M. Allswang, "The Chicago Negro Voter and the Democratic Consensus: A Case Study, 1918–1936," *Journal of the Illinois Historical Society* 60, no. 2 (1967): 159–63. On black Democratic Party workers and the United Colored Democracy in the 1920s, see Gilbert Osofsky, *Harlem: The Making of a Ghetto: Negro New York, 1890–1930*, 2d ed. (Chicago: Ivan R. Dee, 1966), 169–70. "G.O.P. Leaders Point Out Need for Party Reorganization Here," *ESLDJ*, November 8, 1928, 1, 2; "Gerold Deserted by 75 of 77 Members of G.O.P. Committee," *ESLDJ*, April 4, 1929, 1, 2.

58. "U.S. Indicts 4 Local Negroes in Bail Perjury," *ESLDJ*, May 17, 1929, 1. The article claimed Adams worked not as an insurance and real estate agent but as an embalmer for Charles T. Nash, also one of the accused. "Bondsmen to Serve 2 Years in U.S. Prison," *ESLDJ*, June 24, 1929, 1; "Democrats Win 9 of 13 Posts in Board Election," *ESLJ*, April 2, 1930, 1, 2; "Adams Funeral Date Not Set," *ESLJ*, April 19, 1935, 2.

Chapter 6: Breaking the Deadlock, 1930–1945

1. On pre–World War II housing controversies in Detroit and other cities, see Dominic J. Capeci Jr., *Race Relations in Wartime Detroit: The Sojourner Truth Housing Controversy of 1942* (Philadelphia: Temple University Press, 1984), 5–7; Cheryl Lynn Greenberg, *"Or Does It Explode?": Black Harlem in the Great Depression* (New York: Oxford University Press, 1991), 29–31.

2. Christopher G. Wye, "The New Deal and the Negro Community: Toward a Broader Conceptualization," *Journal of American History* 59, no. 3 (December 1972): 621–39.

3. Black military men and women served in segregated units at Scott Field, located twenty miles east of East St. Louis. See "First Negro Squadron at Scott Field," *ESLJ*, August 11, 1942, 5; "Negroes Training at Scott Field," *ESLJ*, January 25, 1943, 3; "Negro WACs Assist in Recruiting Drive," *ESLJ*, November 12, 1944,

3. Although no evidence was uncovered of black military personnel fighting discrimination in East St. Louis during the war, there is ample reason to assume it occurred there as it did elsewhere: see, for example, C. L. R. James et al., *Fighting Racism in World War II* (New York: Monad Press, 1980); Phillip McGuire, ed., *Taps for a Jim Crow Army: Letters from Black Soldiers in World War II* (Santa Barbara, Calif.: ABC-Clio, 1983); Martha S. Putney, *When the Nation Was in Need: Blacks in the Women's Army Corps during World War II* (Metuchen, N.J.: Scarecrow Press, 1992); Neil A. Wynn, *The Afro-American and the Second World War,* 2d ed. (New York: Holmes and Meier, 1993). On cities that experienced racial violence, see Greenberg, *"Or Does It Explode?"* 3–6, 136–37, 211–14; Dominic J. Capeci Jr. and Martha Wilkerson, *Layered Violence: The Detroit Rioters of 1943* (Oxford, Miss.: University of Mississippi Press, 1991).

4. Joe William Trotter Jr., *River Jordan: African American Urban Life in the Ohio Valley* (Lexington: University Press of Kentucky, 1998), 141–43.

5. Unfortunately research in several subgroups of the Work Projects Administration papers at the National Archives did not yield letters by black and white East St. Louisans describing their hardships during the Great Depression. On livelihoods depending upon railroads and other industries, see Duncan C. Smith, Aluminum Ore Company, to Colonel Horatio B. Hackett, Public Works Administration, Housing Division, December 6, 1934, folder "Project File H-4800," boxes 311–12, Project Files (1933–1937), Records of the Public Housing Administration, RG196, entry 2, National Archives, College Park, Md.; "City Must Raise about $18,000 for Relief of Paupers," *ESLJ,* July 12, 1931, 1, 2; "$20,000,000 Bond Issue Drive on as Part of Emergency Relief Program," *ESLJ,* June 23, 1932, 1, 10; "1,000 to Work for 'Dole' to Help Beautify Parks," *ESLJ,* September 1, 1932, 1; "Governor Fears Fate of 700,000 Illinoisans," *ESLJ,* September 6, 1932, 1.

6. U.S. Bureau of the Census, *Fifteenth Census of the United States, 1930;* "7,909 St. Clair County Families Receiving Aid from State Fund," *ESLJ,* October 2, 1932, 4; Mattie Malone, interview by author, September 21, 1999, East St. Louis; William Nash interview, July 14, 1986, tape 209, Illinois Labor History Society, United Packinghouse Workers of America Interviews, 1979–1983 (SC 452), State Historical Society of Wisconsin, Madison; Illinois Emergency Relief Commission, *Annual Report, 1933–1934,* Henry Horner Lincoln Collection, Abraham Lincoln Presidential Library, Springfield; Elizabeth A. Hughes, *Illinois Persons on Relief in 1935* (Chicago: Illinois Emergency Relief Commission, 1937), tables 47 and 49.

7. "Army of 2,205 Starts Work Here as Nation Opens Big Job Drive," *ESLJ,* November 20, 1933, 1; "Jobs for 5,585 Are Provided in New CWA Quota," *ESLJ,* December 10, 1933, 1; "A Report on the Availability of the Services of the United States Employment Office to Negro Applicants in Chicago and East St. Louis, Illinois: August 1, 1936," part 3, 5, folder "Survey—Illinois State Employment Service," Reports of Investigators of Negro Unemployment and Public Placement Facilities for Negroes, 1937–39, Records of the Bureau of Employment Security, RG183, entry 7, National Archives, College Park, Md.; "Only Actually Needy to

Be Given Jobs on New Work Relief Projects," *ESLJ,* March 14, 1934, 1; "Work Relief Plan Will Furnish Jobs for 7,000 Men from List of Needy," *ESLJ,* April 8, 1934, 1; Duncan C. Smith, Aluminum Ore Company, to Governor Horner, January 14, 1935, folder "Housing," Henry Horner Correspondence, 1933–1940, RG101.030, Illinois State Archives, Springfield; "235 Families Are Rejected," *ESLJ,* October 9, 1936, 1.

8. "City Asking Five WPA Projects to Furnish Jobs for 7,000 Men," *ESLJ,* September 6, 1935, 1; "Two-Thirds of Employables to Get Work Soon," *ESLJ,* October 25, 1935, 2; "WPA Put 184 Persons to Work in St. Clair County," *ESLJ,* November 10, 1935, 1; "City Asking Five WPA Projects to Furnish Jobs for 7,000 Men," *ESLJ,* September 6, 1935, 1; "Sewing Project to Employ 696," *ESLJ,* January 7, 1936, 1; "City Has Second Largest Project for Negro Women," *ESLJ,* February 9, 1936, 3. The East St. Louis WPA included black people from Brooklyn and Fireworks Station, an unincorporated suburban village of East St. Louis; "235 Families Are Rejected," *ESLJ,* October 9, 1936, 1; "WPA to Put 600 to Work," *ESLJ,* January 17, 1938, 1; Illinois State Commission on the Living Conditions of the Urban Colored Population (ISCLCUCP), "Transcripts: East St. Louis Proceedings, November 29, 1940," 146, microfilm 30–873, Illinois State Archives, Springfield; "Labor Market Report for East St. Louis, Illinois: October 7, 1941," 36, folder "Problem Areas: East St. Louis, Illinois, Survey," box 99, Area Labor Market Reports, 1940–49, Illinois, Records of the Bureau of Employment Security, RG183, entry 89, National Archives, College Park, Md. (hereafter cited as "Labor Market Report for East St. Louis").

9. "Negro Boys, Girls Are Enrolling in Classes," *ESLJ,* March 22, 1936, 6; "56-Hour Month for NYA Group," *ESLJ,* August 9, 1937, 4; "Labor Market Report for East St. Louis."

10. Mattie Malone, interview by author, September 21, 1999, East St. Louis; Lee Annie Bonner, interview by author, September 22, 1999, East St. Louis; "Negro WPA Worker Sets 27,778 Bricks in a Day for Record," *ESLJ,* March 14, 1937, 1.

11. On Atlanta, see Patricia Sullivan, *Days of Hope: Race and Democracy in the New Deal Era* (Chapel Hill: University of North Carolina Press, 1996), 43. On Harlem, see Greenberg, *"Or Does It Explode?"* 95–97, 216–17. "New Classes to Be Practical," *ESLJ,* January 21, 1934, 5; "Sewing Project to Employ 696," *ESLJ,* January 7, 1936, 1; "WPA Director Would Abolish Relief Set-up," *ESLJ,* January 20, 1938, 1, 2. Will Turner to Roosevelt, January 24, 1939, folder "Illinois—Political Coercion, M-Z," box 1181, Correspondence with State Administrators, Records of the Work Projects Administration, RG69, entry 610; D. Perry, President, East St. Louis NAACP, to Harry L. Hopkins, September 1, 1936, folder "ILL—J-O," box 1279; Sherman Love to Col. F. C. Harrington, April 29, 1939, folder "ILL—A-, box 1184; James Gee to Franklin D. Roosevelt, May 1, 1939, folder "ILL—A-Z, Jan-JE 1939," box 1280, Correspondence with State Administrators, Records of the Work Projects Administration, RG69, entry 693, National Archives, College Park, Md.

12. "Ask Materials for NYA Class," *ESLJ,* June 2, 1937, 12; "55 at Opening of NYA Meeting," *ESLJ,* June 9, 1938, 1; "Prepare Negro NYA Center," *ESLJ,* October 17, 1940, 5; "Shortage of Skilled Labor Opens Training Chances for Young Men," *ESLJ,* March 7, 1937, 1, 8; "Youth Advised to Organize, Demand Work," *ESLJ,* October 1, 1940, 1, 2; "Prepared Negro NYA Center," *ESLJ,* October 17, 1940, 5. "Report of Negro Activities, July 1, 1936–December 31, 1936," folder "Illinois, 1936–1937," Records of the Director. Final Report of the Division Director's File of Reports of State Directors of Negro Affairs, 1936–1939, Records of the National Youth Administration, RG119; ISCLCUCP, "Transcripts: East St. Louis Proceedings," 147, 169–70, 173; "Labor Market Report for East St. Louis," [36]; "Progress of Campaign against Race Discrimination: September 21, 1942," 4, folder "533.21–533.225, 1942, Illinois," Classified State Files {1939–42}, Records of the Bureau of Employment Security, RG183, entry 72, National Archives, College Park, Md.; Wye, "New Deal and the Negro Community," 634.

13. "Negro Boycott Closes Store," *ESLJ,* September 19, 1932, 2; "Grocer Says He Used Fists," *ESLJ,* September 20, 1932, 10; Annette Officer and Weldon Phillips in ISCLCUCP, "Transcripts: East St. Louis Proceedings," 96–103, 129–31; Olga Wayne interview by author, September 21, 1999, East St. Louis. On "Don't Buy" campaigns elsewhere, see, for example, Andor Skotnes, "'Buy Where You Can Work': Boycotting for Jobs in African-American Baltimore, 1933–1934," *Journal of Social History* 27, 4 (Summer 1994), 735–61; Greenberg, *"Or Does It Explode?"* 114–39.

14. Greenberg, *"Or Does It Explode?"* 116–17; Richard W. Thomas, *Life for Us Is What We Make It: Building Black Community in Detroit, 1915–1945* (Bloomington: Indiana University Press, 1992), 214–21; "The Original Illinois Housewives Association," box 038, Negro in Illinois Papers. Statewide, the association had a peak membership of 50,000 in 1942. Using city directories and the list of East St. Louis chapter officers for 1940 and 1942, the author identified the occupations of either the women or their husbands: Pinkie ("Pinksey") Reeves, husband a laborer; president Maude Logan, husband an Illinois Central Railroad employee; assistant secretary Lillie Hunter, husband a packinghouse laborer; treasurer Carrie Brown, husband a carpenter; parliamentarian Irene Yancey, husband a factory fireman; member committee chair Katie McGinis, husband a porter; adult education committee chair Rose Hoard, husband a public school attendance officer; youth and environment committee chair Luaco Gladden, husband a teacher; community welfare committee chair Cora Hughes, husband principal of Lincoln High School; courtesy committee chair Iota (J. R.) Connard (i.e., Conard), husband a school janitor; music committee chair Altha Caldwell, a teacher; finance committee chair Lavader (Joseph A.) Marley, a teacher; national and international relations committee chair Maggie Woods, husband a grocery and meats storekeeper. On black housewives association members as activists and leaders in other cities, see, for example, Thomas, *Life for Us Is What We Make It,* 221, 227.

15. "Lack of Funds Holding Back Adequate Health Work in East St. Louis," *ESLJ,* January 22, 1935, 1; quoted passage from Susan L. Smith, *Sick and Tired of*

Being Sick and Tired: Black Women's Health Activism in America, 1890–1950 (Philadelphia: University of Pennsylvania Press, 1995), 1; "Smallpox at Negro Center," *ESLJ*, February 24, 1935, 10; "Report 8 Cases of Smallpox in Negro District," *ESLJ*, March 30, 1939, 2; "Second Negro School Is Ordered Closed in Fear of Meningitis Spread," *ESLJ*, March 23, 1936, 1, 2; "Death Rate in Slum District Higher Than in Better Areas," *ESLJ*, March 14, 1934, 1; "Negro Health Drive Opened," *ESLJ*, August 14, 1934, 2; "Negro Better Babies Chosen," *ESLJ*, September 26, 1934, 3; "Negro Children Get Attention at VNA Clinic," *ESLJ*, January 30, 1935, 3; "Negro Doctor to Be Named by School Board," *ESLJ*, September 4, 1936, 3; Robert H. Beverley, *Negro Health in the State of Illinois* ([State Department of Public Health, 1937]), 32; "350 Children Vaccinated as New Clinic Is Opened," *ESLJ*, January 18, 1938, 4; "Free Clinics Next Week for Negro Children," *ESLJ*, April 1, 1938, 5.

16. Jeanne A. Faulkner, interview by author, September 24, 1999, East St. Louis; Beverley, *Negro Health in the State of Illinois*, 2, 15–17.

17. "Medics Ponder Negro Question," *ESLJ*, March 29, 1939, 5; "Medics Fail to Admit Negroes," *ESLJ*, May 5, 1939, 8.

18. "Negro Hospital Day Is Set Next Saturday," *ESLJ*, September 17, 1940, 5; "Negro Hospital Plan Rejected by City Council," *ESLJ*, February 14, 1941, 3; "Dr. Hagler to Open New Hospital," *ESLJ*, April 2, 1944, 28; "Here Is a Man Who Refuses to Admit He Is Defeated," *ESLJ*, April 9, 1944, 7; "Negro Hospital to Open," *ESLJ*, May 3, 1944, 5.

19. A series of articles by W. E. B. Du Bois in the *Crisis* in 1934 illustrates the debates then taking place at the national level, much to the embarrassment and anger of the NAACP leadership, about using segregation to strengthen black institutions and communities. On black medical care activism, see Smith, *Sick and Tired of Being Sick and Tired*, 58–82.

20. John Clark, and John Rogers, and E. E. McCarns in ISCLCUCP, "Transcripts: East St. Louis Proceedings," 6, and 19, and 165, 167; "Housing Here Called 'Worst,'" *ESLJ*, September 14, 1934, 1; "Negroes Work for Better Conditions in Local Homes," *ESLJ*, March 12, 1931, 2.

21. On segregated housing during the Great Depression, see Joe William Trotter Jr., *Black Milwaukee: The Making of an Industrial Proletariat, 1915–45* (Urbana: University of Illinois Press, 1985), 175–84; Trotter, *River Jordan*, 140. Also, H. B. Hackett to Col. C. E. Jenks, August 1, 1934; Oliver C. Winston to Robert B. Mitchell, September 21, 1934; Winston to Mitchell, September 21, 1934; Jenks to Hackett, "Personal," October 5, 1934; Jenks to Hackett, Federal Emergency Administration, October 17, 1934, folder "Project File H-4800," Project Files (1933–1937), Records of the Public Housing Administration.

22. Duncan Smith to Hackett, December 6, 1934; Hackett to Smith, December 13, 1934; Smith to Hackett, January 10, 1935; G. E. Fischer to B. M. Pettit, May 4, 1935; Louie F. Orr of East St. Louis NAACP to A. R. Clas, PWA Housing Dept., September 20, 1935, folder "Project File H-4800," boxes 311–12, Project Files (1933–1937), Records of the Public Housing Administration; "USHA Approved of Housing Sites Recorded," *ESLJ*, September 30, 1940, 1.

23. Trotter, *Black Milwaukee*, 183–84; "Security Ar[e]a Map Folder of Metropolitan St. Louis in Illinois: October 15, 1940," folder "Metropolitan St. Louis in Illinois: Security Area Descriptions," and "Map," folder "Metropolitan St. Louis in Illinois: Security Map and Area Descriptions," Records Relating to the City Survey File, 1935–40, Records of the Federal Home Loan Bank Board, Home Owners' Loan Corporation, RG195, entry 39, National Archives, College Park, Md.. On the impact of HOLC on municipalities, see Kenneth T. Jackson, *Crabgrass Frontier: The Suburbanization of the United States* (New York: Oxford University Press, 1985), 195–203. "Negro Housing Site Draws Protests," *ESLJ,* March 5, 1941, 1. On official decisions relating to housing in Detroit, see Capeci, *Race Relations in Wartime Detroit,* 35–37, 76–77; Thomas J. Sugrue, "Crabgrass-Roots Politics: Race, Rights, and the Reaction against Liberalism in the Urban North, 1940–1964," *Journal of American History* 82 (September 1995): 551–78; "Housing Units Completed," *ESLJ,* March 11, 1943, 1, 2; "Permanent Public Housing Projects Accommodating . . . Negro Families (as of August 31, 1943)," folder "Special Lists, Racial, 1938–57," Intergroup Relations Branch, 1936–63, Records of the Public Housing Administration; Simon Stickgold and Rubin Cohn, "Negro Housing Problems" (Research Memorandum 4, Illinois Interracial Commission, Springfield, 1943), 14.

24. "Negroes Observe History Week at Dunbar School," *ESLJ,* February 21, 1932, 2; "Lincoln School Is Rated High," *ESLJ,* December 17, 1933, 25; "Negro Schools to Stage Field, Literary Meet," *ESLJ,* May 21, 1936, 10; "School Enrollment Here Increases 435 in Year," *ESLJ,* May 8, 1931, 1, 2; "Public School Enrollment Shows Gain over Year Ago," *ESLJ,* March 5, 1933, 16; "260 Negro High Pupils Without Place to Attend," *ESLJ,* August 9, 1935, 8; "Potts Reports Lincoln School Is Overcrowded," *ESLJ,* January 8, 1937, 3; "More Negroes Going to School," *ESLJ,* October 11, 1937, 5; "Hold Caucus on Negro Enrollment," *ESLJ,* May 17, 1939, 5.

25. "Local Lincoln (Negro) High under Suspension as College Credit School after a Probe," *ESLJ,* February 12, 1931, 1, 6; "Inspector's Report Caused School Action," *ESLJ,* February 13, 1931, 1, 2; "Unsatisfactory Conditions at Lincoln High School Divulged by Two Local Board Members," *ESLJ,* February 22, 1931, 2; "200 Negroes at Board Meet Issue Ultimatum, They'll Not Send Tots to Annex Building," *ESLJ,* September 4, 1931, 1, 3; "High Schools Here Are Called 'Dirty, Crowded" by State Education Men," *ESLJ,* April 26, 1936, 1, 2; "State Takes Up School Problem in District 182," *ESLJ,* August 2, 1936, 2.

26. ISCLCUCP, "Transcripts: East St. Louis Proceedings," 6, 77, 84–86, 158.

27. On black workers seeing the Communist Party as a vehicle to fight racism, see Nell Irvin Painter, *The Narrative of Hosea Hudson: His Life as a Communist* (Cambridge, Mass.: Harvard University Press, 1979), 13, 87; Mark Naison, *Communists in Harlem during the Depression* (Urbana: University of Illinois Press, 1983).

28. See various issues of the Communist Party USA's newspaper, the *Daily Worker,* from 1930 to 1934; Dan T. Carter, *Scottsboro: A Tragedy of the American South,* rev. ed. (Baton Rouge: Louisiana State University Press, 1979), 147; "Communists Confer," *ESLJ,* June 26, 1934, 1; Granite City in "East St. Louis, Illinois,

Area Report: September 30, 1944," 53, folder "Serial Letter, Region VI," Field Operations Division Community Reports, 1941–1945: Region VI, Illinois-Wisconsin, Records of the Office of Community War Services, RG215, entry 55, National Archives, College Park, Md. On sundown towns in Illinois and other states, see James W. Loewen, *Sundown Towns: A Hidden Dimension of American Racism* (New York: New Press, 2005).

29. "Police Prevent Communist Meet," *ESLJ,* February 26, 1931, 1, 2; "Police Disperse Communists Here at Evening Raid," *ESLJ,* November 8, 1931, 1; "Four Communists Seized as Police Break Up Meeting," *ESLJ,* November 29, 1931, 4-C; "East Saint Louis, Ill., Workers Are Released," *Daily Worker,* December 3, 1931, 2.

30. "Artery Ailment Cause of Detective Combs' Fatal Collapse during 'Red' Raid," *ESLJ,* December 13, 1931, 1; "East St. Louis Police Kill Own Man in Raid on Jobless," *Daily Worker,* December 17, 1931, 1, 3; "Police Used Poison Gas in Raid Friday," *Daily Worker,* December 19, 1931, 5; C. R. F. Smith, "East St. Louis Studies Americanism," *Nation,* March 9, 1932, 283–84; "City Officials Determined to Curb Reds Here," *ESLJ,* December 13, 1931, 1; "Communists in Mass Meet Threat at the City Hall," *ESLJ,* December 30, 1931, 1; "15 Communists on Trial," *ESLJ,* December 22, 1931, 1, 2; "14 Alleged Communists to Be Tried," *ESLJ,* December 23, 1931, 2. Unfortunately, the sources did not name the black Communists.

31. "Police Halt 'Parade' at Nut Factory," *ESLJ,* May 24, 1933, 1; "Strike Appeal Marching Case to Be on June 8," *ESLJ,* June 1, 1933, 10. For the black worker–Communist alliance at the Funsten Nut Company factory in St. Louis, see Paul Dennis Brunn, "Black Workers and Social Movements of the 1930s in St. Louis" (Ph.D. diss., Washington University in St. Louis, 1975); "Women Strike at Nut Factory," *ESLJ,* March 15, 1934, 1; "See Settlement in Nut Strike," *ESLJ,* March 16, 1934, 1; "Strike of Nut Pickers Ended," *ESLJ,* March 29, 1934, 1; "Nut Factory Drops Corporation Papers," *ESLJ,* December 1, 1935, 7. On alliances between black radicals and workers and white radicals and workers, see Keith P. Griffler, *What Price Alliance? Black Radicals Confront White Labor, 1918–1938* (New York: Garland, 1995). On black workers' participation in the Communist Party, see Robin D. G. Kelley, *Hammer and Hoe: Alabama Communists during the Great Depression* (Chapel Hill: University of North Carolina Press, 1990), 17.

32. "Labor Unions Move to Organize Plants under Industrial Bill," *ESLJ,* June 25, 1933, 1; "Alcoa Employes Discuss Union," *ESLJ,* July 9, 1933, 2; "Nesbit Urges Alcoa Employees to Form Union," *ESLJ,* July 13, 1933, 1; "Packing House Workers Meet," *ESLJ,* July 23, 1933, 1; "Factories Here Probed by U.S.," *ESLJ,* July 25, 1933, 1; "Federal Agent Will Probe Labor Trouble in East St. Louis, *ESLJ,* August 20, 1933, 1, 7; "Labor Agreements to Follow Conferences with U.S. Agent in East St. Louis Industries," *ESLJ,* August 23, 1933, 1, 2; "Workers Rap Rules in Code," *ESLJ,* May 22, 1934, 2; "Seek to Settle Bottle Blowers Union," *ESLJ,* August 12, 1934, 1; "Workers at Aluminum Ore Plant Here Join Nation-Wide Walk Out," *ESLJ,* August 12, 1934, 1, 2; "Malleable Iron to Close Plant," *ESLJ,* September 7, 1934, 18; "$625,000 Pay Increase to Stockyards Workers in East St. Louis Area," *ESLJ,* September 25, 1934, 1.

33. ISCLCUCP, "Transcripts: East St. Louis Proceedings," 116–17; "Mepham Paint Workers Strike for Higher Pay," *ESLJ*, September 6, 1936, 1; "A.F.L., C.I.O. Test at Polls Here Tomorrow," *ESLJ*, August 1, 1937, 1, 4; "American Steel Plant Closed When 600 C.I.O. Members Walk Out," *ESLJ*, September 13, 1937, 1, 2; "Ask Aluminum Ore Election," *ESLJ*, February 13, 1938, 1; "30 Employees at 8 Lumber Yards Out on Strike," *ESLJ*, April 26, 1938, 1; "Certain-teed Strike Enters Second Month," *ESLJ*, May 8, 1938, 2; "1,400 Armour Workers Strike," *ESLJ*, November 30, 1938, 1; "Terms Reached, Laundry Strike Is Called Off," *ESLJ*, June 18, 1939, 2; "Workers Strike Monsanto Plant," *ESLJ*, October 2, 1939, 1; "Armour Union Pact Announced for Plant Here," *ESLJ*, February 21, 1940, 1; "Aluminum Ore Plant Strike Is Settled," *ESLJ*, December 1, 1940, 1, 2; "Labor Market Report for East St. Louis." Brief discussion on CIO and packinghouse workers except in East St. Louis and Kansas City, Missouri, in Rick Halpern, *Down on the Killing Floor: Black and White Workers in Chicago's Packinghouses, 1904–54* (Urbana: University of Illinois Press, 1997), 183; "East St. Louis, Illinois, Area Report: September 30, 1944," 53, folder "Serial Letter, Region VI," Field Operations Division Community Reports, 1941–1945: Region VI, Illinois-Wisconsin, Records of the Office of Community War Services, RG215, entry 55, National Archives, College Park, Md.

34. William Nash interview; "C.I.O. Begins Organization of Packing Plants," *ESLJ*, May 18, 1937, 1, 2; "C.I.O. Plans New Drive in Packing Plants," *ESLJ*, October 26, 1937, 2; William Davinroy interview, July 15, 1986, tape 214, and John Condellone and John Matikitis interview, July 17, 1986, tape 220, Illinois Labor History Society, United Packinghouse Workers of America Interviews, 1979–1983 (SC 452); "Labor Market Report for East St. Louis." Lewin-Mathes manufactured metal products and copper ingots and tubing; Rusha Durr in ISCLCUCP, "Transcripts: East St. Louis Proceedings," 116.

35. Progress of Campaign against Race Discrimination: September 21, 1942, 5, folder "533.21–533.225: 1942: Illinois," Classified State Files {1939–42}, Records of the Bureau of Employment Security, RG183, entry 72, National Archives, College Park, Md.; ISCLCUCP, "Transcripts: East St. Louis Proceedings," 13, 50–55, 61, 64, 67, 105–15, 121–26, 148–49; Olga Wayne interview.

36. "Negroes Organize Political Group," *ESLJ*, February 24, 1932, 10; "Negro Democrats Open Headquarters," *ESLJ*, February 28, 1932, 3; "Mrs. Perry Named District Leader of G.O.P. Negro Body," *ESLJ*, September 7, 1932, 8.

37. "Chicagoan to Address Negroes," *ESLJ*, November 3, 1932, 2. On the De-Priest incident, see David S. Day, "Herbert Hoover and Racial Politics: The De-Priest Incident," *Journal of Negro History* 65 (Winter 1980): 6–17; "Illinois Attorney Appointed," *Pittsburgh Courier*, December 17, 1932, in *TINCF*, 41:0718. Summers identified as assistant state's attorney in "City Will Have Three Probes in 'Beating' Case, *ESLJ*, June 27, 1934, 1.

38. "Negro Democrats Hear Kline and Other Speakers," *ESLJ*, September 21, 1933, 6; "Paramount Demos to Initiate 200 at Monday Meet," *ESLJ*, November 19, 1933, 3; "Negro Dentist Is Winner by Narrow Margin," *ESLJ*, April 12, 1934, 1,

3; "Dr. A. H. Smith Is Nominated," *ESLJ*, April 17, 1934, 1. See Smith's terse bi-ography in "Record Breaking Entry List Confronts Voter in Primary," *ESLJ*, April 8, 1934, 15, and Hamilton, *Ebony Tree*, 126. "Negro Politician Says He Was 'Beaten Up,'" *ESLJ*, June 26, 1934, 1; "City Will Have Three Probes in 'Beating' Case," *ESLJ*, June 27, 1934, 1; "Answer Charges within 5 Days, Policemen Told," *ESLJ*, June 28, 1934, 1; "Two Policemen Are Suspended in Beating Case," *ESLJ*, July 5, 1934, 1; "Victory of Negro Dentist Is Surprise of Assembly Race," *ESLJ*, November 7, 1934, 4; "Checkers Reveal Too Many Votes Cast in Brooklyn," *ESLJ*, November 9, 1934, 1; "Adams Funeral Date Not Set," *ESLJ*, April 19, 1935, 2; Richard and Wyvetter Younge, interview by author, September 27, 1999, East St. Louis.

39. To date, the only information on the Paramount Negro Women's Democratic Organization is a membership list. Eliza Hart Thomas, Probation Officer, East St. Louis, to Crystal Bird Fauset, Democratic National Campaign Committee, October 14, 1936; Edna Adams, President, Paramount Negro Women's Democratic Organization, to Eleanor Roosevelt [Mrs. Thomas F. McAllister, Director, Women's Division], January 5, 1938, folder "Organizations, Colored Workers (cont'd)," box 315-Correspondence, 1937–44, Democratic National Committee, Women's Division, Franklin D. Roosevelt Library, Hyde Park, N.Y. On the historical switch from Republican to Democrat, see Nancy J. Weiss, *Farewell to the Party of Lincoln: Black Politics in the Age of FDR* (Princeton, N.J.: Princeton University Press, 1983).

40. Bolen J. Carter, Assistant Principal, East St. Louis High School, to National Youth Administration, October 22, 1940, Letters and Reports Received by the Director from State Directors of Student Work, 1940–1941, Records of the Division of Student Work—Records of the Director, Records of the National Youth Administration, RG119, entry 176; ISCLCUCP "Report, March 1941," folder "1942, 62nd General Assembly Report of the Illinois State Commission on the Condition of the Urban Colored Population," 24, Bills, Resolutions, and Related General Assembly Records, 1st–88th Biennium, 1819–1994, RG600.001, Illinois State Archives, Springfield. G. T. Allen to NLRB, November 13, 1944, [Boilermakers Union file], box 63, [United States Employment Service, East St. Louis file], box 70, Active Case Records, 1941–1946, Region VI, Records of the Committee of Fair Employment Practice, RG228, entry 68, National Archives–Great Lakes Region, Chicago.

41. Annette Officer and Louie F. Orr in ISCLCUCP, "Transcripts: East St. Louis Proceedings," 127, 129, 131, 135, 140.

42. ISCLCUCP, "Transcripts: East St. Louis Proceedings," [15]; ISCLCUCP, "Preliminary Report on Findings," [1], folder "1941, 62nd General Assembly Report of the Illinois State Commission on the Condition of the Urban Colored Population, March 1941," Bills, Resolutions, and Related General Assembly Records, 1st-88th Biennium, 1819–1994, RG600.001, Illinois State Archives, Springfield; "State Hearing for Negroes Begun in City," *ESLJ*, November 29, 1940, 1; "Equality for Negroes Aim of Commission," *ESLJ*, December 1, 1940, 4.

43. F. R. Noack and G. W. Welsh in ISCLCUCP, "Transcripts: East St. Louis Proceedings," 59–61 and 63–64.

44. John T. Clark, and Sidney Williams, and W. K. Allen in ISCLCUCP, "Transcripts: East St. Louis Proceedings," 6–7, and 48–55, and 150–51.

45. Pauline K. Lewis in ISCLCUCP, "Transcripts: East St. Louis Proceedings," 169–70, 173.

46. On the World War I generation setting aside their grievances, see Mark Ellis, "W. E. B. Du Bois and the Formation of Black Opinion in World War I: A Commentary on 'The Damnable Dilemma,'" *Journal of American History* 81 (March 1995): 1584–90; William Jordan, "'The Damnable Dilemma': African American Accommodation and Protest during World War I," *Journal of American History* 81 (March 1995): 1562–83.

47. "Labor Market Report for East St. Louis," 1, 4, 6; "Labor Supply," Serial Letter, no. 50 (March 4, 1942), 321, folder "Newsletters—Region VI, 1941–1943," Field Operations Division Newsletters, 1941–1945, Region V 1941–1943, 1944–1945, Region VI 1941–1943, Records of the Office of the Community War Services, RG215, entry 54, National Archives, College Park, Md.; Sidney Hillman, Associate Director General, Office of Production Management, to All Holders of Defense Contracts, April 11, 1941, folder "1941, 62nd General Assembly, House, Miscellaneous Reports to Report of Committee Appointed Pursuant to House Res. 37," Bills, Resolutions and Related General Assembly Records, 1st–88th Bienniums, 1819–1992, RG600.001, Illinois State Archives, Springfield. "Progress of Campaign against Race Discrimination: September 21, 1942," 2–3, folder "533.21–533.225. 1942, Illinois," Classified State Files {1939–42}, Records of the Bureau of Employment Security, RG183, entry 72, National Archives, College Park, Md.

48. Ernest Allen Jr., "When Japan Was 'Champion of the Darker Races': Satokata Takahashi and the Flowering of Black Messianic Nationalism," *Black Scholar* 24, no. 1 (Winter 1994), 23–46, and "Waiting for Tojo: The Pro-Japan Vigil of Black Missourians, 1932–1942," *Gateway Heritage,* Fall 1995, 38–55; Reginald Kearney, *African American Views of the Japanese: Solidarity or Sedition?* (Albany: State University of New York Press, 1998), 105, 126. On the Nation of Islam and its leader, Elijah Muhammad, see Claude Andrew Clegg III, *An Original Man: The Life and Times of Elijah Muhammad* (New York: St. Martin's Press, 1997), 82, 198. On racism as propaganda and unofficial policy, see John W. Dower, *War without Mercy: Race and Power in the Pacific War* (New York: Pantheon, 1986), 160–61, 173–81.

49. "Police Watch Negro Group," *ESLJ,* January 22, 1934, 2; Report 10110–2666/70 and Report 10110–2666/79, J. Edgar Hoover to Lieut. Colonel C. K. Nulsen, MID, April 10, 1934, and Report 10218–261/92, Lieut. Col. O. A. Dickinson to A. C. of S. G-2, Correspondence of the Military Intelligence Division 1917–41, U.S. War Department, RG165, entry 65, National Archives, Washington, D.C.; United States Federal Bureau of Investigation report made by H. G. Maynor, at St. Louis, November 1, 1933, "The Pacific Movement of the Eastern World," folder "File 235408," Straight Numerical Files, Records of the Department of Justice, RG60, entry 112B. On the FBI's concern about black people's loyalty to the federal government, see Robert A. Hill, ed., *The FBI's RACON:*

Racial Conditions in the United States during World War II (Boston: Northeastern University Press, 1995), 685, 691, 692. "Pacific Movement of the Eastern World: [1942]," folder "File 146–10–2, sec. 2, 6–5–42–7–31–42," FBI Report File 65–305; "Press release, Wednesday, January 27, 1943," folder "146–10–2, FBI Reports and Memos,"; "In the District Court of the United States for the Eastern District of Illinois: Transcript of Testimony and Proceedings before the Grand Jury, September 22, 1942 to and including September 29, 1942," 2 vols., folder "146–10–2, series 22 & 23"; "In the United States Circuit Court of Appeals . . . Statement, Brief and Argument of Appellee: 1943," folder "146–10–2, series 24," Classified Subject Files (Security Classified Files), Class 146–10, Records of the Department of Justice, RG60, entry 114BD. National Association for the Advancement of Colored People, Papers of the NAACP, Manuscript Division, Library of Congress, part 18, series A-Legal Department Files, Special Subjects, 1940–1955, microfilm, 8:00866–00968. "Jap Agent Testifies Here," *ESLJ,* September 29, 1942, 1; "Indict Three in Federal Sedition Probe," *ESLJ,* January 28, 1943, 3; photograph and caption of PMEW leader General Butler, *ESLJ,* January 29, 1943, 3; Hill, *FBI's RACON,* 520.

50. Lee Annie Bonner, interview by author, East St. Louis, September 22, 1999; Lillian Parks, interview by author, East St. Louis, September 22, 1999; "Memorandum for Chief of Branch, Subject: Negro Press Trend," September 28, 1942, October 5, 1942, October 12, 1942, folder "1941–1942" and "Subversive, [January 28, 1943]," 4–5, folder "1943," Office of Public Information Analysis Branch, Press Items, RE: Negro Newspapers, 1944–46, Records of the Assistant Secretary of Defense (Legislative and Public Affairs), RG330, entry 135F, National Archives, College Park, Md.; "Report on Japanese Propaganda in the United States, November 1939," folder "146–10, section 1/10–6–40–4–15–41," Classified Subject Files (Classified Security File Files), Class 146–10, Records of the Department of Justice, RG60, entry 114BD, National Archives, College Park, Md.

51. Lee Finkle, *Forum for Protest: The Black Press during World War II* (Rutherford, N.J.: Fairleigh Dickinson University Press, 1975), 9; Hill, *FBI's RACON,* 694; "Progress of Campaign against Race Discrimination: September 21, 1942," 2–3, folder "533.21–533.225. 1942. Illinois," Classified State Files {1939–42}, Records of the Bureau of Employment Security, RG183, entry 72, National Archives, College Park, Md.

52. On an early assessment of the FEPC, see Louis C. Kesselman, "The Fair Employment Practice Commission Movement in Perspective," *Journal of Negro History* 31 (January 1946): 30–46. Selected examples of FEPC cases: "Strike at Dixie Mills Company, June 24–28, 1943," folder "Dixie Mills Company, East St. Louis, Illinois," box 1830; "Memorandum from J. E. Kuczma, March 29, 1944," folder "Monsanto Chemical Company," box 1826, Records Relating to Strikes, 1944–1945, Region VI, Records of the National War Labor Board, RG202, entry 210, National Archives–Great Lakes Region, Chicago; [Community War Service file], box 106, General Correspondence, 1943–1946, Records of the Committee on Fair Employment Practice, RG228, entry 82; [Aluminum Ore Company file], box

72, [American Steel Foundries, East St. Louis file], box 73, [Cargill, Inc. file], box 75, [Monsanto Chemical Company file], box 85, Closed Cases, 1941–1946, Region VI, Records of the Committee of Fair Employment Practice, RG228, entry 70. George B. Nesbitt, East St. Louis Citizens' Defense and Urban League Organizing Committee to A. H. R. Atwood, Director, Illinois State Employment Service, November 17, 1941, folder "Historical Information, East St. Louis," series 5, National Urban League Records; Leo R. Werts, Acting Director, Illinois State Employment Service, to William E. Officer, January 14, 1942; "Urban League to Stage Benefit," *St. Louis Call*, February 6, 1942, 6; Officer to John J. Corson, Director, United States Employment Service, February 11, 1942; Nesbitt to Lester Granger, February 14, 1942; Granger to Nesbitt, March 4, 1942, folder "Historical Information, East St. Louis," series 5, National Urban League Records.

53. "East St. Louis, Illinois, Area Report: September 30, 1944," 15, 37, "Federal Security Agency, Office of Community War Services: Conference on Community Race Relations Problems, November 11, 1944," 7, folder "Serial Letter, Region VI," Field Operations Division Community Reports, 1941–1945: Region VI, Illinois-Wisconsin, Records of the Office of Community War Services, RG215, entry 55; Elmer W. Henderson, FEPC Regional Director, to P. M. Tompkins, General Manager, Monsanto, January 21, 1944, "Monsanto Chemical Company [file], Exhibit B, Elmer W. Henderson to P. M. Tompkins, April 10, 1944," box 91, Closed Cases, 1941–1946, Records of the Region VI Office (Chicago), Records of the President's Committee on Fair Employment Practice, RG228, entry 70, National Archives–Great Lakes Region, Chicago; Illinois War Manpower Commission, "Monthly Field Operating Report: For Southwestern Illinois, March 1944," folder "VI, Illinois—(Southwestern)," Records of the Reports Processing Section of the Reports Division, Monthly Field Operating Reports, Dec. 1943–July, 1945, VI (Ill.), Records of the War Manpower Commission, RG211, entry 108; Memorandum, Harry H. C. Gibson to Elmer W. Henderson, April 10, 1944, "Monsanto Chemical Company [file], Exhibit B, Elmer W. Henderson to P. M. Tompkins, April 10, 1944," box 91, Closed Cases, 1941–1946, Records of the Region VI Office (Chicago), Records of the President's Committee on Fair Employment Practice, RG228, entry 70, National Archives–Great Lakes Region, Chicago.

54. "Negro Advancement," *ESLJ*, Jubilee Edition, May 26, 1940, 16, section F; "Progress of Campaign against Race Discrimination: September 21, 1942," folder "533.21–533.225, 1942. Illinois," Classified State Files {1932–42}, Records of the Bureau of Employment Security, National Archives, College Park, Md.; Lee Annie Bonner, interview by author, East St. Louis, September 22, 1999; *Serial Letter,* no. 68 (March 6, 1944), 8, and no. 72 (July 15, 1944), 3, folder "Serial Letter, 1944," "East St. Louis, Illinois, Area Report: September 30, 1944," 38, "Federal Security Agency, Office of Community War Services: Conference on Community Race Relations Problems, November 11, 1944," 5, *Serial Letter,* no. 76 (March 1945), folder "Serial Letter: Region VI," Field Operations Division Community Reports, 1941–1945, Records Office of Community War Services, RG215, entry 55; "Demand-Supply Supplement: Illinois WMC Administrative Area #7, East St.

Louis Labor Market Area, November 1944," 6–7, "Monthly Field Operating Report: February 1945," 46–47, folder "VI, Illinois—East St. Louis," Records of the Reports Processing Section of the Reports Division: Monthly Field Operating Reports, Dec. 1943–July 1945, Records of the War Manpower Commission, RG211, entry 108.

55. [Walworth Company file], box 91, Closed Cases, 1941–1946, Region VI, Records of the Committee of Fair Employment Practice, RG228, entry 70; Memorandum, Elmer W. Henderson to Will Maslow, September 1, 1944, General Records, 1941–1946, Records of the Region VI Office (Chicago), Records of the Committee of Fair Employment Practice, RG228, entry 81.

56. "An Important Question to Consider," *ESLJ*, October 17, 1943, 7; "'Job Heaven' to Be Thing of the Past after the War," *ESLJ*, October 31, 1943, 7, 8; "City Post-War Program Described as Five Points," *ESLJ*, November 21, 1943, 7, 8; "East St. Louis Post-War Planning Appears Stagnant," *ESLJ*, April 22, 1945, 7; "The Case of the City of East St. Louis," *ESLJ*, May 2, 1945, 6; "What Is Future of Housing in East St. Louis?," *ESLJ*, July 22, 1945, 7, 8; "Realistic Approach to Area Planning," *ESLJ*, July 29, 1945, 7.

57. "Available Labor Pool to Be Determining Factor in Post-War Jobs Here," *ESLJ*, November 7, 1943, 7.

58. "Available Labor Pool to Be Determining Factor in Post-War Jobs Here," *ESLJ*, November 7, 1943, 7. For discussion of early years of the post–World War II civil rights movement, see August Meier and Elliott Rudwick, *CORE: A Study in the Civil Rights Movement, 1942–1968* (New York: Oxford University Press, 1973), 84, 92, 121; Aldon D. Morris, *The Origins of the Civil Rights Movement: Black Communities Organizing for Change* (New York: Free Press, 1984); John Dittmer, *Local People: The Struggle for Civil Rights in Mississippi* (Urbana: University of Illinois Press, 1994); Charles M. Payne, *I've Got the Light of Freedom: The Organizing Tradition and the Mississippi Freedom Struggle* (Berkeley: University of California Press, 1995).

Postscript

1. On the school desegregation campaign, see Elliott Rudwick, "Fifty Years of Race Relations in East St. Louis: The Breaking Down of White Supremacy," *Midcontinent American Studies Journal* 6, no. 1 (Spring 1965): 3–15.

2. For in-depth discussion of the politics and economy of post-1960 East St. Louis, see Andrew J. Theising, *Made in USA: East St. Louis, The Rise and Fall of an Industrial River Town* (St. Louis, Mo.: Virginia Publishing, 2003), 7–48 passim.

BIBLIOGRAPHY

Primary Materials

Manuscript Collections

Aluminum Company of America Records, 1888–1990. Historical Society of Western Pennsylvania Archives, Pittsburgh.

Bartholomew, Harland, and Associates Records. University Archives, Washington University in St. Louis.

Burlington Archives. Newberry Library, Chicago.

Henry Horner Lincoln Collection. Abraham Lincoln Presidential Library (formerly Illinois State Historical Library), Springfield.

Illinois Central Railroad Archives. Newberry Library, Chicago.

National Association for the Advancement of Colored People Records. Manuscript Division, Library of Congress, Washington, D.C.

National Urban League Records. Manuscript Division, Library of Congress, Washington, D.C.

Negro in Illinois Papers. Illinois Writers' Project, Chicago Public Library.

Sherman, Lawrence Y., Papers. Abraham Lincoln Presidential Library (formerly Illinois State Historical Library), Springfield.

United States Work Projects Administration Federal Writers' Project and Historical Records Survey. Manuscript Division, Library of Congress, Washington, D.C.

Urban League of St. Louis Collection, 1938–1982. Western Historical Manuscripts Collection, University of Missouri–St. Louis.

Urban League of St. Louis Records. University Archives, Washington University in St. Louis.

Official Archives

ILLINOIS STATE ARCHIVES, SPRINGFIELD, ILLINOIS

Bills, Resolutions, and Related General Assembly Records. 1st–88th Bienniums, 1819–1994. RG600.001.

East St. Louis. Office of City Clerk. City Council Proceedings.

Frank Orren Lowden Correspondence, 1917–1921. RG101.027.

Henry Horner Correspondence, 1933–1940. RG101.030.

Illinois State Commission of Human Relations. Minutes of Commission Meetings, October 1, 1943–June 30, 1961. Springfield.

Illinois State Commission on the Living Conditions of the Urban Colored Population, Transcripts of Commission: Hearing by the Illinois State Commission on the Living Conditions of the Urban Colored Population at East St. Louis, Illinois, November 29, 1940: Proceedings. Springfield, 1940.

Illinois State Council of Defense (World War I). Report of the Labor Committee of the State Council of Defense of Illinois Upon the Inquiry into the Recent Influx of Southern Negro Laborers into East St. Louis and Race Riot in Connection Therewith: At a Meeting . . . held at Chicago, June 2, 1917. [Springfield]: Illinois State Council of Defense, 1917. RS517.020, microfilm roll 30-873.

NATIONAL ARCHIVES—GREAT LAKES REGION, CHICAGO, ILLINOIS

Committee on Fair Employment Practice, Region IV. Active Cases, September 1941–April 1946, RG228, entry 68. Administrative Records. General Records, October 1941–1946, RG228, entry 81. Case Records. Closed Cases, August 1941–March 1946. RG228, entry 70. General Correspondence, September 1943–March 1946, RG228, entry 82.

District Courts of the United States. Records of the United States Circuit Court for the Eastern District of Illinois, East St. Louis, 1905–1914. RG21.

District Courts of the United States. Records of the United States District Court for the Eastern District of Illinois at East St. Louis, 1905–1970. RG21.

National War Labor Board. Region VI. Dispute Case Files, 1943–1945. RG202, entry 165. Historical and Policy Documentation Files, 1943–1945. RG202, entry 177. Records Relating to Strikes, 1944–1945. RG202, entry 210.

War Department. Records of the War Dept., General and Special Staffs. Military Intelligence Division. Plant Protection Section, Chicago District Office (No. 11). Correspondence, 1918–1919. RG165, entry 132.

War Manpower Commission. Region VI. Progress Reports, 1942–1945. RG211, entry 272. Reports on Local USES Office Operations, 1942–1945, RG211, entry 281.

NATIONAL ARCHIVES, WASHINGTON, D.C., AND COLLEGE PARK, MARYLAND

Bureau of Employment Security. U.S. Employment Service. Area Labor Market Reports, 1940–49. RG183, entry 89. Classified General Files, 1942–43. RG183, entry 74A. Classified State Files {1939–42}. RG183, entry 72. Reports of Investigations of Negro Unemployment and Public Placement Facilities for Negroes, 1937–39. RG183, entry 7.

Council of National Defense. General Correspondence. RG62, entry 140. General Correspondence, Ap-Dec 1917. State Councils Section. RG62, entry 338.

Department of Defense. Records of the Assistant Secretary of Defense (Legislative and Public Affairs). Office of Public Information Analysis Branch. Press Items, RE: Negro Newspapers, 1944–46. RG330, entry 135F.

Department of Justice. Records of the Department of Justice. Classified Subject Files (Security Classified Records). RG60, entry 114BD. Glasser File, ca. 1938. Internal Disturbance (Geographical File). RG60, entry 126. Straight Numerical Files. RG60, entry 112B.

Department of Labor. General Records of the Department of Labor. General Records, 1907–1942. RG174, entry 1. General Records of the Department of Labor. Office of the Secretary. Secretary William B. Wilson. General Subject Files, 1913–1921. RG174, entry 18.

Federal Bureau of Investigation. Records of the Federal Bureau of Investigation. General Investigative Records. RG65, entry 29, microfilm M1085.

Federal Home Loan Bank Board. Records of the Federal Home Loan Bank Board. Home Owners' Loan Corporation. Records Relating to the City Survey File, 1935–40. RG195, entry 39.

Federal Housing Administration. Records of the Federal Housing Administration. Research and Statistics Division. Housing Market Data, 1938–52. RG31, entry 2. Reports of Housing Market Analysts, 1937–63. RG31, entry 10. State and City Data Re: Economic Conditions, ca. 1934–42. RG31, entry 3.

Housing and Home Finance Agency. Records Relating to Defense Housing (Geographical Dockets), 1941–42. Division of Defense Housing Coordination (Office of Emergency Management). RG207, entry 23. Housing Monographs, 1939–1942. Records of the Division of Research and Statistics (Federal Housing Administration). RG207, entry 34. Records of the National Housing Agency. Subject File of the War Housing Program, May 1, 1943–December 31, 1946. RG207, entry 27.

National Youth Administration. RG119.

Office of the Community War Services. Field Operations Division Community Reports, 1941–1945. Region VI, Illinois-Wisconsin. RG215, entry 55. Public Housing Administration. Records of the Public Housing Administration. Project Files (1933–1937). RG196, entry 2. Records of the Intergroup Relations Branch, 1936–63. RG196, entry 47.

War Department, Military Intelligence Division. Correspondence of the Military Intelligence Division. RG165, entry 65, microfilm M1194 (General Correspondence), microfilm M1440 ("Negro Subversion").

War Manpower Commission. Records of the War Manpower Commission. Records of the Reports and Analysis Service. Records of the Reports Processing Section of the Reports Division. Monthly Field Operating Reports, Dec., 1943–July, 1945. RG211, entry 108.

Work Projects Administration. Records of the Work Projects Administration, Civil Works Administration Central Files, 1933–1934, "State" Series, 1933–1934. RG69, entry 1. WPA Central Files. State Series, 1935–44, Correspondence with State Administrators. RG69, entry 610.

Federal and State Government Publications

Beverly, Robert H. *Negro Health in the State of Illinois.* Springfield: Illinois Department of Public Health, 1937.

Jenison, Marguerite Edith, ed. *War Documents and Addresses.* Vol. 6, *Illinois in the World War.* Springfield: Illinois State Historical Library, 1923.

———. *The War-Time Organization of Illinois.* Vol. 5, *Illinois in the World War.* Springfield: Illinois State Historical Library, 1923.

Shields, Emma L. "Negro Women in Industry." *Bulletin of the Women's Bureau,* no. 20. Women's Bureau, U.S. Department of Labor, Washington, D.C.: GPO, 1922.

Stickgold, Simon. "Illinois Race Riots." Research Memorandum 5, Illinois Interracial Commission, Springfield, 1943.

U.S. Congress. House. Committee on Rules. *Riot at East St. Louis: Hearings. Supplement.* Washington, D.C.: GPO, 1917.

———. Special Committee to Investigate the East St. Louis Riots. *Report of the Special Committee Authorized by Congress to Investigate the East St. Louis Riots.* Washington, D.C.: GPO, 1918.

———. Special Committee to Investigate the East St. Louis Riots. *Transcripts of the Hearings of the House Select Committee That Investigated the Race Riots in East St. Louis, Illinois, 1917.* Washington, D.C.: GPO, 1918. Microfiche and microfilm editions.

U.S. Department of Labor. *Monthly Labor Review.*

———. Bureau of Labor Statistics. *Survey of Negro World War II Veterans and Vacancy and Occupancy of Dwelling Units Available to Negroes in St. Louis Area, Missouri and Illinois, November–December 1946.* Washington, D.C.: GPO, 1947.

———. Women's Bureau. *Negro Women and Their Jobs.* Women's Bureau Leaflet, no. 19. Washington, D.C.: GPO, 1954.

U.S. National Resources Committee. *Regional Planning: Part II—St. Louis Region.* Washington, D.C.: GPO, 1936.

Williams, G. Ishmael, Marlesa A. Gray, and W. Kevin Pope. *Gateway to the Past: Cultural Resources Investigations in East St. Louis, Illinois.* Springfield: Illinois Department of Transportation, 1982.

Books, Articles, Microform Collections, Reports of Nongovernment Organizations, Miscellanea

Bartholomew, Harland. *A Comprehensive City Plan for East St. Louis, Illinois.* Prepared for the War Civics Committee [of East St. Louis]. East St. Louis, Ill.: Daily Journal, 1920.

———. *Guide Plan, Missouri-Illinois Metropolitan Area.* St. Louis: Harland Bartholomew and Associates, 1948.

City directory of East St. Louis (various publishers).

Coffin, Arlyn Wilbur. *Building East St. Louis for Tomorrow. First Annual Report of the War Civics Committee, East St. Louis, Illinois, October 1, 1918–September 30, 1919.* East St. Louis, Ill., 1919.

Comprehensive Plan, East St. Louis, Illinois. Newark, N.J.: Candeub, Fleissig, [1958?].

East St. Louis Branch of the NAACP. *Perseverance and Progress: A History of the East St. Louis Branch of the N.A.A.C.P.* East St. Louis, Ill., 1995.

East St. Louis Centennial Program, 1861–1961. East St. Louis, Ill.: Centennial Committee, 1961.

Fining, Joseph N. *Economic and Other Facts Regarding East St. Louis.* East St. Louis, Ill.: Chamber of Commerce, 1920.

Foner, Philip S., and Ronald L. Lewis. *The Black Worker: A Documentary History from Colonial Times to the Present.* 8 vols. Philadelphia: Temple University Press, 1980.

Grossman, James, ed. *Black Workers in the Era of the Great Migration, 1916–1929.* 25 microfilm reels. Frederick, Md.: University Publications of America, 1985.

Hamilton, Clementine. *The Ebony Tree.* East St. Louis, Ill.: privately printed, [1971?].

Hampton University Newspaper Clipping File. Microfilm collection. Hampton, Va.

Hill, Robert A., ed. *The Marcus Garvey and Universal Negro Improvement Association Papers.* 10 vols. Berkeley: University of California Press, 1983–1986

Olcott, Jane. *The Work of Colored Women.* New York: Colored Work Committee, War Work Council, National Board, Young Women's Christian Associations, [1919 or 1920?].

Records of the National Negro Business League. 14 microfilm reels. Bethesda, Md.: University Publications of America, 1994.

Rudwick, Elliott, ed. *The East St. Louis Race Riot of 1917.* 8 microfilm reels. Frederick, Md.: University Publications of America, 1985.

Standard Atlas of St. Clair County, Illinois, Including a Plat Book. Chicago: Geo. A. Ogle, 1901.

Tuskegee Institute News Clippings File. Microfilm collection. Ann Arbor, Mich.: UMI, 1976. 252 microfilm reels.

Work, Monroe N., ed. *Negro Year Book: An Annual Encyclopedia of the Negro, 1918–1919.* 5th ed. Tuskegee, Ala.: Negro Year Book Publishing, 1919.

Young Women's Christian Associations, War Work Council, Committee on Work Among Colored Girls and Women. *Colored American Women in War Work.* New York: YWCA, 1918.

Newspapers and Periodicals

Chicago Defender
Congressional Record
Crisis
Current History Magazine of the New York Times
Daily Worker
East St. Louis Daily Journal (after 1929: *East St. Louis Journal*)
East St. Louis Today
Illinois Record (Illinois Afro-American Protective League)
Negro World
Opportunity (National Urban League)

St. Louis Argus
St. Louis Post-Dispatch
Survey (National Association of Social Workers)

Interviews—State Historical Society of Wisconsin

Condellone, John, and John Matikitis (tapes 220, 221, 222).
Davinroy, William (tapes 214, 215, 216).
Nash, William (tapes 209, 210).
United Packinghouse Workers of America Oral History Project Interviews, 1985–1986 (SC 452, tape 1117A).
Weightman, Philip (tapes 284, 285).

Interviews by the author in 1999 in East St. Louis (tapes deposited at Edwardsville Library Archives, Southern Illinois University, Edwardsville, Ill.)

Lee Annie Bonner, September 22.
Jeanne A. Faulkner, accompanied by Phillip L. Beck Sr. and William Thomas, September 24.
Mattie Malone, September 21.
Lillian Parks, September 22.
Frances Nash Terrell and Claudia Nash Thomas, September 24.
Olga Wayne, September 21.
Richard Younge and Wyvetter Hoover Younge, September 27.

Secondary Literature

Monographs

Adler, Jeffrey S. *Yankee Merchants and the Making of the Urban West: The Rise and Fall of Antebellum St. Louis.* New York: Cambridge University Press, 1991.
Allen, Robert L. *Reluctant Reformers: Racism and Social Reform Movements in the United States.* Washington, D.C.: Howard University Press, 1974.
Allen, Theodore W. *The Invention of the White Race.* London: Verso, 1994.
Anderson, James D. *The Education of Blacks in the South, 1860–1935.* Chapel Hill: University of North Carolina Press, 1988.
Aptheker, Herbert, ed. *Pamphlets and Leaflets by W. E. B. Du Bois.* White Plains, N.Y.: Kraus-Thomson, 1986.
Arneson, Eric. *Waterfront Workers of New Orleans: Race, Class and Politics, 1863–1923.* New York: Oxford University Press, 1991.
Babb, Valerie. *Whiteness Visible: The Meaning of Whiteness in American Literature and Culture.* New York: New York University Press, 1998.
Baker, Ray Stannard. *Following the Color Line: An Account of Negro Citizenship in the American Democracy.* New York: Doubleday, Page, 1908.
Barrett, James R. *Work and Community in the Jungle: Chicago's Packinghouse Workers, 1894–1922.* Urbana: University of Illinois Press, 1987.

Belcher, Wyatt Winton. *The Economic Rivalry Between St. Louis and Chicago, 1850–1880.* New York: Columbia University Press, 1947.

Berlin, Ira, Barbara J. Fields, Steven F. Miller, Joseph P. Reidy, and Leslie S. Rowland. *Slaves No More: Three Essays on Emancipation and the Civil War.* New York: Cambridge University Press, 1992.

Best, Joel. *Controlling Vice: Regulating Brothel Prostitution in St. Paul, 1865–1883.* Columbus: Ohio State University Press, 1998.

Blee, Kathleen M. *Women of the Klan: Racism and Gender in the 1920s.* Berkeley: University of California Press, 1991.

Boyer, Paul. *Urban Masses and Moral Order in America, 1820–1920.* Cambridge, Mass.: Harvard University Press, 1978.

Brass, Paul R., ed. *Riots and Pogroms.* New York: New York University Press, 1996.

Brooks, Jennifer E. *Defining the Peace: World War II Veterans, Race, and the Remaking of Southern Political Tradition.* Chapel Hill: University of North Carolina Press, 2004.

Brophy, Alfred L. *Reconstructing the Dreamland: The Tulsa Riot of 1921, Race, Reparations, and Reconciliation.* New York: Oxford University Press, 2002.

Brundage, W. Fitzhugh. *Lynching in the New South: Georgia and Virginia, 1880–1930.* Urbana: University of Illinois Press, 1993.

Bunch-Lyons, Beverly A. *Contested Terrain: African-American Women Migrate from the South to Cincinnati, Ohio, 1900–1950.* New York: Routledge, 2002.

Butler, Brian. *An Undergrowth of Folly: Public Order, Race Anxiety, and the 1903 Evansville, Indiana Riot.* New York: Garland, 2000.

Capeci, Dominic J. Jr. *Race Relations in Wartime Detroit: The Sojourner Truth Housing Controversy of 1942.* Philadelphia: Temple University Press, 1984.

Capeci, Dominic J. Jr., and Martha Wilkerson. *Layered Violence: The Detroit Rioters of 1943.* Oxford: University of Mississippi Press, 1991.

Carter, Dan T. *Scottsboro: A Tragedy of the American South.* Rev. ed. Baton Rouge: Louisiana State University Press, 1979.

Cayton, Horace R., and George S. Mitchell. *Black Workers and the New Unions.* Chapel Hill: University of North Carolina Press, 1939.

Cell, John W. *The Highest Stage of White Supremacy: The Origins of Segregation in South Africa and the American South.* New York: Cambridge University Press, 1982.

Cha-Jua, Sundiata Keita. *America's First Black Town: Brooklyn, Illinois, 1830–1915.* Urbana: University of Illinois Press, 2000.

Cecelski, David S., and Timothy B. Tyson. *Democracy Betrayed: The Wilmington Race Riot and Its Legacy.* Chapel Hill: University of North Carolina Press, 1998.

Chalmers, David M. *Hooded Americanism: The First Century of the Ku Klux Klan, 1865–1965.* New York: Doubleday, 1965.

Christian, Garna L. *Black Soldiers in Jim Crow Texas, 1899–1917.* College Station: Texas A&M University Press, 1995.

Clark-Lewis, Elizabeth. *Living In, Living Out: American Domestics and the Great Migration.* Washington, D.C.: Smithsonian Institution, 1994.

Cohen, Lizabeth. *Making a New Deal: Industrial Workers in Chicago, 1919–1939.* New York: Cambridge University Press, 1990.

Cohen, William. *At Freedom's Edge: Black Mobility and the Southern White Quest for Racial Control, 1861–1915.* Baton Rouge: Louisiana State University Press, 1991.

Connelly, Mark Thomas. *The Response to Prostitution in the Progressive Era.* Chapel Hill: University of North Carolina Press, 1980.

Crew, Spencer R. *Black Life in Secondary Cities: A Comparative Analysis of the Black Communities of Camden and Elizabeth, N.J., 1860–1920.* New York: Garland, 1993.

Cumbler, John T. *A Social History of Economic Decline: Business, Politics, and Work in Trenton.* New Brunswick, N.J.: Rutgers University Press, 1989.

———. *Working-Class Community: Work, Leisure, and Conflict in Two Industrial Cities, 1880–1930.* Westport, CT: Greenwood Press, 1979.

Curriden, Mark, and Leroy Phillips Jr. *Contempt of Court: The Turn-of-the-Century Lynching That Launched 100 Years of Federalism.* New York: Faber and Faber, 1999.

Davis, Elizabeth Lindsay. *The Story of the Illinois Federation of Colored Women's Clubs.* Chicago, 1922. Reprint, New York: G. K. Hall, 1997.

Delaney, David. *Race, Place, and the Law, 1836–1948.* Austin: University of Texas Press, 1998.

Diner, Steven J. *A Very Different Age: Americans of the Progressive Era.* New York: Hill and Wang, 1998.

Dittmer, John. *Black Georgia in the Progressive Era, 1900–1920.* Urbana: University of Illinois Press, 1977.

———. *Local People: The Struggle for Civil Rights in Mississippi.* Urbana: University of Illinois Press, 1994.

Dower, John W. *War without Mercy: Race and Power in the Pacific War.* New York: Pantheon, 1986.

Drake, St. Clair, and Horace Cayton. *Black Metropolis: A Study of Negro Life in a Northern City.* 1944. Reprint, Chicago: University of Chicago Press, 1993.

Dray, Philip. *At the Hands of Persons Unknown: The Lynching of Black America.* New York: Random House, 2002.

Du Bois, W. E. B. *Black Reconstruction in America, 1860–1880.* 1935. Reprint, New York: Vintage Books, 1995.

Ellsworth, Scott. *Death in a Promised Land: The Tulsa Race Riot of 1921.* Baton Rouge: Louisiana State University Press, 1982.

English, Edward. *The Good Things of East St. Louis.* Mascoutah, Ill.: Top's Books, 1992.

Fairclough, Adam. *Teaching Equality: Black Schools in the Age of Jim Crow.* Athens: University of Georgia Press, 2001.

Finkle, Lee. *Forum for Protest: The Black Press during World War II.* Cranbury, N.J.: Associated University Presses, 1975.

Fogel, Walter A. *The Negro in the Meat Industry.* Philadelphia: Industrial Research Unit, Department of Industry, Wharton School of Finance and Commerce, University of Pennsylvania, 1970.

Foner, Eric. *Reconstruction: America's Unfinished Revolution, 1863–1877.* New York: Harper and Row, 1988.

Fredrickson, George M. *The Black Image in the White Mind: The Debate on Afro-American Character and Destiny, 1817–1914.* New York: Harper and Row, 1971.

Freund, David M. P. *Colored Property: State Policy and White Racial Politics in Suburban America.* Chicago: University of Chicago Press, 2007.

Gaines, Kevin K. *Uplifting the Race: Black Leadership, Politics, and Culture in the Twentieth Century.* Chapel Hill: University of North Carolina Press, 1996.

Gates, Paul W. *Landlords and Tenants on the Prairie Frontier.* Ithaca, N.Y.: Cornell University Press, 1973.

Gatewood, Willard B. Jr. *"Smoked Yankees" and the Struggle for Empire: Letters from Negro Soldiers, 1898–1902.* Urbana: University of Illinois Press, 1971.

Giddings, Paula. *When and Where I Enter: The Impact of Black Women on Race and Sex in America.* New York: Morrow, 1984.

Gilmore, Glenda Elizabeth. *Gender and Jim Crow: Women and the Politics of White Supremacy in North Carolina, 1896–1920.* Chapel Hill: University of North Carolina Press, 1996.

Godshalk, David Fort. *Veiled Visions: The 1906 Atlanta Race Riot and the Reshaping of American Race Relations.* Chapel Hill: University of North Carolina Press, 2005.

Goings, Kenneth W., and Raymond A. Mohl, eds. *The New African American Urban History.* Thousand Oaks, Calif.: Sage, 1991.

Gordon, David M., and Richard Michael Reich. *Segmented Work, Divided Workers: The Historical Transformation of Labor in the United States.* New York: Cambridge University Press, 1982.

Gosnell, Harold F. *Negro Politicians: The Rise of Negro Politics in Chicago.* Chicago: University of Chicago Press, 1935.

Gottlieb, Peter. *Making Their Own Way: Southern Blacks' Migration to Pittsburgh, 1916–30.* Urbana: University of Illinois Press, 1987.

Grantham, Dewey W. *Southern Progressivism: The Reconciliation of Progress and Tradition.* Knoxville: University of Tennessee Press, 1983.

Greenberg, Cheryl Lynn. *"Or Does It Explode?" Black Harlem in the Great Depression.* New York: Oxford University Press, 1991.

Greer, Edward. *Big Steel: Black Politics and Corporate Power in Gary, Indiana.* New York: Monthly Review Press, 1979.

Gregg, Robert. *Sparks from the Anvil of Oppression: Philadelphia's African Methodists and Southern Migrants, 1890–1940.* Philadelphia: Temple University Press, 1993.

Griffler, Keith P. *What Price Alliance? Black Radicals Confront White Labor, 1918–1938.* New York: Garland, 1995.

Grimshaw, Allen D., ed. *Racial Violence in the United States.* Chicago: Aldine, 1969.

Grimshaw, William J. *Bitter Fruit: Black Politics and the Chicago Machine, 1931–1991.* Chicago: University of Chicago Press, 1992.

Grossman, James R. *Land of Hope: Chicago, Black Southerners, and the Great Migration.* Chicago: University of Chicago Press, 1989.

Gutman, Herbert G. *Work, Culture, and Society in Industrializing America: Essays in American Working-Class and Social History.* New York: Vintage, 1977.

Hahn, Steven. *A Nation under Our Feet: Black Political Struggles in the Rural South from Slavery to the Great Migration.* Cambridge, Mass.: Harvard University Press, 2003.

———. *The Roots of Southern Populism: Yeoman Farmers and the Transformation of the Georgia Upcountry, 1850–1890.* New York: Oxford University Press, 1983.

Hair, William Ivy. *Carnival of Fury: Robert Charles and the New Orleans Race Riot of 1900.* Baton Rouge: Louisiana State University Press, 1976.

Hale, Grace Elizabeth. *Making Whiteness: The Culture of Segregation in the South, 1890–1940.* New York: Pantheon, 1998.

Hall, Jacquelyn Dowd. *Revolt against Chivalry: Jessie Daniel Ames and the Women's Campaign against Lynching.* Rev. ed. New York: Columbia University Press, 1993.

Halpern, Rick. *Down on the Killing Floor: Black and White Workers in Chicago's Packinghouses, 1904–54.* Urbana: University of Illinois Press, 1997.

Halpern, Rick, and Jonathan Morris, ed. *American Exceptionalism? U.S. Working-Class Formation in an International Context.* New York: St. Martin's Press, 1997.

Harlan, Louis R., ed. *The Booker T. Washington Papers.* Urbana: University of Illinois Press, 1972.

———. *Booker T. Washington: The Wizard of Tuskegee, 1901–1915.* New York: Oxford University Press, 1985.

Harrison, William J. *The First 75 Years, 1918–1993: The Urban League of Metropolitan St. Louis.* St. Louis: Urban League of Metropolitan St. Louis, 1993.

Hartshorn, William Newton, ed. *Era of Progress and Promise, 1863–1910: The Religious, Moral, and Educational Development of the American Negro since His Emancipation.* Boston: Priscilla Publishing, 1910.

Harvey, David. *The Limits to Capital.* Chicago: University of Chicago Press, 1982.

Haynes, Robert V. *A Night of Violence: The Houston Riot of 1917.* Baton Rouge: Louisiana State University Press, 1976.

Hendricks, Wanda A. *Gender, Race, and Politics in the Midwest: Black Club Women in Illinois.* Bloomington: Indiana University Press, 1998.

Higginbotham, Evelyn Brooks. *Righteous Discontent: The Women's Movement in the Black Baptist Church, 1880–1920.* Cambridge, Mass.: Harvard University Press, 1993.

Hill, Robert A., ed. *The FBI's RACON: Racial Conditions in the United States during World War II.* Boston: Northeastern University Press, 1995.

Howard, Robert P. *Illinois: A History of the Prairie State.* Grand Rapids, MI: Wm. B. Eerdmans, 1972.

Hunter, Tera W. *To 'Joy My Freedom: Southern Black Women's Lives and Labors after the Civil War.* Cambridge, Mass.: Harvard University Press, 1997.

Ignatiev, Noel. *How the Irish Became White.* New York: Routledge, 1995.

Jackson, Kenneth T. *Crabgrass Frontier: The Suburbanization of the United States.* New York: Oxford University Press, 1985.

———. *The Ku Klux Klan in the City, 1915–1930.* New York: Oxford University Press, 1967.

Jacobson, Matthew Frye. *Whiteness of a Different Color: European Immigration and the Alchemy of Race.* Cambridge, Mass.: Harvard University Press, 1998.

Jaspin, Elliot. *Buried in the Bitter Waters: The History of Racial Cleansing in America.* New York: Basic Books, 2007.

Judd, Dennis R., and Robert S. Mendelson. *The Politics of Urban Planning: The East St. Louis Experience.* Urbana: University of Illinois, 1973.

Kachun, Mitch. *Festivals of Freedom: Memory and Meaning in African American Emancipation Celebrations, 1808–1915.* Amherst: University of Massachusetts Press, 2003.

Katzman, David M. *Before the Ghetto: Black Detroit in the Nineteenth Century.* Urbana: University of Illinois Press, 1973.

Kearney, Reginald. *African American Views of the Japanese: Solidarity or Sedition?* Albany: State University of New York Press, 1998.

Kelley, Robin D. G. *Hammer and Hoe: Alabama Communists During the Great Depression.* Chapel Hill: University of North Carolina Press, 1990.

———. *Race Rebels: Culture, Politics, and the Black Working Class.* New York: Free Press, 1994.

Kelly, Brian. *Race, Class, and Power in the Alabama Coalfields, 1908–21.* Urbana: University of Illinois Press, 2001.

Keyssar, Alexander. *The Right to Vote: The Contested History of Democracy in the United States.* New York: Basic Books, 2000.

Klier, John D., and Shlomo Lambroza, eds. *Pogroms: Anti-Jewish Violence in Modern Russian History.* New York: Cambridge University Press, 1992.

Kornweibel, Theodore. *"Seeing Red": Federal Campaigns against Black Militancy, 1919–1925.* Bloomington: Indiana University Press, 1998.

Kousser, J. Morgan. *The Shaping of Southern Politics: Suffrage Restriction and the Establishment of the One-Party South, 1880–1910.* New Haven, CT: Yale University Press, 1974.

Kusmer, Kenneth L. *A Ghetto Takes Shape: Black Cleveland, 1870–1930.* Urbana: University of Illinois Press, 1976.

Lender, Mark Edward, and James Kirby Martin. *Drinking in America: A History.* Rev. ed. New York: Free Press, 1987.

Letwin, Daniel. *The Challenge of Interracial Unionism: Alabama Coal Miners, 1878–1921.* Chapel Hill: University of North Carolina Press, 1998.

Lewis, David Levering, *W. E. B. Du Bois: Biography of a Race, 1868–1919.* New York: Holt, 1993.

Lewis, Earl. *In Their Own Interests: Race, Class, and Power in Twentieth-Century Norfolk, Virginia.* Berkeley: University of California Press, 1991.

Litwack, Leon F. *Trouble in Mind: Black Southerners in the Age of Jim Crow.* New York: Knopf, 1998.

Locke, Alain, ed. *The New Negro: An Interpretation.* New York: Macmillan, 1925.

Loewen, James W. *Sundown Towns: A Hidden Dimension of American Racism.* New York: New Press, 2005.

Logan, John R., and Harvey L. Molotch. *Urban Fortunes: The Political Economy of Place.* Berkeley: University of California Press, 1987.

Logan, Rayford. *Betrayal of the Negro: From Rutherford B. Hayes to Woodrow Wilson.* 1954. Reprint, New York: Macmillan, 1972.

MacLean, Nancy. *Behind the Mask of Chivalry: The Making of the Second Ku Klux Klan.* New York: Oxford University Press, 1994.

Marks, Carole. *Farewell—We're Good and Gone: The Great Black Migration.* Bloomington: Indiana University Press, 1989.

McLaughlin, Malcolm. *Power, Community, and Racial Killing in East St. Louis.* New York: Palgrave Macmillan, 2005.

McMurry, Linda O. *To Keep the Waters Troubled: The Life of Ida B. Wells.* New York: Oxford University Press, 1999.

Meier, August. *Negro Thought in America, 1880–1915: Racial Ideologies in the Age of Booker T. Washington.* Ann Arbor: University of Michigan Press, 1963.

Meier, August, and Elliott Rudwick. *CORE: A Study in the Civil Rights Movement, 1942–1968.* New York: Oxford University Press, 1973.

Meyer, Stephen Grant. *As Long as They Don't Move Next Door: Segregation and Racial Conflict in American Neighborhoods.* Lanham, Md.: Rowman and Littlefield, 2000.

Miller, Zane L. *Boss Cox's Cincinnati: Urban Politics in the Progressive Era.* New York: Oxford University Press, 1968.

Miller, Zane L., and Patricia M. Melvin. *The Urbanization of Modern America: A Brief History.* 2d ed. San Diego, Calif.: Harcourt, Brace, Jovanovich, 1987.

Mixon, Gregory. *The Atlanta Riot: Race, Class, and Violence in a New South City.* Gainesville: University Press of Florida, 2005.

Mohl, Raymond A. *The New City: Urban America in the Industrial Age, 1860–1920.* Arlington Heights, Ill.: Harlan Davidson, 1985.

Mohl, Raymond A., and Neil Betten. *Steel City: Urban and Ethnic Patterns in Gary, Indiana, 1906–1950.* New York: Holmes & Meier, 1986.

Monkkonen, Eric H. *America Becomes Urban: The Development of U.S. Cities and Towns, 1780–1980.* Berkeley: University of California Press, 1988.

Montgomery, David. *The Fall of the House of Labor: The Workplace, the State, and American Labor Activism, 1865–1925.* New York: Cambridge University Press, 1987.

Moore, Jesse Thomas Jr. *A Search for Equality: The National Urban League, 1910–1961.* University Park: Pennsylvania State University Press, 1981.

Morris, Aldon D. *The Origins of the Civil Rights Movement: Black Communities Organizing for Change.* New York: Free Press, 1984.

Mumford, Kevin J. *Interzones: Black/White Sex Districts in Chicago and New York in the Early Twentieth Century.* New York: Columbia University Press, 1997.

Myrdal, Gunnar. *An American Dilemma: The Negro Problem and Modern Democracy.* New York: Harper, 1944.

Naison, Mark. *Communists in Harlem during the Depression.* Urbana: University of Illinois Press, 1983.

Newby, I. A. *The Development of Segregationist Thought.* Homewood, Ill.: Dorsey Press, 1968.

Nore, Ellen. *St. Louis National Stockyards Company: East Side Story, 125 Years.* St. Louis: St. Louis National Stockyards Company, 1998.

Osofsky, Gilbert. *Harlem: The Making of a Ghetto, 1890–1903.* New York: Harper & Row, 1966.

Painter, Nell Irvin. *Exodusters: Black Migration to Kansas after Reconstruction.* New York: Knopf, 1977.

———. *The Narrative of Hosea Hudson: His Life as a Communist.* Cambridge, Mass.: Harvard University Press, 1979.

Payne, Charles M. *I've Got the Light of Freedom: The Organizing Tradition and the Mississippi Freedom Struggle.* Berkeley: University of California Press, 1995.

Payne, Charles M., and Adam Green, eds. *Time Longer Than Rope: A Century of African American Activism, 1850–1950.* New York: New York University Press, 2003.

Perry, Jeffrey B., ed. *A Hubert Harrison Reader.* Middletown, CT: Wesleyan University Press, 2001.

Phillips, Kimberley L. *Alabama North: African-American Migrants, Community, and Working-Class Activism in Cleveland, 1915–45.* Urbana: University of Illinois Press, 1999.

Powers, Madelon. *Faces Along the Bar: Lore and Order in the Workingman's Saloon, 1870–1920.* Chicago: University of Chicago Press, 1998.

Prather, H. Leon Sr. *We Have Taken a City: Wilmington Racial Massacre and Coup of 1898.* Cranbury, N.J.: Associated University Presses, 1984.

Primm, James Neal. *Lion of the Valley: St. Louis, Missouri, 1764–1980.* 3d ed. St. Louis: Missouri Historical Society Press, 1998.

Putney, Martha S. *When the Nation Was in Need: Blacks in the Women's Army Corps during World War II.* Metuchen, N.J.: Scarecrow Press, 1992.

Rabinowitz, Howard N. *Race Relations in the Urban South, 1865–1890.* Urbana: University of Illinois Press, 1980.

Rachleff, Peter. *Black Labor in the South: Richmond Virginia, 1865–1890.* Philadelphia: Temple University Press, 1984.

Rawley, James A. *The Transatlantic Slave Trade: A History.* New York: Norton, 1981.

Reed, Christopher. *The Chicago NAACP and the Rise of Black Professional Leadership, 1910–1966.* Bloomington: Indiana University Press, 1997.

Richardson, Heather Cox. *The Death of Reconstruction: Race, Labor, and Politics in the Post-Civil War North, 1865–1901.* Cambridge, Mass.: Harvard University Press, 2001.

Roediger, David R. *Colored White: Transcending the Racial Past.* Berkeley: University of California Press, 2002.

———. *The Wages of Whiteness: Race and the Making of the American Working Class.* London: Verso, 1991.

Rudé, George. *The Crowd in History: A Study of Popular Disturbances in France and England, 1730–1848.* New York: Wiley, 1964.

Rudwick, Elliott M. *Race Riot at East St. Louis, July 2, 1917.* Carbondale: Southern Illinois University Press, 1964.

Saxton, Alexander. *The Indispensable Enemy: Labor and the Anti-Chinese Movement in California.* Berkeley: University of California Press, 1971.

Schechter, Patricia A. *Ida B. Wells-Barnett and American Reform, 1880–1930.* Chapel Hill: University of North Carolina Press, 2001.

Schneider, Mark Robert. *"We Return Fighting": The Civil Rights Movement in the Jazz Age.* Boston: Northeastern University Press, 2002.

Scott, Emmett J. *Negro Migration during the War.* New York: Oxford University Press, 1920. Reprint, New York: Arno Press, 1969.

Senechal, Roberta. *The Sociogenesis of a Race Riot: Springfield, Illinois, in 1908.* Urbana: University of Illinois Press, 1990.

Sernett, Milton C. *Bound for the Promised Land: African American Religion and the Great Migration.* Durham, NC: Duke University Press, 1997.

Singh, Nikhil Pal. *Black Is a Country: Race and the Unfinished Struggle for Democracy.* Cambridge, Mass.: Harvard University Press, 2004.

Sitkoff, Harvard. *A New Deal for Blacks: The Emergence of Civil Rights as a National Issue: The Depression Decade.* New York: Oxford University Press, 1978.

Smith, Susan L. *Sick and Tired of Being Sick and Tired: Black Women's Health Activism in America, 1890–1950.* Philadelphia: University of Pennsylvania Press, 1995.

Spear, Allan H. *Black Chicago: The Making of a Negro Ghetto, 1890–1920.* Chicago: University of Chicago Press, 1967.

Stein, Judith. *The World of Marcus Garvey: Race and Class in Modern Society.* Baton Rouge: Louisiana State University Press, 1986.

Strain, Christopher B. *Pure Fire: Self-defense as Activism in the Civil Rights Era.* Athens: University of Georgia Press, 2005.

Sullivan, Patricia. *Days of Hope: Race and Democracy in the New Deal Era.* Chapel Hill: University of North Carolina Press, 1996.

Taylor, Graham Romeyn. *Satellite Cities: A Study of Industrial Suburbs.* New York: Appleton, 1915. Reprint, New York: Arno Press, 1970.

Taylor, Henry Louis Jr., and Walter Hill, eds. *Historical Roots of the Urban Crisis: African Americans in the Industrial City, 1900–1950.* New York: Garland, 2000.

Theising, Andrew J. *Made in USA: East St. Louis, the Rise and Fall of an Industrial River Town.* St. Louis: Virginia Publishing, 2003.

Thomas, Richard W. *Life for Us Is What We Make It: Building Black Community in Detroit, 1915–1945.* Bloomington: Indiana University Press, 1992.

Tregillis, Helen Cox. *River Roads to Freedom: Fugitive Slave Notices and Sheriff Notices Found in Illinois Sources.* Bowie, Md.: Heritage Books, 1988.

Trotter, Joe William Jr. *Black Milwaukee: The Making of an Industrial Proletariat, 1915–45.* Urbana: University of Illinois Press, 1985.

———, ed. *The Great Migration in Historical Perspective: New Dimensions of Race, Class, and Gender.* Bloomington: Indiana University Press, 1991.

————. *River Jordan: African American Urban Life in the Ohio Valley.* Lexington: University Press of Kentucky, 1998.

Trotter, Joe William Jr., and Earl Lewis, eds. *African Americans in the Industrial Age: A Documentary History, 1915–1945.* Boston: Northeastern University Press, 1996.

Tuttle, William M. Jr. *Race Riot: Chicago in the Red Summer of 1919.* New York: Atheneum, 1970.

Tyson, Robert A. *History of East St. Louis: Its Resources, Statistics, Railroads, Physical Features, Business and Advantages.* East St. Louis, Ill.: John Haps, 1875.

Vaz, Kim Marie, ed. *Black Women in America.* Thousand Oaks, Calif.: Sage, 1995.

Wade, Richard. *The Urban Frontier: Pioneer Life in Early Pittsburgh, Cincinnati, Lexington, Louisville, and St. Louis.* Chicago: University of Chicago Press, 1959.

Weiss, Nancy J. *Farewell to the Party of Lincoln: Black Politics in the Age of Lincoln.* Princeton, N.J.: Princeton University Press, 1983.

————. *The National Urban League, 1910–1940.* New York: Oxford University Press, 1974.

Wells-Barnett, Ida B. *Southern Horrors: Lynch Law in All Its Phases.* New York: New York Age Print, 1892.

Williams, Eric. *Capitalism & Slavery.* Chapel Hill: University of North Carolina Press, 1944.

Williamson, Joel. *The Crucible of Race: Black-White Relations in the American South since Emancipation.* New York: Oxford University Press, 1984.

Woodruff, Nan Elizabeth. *American Congo: The African American Freedom Struggle in the Delta.* Cambridge, Mass.: Harvard University Press, 2003.

Woodward, C. Vann. *Origins of the New South, 1877–1913.* Baton Rouge: Louisiana State University Press, 1951.

Wynn, Neil A. *The Afro-American and the Second World War.* 2d ed. New York: Holmes & Meier, 1993.

Yelvington, Ruben L. *East St. Louis: The Way It Is.* Mascoutah, Ill.: Top's Books, 1990.

Zangrando, Robert L. *The NAACP Crusade against Lynching, 1909–1950.* Philadelphia: Temple University Press, 1980.

Dissertations

Brunn, Paul Dennis. "Black Workers and Social Movements of the 1930s in St. Louis." PhD diss., Washington University in St. Louis, 1975.

Barbara A. Gannon. "The Won Cause: Black and White Comradeship in the Grand Army of the Republic." PhD diss., Pennsylvania State University, 2005.

Gard, Lura Mary. "East St. Louis and the Railroads to 1875." Master's thesis, Washington University in St. Louis, 1947.

Grimshaw, Allen D. "A Study in Social Violence: Urban Race Riots in the U.S." PhD diss., University of Pennsylvania, 1959.

Holmes, Harry Dadisman. "Socio-Economic Patterns of Non-Partisan Political Behavior in the Industrial Metropolis: St. Louis, 1895 to 1916." PhD diss., University of Missouri, Columbia, 1973.

Landis, Anthony M. "They Refused to Stay in Their Place: African American Organized Resistance During the Springfield, Illinois, Race Riot of 1908." Master's thesis, Southern Illinois University, Edwardsville, 2002.

Lightner, David Lee. "Labor on the Illinois Central Railroad, 1852–1900." PhD diss., Cornell University, 1969.

Schmidt, Elizabeth Noel. "Civic Pride and Prejudice: St. Louis Progressive Reform, 1900–1916." Master's thesis, University of Missouri, St. Louis, 1986.

Articles and Essays

Abell, John B. "The Negro in Industry." *Trade Winds,* March 1924, 17–20.

Allen, Ernest Jr. "Waiting for Tojo: The Pro-Japan Vigil of Black Missourians, 1932–1943." *Gateway Heritage,* Fall 1995, 38–55.

———. "When Japan Was 'Champion of the Darker Races': Satokata Takahashi and the Flowering of Black Messianic Nationalism." *Black Scholar* 24, no. 1 (Winter 1994): 23–46.

Allswang, John M. "The Chicago Negro Voter and the Democratic Consensus: A Case Study, 1918–1936." *Journal of the Illinois Historical Society* 60, no. 2 (1967): 145–75.

Altes, Jane A. "East St. Louis: A Persevering Community." In *The Middle-Size Cities of Illinois: Their People, Politics, and Quality of Life,* edited by Daniel Milo Johnson and Rebecca Monroe Veach, 89–101. Springfield, Ill.: Sangamon State University, 1980.

Anderson, Sherwood. "Nobody's Home." *Today: An Independent National Weekly,* March 30, 1935.

Baldwin, Carl R. "East St. Louis." Pts. 1 and 2. *St. Louis Commerce,* November 1982, 68, and December 1982, 42.

Barrett, James R., and David Roediger. "Inbetween Peoples: Race, Nationality and the New Immigrant Working Class." In *American Exceptionalism? U.S. Working-Class Formation in an International Context,* edited by Rick Halpern and Jonathan Morris, 181–220. New York: St. Martin's Press, 1997.

Barton, John W. "Negro Migration." *Methodist Quarterly Review* 74 (January 1925): 84–101.

Biles, Roger. "Black Mayors: A Historical Assessment." *Journal of Negro History* 77, no. 3 (Summer 1992): 109–25.

Budenz, Louis F. "The East St. Louis Riots." *National Municipal Review* 6 (September 1917): 622.

Cha-Jua, Sundiata Keita. "'A Warlike Demonstration': Legalism, Armed Resistance, and Black Political Mobilization in Decatur, Illinois, 1894–1898." *Journal of Negro History* 83, no. 1 (Winter 1998): 52–72.

Chesson, Michael B. "Harlots or Heroines? A New Look at the Richmond Bread Riot." *Virginia Magazine of History and Biography* 92, no. 2 (April 1984): 131–75.

Colten, Craig E. "Environmental Development in the East St. Louis Region, 1890–1970." *Environmental History Review* 14, nos. 1–2 (Spring/Summer 1990): 93–114.

————. "Environmental Justice on the American Bottom: The Legal Response to Pollution, 1900–1950." In *Common Fields: An Environmental History of St. Louis,* edited by Andrew Hurley, 165–75. St. Louis: Missouri Historical Society Press, 1977.

Davis, P. O. "The Negro Exodus and Southern Agriculture." *American Review of Reviews* 68 (October 1923): 401–7.

Day, David S. "Herbert Hoover and Racial Politics: The DePriest Incident." *Journal of Negro History* 65 (Winter 1980): 6–17.

Dilliard, Irving. "Civil Liberties of Negroes in Illinois since 1865." *Journal of the Illinois State Historical Society* 56, no. 3 (Autumn 1963): 592–624.

Ellis, Mark. "W. E. B. Du Bois and the Formation of Black Opinion in World War I: A Commentary on 'The Damnable Dilemma.'" *Journal of American History* 81 (March 1995): 1584–90.

Fairclough, Adam. "'Being in the Field of Education and Also Being a Negro . . . Seems . . . Tragic': Black Teachers in the Jim Crow South." *Journal of American History* 87 (June 2000): 65.

Farnham, Dwight Thompson. "Negroes, a Source of Industrial Labor." *Factory and Industrial Management,* August 1918, 123–29.

Fields, Barbara J. "Whiteness, Racism, and Identity." *International Labor and Working-Class History* 60 (Fall 2001): 48–56.

Fishback, Mason McCloud. "Illinois Legislation on Slavery and Free Negroes, 1818–1865." *Transactions of the Illinois State Historical Society* 9 (1904): 414–32.

Franklin, Vincent P. "The Philadelphia Race Riot of 1918." *Pennsylvania Magazine of History and Biography* 99, no. 3 (1975): 336–50.

Gertz, Elmer. The Black Laws of Illinois." *Journal of the Illinois State Historical Society* 56, no. 3 (Autumn 1963): 454–73.

Glymph, Thavolia. "'Liberty Dearly Bought': The Making of Civil War Memory in Afro-American Communities in the South." In *Time Longer than Rope: A Century of African American Activism, 1850–1950,* edited by Charles M. Payne and Adam Green, 111–39. New York: New York University Press, 2003.

Gordon, Rita Werner. "The Change in the Political Alignment of Chicago's Negroes during the New Deal." *Journal of American History* 56 (December 1969): 584–603.

Hanna, William F. "The Boston Draft Riot." *Civil War History* 36, no. 3 (1990): 262–73.

Hardwick, Kevin R. "'Your Old Father Abe Lincoln Is Dead and Damned': Black Soldiers and the Memphis Race Riot of 1866." *Journal of Social History* 27, no. 1 (Autumn 1993): 109–28.

Haynes, Elizabeth Ross. "Negroes in Domestic Service in the United States." *Journal of Negro History* 8, no. 4 (October 1923): 384–442. Reprinted in *Unsung Heroes; The Black Boy of Atlanta; "Negroes in Domestic Service in the United States"* (New York: G. K. Hall, 1997), 537–96.

Haynes, George Edmund. "Effect of War Conditions on Negro Labor." *Proceedings of the Academy of Political Science* 8 (February 1919): 299–312.

Hill, Joseph A. "Recent Northward Migration of the Negro." *Monthly Labor Review* 18, no. 3 (March 1924): 475–89.

Hill, T. Arnold. "The Negro in Industry." *American Federationist* 32 (October 1925): 915–20.

Hine, Darlene Clark. "Black Migration to the Urban Midwest: The Gender Dimension, 1915–1945." In *The New African American Urban History*, edited by Kenneth W. Goings and Raymond A. Mohl, 240–65. Thousand Oaks, Calif.: Sage, 1991.

Horney, Helen, and William E. Keller. "The Negro's Two Hundred Forty Years in Illinois: A Chronology." *Journal of the Illinois State Historical Society* 56, no. 3 (Autumn 1963): 435–36.

Jenkins, Philip. "'A Wide-Open City': Prostitution in Progressive Era Lancaster." *Pennsylvania History* 65 (Autumn 1998): 509–26.

Johnson, Marilynn S. "Gender, Race, and Rumours: Re-examining the 1943 Race Riots." *Gender & History* 10, no. 2 (August 1998): 252–77.

Jordan, William. "'The Damnable Dilemma': African American Accommodation and Protest during World War I." *Journal of American History* 81 (March 1995): 1562–83.

Kesselman, Louis C. "The Fair Employment Practice Commission Movement in Perspective." *Journal of Negro History* 31 (January 1946): 30–46.

Kilson, Martin. "Political Change in the Negro Ghetto, 1900–1940s." In *Key Issues in the Afro-American Experience*, edited by Nathan I. Huggins, Martin Kilson, and Daniel M. Fox, 2:167–92. New York: Harcourt Brace Jovanovich, 1971.

Kirshenbaum, Andrea Meryl. "'The Vampire That Hovers Over North Carolina': Gender, White Supremacy, and the Wilmington Race Riot of 1898." *Southern Cultures* 4, no. 3 (Fall 1998): 6–29.

McLaughlin, Malcolm. "Reconsidering the East St. Louis Race Riot of 1917." *International Review of Social History* 47 (2002): 187–212.

Ngozi-Brown, Scot. "African-American Soldiers and Filipinos: Racial Imperialism, Jim Crow and Social Relations." *Journal of Negro History* 82, no. 1 (Winter 1997): 42–53.

Norvell, Stanley B., and William M. Tuttle Jr. "Views of a Negro During 'The Red Summer' of 1919." *Journal of Negro History* 51 (July 1966): 209–18.

Portwood, Shirley J. "'We Lifted Our Voices in Thunder Tones': African American Race Men and Race Women and Community Agency in Southern Illinois, 1895–1910." *Journal of Urban History* 26 (2000): 740–58.

Reardon, Kenneth M. "State and Local Revitalization Efforts in East St. Louis, Illinois." In "Globalization and the Changing U.S. City," edited by David Wilson, special issue, *Annals of the American Academy of Political and Social Science* 551, no. 1 (May 1997): 235–47.

Reich, Steven A. "Soldiers of Democracy: Black Texans and the Fight for Citizenship, 1917–1921." *Journal of American History* 82 (March 1996): 1478–1504.

Rudwick, Elliott M. "Fifty Years of Race Relations in East St. Louis: The Breaking Down of White Supremacy." *Midcontinent American Studies Journal* 6, no. 1 (Spring 1965): 3–15.

Skotnes, Andor. "'Buy Where You Can Work': Boycotting for Jobs in African-American Baltimore, 1933–1934." *Journal of Social History* 27, no. 4 (Summer 1994): 735–61.

Smith, C. R. F. "East St. Louis Studies Americanism." *The Nation*, March 9, 1932, 283–84.

Smith, Duncan C. "Know Your East St. Louis: Aluminum, an Interesting Story about an East St. Louis Industry." *East St. Louis Today* (East St. Louis Chamber of Commerce) 4, no. 10 (April 1936): 7–8.

Sugrue, Thomas J. "Crabgrass-Roots Politics: Race, Rights, and the Reaction against Liberalism in the Urban North, 1940–1964." *Journal of American History* 82 (September 1995): 551–78.

Thornbrough, Emma Lou. "The National Afro-American League, 1887–1908." *Journal of Southern History* 27 (November 1961): 494–512.

Watkins, Sylvestre C. Sr. "Some of Early Illinois' Free Negroes." *Journal of the Illinois State Historical Society* 56, no. 3 (Autumn 1963): 495–507.

INDEX

300 — Index

Chism, Mary, 18, 215n12
Christian Welfare Hospital, 182, 183
Chunn, Joe, 170
Cincinnati, Ohio, 4, 21, 91, 176
CIO. *See* Congress of Industrial
  Organizations (CIO)
Citizens Defense and Urban League
  Organizing Committee, 200
citizenship, 11, 15, 35–36, 39–40, 93, 130,
  155, 197, 199
Citizens' Party of East St. Louis, 33, 38–39,
  41–42, 64–67, 230n37
Citizens' Welfare Committee, 168
city government. *See* municipal government
city hall. *See* municipal government
civil rights, 9, 35, 69, 109, 140, 142, 166,
  168, 180–81, 191, 204
  post–World War II, xii, 10, 176, 205, 246
  World War II years, 194–96, 199
Civil War, role of African Americans in,
  18, 34–35, 37
Civil Works Administration, 177, 181
Clark, John (Colored Democratic
  League), 81
Clark, John (social worker), 183
Clark, R. Vernon, 148
Clark, Scott, 116
Clarke, James, 56
Clark Realty Company, 148
Class, Angelo R., 184
Clay, Henry, 230n40
Clayton, E. P., 100, 114, 122, 125
Cleveland, Ohio, 4, 6, 13, 30, 58,
  138–39, 179
Coddington, Eugene S., 230n37
Coffey, E. J., 134
Coffin, Arlyn Wilbur, 161
Colby, W. G., 221n51
Collier, A., 221n51
Collins, William M., 222n56
Collinsville Avenue, 98–99, 122
Colored Citizens' Community Committee
  of the Bond Avenue YMCA, 165
Colored Democratic League, 81–82
Colored Lincoln-Roosevelt Republican
  League, 66
Colored Men's Progressive Club, 66
Colored Mothers' Craft Club, 164
Colored Old Folks' Home and Orphans'
  Association, 60, 128, 164
Colored Progressive Republican League of
  East St. Louis, 68

Colored Welfare Association, 163, 168
Colored Women's Republican Club, 167
Colored Women's Welfare League, 182
commission form of municipal govern-
  ment, 110, 139–40, 144, 147, 167
Commission on the Condition of the
  Urban Colored Population, 195
Committee of One Hundred, 132–34
Committee on Industrial Relations of the
  Illinois State Employment Service, 200
communism and communists, 145,
  187–89, 191, 254n2
Communist Party of the United States of
  America, 9, 158, 175, 187–89
community building, xi, 3, 35
Conard, Iota, 268n14
Congress of Industrial Organizations
  (CIO), 9, 158, 175, 190–91, 200, 202
Connecticut Land Company, 22
Connors, John T., 170, 202
Conway, Robert, 56, 73, 76, 88, 140
Cook, Edward, 120
Cook, Lena, 120
Cook, Silas, 66
Cooksey, Joseph, 222n56
Cooper, General, 231n44
Coppedge, Samuel, 111–13, 135, 137–38,
  238n49, 241n5
corruption, 32–33, 46, 48, 52–53, 66, 68,
  70–71, 82, 134, 139–40
Cosby, Madison, 223n58
Cotton, Calvin, 113, 168, 263n50
Cox, J. M., 138
Creath, Gertrude, 162, 260–61n37
crime and criminality, 2, 53, 68, 83, 102,
  105–6, 110, 115, 134, 137, 147
  accusations of black involvement in, 75,
  92–93, 105–6
  by politicians, businessmen, city em-
  ployees, 51–52, 111, 132, 140
Crittenden, Henry, 113
Crook, Gordon, 56
Crow, George, 137
CTLU. *See* Central Trades and Labor
  Union (CTLU)

dance halls, 51–53, 59, 82, 147
Daughters of the Tabernacle, 19
Deaconess Hospital, 112
debt. *See* municipal debt
Decatur, Illinois, 107
deindustrialization, 205

Demery, Walter, 81
Democratic Party, 9, 32, 38, 64–68, 70,
    79–80, 105, 131, 146, 167, 175
  black politicians and supporters of, 38,
    62–63, 67–68, 81–83, 128, 170–73, 175,
    192–94, 201
Denverside (East St. Louis), 18, 49, 90,
    111, 159, 165
Denverside Improvement Association,
    166
De Priest, Oscar, 192
Derleth, C. G., 230n37
desegregation, 187, 205
DeShields, Annie Mae, 182
DeShields, John, 163, 222n56, 231n44
Detroit, Michigan, 3–4, 6–7, 18, 30, 141,
    175–76, 181, 185, 202, 205
Dickson, F. S., 114
Dickson, James, 81
discrimination. *See* segregation and
    discrimination
Domhoff, John, 82
Donohue, D. J., 222n56
"don't buy where you can't work or shop
    in dignity," 180–81
Double V campaign, 197–99, 204
Dowling, Edward F., 231n42
Downtown Business Men's Association,
    149
Doyle, Frank, 166, 188
Doyle, John, 24
Draggon, Louis, 230n37
Drury, John H., 83
Du Bois, W. E. B., 40
Duncan, Gran A., 222n56, 230n40
Dunlap, Harry, 165
Durr, Rusha, 191
Dutcher, John B., 22

Eads Bridge, 22, 31, 47, 124, 149
Eagleson, William, 37
Easterly, Dora, 231n44
Easterly, William M., 231n44
Eastman, Harry, 31–32
East Side Levee and Sanitary District, 46,
    135. *See also* levee board
East Side Packing Company, 85
East St. Louis and Suburban Railroad
    Company, 79, 84–85, 94
East St. Louis Casting Company, 190
East St. Louis Cotton Seed Oil Company,
    49, 89

East St. Louis Housing Board, 184
East St. Louis Overseer of the Poor, 160
East St. Louis Real Estate Exchange. *See*
    Real Estate Exchange
East St. Louis United Labor Defense
    League, 134
East St. Louis War Civics Committee,
    161–63
East St. Louis Welfare League, 165
Eckert, Henry J., 230n37
economy
  decline of, 206
  development of, xii, 4–5, 21, 69, 95, 147
  growth of, machine for, 22, 43, 46, 95
  rivalry, St. Louis–Chicago, 22–23
Edgemont (East St. Louis), 50
Edinger, William J., 26
Edward, Lawrence, 159
Eldorado, Illinois, 61
elections, local and state, 5–6, 9, 54–55, 79,
    139, 145–46, 167, 169, 171
  of 1859, 22
  of 1878, 32
  of 1885, 32
  of 1886, 38
  of 1887, 33
  of 1893, 38
  of 1895, 38–39
  of 1903, 66
  of 1908, 67
  of 1910, 67
  of 1915, 70–72
  of 1916, 80–82
  of 1917, 95, 97
  of 1919, 167
  of 1920, 168
  of 1922, 168
  of 1924, 168
  of 1926, 170–71
  of 1934, 193
elections, national, 167
  of 1894, 34
  of 1908, 67
  of 1916, 79, 81
  of 1917, 81–82
  of 1928, 171–72
  of 1932, 172, 192
  of 1936, 193
Ellington, Henry, 221n48
Elliott Frog and Switch Company, 26, 48
Ellis, J. E., 229n29
Emancipation Proclamation Day, 154

employment and occupations
  black, 5, 42, 60, 77–79, 151–54, 176–80,
    196–97, 199
  white, 28–30
employment discrimination. *See* segregation and discrimination: employment
Erwin, David, 198
ethnic cleansing. *See* pogroms
Eubanks, John, 80, 235n12
Evanhoff, Mike, 124
Ewing, Quincy, 53
Executive Order 8802, 196
"Exodusters," 16–17. *See also* Great Migration; migrants and migration, black

Fair Employment Practice Committee
  (FEPC), 9, 196, 199–201
Faulkner, Jeanne, 150, 165
Federal Bureau of Investigation, 198
Federal Emergency Relief Administration
  (FERA), 184
Fekete, Thomas L., Sr., 46
FEPC. *See* Fair Employment Practice
  Committee (FEPC)
FERA. *See* Federal Emergency Relief
  Administration (FERA)
Ferguson, Jack, 221n48
Fining, Joseph N., 147
First World War. *See* World War I
Fisher, Farley, 166
Flake, Mrs. Willie, 128
Flannigan, Alexander, 97, 101, 105, 135
Flannigen, Walter, 149
Flood, Richard, 228n25
Flood, Sarah, 60, 228n25
floods and flood control, 23–24, 46. *See
  also* East Side Levee and Sanitary Dis-
  trict; levee board; grading, high
Florence, Frank, 51–52
Forster, Charles, 137
Fortune, Timothy Thomas, 39, 41
Fowler, Lester, 137
Fox, Charles B., 87–88, 91, 94, 102
fraternal societies and lodges, 18–19, 42,
  100. *See also individual organizations*
Free Bridge. *See* Municipal Bridge (Free
  Bridge)
Freeman, Maggie, 162, 260n37
Freeman, Richard, 67
Freeman, Ruth, 60
Freeman, William, 230n40
Funsten Nut Company, 189

Gardner, Myrtle, 52
Garrett, William, 231n44
Garvey, John E., 230n37
Garvey, Marcus, 138, 146, 155, 157, 198
Gas Fitters and Helpers Union, 195
Gates, B., 228n25
General Assembly. *See* Illinois General
  Assembly
General Maceo Club
Gerold, Fred, 70, 170, 172, 230n37
ghettos and ghettoization. *See* segregation
  and discrimination: housing
Gibbs, John, 222n56
Gibbs, Parnell, 66
Gibson, Harry H. C., 200
Giesing, Fred, 134
Girls' Reserves, 164
Gladden, Luaco, 268n14
glass industry, 2, 5, 19, 25, 42, 151–52
Glessing, Fred, 230n37
Goedde, Edmund, 147–48
Goff, B. F., 38
Gold Bank Boosters' Club, 164
Gold Star Mothers, 192
Gompers, Samuel, 86
Goose Hill (East St. Louis), 18, 90, 122,
  151
Gould, Jay, 47
Gow, John, 120, 244n21
grading, high, 23–24. *See also* East Side
  Levee and Sanitary District; floods and
  flood control; levee board
Granby Mining and Milling Company,
  159
Granite City, Illinois, 20, 188
Gray, C. L., 26
Great Depression, 174, 176–177, 181, 187
Greater East St. Louis Party, 70
Great Migration, 2, 7, 12, 71, 76–79, 86,
  91–92, 107, 109–10, 153, 205. *See also*
  immigrants; migrants and migrations,
  black
Great Railroad Strike of 1877, 31–32
Green, John, 69
Green, Peter A., 61
Green, Russell M. C., 62, 80, 83, 106, 137,
  157, 229n29, 247n35
Green, Thomas, 223n58
Green, W., 93
Greenberg, Cheryl, 180
Greer, Edward, 5
Grimshaw, Allen D., 3

Grimshaw, William J., 4
Guenther, Charles E., 150

Hackett, Horatio B., 184
Hagler, Nathaniel G., 182–83
Haines, G. H., 162
Halpert, Ben, 191
Halsey, Fred, 62, 229n29
Hamilton, Nevada, 168, 263n48
Hanna, Charles, 120
Harding, Fred, 131
Harrison, Hubert H., 127
Hart, Eliza, 167
Hawkins, Morton, 39, 42, 128
Hawkins, S. W., 223n58
Hayes, Edwin, 221n48
Hayes, M. M., 37
Hayes, Matt, 80, 135, 137, 164, 168
Hayes, William, 168
Haynes, Maude, 162, 182, 260n37
health care and public health, 25, 91, 154,
    162, 164–65, 170, 179, 181–83, 194
Hearst, Mack, 113
Heim Brewery, 133
Henderson, Charles, 168
Henderson, Elmer, 200
Henry, Edward, 221n48
Henry, John, 221n48
Hepler, Chester, 199
Hickey, Cornelius, 111, 134
high-grading. See grading, high
Hightower, James, 221n48
Hill-Thomas Lime and Cement Company,
    121–22
Hisrich, C. R., 131
Hoard, Rose, 268n14
Hod Carriers and Common Laborers
    Union, 195
Home Owners' Loan Corporation, 185
Home Protective Association of East St.
    Louis, 166
Hood, Ralph, 115
Hoover, Herbert, 171, 192–93
Hoover, Lou Henry, 192
Hoover-Curtis Club, 167
Hormel Packing Company, 196
Horner, William H., 149, 182
hospitals, 165, 182–83
House, Charles, 131
House, Mattie, 119
housing, 51, 90–91, 140, 150, 183–86
    black southern migrants, 74–75, 77–78,
    83, 89–91, 107–8

housing discrimination. See segregation
    and discrimination: housing
Houston, Texas, 8, 141–42, 240n1
Howard, Douglas, 168
Howard, Fred, 230n40
Howard, Kate, 118
Huddleston, Tom, 80, 168, 234–35n12
Hughes, Albert, 137, 168
Hughes, Cora, 184, 268n14
Hughes, John W., 129, 161–62, 184,
    260n37
Human Rights Commission, Illinois. See
    Illinois Human Rights Commission
Hunter, Frank A., 56, 160
Hunter, Lillie, 268n14
Hunter, Thomas, 113, 127
Hunter Packing Company, 196, 199
Hurd, Carlos F., 116
Hutchinson, Park, 37, 221n48
Hutter, William, 111–12

Illinois Central Railroad, 56
Illinois Commission on the Condition of
    the Urban Colored Population. See
    Commission on the Condition of the
    Urban Colored Population
Illinois Craftsmen's Association, 191
Illinois Federation of Colored Women's
    Clubs, 59
Illinois Federation of Labor, 102
Illinois General Assembly, 36, 41, 133, 145,
    168, 176, 193, 195
Illinois Human Rights Commission, 2, 204
Illinois-Iowa Power Company, 195
Illinois Relief Commission, 176
Illinois State Committee of the North
    Central Association of Colleges and
    Secondary Schools, 186
Illinois State Convention of Colored Men,
    35
Illinois State Council of Defense Labor
    Committee, 102–3, 105
Illinois State Employment Service,
    Committee on Industrial Relations
    of the. See Committee on Industrial
    Relations of the Illinois State Employ-
    ment Service
Illinoistown (East St. Louis), 21, 23
immigrants, 20, 27–30, 53–54, 93, 118–9,
    152, 169. See also Great Emigration; mi-
    grants and migrations, black
Imperial Social Club, 62
incorporation, 59, 149. See also annexation

Soellinger, Theodore, 231n42
Soffer, Harry, 180
Sorrell, E. M., 94
South End (East St. Louis), 18, 90, 99, 111, 125, 150. *See also* Denverside; Rush City
Southern Illinois Construction Company, 26
Southern Illinois National Bank, 132–33, 135
Southern Malleable Iron Company, 190
Southern Railway, 134
Spanish-American War, 41, 44
  veterans, 41, 62
Springfield, Jerseyville & St. Louis Railway, 23
Stanisic, Harry, 102
State Bar Association of Illinois, 135
state legislature. *See* Illinois General Assembly
St. Clair County Board of Assessors, 48–49
St. Clair County Board of Review, 48–49
St. Clair County Board of Supervisors, 83, 106, 128, 131, 193
St. Clair County (Colored) Republican League, 80–82
St. Clair County Medical Society, 182
steel and iron industry, 2, 5, 25–26, 42, 55, 151–52, 158, 177, 190
Stephens, Melbern M., 5, 14, 24, 31, 38–39, 41, 49, 66, 140–41, 160, 167, 230n37
Sterling Steel Castings Company, 199
Stevenson, Sarah, 221n48
St. George Lodge No. 1524 of the Grand United Order of Odd Fellows, 18, 100
St. John's AME Church, 79
St. Louis Bridge Company, 48
St. Louis National Stockyards Company, 22, 25–26, 50, 116, 133, 135, 190
St. Louis Transfer Railway Company, 24
St. Luke's African Methodist Episcopal Church, 18, 228n25
St. Mark's Baptist Church, 90
St. Mary's Hospital, 165, 182–83
Stone, I. S., 229n29
St. Paul Lodge No. 42, 18
St. Paul's Baptist Church, 18, 163, 231n44
Street Railway, Light and Power Company, 91
strikes, 7, 31–33, 83–89, 94–96, 101–4, 110, 146, 158–61, 189–91, 200
Sullivan, Jerry, 135

Summers, Frank E., 193
Summers, Neil, 231n42
sundown towns, 4, 61, 98, 101, 108, 112, 114, 127, 188. *See also* pogroms
Sunrise Council of the Daughters of Africa, 19
Suttles, Joseph, 67
Swift and Company, 26, 49–50, 55–56, 85, 121, 133, 160–61, 164, 190

Tackett, "Slim," 137
Taft, Howard, 65, 68
Tamblyn, W. L., 47
Tarlton, George Locke, 5, 14, 46, 52, 65, 67, 69–71, 81–83, 105, 110–11, 134–35
Taylor, James, 119
Tecklenburg (state's attorney of St. Clair County), 67
Terminal Railroad Association, 47–48, 56, 69, 129, 148
Theising, Andrew J., 20, 25
Third Ward Independent Club, 63
Thomas, Ephiriam, 128
Thomas, Horace, 137, 168
Thomas, Jennie, 18, 128
Thomas, John W. E., 36
Thomas, Laura, 167
Thomas, Lulu, 128
Thomas, Richard W., 3
Thomas, Robert, 122
Thompson, C. W., 156
Thompson, William Hale, 145, 171–72
Thornton, Ida, 167, 263n48
Tieje, Claus E., 231n42
Tillman, Benjamin, 130
Towers, Alois, 84, 86, 88, 92
Townsend, Bud, 137
Townsend, Russell, 75
Trade Union Unity League, 189
Trafton, H. F., 52
tri-city area. *See* Granite City, Illinois; Madison, Illinois; Venice, Illinois
Tripp, S. O., 114, 116, 122
Trotter, Joe William, Jr., 6
Trotter, William Monroe, 40
Truelight Baptist Church, 18
Tudor Iron Works, 26
Tunstell, J. R., 129
Turley, James, 67
Turner, Fannie, 128, 162, 260n37
Turner, Lucy Mae, 128, 162, 260n37
Tuttle, William, Jr., 3, 118